All Kinds of Writing

Book 1

Contents

Cambridge University Press

Cambridge London New York New Rochelle Melbourne Sydney

Note to the teacher

This series aims to broaden the range of writing encountered by older junior and middle school children and to draw them into areas of written work that have been stressed by recent major reports but are nevertheless often neglected in school.

Each book contains eight units. A unit contains work for several lessons and thus, overall, each book should provide a range of written work stretching over a full school year. The units may be used in any order as the teacher sees a need for experience in a particular type of writing.

The written work is intended to be challenging but is based on topics which draw upon experience common to most children. There is therefore no need for elaborate preparation by the teacher or preliminary activity by the children before they begin to write. There is, however, an emphasis on discussion as a class before any writing is undertaken, and in the sharing of the responses in groups afterwards. In many of the activities there is the opportunity for children to work together in pairs or in small groups.

The response asked of the children will lead them into new kinds of writing and make fresh demands upon their imagination and creativity. It is therefore suggested that in most units teachers concentrate on the content of the pupil's response rather than the technical accuracy with which it is expressed.

All kinds of writing may be used in classes of mixed ability. The written activity allows for responses at the level appropriate to each individual child.

The chart on page 64 is intended to help the teacher plot the types of writing the class has covered as the term progresses. A teacher making such a chart for his or her own use (it is not intended that there should be a copy for each child)

a will ensure that the class is encountering a range of writing modes and be able to spot the gaps;

b have some indication of the source of the various types of writing undertaken, across the curriculum.

Thus ES in the Description row would mean that Environmental studies had provided an opportunity for some descriptive writing. RE in the Story row would mean that a story had been written in Religious education.

Teachers will thus be alerted not only to neglect of any one type of writing but also as to whether they are making full use of the whole curriculum as a source for variety in written work. Poems can flow as readily from a nature lesson as from a language lesson. Again, the importance of discussion between teacher and children before activities are undertaken is underlined.

R. W. Forward
1986

Acknowledgements

The author would like to thank Miss Isobel Gaffney, Headteacher of Rosary R.C. Junior School, Hampstead, for her most helpful suggestions. He would also like to thank Mr John Gulliver, Primary Adviser for English, Devon, who first introduced him to the full list of writing areas used in this book.

The author and publisher would like to thank the following for permission to reproduce material in this book:
p.9 'Terrific Teachers' by Roger McGough, reprinted by permission of A. D. Peters & Co Ltd; p.10 'Timothy Winters' by Charles Causley, from *Figgie Hobbin*, Macmillan; p.15 Gwen Dunn; p.15 'The Name of the Game' by Jenny Craig from *The Beaver Book of School Verse*, ed. J. Curry; p.20 'Cold Feet' by Brian Lee, from *Late Home*, Kestrel Books, 1976, copyright © 1976 by Brian Lee; p.28 Roy Fuller; p.41 *The Village by the Sea* by Anita Desai, reprinted by kind permission of William Heinemann Limited; p.41 *George's Marvellous Medicine* by Roald Dahl, illustrated by Quentin Blake, Jonathan Cape Ltd and Alfred A. Knopf, Inc.; p.45 *Ludo and the Star Horse* by Mary Stewart, Hodder and Stoughton Ltd; p.53 'Ole Biscuit' by Jan Stewer and and A. J. Coles, Herbert Jenkins, 1925.

Every effort has been made to reach copyright holders; the publishers would be glad to hear from anyone whose rights they have unwittingly infringed.

In the same series
All Kinds of Writing Book 2

Published by the Press Syndicate of the University of Cambridge
The Pitt Building, Trumpington Street, Cambridge CB2 1RP
32 East 57th Street, New York, NY 10022, USA
10 Stamford Road, Oakleigh, Melbourne 3166, Australia

© Cambridge University Press 1987

First published 1987

Printed in Great Britain by Scotprint Ltd, Musselburgh, Scotland

ISBN 0 521 33985 5

Designed by Ann Samuel
Illustrated by Kim Blundell, Terry Burton, Di Lorriman, Jan Nesbitt, Lesley Smith, Nicola Spoor, Lynne Willey

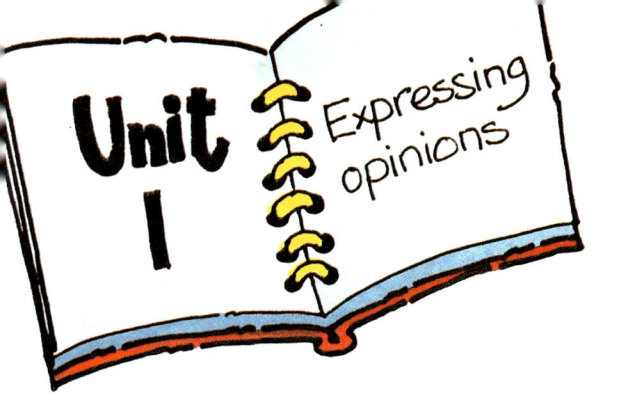

Unit 1 — Expressing opinions

Do you argue with your friends?
Do you have different opinions?

We have opinions on all sorts of things – from which is the best pop group to whether schools should open on Saturday mornings.

This unit will help you express **your** opinions clearly.

Life is very different for the lion in the wild and the lion in the zoo.

1 Write down all the ways you can think of in which the life of a wild lion is different from that of a zoo lion. Which lion do you think is more content?

2 **Discussion time**
Share your ideas with the rest of the class.
Did you have different opinions on which lion was better off?

Many people think it wrong to keep wild animals in captivity. They say the only place for wild animals is in the forests, plains and deserts where they have always lived.

Imagine you belong to a society called the SAFS – the Set Animals Free Society. You are trying to close down a small local zoo and have the animals returned to the wild. The town is called Bidpark.

What you do

1 Write a letter to the Mayor of Bidpark asking the council to close the zoo. Explain why you think it wrong to keep animals in captivity and how they would be better off in the wild.

Start your letter like this:

> 'THE SET ANIMALS FREE SOCIETY'
>
> Dear Mr Mayor
>   As a member of the S.A.F.S. I strongly object to Bidpark Zoo It should be closed and the animals returned to the wild.
>   The reason for doing this . . .

2 Design a badge for the SAFS.

3 Design a poster for display in Bidpark to get the support of local residents.

4 Write down other ways you could use to get people to support your opinion.

Another opinion

Many people strongly support zoos.
In this picture our wild lion has been caught in a drought. There is no water, he is too weak to hunt and there are hunters about.

Our zoo lion is looking well fed and is safe from harm. He has a large enclosure with trees and water holes. There are other lions for company.

What you do

1 **Discussion time**
   Have a class discussion about the good things that zoos do.
   They are not just there so that we can look at wild animals.

2 Imagine you are the head keeper at Bidpark Zoo. Write a letter to the Mayor in support of zoos.

Start your letter like this:

> BIDPARK ZOO
>
> Dear Mr Mayor
> The S.A.F.S. is trying to close this zoo. They do not understand all the good work zoos can do. For instance . . .

3 Design a 'Save our Zoo' badge and poster.

4 Some things to think and write about, and talk about:
   ★ Is it kind or sensible to return animals to the wild if they have lived in a zoo for a long time?
   ★ Do animals really understand what being free means?

5 Now you have thought about animals and zoos carefully, give your own opinion on whether animals should be kept in zoos. If you are in favour of zoos, what do you think they should be like?

Nature's Ark

Our planet Earth is sometimes called 'Nature's Ark'. People and animals have to share it. There is nowhere else for each to go.

Each year the population of the world grows by millions. Each year we cut down an area the size of Scotland from the great rain forests of South America and Africa, to make room for farming. Animals' natural habitats are disappearing; wild animals have less space to live in.

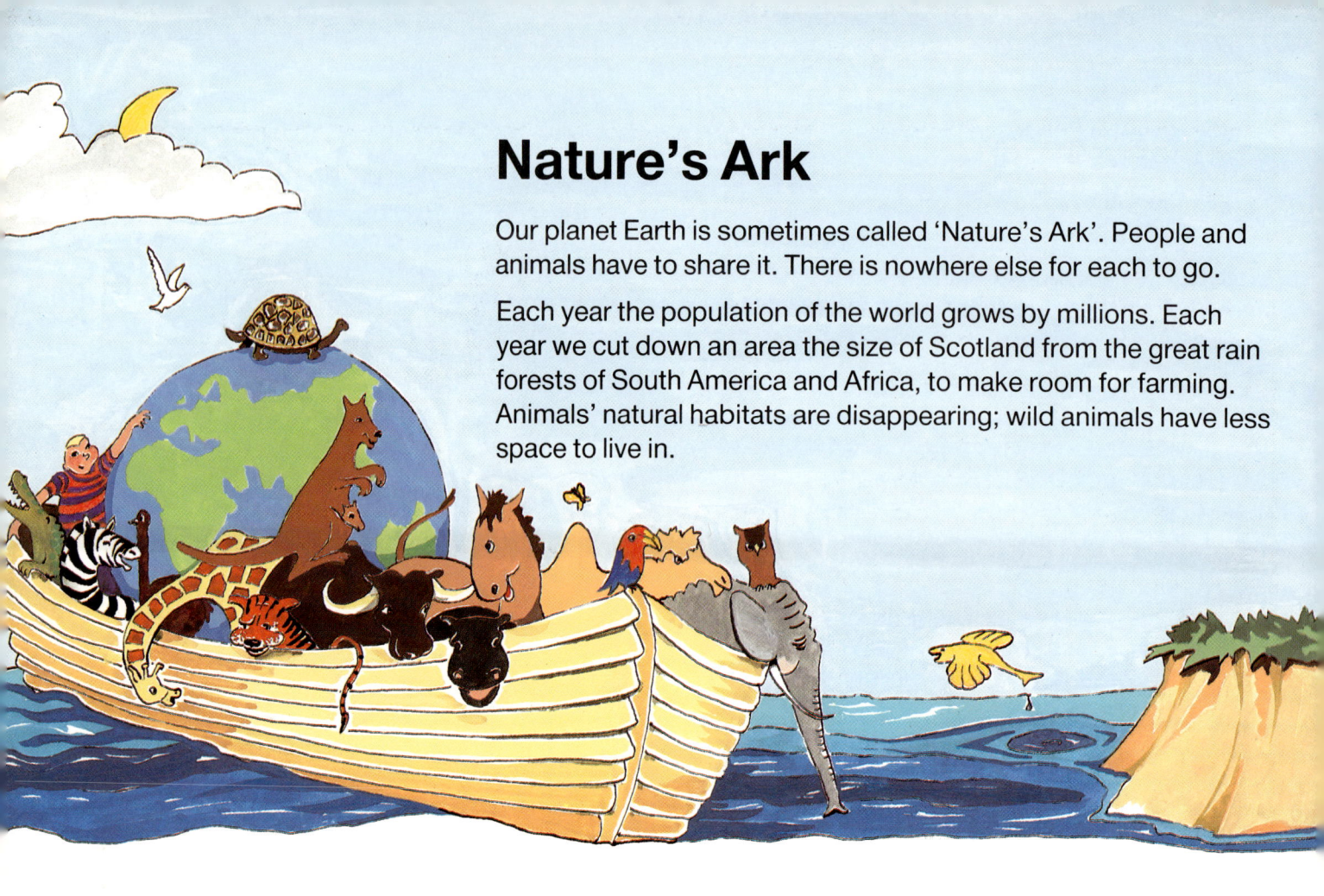

N'Gobani's story

Hello! My name is N'Gobani. I live in Kenya and I am a farmer. I grow fruit and corn on my farm to sell in the market and to feed my large family.

The soil of my farm is not very fertile and often we are short of water. I need more land, especially as my wife is soon to have our fifth baby.

I am getting worried because I shall not be able to feed my family much longer as they grow and need more to eat.

On the edge of my land the great forest begins. It has a big river and the soil is moist and good. I have asked the Government if I may have a little of the forest to clear.

I could grow more crops to feed my family and to sell to others. The Government says I cannot have the land because it is an Animal Reserve. They seem to think animals are more important than people.

What you do

1 Do you feel sorry for N'Gobani? In your opinion should he be given more land or should the forest be saved for the wild animals? Write down what you think and say why you think what you have decided is the right thing to do.

2 When you have written down your opinion, have a class discussion and tell the class what you think. Take a vote for N'Gobani or the animals. Before you take a vote make sure that all the points in favour of N'Gobani or the animals have been made.

Ideas needed

Can we help N'Gobani feed his children and still keep plenty of grassland and forest for the wild animals?

Yes we can. Here are some ideas:

★ We can share the world's food more fairly. Europe has more food than it needs stored in 'Butter Mountains' and 'Wine Lakes'.

★ We can help N'Gobani become a better farmer. He needs machinery and water to start with.

★ We can keep parts of the world wild, just for animals.

What you do

1 Discussion time
Talk about the three ideas above for helping N'Gobani and the animals. What will N'Gobani need to farm his land better? How will we share the food from rich countries? Where will the best places be for the animal reserves?

2 When you have had your discussion, write down your ideas in a little booklet called *Helping N'Gobani*. Try to explain the problem and give your opinion on what could be done. Draw pictures to illustrate your booklet. Look in the papers and collect any writing or pictures to do with helping people like N'Gobani.

3 Can you think of ways your school can help?

Remember.

Our opinions will be listened to if we:
★ support them with facts stated clearly;
★ listen to other opinions and try to understand them.

Unit 2

Writing descriptions

What better place to practise descriptions than school!

Let's start with a rather unusual teacher.

Imagine a dragon; fierce with yellow fangs and evil-smelling breath; bulging eyes and green scaly skin. If you can imagine that dragon with nail varnish on its claws, wearing a brown tweed suit and ginger hair tied in a bun, then you can imagine Miss Bolger.

Miss Bolger, the scourge of Junior 2, Terror of the Tongue, Attila the Hun. She was a sorceress who could turn a classroom into a torture chamber with a wave of her magic cane . . . She taught us the three Ss – sweating, stammering and skins (how to jump out of).

Roger McGough

Roger McGough seemed a little unlucky with his teacher. Perhaps Miss Bolger's friends saw her quite differently. We usually describe things the way that we see them.

What you do

1 Describe Miss Bolger as if she were a friend of yours. You may think her brown suit smart and her hair attractive. Start like this:

   Sue Bolger is a good friend of mine. She is a very pleasant, smart lady . . .

2 Compare your descriptions with your friends'. Did you imagine Miss Bolger in different ways?

Similes

Look at the way Charles Causley uses words in
the first verses about Timothy Winters.

Timothy Winters comes to school
With eyes as wide as a football-pool,
Ears like bombs and teeth like splinters:
A blitz of a boy is Timothy Winters.

His belly is white, his neck is dark,
And his hair is an exclamation mark,
His clothes are enough to scare a crow
And through his britches the blue winds blow.

Charles Causley

10

Describing something is a little like drawing a picture in words. Often we can make our descriptions more interesting by using phrases or groups of words called **similes**. We can spot them easily because they always include the words 'like' or 'as'.

as quiet as a mouse

Charles Causley uses similes in his poem on Timothy Winters.

hair like straw

1 Read the verses about Timothy Winters and pick out all the similes. Remember, look for 'like' and 'as'.

2 Look at the picture of Timothy Winters. Can *you* make up some similes that would fit him?

3 **Discussion time**
With your teacher make a collection on the board of all the similes you can think of, not just about Timothy.

Sometimes we use sentences such as 'He is a devil' or 'She is a little monkey'. We leave out the 'like' or 'as'. These sentences are called **metaphors**.

4 Look around the class, choose one person and describe them in the most interesting way you can. After you have finished, see if your friends can guess who you have described.

5 Choose someone famous – a pop star perhaps – and describe him or her. Would your friends have described the person in the same way?

Billy the Kid

Have a good look at Billy. His teacher sees him quite differently from his mother. She thinks he's an angel – his teacher thinks he's a devil!

What do you think Billy is like at home? How does he act? How does his Mum see him?

How does he act at school? How does his teacher see him? What sort of things does he do?

1   Write two short descriptions of Billy, one by his mother and one by his teacher.
    Start like this:

> My Billy is a dear little boy

> Billy is a terrible nuisance.

2   **Discussion time**
    Compare your descriptions of Billy with those of your friends. Try to decide with your teacher what made some of the descriptions more interesting. Was it the way the words were used, or the choice of words? This makes all the difference when we are describing someone or something.

3   When you have had your discussion, choose someone you all know – your teacher perhaps – and describe her or him. When we are describing we need to say how people act as well as how they look. When you have finished, compare your descriptions. You will find you see the person in lots of different ways.

Remember

You can make descriptions much more interesting if you:

★ Choose words carefully
★ Look for the right word – use similes
★ Use your imagination. Not just how something looks but what it is like.

All about you

Have you ever thought about the way other people may describe you?

Worst enemy

Family

Best friend

Older children

Teacher

Small children

What you do

Write some short descriptions of the way each of the people above may describe you. Start with your best friend's description. Each person will see you in a different way.

Facts, facts, facts

The descriptions we have written so far have been impressions of how we think people look and what they are like. Sometimes descriptions have to be very detailed, giving only facts, rather like a police or passport photograph.

WANTED

HANDSOME HARRY JONES

Jones is 1.84 m tall. He has dark brown hair cut very short (crew cut). His eyes are brown and set close together. His nose has been broken at some time. He has yellow teeth with two missing in the front. Normally clean shaven, but may be growing a beard.

Well built. Last seen wearing a green anorak and brown trousers. Contact the police, do not approach – this man is dangerous.

What you do

Do a drawing and write a 'wanted' notice for someone in your class. Remember just to describe his or her appearance, as exactly as you can.

Not all descriptions are about people.
We describe:

Places

How observant are you?
Do you notice the places you visit?
Do you walk around with a sack over your head?
Some people see so little they might just as well.

or **Special times**

Saturday

When I was ten, a Saturday
Stretched its barefoot, hungry way
From waking up and hearing Mum
And seeing if the post had come
To breakfast . . . curly bacon . . . then
Begin again . . .
With fried bread central on the plate . . .
Still only half
past eight.

Then the long freedom of the day
For play
And pocket money.
Every Saturday was sunny.

Gwen Dunn

or **Feelings**

The name of the game

'Catch the *ball!*' the teacher cried
I ran, I jumped, I stretched, I tried.
I really did
      – I missed.

'Useless!' she yelled. 'Silly girl!' she spat.
'What on earth d'you think you are playing at?'
'A game' I said
      – and wept.

Jenny Craig

15

What you do

1 Places   How observant are you? Give yourself an observation test.
Describe
   a   The street outside the school
   b   The front of your house
   c   Your bedroom
   d   Look around your classroom. Look at its shape, its size, the colour of the walls, the furniture, the shape and number of windows and doors. Write a very accurate description of it.

2 Special times   In the poem Gwen Dunn describes a time special to her – Saturdays. Choose a time that is special for you. It could be a Saturday, Sunday, Monday morning, the first day of the holiday or Christmas Day. Describe it and say why it is important for you.

3 Feelings   Can you imagine how Jenny felt when the teacher was angry with her? Can you remember a time when something happened that made you very sad, happy, angry or frightened? Try to describe it. Don't be afraid to use similes. Look for just the right words to describe your feelings at that moment.

4 Discussion time
Share your descriptions with the class. Discuss with your teacher what makes some of the descriptions more interesting than others.

Unit 3 — Writing about feelings

Everyone has feelings. We get sad and happy, frightened and lonely, angry and jealous. We are always feeling something.

Writing about our feelings can help us to understand them.

Have you ever felt the way some of these people are feeling? Of course you have.

**Lonely   Happy   Jealous   Sad
Worried   Scared   Angry**

What you do

1   Pick out the correct title to put under each picture.

2   **Discussion time**
    Make a list together of all the different sorts of feelings people have. Talk about the kind of happenings that make us feel that way. Do we all feel the same when something happens, or have different feelings about it?

Feeling happy

Being happy is what everyone wants to be.
Different things make people happy.

Climbing cliffs is some people's idea of fun

. . . or swimming

Others just enjoy a good read.

What makes you happy?

What you do

1   Write down the things that make you happy.
    Start your list like this:

> "I feel happy when I'm playing with my friends."
> "I feel good when someone gives me a present."
> "I feel . . . . ."

2   **Discussion time**
    Share your list with your friends. Compare what makes you
    happy with what they have written. Are there any surprises?
3   Write about a time when something happened that made you
    very happy. You will need to think hard about it.

Helping other people can make us feel happy.

Why do we feel happy sometimes, even though nothing special has happened?

What you do

1 Write down some ways in which you could make someone at home happy. When you get home this afternoon, try it.

2 Write about a time when you were feeling unhappy and someone cheered you up.

3 Some people always seem cheerful. Do you know someone like that? Do you like being with them? Write about it.

4 **Discussion time**
Do you think when you are happy you make those around you a bit happier, or doesn't it make any difference to them?
Why do we feel good some days even though nothing special has happened? Talk about these things with your teacher.

Feeling scared

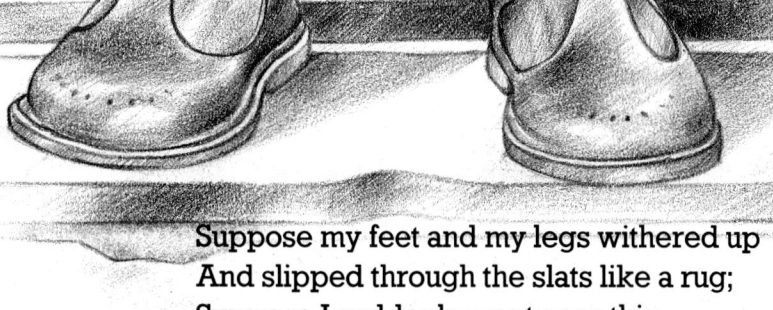

Cold feet

They have all gone across
They are all turning to see
They are all shouting 'Come on'
They are all waiting for me.

I look through the gaps in the footway
And my heart shrivels with fear,
For way below the river is flowing
So quick and so cold and so clear.

And all that there is between it
And me falling down there is this:
A few wooden planks (not very thick)
And between each, a little abyss.

The holes get right under my sandals,
I can see straight through to the rocks,
And if I don't look, I can feel it,
Just there, through my shoes and my socks.

Suppose my feet and my legs withered up
And slipped through the slats like a rug;
Suppose I suddenly went very thin
Like that baby that slid down the plug?

I know that it cannot happen,
But suppose that it did, what then?
Would they be able to find me
And take me back home again?

They have all gone across
They are waiting to see
They are all shouting 'Come on'
But they'll have to carry me.

Brian Lee

Everybody gets frightened sometimes.

What you do

1 **Discussion time**
   Read this poem together. Talk about the way the boy felt when he found he was afraid to cross the bridge. What was he afraid of? Could he help feeling that way? Was he ashamed? Should he be?

2 Have you ever been scared like the boy in the poem? Write a good story about your most frightening experience.

3 Describe how you feel when you are scared. Do you shiver? Do you shake? Does your heart beat faster?

4 Make a list of the things that scare you. Compare your list with your friends'.

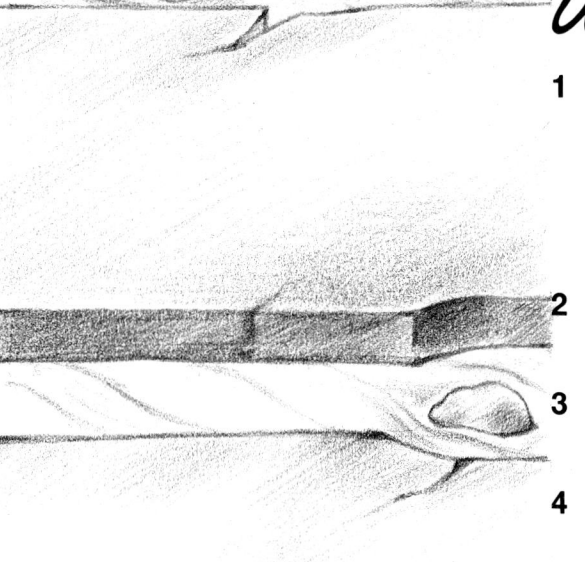

Some things that scared us when we were little don't scare us any more.

Is it unkind to frighten someone even in fun?

We may be frightened of being hurt inside – in our feelings. We're afraid that people will laugh at us, or that we'll be 'told off'.

Or it might be the thought of doing exams that scares us.

What you do

1. Write a few sentences about the things that used to scare you but don't now.

2. Write about what makes you afraid of being hurt in your feelings, for example, being laughed at.

3. When is it all right to give someone a scare? Or is it always wrong to frighten people? What sort of people should we never scare even in fun? Have a **Discussion time** on this before you write anything.

4. We sometimes scare ourselves deliberately. We read spooky stories or watch frightening films or TV. Why do we do this? Can you write a spooky story to scare your friends?

5. The boy was ashamed of being afraid to cross the bridge, yet no-one is ashamed of being scared of spiders, snakes, or the dark. Talk and write about this idea.

Feeling sad

All sorts of things can make us feel sad:
– being lonely
– having someone in the family sick
– losing a pet or something we are fond of
– feeling different from others, being left out
– when nobody seems to care how we feel.

What do you think is happening in this picture?
Yes, you are right.
The girl has been left out of the game and has
no-one to play with.

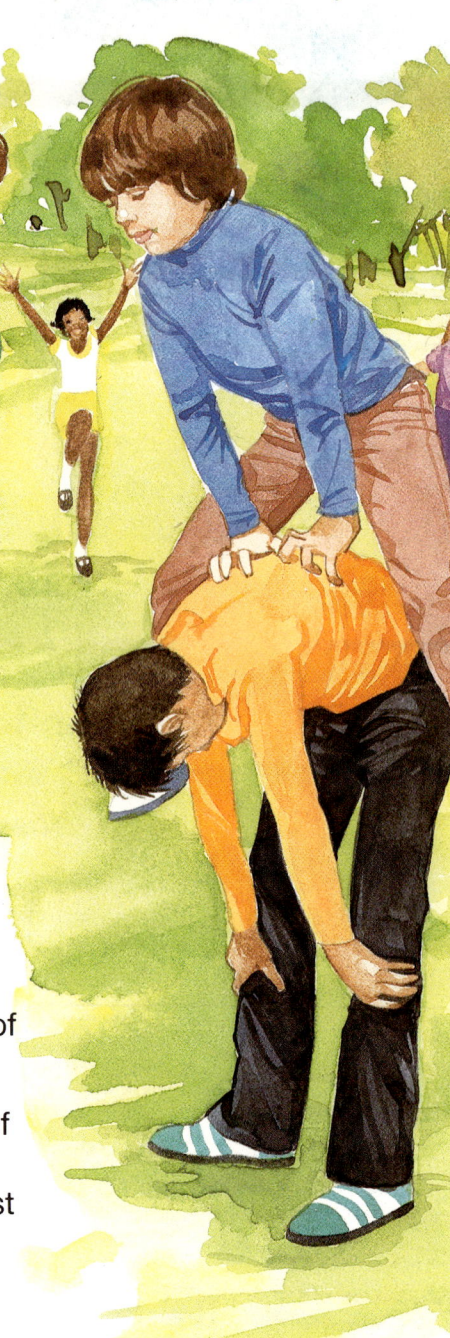

What you do

1 **Discussion time**
   Talk about feeling sad. Think of all the things that can make
   people feel unhappy.

2 Write about the things that make you unhappy. What sorts of
   happenings make you sad?

3 The girl in the picture is sad because she has been left out of
   the game. She has no-one to play with. Has this ever
   happened to you? Are the other children being unkind or just
   thoughtless? What could they do to cheer her up?
   Talk about the picture and then write a story with a happy
   ending called 'Left out'.

Being lonely often means being unhappy. Some people are more likely to be lonely than others. Because they are old, sick, handicapped, or new to a school they find it difficult to join in.

What you do

Write down all the sorts of people you think may be most likely to be lonely. Say what you think you and other children could do to help such people feel needed and happy again. Find out a little about organizations like 'Age Concern' that help old or lonely people.

There are lots of other feelings and moods we can talk and write about.

Worried **Jealous** **Anxious** **Angry**

These are just some of them.
You could make a booklet about your own feelings. It would be interesting to read when you grow up.
You might like to try expressing your feelings by acting a play, writing a poem or playing music.
Doing these things can help us understand our feelings better.

Unit 4

Writing instructions

Have you ever thought how difficult it is to be a driving instructor? Especially when you have a pupil like this one!

When we give instructions there are some simple things to remember. The first is to put things in the right order.

What you do

Put the following instructions from our driving instructor in the right order:

Fasten your seat belt

Look in the mirror

Drive off

Start the engine

Open the door

Get in the car

Put the car in gear

Take off the brake

Now you have to mend a bicycle puncture. Don't worry if you have never done this. If you read the instructions carefully and think hard you will get it sorted out.

What you do

Put these instructions in the right order:
Put the tube and tyre back on the bike
Put the sticky rubber solution over the hole
Dip the tube into a bowl of water, watch for
 the bubbles that show where the hole is
Take the tyre off and remove the inner tube
Blow the tube up a little
Put on the patch
Allow the rubber solution to dry a little
Dry the area around the hole and mark it with chalk.

Now you have to write all the instructions yourself. It is not as easy as it may seem. Write out your instructions on rough paper first so that you can change them.

What you do

Write instructions for the following activities. Start a new line for each instruction.
Making a cup of tea
Making a cheese sandwich
Planting seeds
Putting a plaster on a cut finger
Cleaning the hamster's cage

Here is a really hard one to finish. Give instructions for tying a shoe lace.

Unusual instructions

You have been appointed Chief Keeper of Addlepate Zoo.

You have to write out some instructions for the assistant keepers who have to do some of the more dangerous jobs in the zoo.

Write clearly, start new lines for each instruction and make your instructions simple. They are new to the job – just like you.

What you do

1 Write instructions for your assistant keepers on how to:
   a Put a large poisonous snake in a box for transport.
   b Take a thorn out of the lion's foot.
   c Wash the elephant.
   d Put the polar bear in a new enclosure on the other side of the zoo.
   e Take an underwater picture of the killer whale in its large pool for the newspapers.
   f Take a bad tooth out of the crocodile's mouth. You must not drug it.

Do get your instructions right. It could be very unpleasant for your keepers if you don't.

Buck Star's puzzle

Here is an old puzzle in a new form for you to try. You may have to tackle this in groups to find the answers before you write it down.

Buck star has a problem. He has to take a Zarcat from Planet X2 to his spaceship in his small shuttle craft. The Zarcat is a fierce meat-eater. He also has to take a Perican, a large gentle plant-eater. He also has a large sack of rare plants to take. He can only take one thing at a time in his small craft to the spaceship.

If he leaves the two animals alone the Zarcat will eat the Perican. He can't leave the Perican alone with the plants or it may eat them. The only two things he can leave alone together on planet or spaceship are the Zarcat and the plants.

What you do

Write out instructions for Buck Star telling him how to get the two animals and the plants safely to the spaceship. The first instruction is done for you.

> a Take the Perican to the space ship.
> b Return to the planet and pick up the.....

Now you finish the instructions for Buck.

This is quite a hard puzzle so you may like to work in groups to find the answer before you write it down. See which group is first to find the right instructions.

Robin

I stop myself sliding a morsel
Of bacon fat into the bin.
It will do as a meal for the robin,
His legs are so terribly thin.

Roy Fuller

What you do

Instructions for someone to build something have to be written carefully or the construction will fall to pieces. Write instructions for building the bird table you can see in the picture.

Explaining

Explaining is not quite the same as instructing. You don't expect anyone to go and **do** what you have explained. If you are instructing someone you expect him or her to carry out your instructions.

Suppose you had to explain a number of things to a very inquisitive stranger who had just landed on earth. Fortunately he can read English.

1 The spaceman wants all sorts of things explained to him. Do the best you can to write out:

How a bird builds its nest
How a tadpole becomes a frog
What a motor car looks like
The difference between an aeroplane and an airship.

2 Imagine you are from outer space. Ask one of your friends to write out an explanation of something that puzzles you.

Games

Have you a favourite game?
Explaining how games are
played is quite difficult.

Before you explain how to play your favourite game, talk over
these suggestions as a class with your teacher. Start by saying:

What the game is called and where it is played . . . on a field, a
    court, a table, outdoors or indoors.
How many players are involved.
What equipment is used (posts, nets, bats, etc.).
What the players try to do.
How they win the game.

Give just one or two of the most important rules. In football, for
example, players must not handle the ball.

Say why this is your favourite game.

What you do

Explain your favourite game and why you like it. Use the plan you
have just talked about as a class to help you.

Inventions

Ever tried your hand as an inventor? Here is a chance to do some inventing and explaining at the same time.

'Extending arm'

'Eyes to look around corners'

1 In the picture the artist has suggested two ways of improving the human body. Can you think of one or two more? Explain what they are and how they would work.

2 Invent a device to protect postmen from dogs.

3 Invent a machine to get you out of bed in the morning.

4 Invent a new mouse trap.

5 Invent a safer bicycle.

If you are not very good at inventing, have a chat in groups first to get your ideas going. Use some drawings to help your writing.

More ideas to think about

Imagine you have a dangerous hobby like hang-gliding, potholing or mountain climbing. Perhaps you have a dangerous job working as a steeple jack, stunt man, tight-rope walker or lion tamer. Try to explain to a friend why you choose to do these dangerous things.

Unit 5 — Making Plans

'Be prepared' is the motto of the Scouts and Guides.

One way of being prepared is to make careful plans for what you are going to do . . . and being ready if things go wrong.

Some events need a lot of planning and preparation.

Even less important events are helped if we think ahead a little.

It often helps to write plans down. This unit is about writing plans out clearly, and thinking ahead.

What you do

1 **Discussion time**
   What makes a good plan? We have to give ourselves time to plan, for instance. Talk about all the things that should go into a good plan.

2 Write what you think makes a good plan. List a few of the events and activities that you think need careful planning.

The school trip

In some schools the children help to organize the school trips. Have you ever done this?

Try planning a visit to a local zoo or some other interesting place. If you plan this imaginary trip well you may be able to help plan the next real visit.

What you do

1. Plan a class trip to the zoo or some other place of interest. You will need to:

   write to the bus company and arrange the seating and times of the bus;
   book the entrance to the zoo;
   decide how many children will go;
   what you will need to charge;
   what you will do when you get there.

   You are supposed to learn something as well as have a good time. Plan what to do if the weather is bad.

2. When you have made your plans, compare them with your friends'. Did you miss anything out?

3. Write a short description of the best school trip you have ever had and why you thought it was such good fun.

Remember

To make good plans you need to:
Know exactly what you are going to do.
Plan well ahead – don't rush.
If others are going to use your plans, it is even more important to write clearly, use language everyone understands and not waste words.
Have a check list of the things you will need.
Make sure everyone with a job knows what he or she has to do and is prepared if things go wrong.

Jane's picnic

Calamity Jane does it again.

Poor plans are worse than no plans.

Jane is always organizing something for her friends, but she never does it properly. Things are going to go terribly wrong at her picnic.

Jane has forgotten the cups to drink from, but that's the least of her problems. Look at the bull charging through the gate, the bees, the angry landowner, and much else besides.

What you do

1   Calamity Jane really got her plans wrong for this picnic. Can you imagine what the picture would look like in a few more minutes? Describe what you think will happen to Jane's picnic.

2   Draw a picture to show how you think the picnic may look in a few minutes' time.

3   **Discussion time**
    Talk about the mistakes Jane made in planning her picnic. Where did she go wrong?

Careful Carol made no mistakes about planning her picnic.

She planned the right place, the right time, the right food and plenty of things to do.

So everyone had a good time.

What you do

1   Plan a picnic for yourself and five friends. If you can't get to the country, plan it for the park.

   Here are some of the things you will need to think about when you are making your plans.
       Choose a good place for your picnic. It must be a real place you know. Say why you chose that spot.
       What day will it be on and how will you get there? What time will you all set off?
       Decide what food to take. Remember some food isn't easy to carry. Which friend brings what food?
       What else will you need besides food? Make a list.
       Plan some things to do after the picnic.
       Have some plans for what to do if it rains.

2   When you have written out your plans carefully, get together in small groups with your friends and compare what you have written. Decide which was the best planned picnic in your group. Remember the neatest writer and best speller may not have written the best plans. Just be as neat as you can.

3   **Discussion time**
   As a class, look at the best entry from each group and discuss with your teacher why they were such good plans.

Indigo Bones and the Temple of Gloom

Forest

Indigo Bones is an explorer. He knows that in the Temple of Gloom lies a priceless treasure of diamonds. To get to the temple he has to face many dangers and he needs to plan his journey to the temple very carefully.

Between Indigo and the temple are 20 miles of dense jungle. He will have to cut his way through it. There are many wild animals – particularly snakes. It is also full of insects – some of which are poisonous.

At the end of the jungle is a fast-flowing river, which is known to contain crocodiles and dangerous fish. It is very muddy and no good for drinking.

Beyond the river lies the mountain. It has steep cliff sides with falling rocks. It can only be climbed with ropes. At the top Indigo will come to the temple but all round it lies a very deep ditch with sharp metal spikes at the bottom. He will have to bridge it somehow.

When he gets through the heavy doors of the temple, long rusted together, he will be in complete darkness; there are no windows in the Temple of Gloom. The temple is supposed to be deserted, but lights have been seen and no-one knows if a mysterious person or tribe guards the treasure.

The jewels lie high up on a ledge in the central hall. They are locked in a heavy iron box.

Indigo has a few problems to face, doesn't he?

Temple

Crocodile River

Indigo's camp

Just suppose you were Indigo Bones.

You want to get those jewels. You will need to make some careful plans if you are to succeed.

Will you take anyone with you? – if so, what sort of person?
What time of year will it be best to start? Why?
How long will it take? How much food will you need?
How will you get through the jungle, over the river, up the mountain and over the ditch?
What tools, equipment and medical supplies will you need? (Don't forget the insects.)
In the temple it will be dark. There may be danger from someone guarding the treasure. The great doors have to be opened, and there may be traps in the floors of the hall.
The treasure is on a high ledge. How will you reach it? Now you have to open the iron chest and get back to base again.

What you do

1   Plan your journey to the Temple of Gloom. Write out carefully what you intend to take and how you will overcome the problems.

2   **Discussion time**
    When you have written out your plan, talk it over with your friends in a class discussion. What did you miss out?

3   When you have had your discussion, write a story about your journey to the temple, what happened to you and whether you got the jewels. You could write it as a diary if you wish. Maybe you didn't get back and the diary was found later. You decide.

The perfect holiday

Have you ever dreamt of the perfect holiday?

Everyone enjoys going on holiday. We can't always go exactly where we would like, or do what we would really like most to do.
Just suppose you could have any holiday you want. All you have to do is plan it very carefully.

What you do

1   Decide what you think would be a perfect holiday – at the seaside, in a big city, abroad, on a boat, a holiday camp. There are lots of choices. Share some ideas with your class first.

2   Plan your holiday.
Where will you go and when?
How will you get there?
What will you take?
What will you do?
Where will you stay?
You will need a passport if you go abroad. How will you get one?
There are lots of things for you to plan. Write it all down.

3   Write a story called 'A very unusual holiday' about a holiday that didn't turn out as it was planned.

Practise your planning

If you have enjoyed making plans, here are some other ideas to try. Make plans for:

an enjoyable day for some old folk who don't get out much
a school disco
an outing for some handicapped children
an event to raise money for a charity
school sports day.

Unit 6 — Writing stories

Do you like making up stories? Telling stories has been going on since people began to talk.

In the Far East there are still a few story tellers who go from village to village telling the ancient tales to anyone who will listen.

What shall we tell you? Tales, marvellous tales
Of ships and stars and isles where good men rest,
Where never more the rose of sunset pales
And winds and shadows fall towards the west.

So writes the poet in the *Golden Road to Samarkand*.

We can all learn to write interesting, exciting stories. This unit will help you to do that.

Making a good start

Read this story.

Strange goings on at the manor

It had been a smashing party. There had been ten boys and ten girls at Jim's place. We had a great time, plenty to eat, games, disco dancing and a present for everyone to take home.

It was ten o'clock and Kate, Ranji, Justin and I were walking home. It wasn't very far, but we had to go up the lane beside the old manor house. No-one had lived there for a long time and everyone thought it was a spooky old place.

We all kept together and just as we reached the middle of the lane where the gateway leads up through an overgrown drive to the manor Ranji stopped.

'Hey!' he said, 'Look at that.' He pointed up the drive. We could all see what he meant. There was a very bright light in front of the manor. It was no ordinary light – it seemed to glow and then brighten and go dim again.

Most strange of all, it seemed to be coming from a huge machine, the shape of a discus or a large saucer. We couldn't see very clearly what it was because of the overgrown drive.

'Come on', said Justin in an excited voice, 'We've got to see what this is.'

What you do

1 Finish off the story. Say what happened when the children went up the drive.

2 **Discussion time**
   Have a class discussion on whether this was a good start for a story.
   Did it get your interest quickly?
   Did you want to know what was going to happen next?
   Could you imagine yourself as one of the children?
   Did things begin to happen quickly in the story?
   Can you spot other ways the writer got your attention?

When you write your next story think about what you have discussed and what makes a good start to a story.

Good starts

Read these beginnings to stories by well-known writers.

'When Lila went out on the beach it was so early in the morning that there was no one else there. The sand was washed clean by last night's tide and no one had walked on it except the birds that fished along the coast – gulls, curlews and sand pipers. She walked to the sea with the small basket she carried on the flat of her hand, filled with flowers from the garden around their house– scarlet hibiscus blooms, sweet smelling spider lilies and bright butter-yellow allamanda flowers.'

from *The Village by the Sea* by Anita Desai

'I'm going shopping in the village,' George's mother said to George on Saturday morning. 'So be a good boy and don't get up to mischief.'
This was a silly thing to say to a small boy at any time. It immediately made him wonder what sort of mischief he might get up to.
'And don't forget to give Grandma her medicine at eleven o'clock,' the mother said. Then out she went, closing the back door behind her.
Grandma, who was dozing in her chair by the window, opened one wicked little eye and said, 'Now you heard what your mother said, George. Don't forget my medicine.'
'No, Grandma,' George said.
'And just try to behave yourself for once while she's away.'
'Yes, Grandma,' George said.

from *George's Marvellous Medicine* by Roald Dahl

The Mole had been working hard all the morning, spring cleaning his little home. First with the brooms; then with the dusters; then on ladders and steps and a pail of whitewash; till he had dust in his throat and eyes, splashes of whitewash all over his black fur, and an aching back and weary arms.

from *The Wind in the Willows* by Kenneth Grahame

What you do

1. After you have read these beginnings, write them down in order, starting with the name of the story you feel is going to be most interesting, the one you would most like to read.

2. When you have written your list, write down why you think your first choice is the best. Write a little about each story.

3. **Discussion time**
   Did you notice that the writers tried to get your interest in different ways? They made you want to know more about where Lila lived, George's Grandma, or a mole that does housework.
   Take a class vote on the best beginning and talk a little more about what makes a good start to a story.

4. Try to read at least one of the stories all the way through – just to find out what happens.

More on good starts

Look at the titles of these four books: *The Vanishing Magician*, *The Trouble with Suzy*, *Dangerous Planet* and *The Adventures of the Invisible Boy*.

What you do

1   As far as we know no-one has written these books yet. They are waiting for someone to begin writing them. You try. Write a good start for each of these four stories. It doesn't have to be very long – just three or four paragraphs. Remembering how the professional writers started their stories and what you have discussed, try to make the beginnings really interesting or exciting.

2   When you have written your story beginnings, come together in groups of four. Pick out your group's best effort for each story. Have someone read your selection to the class. Take a class vote on the four best ones.

3   **Discussion time**
    Have a discussion on what made the winning openings the best.

4   Write one of the stories in full and design a cover for it.

Story plans

Before we start a story we should have some idea how it will develop, and what will happen next. Authors have to plan a story before they start to write it.

Look at these three simple plans for stories. It helps to think of a title before you begin. You can always alter it later if you wish.

One good turn
Girl on way to school – man hitting dog – stops him – feeds dog from lunch pack – next weekend – playing near old mine – falls down mine shaft – trapped – rescue search – parents – giving up hope – found by dog she had befriended.

Spanish treasure
Children on holiday – find old map in book – tell explorer friend – expedition planned – arrival in Amazon forest – adventures (savage animals) – find temple – haunted – dangers – find treasure – betrayed by guide – left trapped – escape – catch guide – help from friendly Indians – home.

A narrow escape
At a circus – lion tamer act – lion escapes – panic – alone in circus tent with lion – lion stalking you – see cage – get inside – lion outside – return of tamer – capture of lion.

We don't always have to write a plan for our stories, but it can help sometimes. We must always have some idea how our story will grow. Be ready to alter your plan if you get a better idea.

What you do

1 **Discussion time**
   What do you think of the story plans above? Do they give a good idea how the story will develop? Is there enough detail?

2 Choose one (or more if you wish) and write the story.

3 Make a simple plan for a story called *Just in time*. Exchange your plan with a friend and write each other's story. Afterwards, see if you wrote what was expected.

4 Try writing a complete story, not a plan, in 30 words, just for fun.

Good endings

It is just as important to finish your story well.

Stories should always end with an exciting climax or ending. The last chapter is very important in every book and story.

What you do

1 Look at the picture strip. Think what the last picture might show. Write down what happened to Nosey Parker. You can draw the picture if you like.

2 **Kidnapped**
A girl has been kidnapped and held to ransom. The police are being led to an old windmill by some children who have seen lights there and heard a child crying. Write the last chapter of the story as the police break into the mill to try and rescue the girl and capture the kidnappers.

3 **Discussion time**
Have a class discussion and compare the way some of you have finished the story. Are there some really good endings? What made them good? Was there a surprise? How did the best endings hold your attention?

Description in stories

Using description properly in stories is very important. It can help us to make our writing much more interesting. Read this page from *Ludo and the Star Horse* by Mary Stewart. Ludo, a German boy, is having some very strange adventures with his horse Renti. They have come to a great forest – nothing like the forests Ludo was used to in Germany.

But this forest. You and I would have known it was a tropical forest and that Ludo was very near the sun; but Ludo had never heard of the tropics, and gaped amazed from Renti's back as he looked about him.

To begin with, the trees were half as high again as they were at home, and beneath them the growth of tree-ferns and flowering bushes was so thick that you couldn't see even half-way up the tallest trunks. Creepers hung like ropes from bough to bough, some of them with leaves as big as paddles, and great scarlet or purple flowers shaped like trumpets or huge star-fish. Whole clusters of orchids sprouted from the crotches of trees. Fireflies floated by like clouds of sparks.

The forest was rich with a sort of steamy warmth, and heavy with all the scents you can imagine. It was humming with cheerful bees all stacking the honey away in their own secret combs for their own use; and all a-whistle with birds stuffing themselves with fruit and fat insect-grubs and delicious caterpillars.

If Mary Stewart had written, 'Ludo and Renti came to a great tropical forest' and then continued with her story, you would not have felt what it was like in that strange forest which she describes so well. It sets the scene for the amazing things that happen next to Ludo and Renti. When you have a chance, read *Ludo and the Star Horse*. It is a great story.

What you do

1 Discussion time

Look at the description of the tropical forest with a friend. Pick out together all the describing words (**adjectives**) and the phrases that start with 'like'. It is these words and phrases that make the description interesting.

Have a class discussion with your teacher about the use of these adjectives and descriptive phrases (which are called **similes**).

2 On your own, rewrite these short, bare sentences and make them more interesting by describing the loft; the room; the teenagers and how the people felt.

'The burglar entered the room and took the silver from the safe.'

'Amy climbed the steps and shone her torch into the loft.'

'The gang of teenagers came on the pitch and spoilt our game.'

Remember

Get a good, exciting, interesting start.

Have some idea about the way your story will grow.

Keep the reader's interest by having something new or unexpected happening often.

Make sure you have an exciting, interesting ending.

Write as neatly as you can.

Spell as well as you can, but don't let being a poor speller stop you being a good story teller and enjoying it. Some very famous writers are poor spellers.

Use your dictionary to help, but don't be afraid to use interesting words because they are hard to spell.

Make a proper book. Design a cover, illustrate it, put your name on it.

Use pictures with your story to make them more interesting.

Use loose sheets so that your story can be as long or as short as you like.

Have a shelf in the classroom just for the books your class have written.

Suggestions for stories

Adventure stories
About lost treasure, distant jungles, hidden cities, strange lands and dangers in space or on other planets.

Unusual happenings in ordinary places
Discovering robbers, spies, smugglers in your own area or on holiday; strange encounters; visitors from space.

Mystery stories
Unexplained mysteries; crimes; disappearances; invent your own famous detective like Sherlock Holmes.

Animal stories
Pets and wild animals. Try imagining you are an animal.

School stories
Sports days; unusual happenings; the school bully getting paid out; quarrels and funny events.

Time stories
Stories set in other times in history. You may have to find out a little about those times before you start, but that's what story writers have to do.

Ghost stories
Great fun. See if you can write a really spooky one.

Funny stories
Probably the hardest of all to write but worth a try.

You could also try writing a series of stories about one character or a group of people. You can work with your friends on this.

Write a book of short stories all on the same theme, for example, stories with a surprise ending entitled *Tales of the Unexpected*.

Write stories for a special audience – the infant class, perhaps.

Remember

Stories were told long before they were written. Make time in class for reading your stories to each other. Encourage each other. Never make fun of someone else's story. That would be very unkind. Think how you would feel. The important thing is to enjoy being a writer.

Unit 7

Writing Conversations

Cave men had very few words. It must have made life difficult at times.
Talking together – conversation – is a very important part of our life.

When we write stories or reports it helps if we know how to write out what people say properly. This Unit will help you to do this.

Have you met these two yet?

They are the 'Quotation Twins'.

We use Mr Start ❝ when we start speaking and Mr Stop ❞ when we finish. We have to learn to use Start and Stop quotation marks if we want to write real conversation.

Mr Start   **Mr Stop**

What you do

For a start, write down what you think the cave man might have said to warn his friend and what his friend may have replied. Put quotation marks around the words that were actually spoken: . . .

Highwayman

The great black horse and its rider leapt in front of the stage coach.

'Stand and deliver!' cried Black Jake.

There was a startled cry from the coach and a young woman thrust her head through the window.

I have no money, Sir, please spare me she said fearfully.

The highwayman gave a sinister chuckle.

Well now, I'll be content with that handsome necklace you are wearing, pretty lady.

Quickly the frightened girl undid the necklace and gave it to him.

With a cry of Away Beauty the robber galloped off into the night.

What you do

Write out the passage about the highwayman and put in quotation marks where you think they should go. Put them around any group of words that were spoken. The first quotation is done for you. Note that in printed conversation (as in books), the printer often uses single quotation marks, as here.

The inspector investigates

We usually start a new line for a fresh speaker.

'When you entered the room was the body lying in this position?' asked the inspector. 'Exactly where it is now, Sir,' replied the butler. 'I have not moved anything.' The inspector looked thoughtful. 'Has anyone entered the room since you found the body?' he asked. 'No. I have kept everyone out of the room and the door locked until you arrived,' the butler answered. 'Very well, I shall need to see you again later. Please ask his lordship to step this way.' The butler bowed and turned to leave the room.

What you do

Write out the passage about the inspector. All the quotation marks are written in, but you have to start a new line each time the butler or the inspector starts to speak.

Too many 'saids'

Sometimes we spoil the conversations we write by using the word 'said' too often.

There are plenty of other more interesting words to use. You can also add words like 'wearily', 'sadly' or 'firmly' to 'said' to make it more interesting. These are called adverbs. (Added to the verb – add verb.) They often end in -ly.

Here are a few words we can use instead of 'said'. Can you think of some more?

asked
jeered
cried
hissed
answered
shouted
murmured
replied
whispered
laughed

The haunted house

'Gosh! That house does look creepy,' said Dick.
'Well, we've got to get inside somehow,' said Matt.
'But it's so dark, we won't be able to see anything – or anyone,' said Dick.
You could almost hear his knees clacking together.
'Come on – you're not chicken are you?' said Matt, looking hard at his friend.
'Me! Scared! Of that silly old house!' said Dick, putting on a brave front.
'Of course I'm not scared – much.'

What you do

Copy out the conversation between Dick and Matt but don't use the word 'said'. Find other more suitable words to use. When you have finished, compare your words with your friends' and ask the teacher to write them all up on the board.

Conversation in stories

The cave

The two girls entered the cave slowly, Kate holding tight to her sister's hand. The darkness seemed to reach out for them as they moved away from the bright sunlight of the hillside. Kate felt suddenly cold and rather frightened and began to wish they had never decided to explore the cave.

★★
June's comforting hand squeezed hers, and they went carefully on. June's torch picked out faint patterns on the walls of the cave.

Kate didn't like those shapes she could see among the jutting rocks, shadows which looked like witches or goblins. Her fears returned.

★★
Reassured once more by what her sister had said, Kate saw ahead a passage which led from the main part of the cavern into a much smaller cave from which came a very faint glow. June didn't appear to have seen it and Kate pulled her sister to a halt.

★★
Together they moved into the passage and quite quickly the glow got brighter and there at the end of the passage, on a ledge in the small cave, stood the most unusual object the girls had ever seen.

This story would be much better with some conversation.

1   **Discussion time**
    Read through the short story above together as a class. When you come to the ******** lines get some suggestions from the class on what the sisters might have said to each other at that point in the story.

2   When you have heard lots of suggestions, copy out the story and write in a few sentences of conversation where the ****** lines are.

3   What was the strange object in the small cave? What happened next? Finish off the story in as exciting a way as you can.

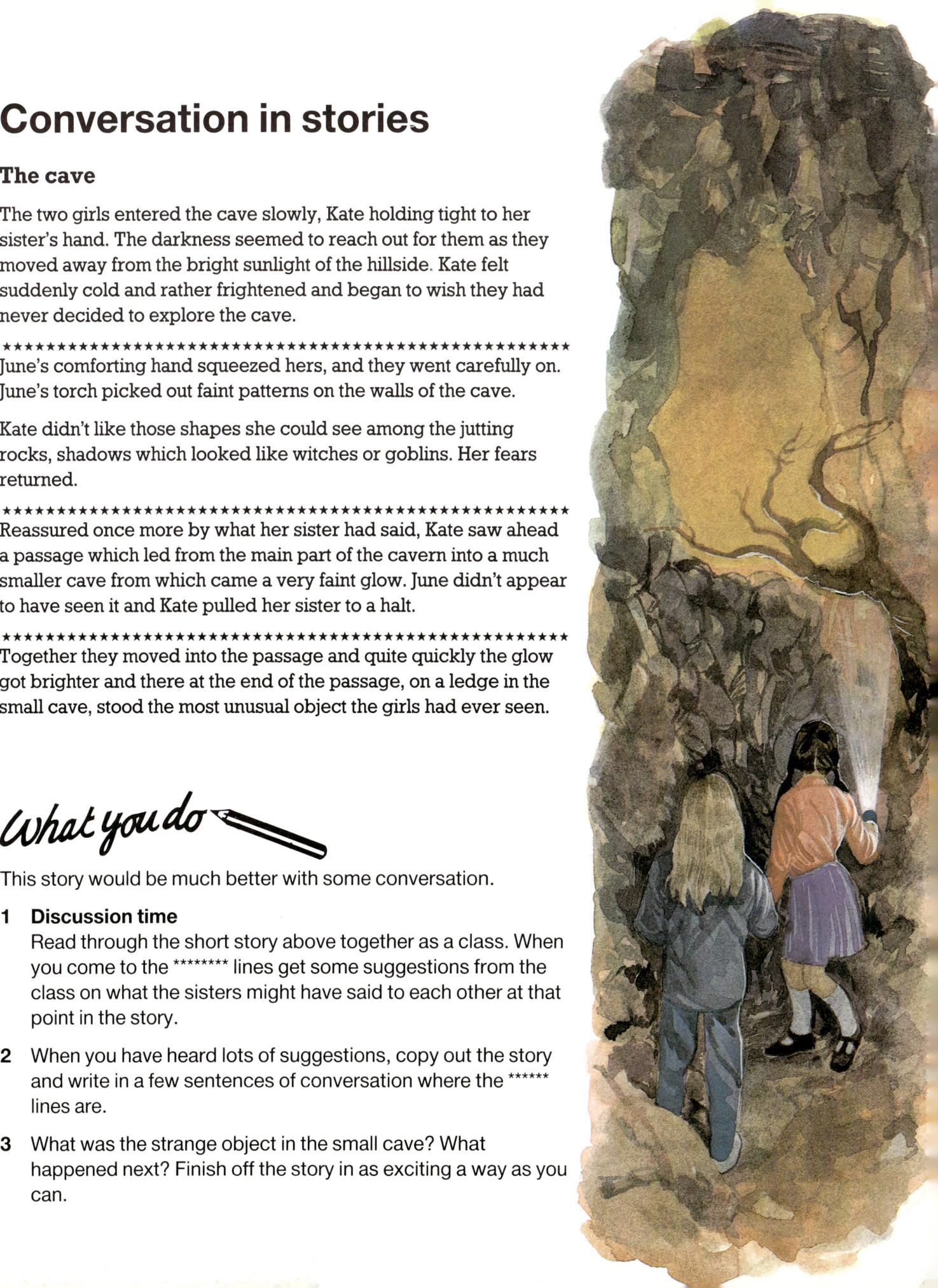

No names

'What's the difference between a nightwatchman and a butcher?'
'I don't know, what is the difference?'
'One stays awake and one weighs a steak!'

'Doctor, doctor, I keep seeing little black spots before my eyes!'
'Have you seen a doctor before?'
'No, just little black spots'.

When just two people are talking, we do not have to say which person is actually speaking each time. We can just write what is said as long as we start a new line for each speaker.

What you do

Finish a conversation between these two girls who are trying to decide what to do on a Saturday morning. You must only use their names in the opening sentences, which have been done for you.

> "Hi Jill! What a great morning. How are we going to use it?" greeted Susan.
> "Let's do something really different," replied Jill.

Is it a foreign language?

'Jan,' her said, 'I ricken you should have a moter-car fer yerzel, getting about like you do to zo many places.'

'Daun ee tell up sitch ole rummidge missis,' I says, 'Whatever should I do with a motor car?'

'Do with 'en? Why, ride in 'en,' her says.

'You daun think I meaned for 'ee to ait 'en do 'ee?'

'He'd ait me, more likely,' I says. 'You'll be saying next I ought to have a vlying machine, or a subtareen.'

'Well you never knaws,' her says.

'No, that's very true,' I says. 'Pigs might fly but they'm most unlikely burds. When you zees me with a moter you can expec' pigs to start sprouting wings any minute.'

If you read the conversation between Jan Stewer and Mrs Endycott just as it is written you will sound just like them.

Not many people in Devon speak just like this any more, but there is still a strong Devon dialect and Devonians are proud to speak it. Perhaps you speak a different language from some of the children in your class.

We should all be proud of the language we speak or our regional dialect from London, Liverpool, Scotland – wherever we live.

What you do

Have a discussion about the dialect in your town or village. Try to write the conversation between the two people above in your dialect. It is hard but you can have a lot of fun trying.

All kinds of talk

Here's a chance to try different kinds of conversation.

What you do

1 Imagine what these famous people might have said to each other when:
Neil Armstrong and Buzz Aldrin set foot on the moon;
Columbus and his ship's captain first caught a glimpse of the coast of America;
Edmund Hillary and Sherpa Tensing set foot on the top of Mount Everest.

Write a short conversation between each pair when they finally reached their goals. You could work it out in pairs – each taking a part – before you write anything.

2 The mood we are in has an effect on our conversation.

Angry
Write a conversation between a youth club leader and two teenagers who have made a nuisance of themselves.

Happy
Write a jolly conversation between two children who have just watched a funny TV programme together.

Sad
Write a sad conversation between a girl who has lost her pet cat and her mother who tries to comfort her.

Try some other conversations which reflect moods.

3 Have fun! Two space travellers have landed on a strange planet and meet a 'back-to-front' person who says all his sentences backwards:
'Sregnarts ginrom doog' said the back-to-front man.

Finish the conversation.

Write a radio play

In radio plays we can't see what people are doing or where they are as we can in TV or films. Everything has to be explained to us through the conversation of the people in the play or someone speaking their thoughts aloud.

Sound effects, of course, help us to imagine what is happening.

Read this example of Dr Who talking to his assistants as the 'Tardis' lands on a new planet. The script may look a little like this:

DOCTOR   'Hold tight everyone, we are just about to materialize and the ground seems very uneven.'
(Crashing sounds and then silence.)

LEILA   'Phew! That was a nasty moment.'

DOCTOR   'Don't move, anyone. There is a strange creature probing round the Tardis. It seems to be of unbelievable strength and it wants to get in – don't move!'
(There are soft thudding noises.)

What you do

1 Write a little more of this play about Dr Who. Afterwards, record your play on a tape recorder and play it back. Use sound effects to make it more exciting. You will need to experiment to get this right.

2 Try writing the script for a radio play. It need not be very long. Write in instructions for the sounds you need. Remember you have to use the conversation of the characters in the play to make it clear to listeners what is happening, who the people are, where they are, etc.
You may need to talk about this as a class first with your teacher.

Remember.

Quotation marks around spoken words.

New lines for new speakers.

Use other 'speaking' words as well as 'said'.

Keep full stops, commas and question marks inside quotation marks.

56

Unit 8 — Predicting

When we forecast something that will happen in the future we are making a **prediction**. This unit helps you understand what predictions are.

There was a young man of Bellaire
Who thought he was lighter than air,
One day from a loft
He tried to take off
And landed . . .

What you do

1 Here is something very easy to start with. What do you predict will happen to the skater in the cartoon strip?

2 Finish the limerick about the young man from Bellaire.

Newspaper predictions

Predictions are being made in newspapers all the time: on the weather, the tides, football results, horse races, the harvest, elections and so on.

Tides

BARNSTAPLE

	Time	Hght	Mtrs
Thursday	03.59	16.30	2.9
Friday	04.54	17.21	3.3
Saturday	05.47	18.13	3.7
Sunday	07.33	19.57	

Look ahead with the stars

Cancer
22 June–23 July
Treats, gifts and luxuries are abundant from Sunday until mid-July. While the influence of Venus is pres...

Virgo
24 August–23 September
Have a pleasant trip! Someone, somewhere...

Scorpio
24 October–22 November
The week...

ONE DAY THESE STAMPS WILL BE VALUABLE.

Yamani warning of new oil crisis

The Saudi Arabian ... ister, Sheikh Yaman ... new oil crisis could ... the 1990s, leaving ... supplying as much ... quart... of the world's ...

In Saud... said ... prod...

Orlov expected to leave for America

By Nicholas Beeston, and Mohsin Ali in Washington

...e returned to Moscow in ...itted to ...

Helsinki group until his arrest in October 1977. ... "The Hel-

for particular attention fro... the KGB and was caught up ... the first wave of arrests ... ...mbers. Since 198...

Labour 'will need 1.3 m jobs to keep pledge'

By David Hencke, Westminster Correspondent

Labour will have to create 1.3 million jobs if it is ... ceed in taking a m... off the regis... years of ... the...

Crisis in store for Panama Canal

GEOFFREY LEAN
■ Environment Correspondent

THE Panama Canal is slow-... ...up because of the ... ...l rain-

What you do

1 You will need a newspaper, a few days old.
Work in pairs and try to find as many examples of predictions as you can.
Cut them out and mount them as part of a class display called 'Whatever next'.
Find out if any of the predictions came true.

2 Try your hand at predicting. Write down what you think will happen, and why:
    in your school or favourite team's next match
    in the TV serial you are watching
    in a book you are half-way through.

You might prefer something easy like what will happen when you get home tonight. Choose any subject on which you think you can make a good prediction.

Merlin's time goes backwards

Do you write diaries or news books in school saying what you did yesterday?

Merlin the Magician in T H White's Book *The Once and Future King* kept living time backwards. For him yesterday was tomorrow and tomorrow was yesterday. Predicting the future was easy for him.

Try turning tomorrow into yesterday yourself.

What you do

1   Instead of writing a diary on what happened to you last weekend, write a diary for next weekend.
    Write it as Merlin would have written it, as if it had already happened. Think carefully about what you are likely to do and then write it up as if it had already taken place.

2   This exercise is for later. Next Monday, after the weekend, have a look at your 'Merlin Diary'. How much that you predicted actually happened? Write up what actually happened.
    Compare the two. How accurate was your prediction?
    Share your diary by reading your two versions to the class if you wish. You should have some laughs.

You need to be very careful and look at all the information if you are going to make sensible predictions.

Science fiction

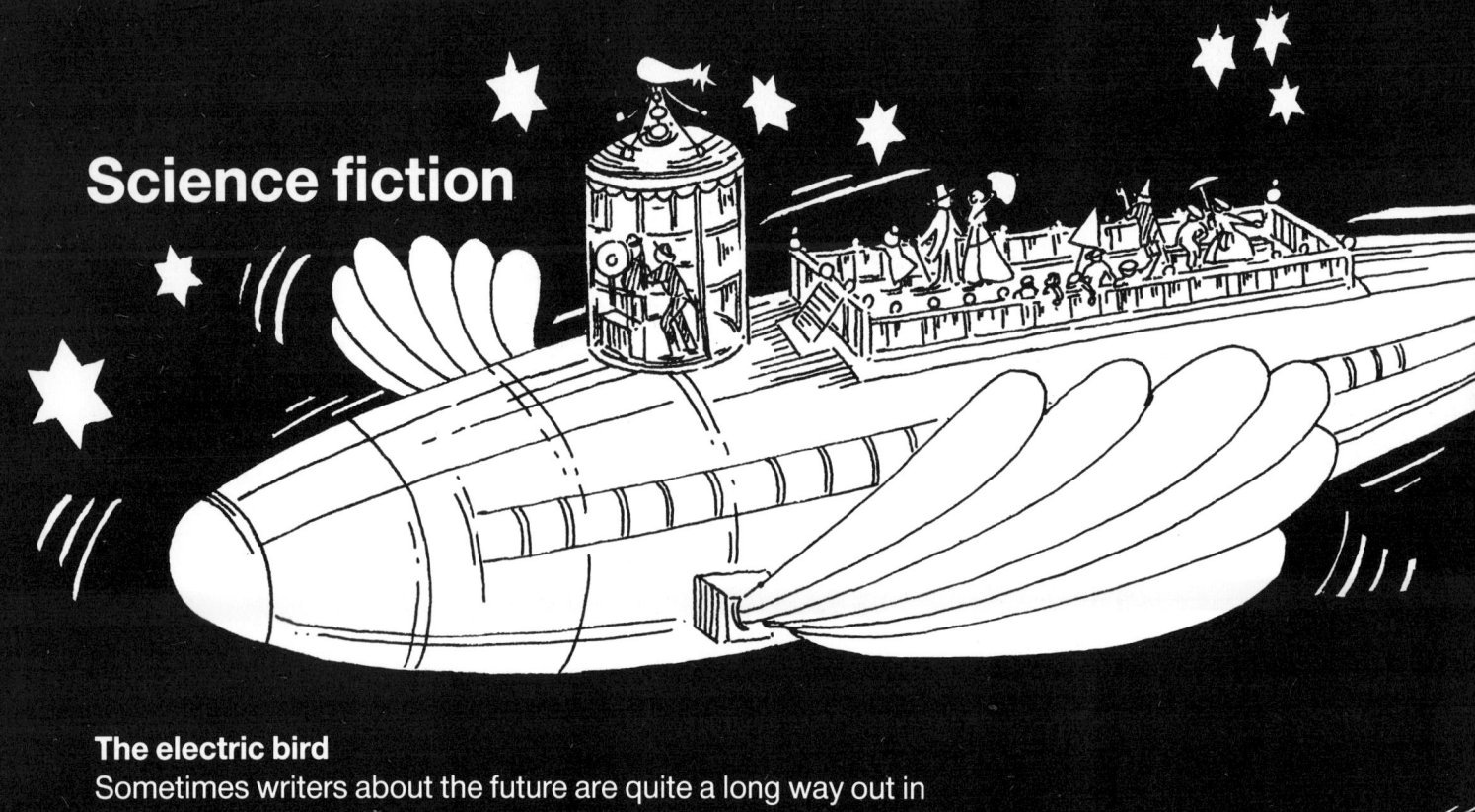

The electric bird

Sometimes writers about the future are quite a long way out in their predictions. This flying machine is from the front page of a popular comic of a hundred years ago. It isn't much like the real aeroplanes of today.

Science Fiction writers often imagine a world of the future, sometimes not too seriously. The writer H G Wells got his first men on the moon by firing them out of a giant cannon! But he also wrote seriously and with great skill about what the world would really be like.

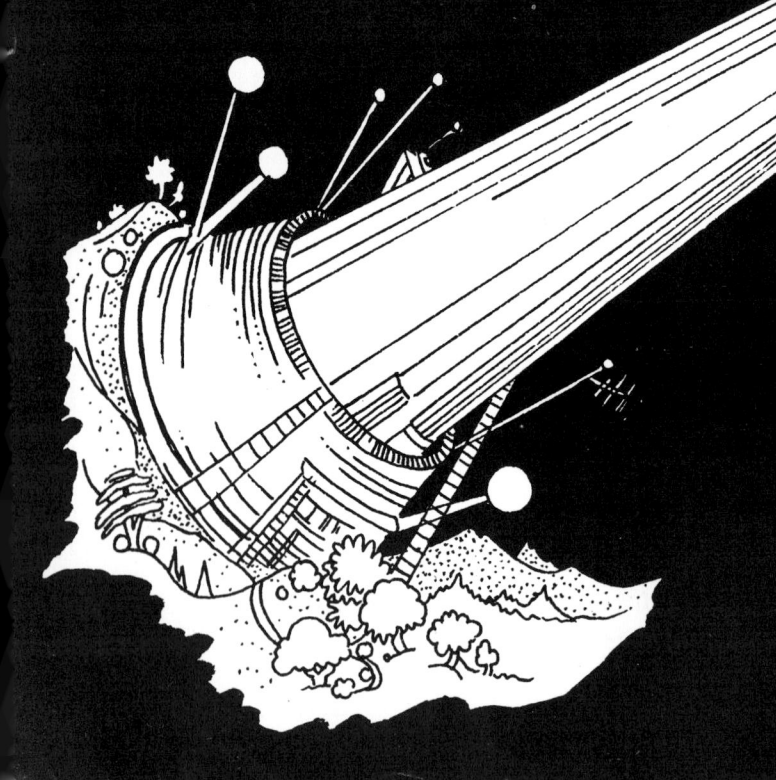

Dr Who and Captain Kirk move through space and time in the 'Tardis' and the star ship 'Enterprise'.

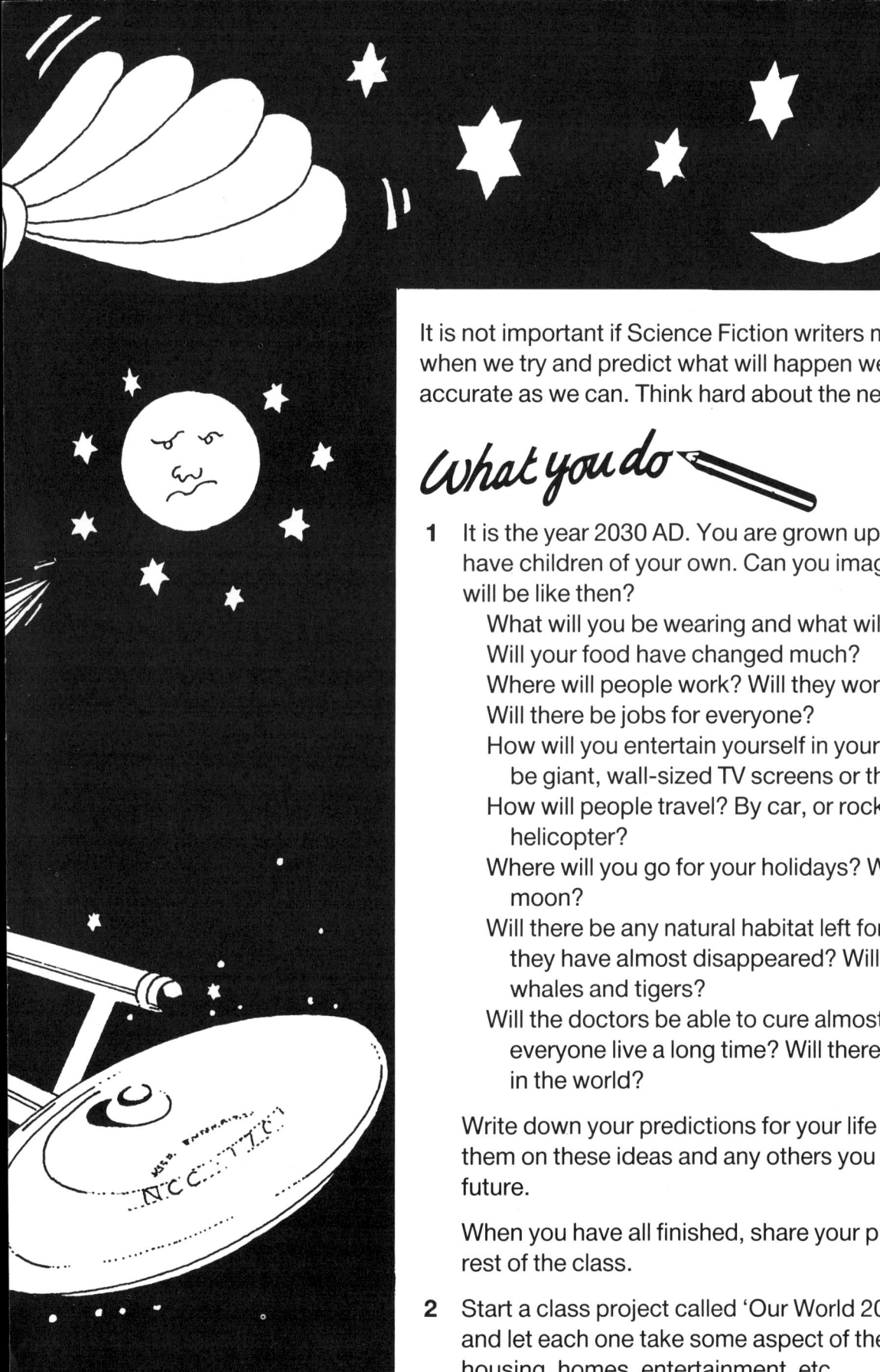

It is not important if Science Fiction writers make a mistake. But when we try and predict what will happen we should be as accurate as we can. Think hard about the next questions.

What you do

1 It is the year 2030 AD. You are grown up; you may possibly have children of your own. Can you imagine what the world will be like then?

What will you be wearing and what will houses be like?
Will your food have changed much?
Where will people work? Will they work as long or as hard? Will there be jobs for everyone?
How will you entertain yourself in your spare time? Will there be giant, wall-sized TV screens or three-dimensional TV?
How will people travel? By car, or rocket, or personal helicopter?
Where will you go for your holidays? Will there be trips to the moon?
Will there be any natural habitat left for wild animals, or will they have almost disappeared? Will we have saved the whales and tigers?
Will the doctors be able to cure almost any illness? Will everyone live a long time? Will there still be hungry people in the world?

Write down your predictions for your life in 2030 AD. Base them on these ideas and any others you may have about the future.

When you have all finished, share your predictions with the rest of the class.

2 Start a class project called 'Our World 2030 AD'. Form groups and let each one take some aspect of the future, like travel, housing, homes, entertainment, etc.
Do drawings and models to go with your writing.
Tape imaginary interviews with adults from the year 2030.

Predictions about people

Predicting how people will act when something unexpected happens isn't easy, but it can be fun.

What you do

Can you predict how these people will act?

Dad, if you give him an unexpected present.
Mum, if you help to wash the dishes.
Your sister, when you take her breakfast in bed.
Your friend, who has never had a bike, when you boast about your new one.
A man who has thoughtlessly thrown an empty packet on the ground, when you pick it up and give it back to him.

Remember how they act as well as how they feel.

The lift

A lift gets stuck between two floors and the lights go out. In the lift are six people: Mrs Dibble, an old lady of 80 who is rather nervous; Mr Harris, 45, a headmaster; Miss Chugg, a rather giggly young lady of 19; her brother Richard who is 10 and always up to mischief; Mrs Ring, a quiet lady who was a nurse.
They are stuck in the lift with very little light for half an hour.

What you do

1 Can you predict what will happen in the lift during that half an hour? Who will panic? Who will take charge? What will they all do? Unexpected happenings and problems bring out the best, and sometimes the worst in people.
Write down your own story about what will happen and also how they acted when rescue came. By the way, you have to invent the sixth person.

2 **Discussion time**
Share your stories. Did the people all act in the way you would have expected? Did some of them behave in an unexpected way?

Personal predictions

People have always been interested in knowing about their future. They use all sorts of ways to try and find out what it will be: crystal balls; cards; hand palms; stars; even tea leaves.

The Bible, The Qur'an and other religious books are full of the stories of prophets, who told people what was going to happen. There are still plenty of prophets around today, as you can see from reading the newspapers.

It is useful to know what the weather is likely to be, if prices will rise and so on, but would you really like to know exactly what your future is, exactly what will happen to you in the years ahead?

What you do

1 If someone offered to tell your fortune, would you want to know or not? Write down what you think would be the advantages and disadvantages.

2 **Discussion time**
   Finish your work on predictions by having a class discussion on when it is good to be able to predict the future, and when it is not.

Type of writing	1st Term				2nd Term				3rd Term			
	1st Qtr	2nd Qtr	3rd Qtr	4th Qtr	1st Qtr	2nd Qtr	3rd Qtr	4th Qtr	1st Qtr	2nd Qtr	3rd Qtr	4th Qtr
Opinions												
Descriptions												
Express feelings												
Instructions												
Plans												
Stories												
Conversations												
Predictions												
Directions												
Present arguments												
Poetry												
To persuade												
To report												
To record												
To justify												
To reflect												

Social studies	SS	Language session	LS	Nature study	NS
Environmental studies	ES	Religious education	RE	Mathematics	M
Science	SC	Integrated project	IP		

CONTENTS

1982
Ian Moss, Family Hotel,
August

1)

I FIRST SAW COLD CHISEL PERFORM AT THE INFAMOUS STATION HOTEL IN PRAHRAN, AN INNER CITY PUB IN MELBOURNE, WHERE MANY IMPORTANT BANDS THAT EMERGED IN THE 70'S GOT THEIR START.

THE STATION HOTEL HAD A SPECIAL AURA ABOUT IT. YOU KNEW THAT NO MATTER WHO THE UNKNOWN BAND WAS ON ANY GIVEN NIGHT (OR DAY), ON THE OFF CHANCE THEY WEREN'T MUCH GOOD, YOU'D STILL ENJOY THE TIME SPENT. I THINK IT WAS LATE 1977 THAT STEVE HANDS PERSUADED ME TO CHECK OUT AN ADELAIDE BAND THAT HE WAS KEEN TO SIGN. BACK THEN, STEVE WAS WARNER MUSIC'S PROMOTIONS MANAGER, AND HIS ABILITY TO SPOT RAW TALENT AND DO SOMETHING TO EXPOSE IT WOULD EARN HIM THE RESPECT OF MUSICIANS AND HIS PEERS AUSTRALIA WIDE.

Cold Chisel's live set on that night included lots of covers (I recall a Led Zeppelin song) and some originals written by the keyboard player, as I found out during the performance (which was witnessed by only a few die-hards on this occasion). What stuck in my mind on the drive home was a song about a disillusioned Vietnam vet, and the last song, when the keyboard player backed the guitarist, who sang "Georgia on my mind" while the lead singer and the rhythm section retired to the bar.

Over the next ten years, I would be privileged to attend many Cold Chisel performances and appreciate the intelligent, melodic rock and roll of one of the best bands Australia has ever produced. On the eve of their reformation it is appropriate that Michael Lawrence, a fan, has painstakingly traced every step in Cold Chisel's journey to success and acceptance as the ultimate people's band.

Michael's book is about people: those who made Cold Chisel great; those who played lesser roles; the characters that bands like Cold Chisel attract; the performances; and the recordings. In fact, I can't recall a more thorough account of any band's career.

All the major players are revealing in their conversations with Michael. They obviously enjoyed retracing their steps, as I'm sure any Cold Chisel fan will. The Chisels were that kind of experience.

Billy Pinnell
RADIO PROGRAMMER/PRESENTER.

Faust

Donald Hugh Walker was born in the Northern Queensland town of Ayr in 1951 on a sugar cane plantation owned by his father, a subject he would later return to in his songs. He took piano lessons from a lady on a neighbouring farm when the family moved to Grafton in NSW during his primary school years, leaning towards rock'n'roll in high school. During these early years Don was exposed to the black music his father loved, by artists such as Pearl Bailey and Fats Waller, "Not quite Chicago blues, more like gospel, torch songs and Broadway music." Other early influences included Winifred Atwell and Oscar Peterson. When he later discovered rock music he listened to Stevie Winwood, Brian Auger, Ray Manzarek (The Doors) and Richard Manuel (The Band). By 16 he was playing in bands, while still doing well enough at school to earn a teaching scholarship at the University of New England in Armidale. He majored in Quantum Mechanics and topped three of his four classes in his first year.

Don then went on to join Bogislav ("named after a white Russian General") because they "were crash hot excellent musicians and also had a great reputation around town. I was swept in by the prestige of playing with them". Bogislav were led by drummer/singer/pianist and composer Ron Carpenter, whom Don feels taught him as much as anyone. Other members included guitarist David Froggat who had just arrived from London and brought with him a Marshall stack, truly a rarity in those parts at the time. David is now involved with the Twelfth Man comedy records along with Billy Birmingham, who was at one time Aleph's (the name of a later Bogislav incarnation) manager.

Ian Moss was born and raised in Alice Springs. Although not a musical family, as television had not yet reached that part of the world, music was always heard in the household. The source was usually ABC radio in Darwin. Ian would often write to the station and request his favourite songs. Ian's mother clearly remembers a seven year old Ian requesting 'Hard Headed Woman', which the station didn't have. As a six year-old Ian would perform for the family as they sat outside in the warm evenings. He would announce the title of the song, sing it and take a bow. At about nine years of age he sang 'The Battle of New Orleans' at his school.

Ian's older sister was an accomplished pianist and Ian began taking piano lessons from the age of eight. But it was his older brother Peter's guitar which soon took his interest. Peter recalls going away to university, having shown Ian a few basic chords on the guitar, and returning home 12 months later to be astounded by his little brother's development as a guitarist. Ian's school grades suffered and his teachers told of how he was always tapping out the rhythms to songs instead of getting on with his work.

At the same time guitarists such as Jimi Hendrix, Jimmy Page, Ritchie Blackmore and Jeff Beck, all major influences, were emerging on the music scene. At fourteen Ian was asked to join The Scene, a successful local band. The Scene played about once a week at venues such as The Riverside Hotel, beside the Todd River and the Stuart Arms Hotel. The band's leader Robert Fortunaso (his brother John played bass) recalls that Ian got the gig because "he was the only guy we knew in Alice Springs who was learning to play the guitar." Their material was a mixture of current rock and standards such as Creedence Clearwater Revival's *Proud Mary* and *Green River*, Cream's *Sunshine Of Your Love* and *Spoonful*, Blind Faith, Beatles, and classics such as *Rock Me Baby*.

Ian played rhythm guitar, which involved plugging an acoustic guitar into the bass player's amplifier.

"And then I got kicked out of the band - the first night. Robert was the lead, and not the most reassuring type person. And it was the first time I'd got up on stage. So I was petrified.

"Robert stood there strumming away at his guitar, looking dead serious and I stood there, looking at him for approval to make sure I was doing the right thing. So at the end of the first bracket Robert walked around, paced up and down the back, then after a while came up to me with a blank look and said 'Look, would you mind not playing the next bracket? We want to see how it goes three-piece again."

This was not the end of Ian's time with the band, *"Robert decided to try singing without his guitar and stood out in front holding the microphone and I played his guitar - so it worked out really well."* The Scene played the local youth centre and soon started organising their own dances. Ian was soon singing a

couple of songs himself and he did purchase an electric guitar to replace his acoustic.

The band's most regular gig, The Riverside Hotel was a lively venue and they usually played to about a hundred people. The hotel also had an aboriginal bar, which adjoined the left-hand side of the stage. Chicken wire prevented aboriginal patrons from entering the band room. Robert Fortunaso recalls Ian forgetting his guitar at one gig, and starting another late because he had no strings.

The Fortunaso brothers would later move to Adelaide and play in a band called Simon Gray, at the same time as a young Cold Chisel were starting to make a name for themselves.

As for Ian: *"I was with them (The Scene) for about a year and by that time I was starting to get my own band happening."*

That band was Anger & Tears. Comprising Roger Harris on second guitar, David Michel on drums (David's father owned a menswear shop and helped the band with costumes), a keyboard player and a bassist. "We debuted at the Alice Springs High School in 1970 with *Proud Mary* and *Who'll Stop The Rain*, two Creedence Clearwater songs. I think they went down well." Ian also recalls a Battle of the Bands competition where they played Black Sabbath's 'Paranoid', Chain's 'Black and Blue' and 'Race with the Devil' by a group called The Gunn.

The band played at a school assembly and Ian's mother was so concerned about the length of her son's hair that she insisted he get it cut.

Adelaide, Sth Australia

(4

When he sheepishly returned from the barber, it had been cut extremely short. Realising how much Ian disliked it, Lorna Moss never again asked him to cut his hair. Anger & Tears were then invited to play the school dance but arrived late and had their payment docked. As they only had four or five songs in their repertoire, they continually repeated these to fill the time required.

In 1972, at the age of seventeen, Ian left Alice Springs and moved to Adelaide (Ian's older sister was already there, studying at teacher's college) to attend Marion High School, where he repeated Year 11. During this time he jammed in a 'band' with drummer Rob Young, bassist Phil Small, and a singer who was something of a Paul Rogers clone. Ian showed up for rehearsal in his school uniform, hopeful that this combination would justify his decision to go to Adelaide. Unfortunately the band rarely left the bedroom they rehearsed in.

"That was the big courageous step out of the country into the city, to get near what was happening. My sister used to talk to me a lot and really encourage me, tell me how fantastic it was to be in the city, where it was all happening and it was all incredibly different."

In 1979 Ian stated his influences as the previously mentioned British heavy metal players, as well as blues players such as Muddy Waters and B.B.King.

"I suppose I lean toward the English heavy rock style, but I also admire jazz-rock players like Bill Connors from Return To Forever."

(Ian Moss, 1979)

"I never consciously studied anything. I listened to anything. I've always liked Elvis Presley a lot, anything that swings. If somebody's good, they're good, from jazz to rock to classical. There's obvious things in my playing, like Blackmore, Beck, Hendrix...My style's definitely a real blues style - you can easily say, "Oh yeah, Beck did that, or Hendrix. But then you can go back like that with anything."

(Ian Moss 1982)

5)

1973
Gawler Raceway,
South Australia

No V-Day heroes

I LEFT MY HEART TO THE SAPPERS ROUND KHE SANH,

AND MY SOUL WAS SOLD WITH MY CIGARETTES TO THE BLACK MARKET MAN,

I'VE HAD THE VIETNAM COLD TURKEY FROM THE OCEAN TO THE SILVER CITY,

AND IT'S ONLY OTHER VETS COULD UNDERSTAND.

HOW WE SAILED INTO SYDNEY HARBOUR, HOME AND FREE (BUT) THERE WERE NO V-DAY HEROES

BACK IN NINETEEN SEVENTY THREE;

HOW I BOUGHT A KING'S CROSS WHISPER, I FOUND AN OLD FRIEND BUT I COULDN'T KISS HER,

SHE SAID "BOY I'M GLAD YOU DIDN'T SEE NO HARM."

SHE WAS LIKE SO MANY OTHERS FROM THEN ON,

THEIR LIVES WERE ALL SO EMPTY

'TILL THEY FOUND THEIR CHOSEN ONE

The original lyric to Khe-Sanh. Taken from the 1977 demo tape. Reprinted with kind permission of Don Walker. (For complete lyrics see Appendix One.)

When Don Walker left for Adelaide in 1973, Bogislav changed their name to Aleph, extended their line-up, learnt a new batch of Ron Carpenter's music and moved to Sydney where they later recorded an album. Ron Carpenter also played drums briefly with AC/DC in 1974, before they recorded their debut LP.

Part of a cadetship the government gave him while in Armidale included the offer of a job, which in Don's case turned out to be at the Defence Department's Weapons Research Establishment, in Adelaide. His work there was top secret, but not all that interesting and the paperwork of the aeronautics division was not his idea of excitement.

Don Walker first met 17-year-old guitarist Ian Moss at a public jam session at Norwood Town Hall in Adelaide around April 1973. The feeling was good when the two played together, and both preferred a more bluesy style, unlike the Yes styles that everyone in Adelaide seemed to be interested in at the time. From that day on the pair kept running into each other in unlikely places - street corners, music stores and on one occasion, Adelaide Railway Station.

During that time Don was playing in a band called Queen which featured Swanee (John Swan) singing in its last few gigs. When the band broke up

Don answered an advertisement in a music shop in the winter of 1973, which led him to Les Kaczmarek's house. There he again ran into Ian. They rehearsed the chords for *Georgia* and Ian sang a Stevie Wonder song as means of an audition. Les' previous band, McCabe, had broken up so he was looking to put together a new band. He already had a keyboard player, who happened to be away in Sydney buying all the latest keyboard equipment, but Les wasn't happy with him anyway, and Don was brought in immediately.

The new band did some rehearsals, but Don didn't feel that the drummer was up to scratch, and they auditioned Steve Prestwich, who was great, and sacked the previous drummer. Don and Ian had the job of catching a bus across town to tell the drummer of his fate. As soon as he opened the door and saw Ian and Don standing there, he knew what they were about to say and slammed the door on them!

Ian indicated that he'd like to get a singer into the band so that he could concentrate on his guitar playing. Steve had a good friend, John Swan who had an excellent reputation around town as a singer and knew Don from Queen. But he was really out of their league, so the band auditioned his little brother, Jim, who joined the same day.

(6

"My first idea was to entice John Swan to sing with us, but he was committed to other things and didn't show a lot of interest."

(Les Kaczmarek, 1997)

James Dixon Swan was born in the Gorbals section of Glasgow, the night his father, Jim Senior, became the featherweight boxing champion of Scotland. James (Jr), the fourth of six children, arrived in Australia as a five-year-old on the 7th of January 1961. After spending some time in hostels and nearly buying a house at Tea Tree Gully, the family eventually settled in Elizabeth West, a satellite city just outside of Adelaide.

Although music was not his parents' profession, it was a very musical household. Both Jim's parents sang, and R & B was the music of choice. Nat King Cole, Little Richard and Jerry Lee Lewis were among the sounds emanating from the Swan household. Jim's older brother John recalls playing the new Jimi Hendrix album quite loudly in his bedroom when there came a knock on the door. John was concerned that his father would not accept this new music; Jim Snr. asked him to play the song *Red House* again and after listening very closely assured him that it was one hell of a song.

Unfortunately, the Swan family's marriage didn't last and the children found themselves living with a stepfather, Reg Barnes. When younger sister Lisa was taunted at school about being adopted, the prospect of changing their surname to Barnes was put to the Swan children and all but John elected to do so.

It was John's interest in music - he played the drums - that inspired Jim, and when he heard Paul Rogers singing with Free (*Alright Now* is still one of his favourite songs), Jim decided that singing was the way to go, although he did play bass for a brief period also.

Steve Prestwich had not been in the country all that long and was, in fact seriously considering heading back to his native England when the offer to join the band came up. The Prestwich family, including seventeen - year - old Steve had arrived in Adelaide on the 24th of August 1971. Steve's father, Bill, was a drummer/vocalist with a local beat group called The Victors, who occasionally played at Liverpool's Cavern Club (among other venues), later made famous by The Beatles. It was while watching these early gigs as a child that Steve decided where his future lay.

Steve grew up in a musical environment, singing in the school choir and playing his first gig (filling in for his father) when he was just eleven. The band was called The Three Js. 'Junior', as he was christened for the night, was paid two pounds, which he put towards a drum kit of his own.

Growing up in Liverpool in the '60s, the height of Beatlemania and the Mersey Sound, left a distinct musical impression on young Steve. Its accent on melody would be an undeniable influence on his writing in later years. On one occasion a young Steve witnessed a very drunk George Harrison, Eric Clapton and various members of Delaney and Bonnie and Friends jamming at the restaurant at which The Victors were playing.

Steve's first group was a folk/rock band Sandy, which covered artists such as Bob Dylan, Fairport Convention, Sandy Denny (one-time Fairport singer, best known perhaps as the voice on the Led Zeppelin track *The Battle Of Evermore*), Steeleye Span and John Lennon. In the late sixties he identified with the Mods, both in their dress and love of soul music. Steve was also starting to be influenced by the new generation of heavy, blues-based bands, such as Led Zeppelin, Deep Purple, Jethro Tull and Colosseum, all of whom Steve saw play when they visited Liverpool.

By the time the Prestwich family's immigration application was accepted, Steve's band were doing small tours outside of Liverpool. Steve decided to stay in England, where he also had a secure day job, and pursue a musical career.

Correspondence with a cousin in Adelaide (which included newspaper clippings and copies of Go-Set magazine) confirmed a thriving music scene in that city and at the last minute he decided to join his family on the trip to Australia.

The uncertainty of the local job market only served to make Steve even more determined to pursue music. Elizabeth, the migrant town where the family had settled, contained a wealth of musicians from various countries and Steve was soon (early 1972) playing in a three piece band with two other English lads; John Pryor (gt) and Mike Smith (bs). The band was called Ice.

They played covers and some originals penned by the guitarist and it was with this band that Steve wrote his first song which, contrary to the music he was listening to, was a blues. Steve had also met John Swan at a Christmas party in 1971. John was AWOL from the army (and still in uniform). Being drummers, the two became friends.

It was while playing a gig with Ice that Steve met Les, who had played in another band (McCabe) on the same bill. Ice folded when John Pryor returned to Liverpool, a move that Steve was also seriously considering. He was still suffering culture shock and homesickness. It was at this time that the call came from Les, asking if he was interested in joining another band. Steve still recalls arriving at an audition at the Women's Liberation Hall (Bloor Court, off Currie Street, about 500 metres from the Western end of Rundle Mall) and being greeted by Les, Don and Ian. The audition consisted of a drum solo and a couple of songs. The shoeless guitarist with the voice which conveyed a maturity way beyond his years instantly impressed Steve.

Les, who played bass, had been the original founder of the band and his connections with the local Italian club got them their first gigs.

When asked to rate Ian's guitar playing in 1994, Don told JJJ's Richard Kingswell:

"Well he's the best around that has ever been, with the possible exception of Steve Murphy, in this country. He could play like that when I met him and he was 17. He's just born with it...Not all of us are born equal and Ian was born with this incredible set of talents.

"When we first started the band, the strongest aim was to avoid nine-to-five jobs... just to get some lifestyle different from people our age... so we don't have to get up in the morning."

(Don Walker, 1978)

"We called ourselves Orange, I don't know why...it was appealing."

(Jimmy enjoys a joke in Playboy, 1988)

Early sets at this point included Free's *Alright Now* (Jimmy cites Paul Rogers as one of his main influences and one of his favourite singers), *Ride On Pony* and *Fire and Water* as well as Deep Purple's *Rat Bat Blue*. In a December 1980 story the band's one time manager/agent, Vince Lovegrove, cited the band's early influences as Led Zeppelin, Free, Bad Company, and Dylan. Following a gig at Gawler Raceway the band decide a change of name is necessary.

"I'd written one or two songs a year over that whole period, but I hadn't really gotten into it to the extent that I could say that I 'wrote songs'. But then I started to try and learn."

(Don Walker, 1978)

OCTOBER / NOVEMBER

Orange debut at an Italian workingman's club.

OCT/NOV   Gawler Raceway, with Bullet and other bands. Ian Moss recalls that one of the songs played at this gig was Deep Purple's *Rat Bat Blue*.

The band changed their name to Cold Chisel, as this type of double-barreled, soft/hard names were common at the time (e.g. Led Zeppelin, Deep Purple).

(8

1973
From left Les, Steve, Jim, Don & Ian.

Armidale

COLD CHISEL MOVE TO ARMIDALE (NSW) FOR TEN MONTHS WHILE DON WALKER COMPLETES HIS POST-GRADUATE DEGREE IN QUANTUM MECHANICS, A BRANCH OF PHYSICS WHICH DEALS WITH THE SUB-ATOMIC WORLD. WHEN MATTER IS BROKEN DOWN TO ITS MOST MINUTE FORM - THE ATOM - THE TRADITIONAL RULES OF PHYSICS NO LONGER APPLY. THOSE WHICH DO, COMPRISE THE FIELD OF QUANTUM MECHANICS, WITH APPLICATIONS IN COUNTLESS AREAS OUTSIDE OF WEAPONS AND ATOMIC POWER, SUCH AS COMPUTERS AND OTHER ADVANCED ELECTRONICS, TO NAME A FEW.

9)

Jimmy quits his apprenticeship with the railways. Les had been working with the Commonwealth Bank in Adelaide and was able to arrange a transfer to the Armidale branch, although he did not stay there very long.

The band set up house in the middle of an apple orchard in Kentucky, about 45 kilometres out of town. They shared with two road crew, Mick Porter and Gary Skinner, while Don stayed in town to concentrate on his studies. The band organised their own gigs at local halls, playing as a 4-piece while Don studied.

"The attitude there was that we'd become a really good band with the ideal of moving to Sydney as a top band starting off at a good level. I had a theory originally that if we stuck it out for three years, by the end of that time we'd be a top band and come in at a top level. For some reason we thought if we came in at a certain standard the level would progress. But it was a pretty way out theory - it doesn't work like that at all."

(Ian Moss, 1981)

Gary Skinner, whose family had taken in Ian Moss as a boarder when he first arrived in Adelaide, recalls that the band rehearsed almost daily, working towards a master plan Don had devised, finding popularity much as the Allman Brothers had done. John Swan remembers that the band had their differences of opinion, but were united by Don's ideas.

Gary, who was mixing the sound, also recalls that the band's insistence on playing the music it wanted to play, at the volume it played at, occasionally caused fights in those venues which were not accustomed to that style of rock'n'roll. Mainstream Armidale and surrounding country were anything but rock'n'roll areas, the university being the only reason a band like Cold Chisel could develop a following there. A look through the local paper suggests that possibly the musical highlight of 1974 was a visit to town by Mulga Bill's Bicycle Band! It was as though rock'n'roll didn't exist, no reviews of albums or advertisements for bands playing in town, nothing.

MARCH 2

Armidale Town Hall, with the Maitland Bush Band. 8 p.m.-1 a.m. Supper was supplied and admission was $1.00.

Due to a scarcity of records (most shows were simply advertised on posters in Armidale's main street or on the Uni campus), it is difficult to trace actual dates played by the band during this period. The show listed above was from a classified advertisement in the local newspaper.

The band's set at this time included Deep Purple's *Rat Bat Blue, Lazy, Stormbringer, Hold On* and *Smoke On The Water* as well as a number of tracks from Purple's latest album *Burn*; Jimi Hendrix's *The Wind Cries Mary*, a version of *Georgia* with Ian playing on guitar (Don was not gigging with the band at this point) and some innovative drum patterns from Steve, The Doors' *Roadhouse Blues*, Free's *Ride On Pony* and *The Stealer*, Stevie Wonder's *Superstition, Rock'n'Roll Hoochie Coo* and *Keep Playin' That Rock'n'Roll*, songs originally performed by Johnny Winter. A number called *Underground Railway* by another obscure band called Redwing was a selection from Don's record collection.

Gary Skinner recalls the band (with John Swan) playing *Wild Thing* by request at a gig in a barn although it was not a regular in the set. Jimi Hendrix's *Foxy Lady* was also in the set at this point and Gary remembers the band spending some time rehearsing Led Zeppelin's *Stairway To Heaven* - although it was not included in the set.

Les remembers a trip back to Adelaide for Easter where they convinced Jim's brother John Swan to return with them to Armidale, joining the band as second vocalist and percussionist. Stories of what a great place it was persuaded him to come. John had initially started his career as a drummer, playing with bands such as Blackfeather, The Masters Apprentices and James Wright. He had only been in Armidale a few months before getting the sack for hitting roadie Mick Porter. When John sang lead vocal, Jim would play second guitar, something he would again do later in the band's career. John remembers the Armidale period as a "real growing period, when the band went from being a real rough house band to a serious act who rehearsed every day."

It was around this time that Don first started to seriously develop his songwriting, realising the importance of original material if the band were to achieve the long-term goals it had set. Some songs he was working on included *Just How Many Times, Letmenotforgetme, Cold Chisel,* and *One Long Day*. John Swan also contributed some original material at this time; notably a song called *The Man From Yesterday*.

May 21	Wool Shed, Therley Research

The band (with John Swan) play *Wild Thing* as an audience request.

Sometime between these shows, John Swan returns to Adelaide (see previous) after what Don described as "something of a kangaroo court" (over the Mick Porter incident).

June 8	Armidale Teachers College

The band travelled in a blue Morris van owned by Mick Porter. They often ventured to coastal towns such as Coffs Harbor to play gigs. The van was to be the venue for many a travelling sing along, although Les recalls that Jim's habit of singing all the time nearly drove the others insane! Other gigs included university balls for Wright, Page, Duval, Drummond, Robb, Mary White and St Alberts Colleges as well as a school formal at Glen Innes and an appearance at the Armidale Show.

Life was relaxed at the farm in Kentucky, the band rehearsing three or four times a week and planning for the future while experimenting with whatever substances came their way. Ian was known to "serenade the moon", getting as many extension leads as he could find, setting his guitar and amp up as far away as possible from the house and just sitting and playing at full volume, often after playing a gig earlier that night. He was also known to wait for one of the chickens to lay an egg so that he could have a fresh one.

(10

1974
The house the band shared in Kentucky, photo courtesy of Gary Skinner.

May 21, 1974
Possibly the only photo of John Swan with Cold Chisel, at the Wool Shed, Therley Reasearch. Photo courtesy of Gary Skinner.

AUGUST

11)

The band returns to Adelaide, with Don staying in Armidale to complete the final exams for his degree. It was around this time that Ian's brother, Peter started working with the band, his status eventually growing to that of a sixth (offstage) member. This arrangement also included a six-way split (when the band were five-piece) of the money made, which meant that Peter was close to broke for the next five years.

He was to be the band's sole roadie for much of that time, assisted of course, by the band. In late '75/ early '76 a Latvian by the name of Leon was second roadie, the band also using his V8 Ford "shaker" for at least one interstate trip. After Leon, two of Jim's mates from the Largs Pier, Charlie and Kevin, assisted Peter Moss. Don had the job of trying to collect the band's fee, dealing with excuses such as "my instructions are to send the cheque to the agency".

On returning to Adelaide, Ian found the band a Sunday afternoon residency at the Melbourne Hotel and the band soon found some local success as a cover band. It was at this time that Vince Lovegrove became involved with them.

Pictured right:
Jim in make-up, Armidale, 1974
Photo courtesy of Gary Skinner.

"I met them because my wife, at the time, and I had Adelaide's hippest booking agency and were running Adelaide's hippest venues at the time. The band's original bass player, Les, approached me and asked me if I would manage the band. I went and saw the band, met them, loved them as people and as a band and decided I would manage them as I believed they were the most unique band in the country at that stage, although I felt they should perform more original stuff and was looking forward to Don rejoining them as I was led to believe he was really the main man.

"The band had an unusual allegiance to this man, something that was quite unique and it was clear he had something they accepted as being part of their destiny. It was not an overt thing, but a hidden, subtle belief that they were only treading water until he re-joined them."

Meanwhile, in Armidale, Don enters and wins a song competition at University with a composition titled *Bunny's Blues*, a song which would later be performed by Cold Chisel.

SEPTEMBER	New management takes over the Largs Pier Hotel.
OCTOBER 10	Largs Pier, with the Colored Balls and Buster Brown
OCTOBER 11	Largs Pier, with the Colored Balls and Buster Brown
OCTOBER 12	Largs Pier, with the Colored Balls and Buster Brown
OCTOBER 12	The Ritz, Mansfield Park Hotel

quict. | ROGBY League travelling | . |
ford X | competition, W. Winney, | FOR |
5. | Wicklow Hotel. | tract |
| | only |
ner $8. | DANCE, Saturday night, | with |
$ 8. | March 2, Armidale Town | and |
inner- | Hall, Maitland Bush Band, | good |
sk $4. | Cold Chisel. Supper, | at $3 |
5. 180 | B.Y.O.G. 8-1 a.m. $1 ad- | and |
| mission. | 6094 |

*OCTOBER 17-19

Bakery, with Peter Walker (who would later figure in Cold Chisel's career) on guitar, play three nights at the Largs Pier Hotel. Among the audience on one of these nights was Ian Moss, who always made a point of checking out any guitar player with any sort of reputation who came to town. Peter Walker recalls that from then on, whenever Bakery was in town, they would catch up with Cold Chisel and music was the topic of conversation.

OCTOBER 24	Largs Pier, with AC/DC and Flash
OCTOBER 25	Largs Pier, with AC/DC and Flash
OCTOBER 26	Largs Pier, with AC/DC and Flash

*Not a Cold Chisel gig.

At this stage the band are playing as a four-piece, without Don Walker, who is still in Armidale. Even after his return (sometime in December), Don did not immediately rejoin the band onstage, instead rehearsing a set of original songs with them to mark a new direction for the band.

NOVEMBER 1	The Ritz, Mansfield Park Hotel
NOVEMBER 7	Largs Pier, with Madder Lake
NOVEMBER 9	Largs Pier, with Madder Lake

Gary Skinner recalled that Jim's singing during the Armidale period had been very experimental. Soon after returning to Adelaide the band decided that Jim's singing was not developing as quickly as they would have liked. The specific areas they were concerned about were his range - most of the singers in the bands they admired (and covered in their repertoire) had remarkable vocal ranges.

There were also concerns about his pitching. Ian's voice, even at this time was exceptional, and Jim could not duplicate the vibrato and tone that Ian possessed. The band met without Jim and it was decided that, for the sake of the band Jim would

have to go. A meeting with Jim was arranged to break the news. As the band waited for Jim's arrival, Les suggested that perhaps it was not necessary to sack him and perhaps they could simply tell him what they thought the problems were and hopefully he could work on those areas. With this suggestion Jim's position in the band was secure for another day, although Ian recalls Jim telling him at a party soon after that he wasn't sure if he could do the things the band wanted.

"It was Jim who had a unique charisma and attitude. His was the classic rebel stance, the one that mattered. He had attitude to die for. It was clear he was a star in the making even though he was anti-star. I can remember Steve's position in the band being a precarious one on account of the confrontational relationship between he and Jim. Jim was a speed freak to the core, and he felt sometimes that Steve wasn't playing as fast as he should have been. This was probably a mistake on Jim's part as he was just a fast human being. But I believe the same problem dogged the duo forever more. That is, differences of opinion on how the pace of each song should be."

(Vince Lovegrove, 1998) (12

May 21, 1974
Ian Moss, Wool Shed,
Therley Reasearch

NOVEMBER 14	Largs Pier, with Skyhooks
NOVEMBER 15	The Ritz
NOVEMBER 16	Burnside Town Hall, U/18 dance with Skyhooks and Flash
NOVEMBER 21	Largs Pier Hotel
NOVEMBER 22	The Ritz, Cold Chisel are billed as "Adelaide's amazing new act!"

NOVEMBER 23

Memorial Drive, Uriah Heep support. Ian Moss recalls being as nervous as he's ever been before this show about having to play one of John Swan's originals - *The Man From Yesterday*, which featured an extended guitar solo. Nobody is sure why this song was still in their set at this point, as Swan hadn't been with the band for almost six months.

Before the solo was even over, loud applause filled the auditorium, confirming the band's belief that their guitarist was something special.

DECEMBER 5	Largs Pier, $1.50 admission
DECEMBER 6	Largs Pier, with Flintrock

Cold Chisel continues rehearsing in the offices of the Women's Electoral Lobby in Adelaide. The band rehearsed at this hall for some time until one day Vince Lovegrove, who was managing the band at the time, decided to pen a little essay stating his views on feminism on the telephone message pad. It may have helped to pass the time at a long rehearsal session, but the feminists did not appreciate it.

"I happened to know a few women who were part of the original Women's Electoral Lobby movement and they were hard nosed, man-hating women. My feelings were that they were being hypocritical about their beliefs because of what some of them were doing to their families, and whilst I believed in the notion of equality, indeed I was married to an emancipated woman, Helen, who was a strong, free-thinking woman, and as time has gone by I have realised, an absolutely wonderful woman, the fact is I did not think their created atmosphere of hatred towards all men was the way to go.

"I was very, very cynical about the Women's Electoral Lobby and its aims and its hypocrisy. They were doing in real life what they criticized men for doing. I was also going through a crisis in my marriage, was a bit of a smart arse, was a bit of a jack the lad, with a bit of chip on my shoulder about women in general.

"I remember writing something in their log book one day at their office headquarters which is where Cold Chisel were rehearsing. To this effect, although knowing what an arrogant prick I was, I am sure it was mean and nasty."

(Vince Lovegrove, 1998)

13)

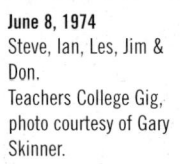

June 8, 1974
Steve, Ian, Les, Jim & Don.
Teachers College Gig, photo courtesy of Gary Skinner.

[1974]

1974
From left Jim, Mick Porter, Don & girlfriend, Ian, Steve & Les

ARMIDALE

COLD CHISEL STORY

[1975]
Lean & Hungry

THE ARMIDALE EXPERIENCE HAD STRENGTHENED THE BAND'S SELF-BELIEF AND FOCUSSED THEIR AMBITION. BIG NAME SUPPORT SHOWS AND INROADS INTO THE ADELAIDE PUB SCENE (VIA THE SUPPORT OF PROMOTER VINCE LOVEGROVE) SAW THE BAND EXPECTING BIG THINGS FROM 1975

15)

It does prove to be a year of great change internally for the band, their ambition bringing more self-examination (and examination of the others in the band!).

JANUARY 3	Countdown, with Ayers Rock
JANUARY 4	Countdown, with Ayers Rock
JANUARY 12	Countdown, with Iron Knob and Ova
JANUARY 18	Countdown, with Daddy Cool

JANUARY 19 - COUNTDOWN WITH JAMES WRIGHT

The band decide to concentrate on original material and rehearse a batch of new songs at a church hall in Hindmarsh before playing one of their usual venues, Countdown (The Mediterranean Hotel). The usual covers repertoire is replaced with the new original material (including *One Long Day*) and Don's keyboards are added.

Footnote: Steve was always keen to move away from covers to original material, but felt that such a total change was not the way to do it.

The audience responded with stunned silence, causing something of a crisis within the band. Steve and Les felt that the band should stick to its covers format, and they had some support from Jim on that, while Ian remained unsure. There was even talk of ousting Don from the band at this point, although a band meeting quickly saw things back on an even keel. The rest of the band, including manager Vince Lovegrove, were keen to sack Don. They had done well without him for virtually the last twelve months. Ian was against the idea and said that if Don went, he too would go, and such was everyone's faith in Ian's abilities that Don's position was secured. Vince quit, although he did put the band in contact with their next manager, Ray Hearn. The number of covers in the set was restored, although original material would now almost always be present also.

Vince Lovegrove has no recollection of wanting to sack Don:

"I never wanted to sack Don, and I can not remember any move to have him sacked, so if there was one, it was certainly clandestine. In terms of sacking Don, the only thoughts I had were that original songs <u>had</u> to be done, but I felt strongly that some of Don's songs were too left of centre. But it was clear to me that his presence provided the glue, the ignition if you like, for the band to be fully functional. Anyone with a brain could see that. I remember at the start I had a little difficulty relating to Don because he was so adamant about how the band should be, and my job was made a little more difficult because of this. Perhaps this is where the feeling came from that I wanted him out, but this was never ever the case. My feelings were that without Don, there would be no Cold Chisel. Indeed, although Jim and I continued a friendship for life from that point on, it was Don to whom I turned for sanity, for reality and for the truth about exactly what the band would and would not do. There is no doubt that time has proven it was Don whose strong beliefs and principles gave the band their unique stance in the music industry, and we haven't even looked at his songs, that <u>was</u> the difference between Chisel and every other Australian band in history."

In hindsight, Ian feels that the material was under-rehearsed and the PA equipment unsuitable for the occasion. When the band had previously played that venue they had been using a PA belonging to the band they were supporting and this was the first time they had had to put together their own PA for such an important gig. Don did not have an amp for the early part of the show, while Les had the largest bass rig in town. The material played that night was heavily biased towards what Don calls 'pseudo sophisticated' material, slow jazz/rock style ballads such as *Letmenotforgertme, Bunny's Blues, Just How Many Times* and *Georgia*. While these may have been just the thing in the country back blocks of Armidale and Kentucky, they were not appreciated in the inner-city nightclubs of Adelaide.

"I handed over management of the band, in a caretaker's position, to Ray Hearn. They did not like him much because he was not really a 'rocker' at heart, his taste being more in the line of 'art rock',

something Chisel despised with a vengeance. I had to talk them into him looking after them."

(Vince Lovegrove, 1998)

JANUARY 20

Perhaps having had time to reflect on the events of the night before, Steve leaves the band and John Swan is recruited as a temporary replacement.

JANUARY 29 - COUNTDOWN

The band play this show as a 4-piece, reverting to the keyboard-less lineup, which had previously proven successful.

During this period the band was struggling to find a direction. The original material was still in question, and the absence of Steve testing everyone. They had tried a number of drummers. All had been disappointing, although Don and Ian continued to work on new songs.

FEBRUARY 8	(Sat) Countdown

The Mediterranean Hotel, with The Dingoes

FEBURARY 9	Following a meeting the band go to see The Dingoes at Countdown. Continue auditioning drummers.

FEBRUARY 12	Countdown

The Mediterranean Hotel, with Skyhooks. The band receive a good response from the audience and stay to watch Skyhooks. Don watches both bands, having not yet rejoined Cold Chisel in an onstage capacity.

FEBRUARY 13	Countdown

The Mediterranean Hotel, with Skyhooks. Don again watches. Peter Moss has now joined the band as roadie and shares a house with Don, Steve and Ian. Still auditioning drummers.

FEBRUARY 15	(Sat) Burnside Town Hall, with Skyhooks

FEBRUARY 15	Ampitheatre

FEBRUARY 16 - COUNTDOWN

The Mediterranean Hotel, with The James Wright Band (John Swan played with this band in 1973.) One of the reasons for the tensions within Cold Chisel was that cover bands such as the James Wright Band (there was no James Wright!) were making very impressive amounts of money on the covers circuit. As they mixed with the members of Cold Chisel, it was hard to not notice the apartments they lived in and the cars they drove.

FEBRUARY 17	Steve rejoins the band. John Swan goes on to play with Salvation Airforce.

(16

FEBRUARY 19 Countdown

The Mediterranean Hotel, with Ariel. Having practiced the day before, Steve plays this show. The band rehearse the next day in preparation for Don's return to the band.

FEBRUARY 20 Hotel Finsbury

FEBRUARY 22 (Sat) The Pooraka Hotel, with Spare Change. Don's return gig. The next day Don writes 'Mona and the Preacher'.

FEBRUARY 26 Memorial Drive, Joe Cocker support.

Crowd response is only average, especially as the band had rehearsed extensively in the days before the show.

FEBRUARY 28 Flinders Uni with The Dingoes and Smokestack Lightning

MARCH 1 Paravista High School

MARCH 8 (Sat) Countdown

The Mediterranean Hotel with Kush. At this stage the band was transporting their gear on hired trailers behind Peter Moss's car.

MARCH 9 - LARGS PIER

The following night the band skips rehearsal in favor of seeing Jim's favourite vocalist Paul Rogers, singing with Bad Company. Another new song is being worked on - *Necrophiliac's Blues*, a band composition. After the turmoil of the previous months, band morale is reaching a new high. Peter Moss had just purchased a new Bedford van, this capital investment ensuring him an equal partnership in the band. The only 'problem' was the fact that Les' day job was restricting rehearsal options for the band.

MARCH 15 (Sat) Victor Harbour Hotel

The set includes the two new songs, *Mona and the Preacher* and *Necrophiliac's Blues* in addition to *Georgia* and *Letmenotforgetme*. The band receive a positive reception.

MARCH 19 Countdown, with The La De Das. Kevin Borich expresses his admiration of Ian's playing.

MARCH 20 Countdown

The Mediterranean Hotel with The La De Das. The band plays a great show, despite the crowd being slow to respond. They preview a new song learnt a couple of days previous called, *I'm Gonna Roll Ya All Night Long* which steals the show, becoming an audience favourite like no other original had up to that time.

MARCH 21 Burnside Town Hall.

A great crowd, although not as good a show as the previous night's. *Just How Many Times* is outstanding.

MARCH 22 (Sat) Walunga Town Hall.

A young crowd who get into the band's music even though the band don't play all that well.

MARCH 29 - (SAT) WHYALLA

The band play a good show which is taped and played to anyone who'll listen over the next few days during a trip to Armidale.

APRIL 4 Shandon Hotel with Chariot. Not a good night.

APRIL 5 (Sat) Pooraka Hotel

APRIL 6 Countdown, The Mediterranean Hotel with Chariot A much better night for the band.

APRIL 9 Countdown with Renee Geyer, another good gig.

APRIL 10 Finsbury Hotel

APRIL 11- POORAKA HOTEL WITH KHAN

Ian and Jim overdo it on the alcohol, but not to the extent where it affects their playing. The crowd go wild as the band play as well as they've ever played.

APRIL 12 (Sat) Countdown. Another great gig.

APRIL 17 Pooraka Hotel, admission $1.50

This is the beginning of a residency at this venue and although door takings are up some 50%, the band play poorly. To publicize the residency, the band distributes handbills to cars in town (Adelaide).

APRIL 18 Countdown, The Mediterranean Hotel with Pantha

APRIL 19 (Sat) Pooraka Hotel with Spare Change (a Melbourne band who released a single in 1976). Another good night.

APRIL 20

Following a mix-up (the band thought they were playing Countdown), the band play at The Largs Pier (8.00 - 9.00 p.m.) with Macarthur.

APRIL 24 Pooraka Hotel. Don has a new piano amplifier and the crowd has built up to 180 people!

APRIL 25 Brighton Town Hall, the band plays to a young crowd and go down a storm.

APRIL 26 (Sat) Countdown with Captain Matchbox.

17)

SUNDOWNER
POORAKA HOTEL, 8 to MIDNIGHT

COLD CHISEL

TONIGHT

$1.80

★ **JAMES WRIGHT**

COMPERE RICK LENNON

Sat. ★ SPARE CHANGE ★ COLD CHISEL ★
NEAT CASUAL DRESS. PROCEEDS AID RED CROSS.

COUNTDOWN COUNTDOWN COUNTDOWN COUNTDOWN COU

COUNTDOWN
WED. to SUN. 8-1.30
THE BOYS FROM THE JUNGLE ARE HERE
WITH US AGAIN

PANTHA
Tonight ★ COLD CHISEL ★
Saturday ★ HUMBOLT ★
SUNDAY SUPERSESSION
PANTHA ● COLD CHISEL

MEDITERRANEAN HOTEL
111 HINDLEY ST.

APRIL 27   Countdown

The first night of a residency there. Only 60 people in the crowd. The following night is Jim's 19th birthday and the band party at his house.

MAY 1   Gawler Institute

Jim is suffering terribly from laryngitis and Rick Morris, singer and guitarist from another Adelaide band Salvation Airforce fills in. Rick was a Vietnam veteran and would be an influence on Don's later writing on this subject.

MAY 2 - ELIZABETH HOTEL

Jim's laryngitis does nothing to help a poor showing from the band. Brawls in the audience complete a forgettable night and ensure that they will not play there again for months.

MAY 3	(Sat) Sundowner, Pooraka Hotel, with Headstone. Another poor show without Jim.
MAY 4	Countdown, The Mediterranean Hotel
MAY 6	Paravista High School
MAY 7	Woodville High School
MAY 8	Grange Golf Club to a crowd from Woodlands Girls High School.

MAY 9 - CASTLE HOTEL

Grand opening of the Rock'n'roll Ballroom with Renee Geyer and Sanctuary. Not a great night.

MAY 10 - (SAT) CASTLE HOTEL

Grand opening (continues) of the Rock'n'roll Ballroom with Renee Geyer and Sanctuary. Steve and Les arrive an hour late.

| MAY 14 | Countdown |

The band plays their first really good one since Jim's laryngitis. Swanee joins the band for the last bracket.

MAY 15 - SUNDOWNER, POORAKA HOTEL

Admission $1.50. Cold Chisel at this time were the resident Thursday night band at the Pooraka. Despite advertising in the papers and handbills, tonight's gig is a little dismal.

| MAY 16 | Christies Beach. A young and appreciative audience. |
| MAY 18 | Elizabeth Octagon. Jim and Les are very drunk and the gig is not a good one. |

MAY 22 - POORAKA HOTEL

Admission $1.50 The band play this show as a 4-piece as Jim has decided to take a month off from singing. The show goes well. The band are still working on new material (*On The Road* and *Desperation Blues*) and decide to continue as a four-piece until Jim's return.

MAY 23 - POORAKA HOTEL

Admission $1.80 Fraternity's "Uncle" joins the band on harp, impressing Ian and Don immensely.

MAY 24 - (SAT) COUNTDOWN

The Mediterranean Hotel. Uncle joins the band for the entire show. Uncle has done so well with the band that the decision is made to let him join, (he also wanted to save some money and needed the extra income) an arrangement which lasts for about six weeks.

MAY 29   Pooraka Hotel.

The band play *On The Road* and *Georgia* with Uncle, among other songs in what would be their last night at this venue for some time.

MAY 31   (Sat) School gig.

JUNE

In one of their first mentions in the national music press, Helen Barrett at 'Juke' magazine, showing great taste and judgement (Helen was from Adelaide) is obviously very impressed with the band:

"If someone would sign 'Cold Chisel' from Adelaide we're sure they'd make our charts."

(Juke magazine)

JUNE 7- (SAT) LARGS PIER

The band made the Largs Pier Hotel their home, creating a family-like relationship with the regulars there. Adelaide journalist Tony Lewis described the Largs Pier at that time: "The Largs Pier is (always has been and probably always will be) the HQ for the genuine street punk. Punk rockers and heavy metallists reign supreme here, and it's definitely not the place to go if you want to show off the latest fashions from Gay Paree." The Largs Pier is also the latest opening venue in Adelaide at the time, opening until 2 a.m. on a Saturday night

JUNE 13 - COUNTDOWN, WITH THE DINGOES

A good show, new songs debuted include *Faust*, which goes down well and *On The Road*, which the band messes up. Uncle dances on his amp during *I'm Gonna Roll Ya*, which is still going down a storm. The band is playing without Jim (still resting his voice), although he is present at some rehearsals.

JUNE 14	(Sat) Countdown, with The Dingoes

Another good night, Broderick Smith, vocalist with The Dingoes joins the band for the last set.

JUNE 15	Private party, Underdale

An unusual gig to a Greek audience. Broderick Smith joins the band again for their last set, The Dingoes having played earlier at Countdown.

JUNE 20 - ELIZABETH HOTEL

John Swan and Uncle jam with the band, but like the last time the band played here, this was not a good show musically. It was in the aftermath of shows like this that some members start to question Les' commitment. Les was entrenched in working a day job and didn't have the same aspirations as the others, a fact which had already created problems with rehearsal times.

JUNE 21	(Sat)Largs Pier Hotel with Mainstreet. A good show, everyone plays well.

JUNE 22

The band meet and discuss Les. This was not the first such meeting, but a decision is made that a new bassist must be sought. The meeting concludes at 3 a.m. The following day Jim is given the job of informing Les. Les will play with the band for a few more weeks.

"I can clearly remember the move to sack Les. It was a strong feeling within the band, but a difficult feeling as he was the founding member and was kind of like the manager, pr person until I came along. It is a common story with many bands from that era...that is, the founding member, or fill-in manager being the weakest person musically. They did not want to sack him and there was quite a dilemma about how it should be done. I don't quite recall who actually did the dirty deed or when. It may have been me, I cannot remember."

Vince Lovegrove, 1998.

Les' full-time job was managing a record store at that stage, "It was handy for someone in the band to have money" and as he put it, "It was probably a case of not being as devoted to the change in the band from covers to originals, which was fairly sudden and I should have given more thought as to my role in it." Les also adds that his enthusiasm for the musician's lifestyle was waning and in hindsight feels that while the others had plans to leave Adelaide, he was always happiest in his hometown, where he still happily resides.

Les went on to enjoy some success with a band called Dirty Alice in the late '70s and ran a recording studio in Adelaide in the early '80s while continuing to dabble in the playing side of things, filling in as a sideman for such acts as The Drifters.

JUNE 25

The band jam with Phil Small. Also considered for the bass role were Michael Kiely (now a top Sydney advertising executive), a friend, and former Aleph/Bogislav bassist Dave Hiatt, the former doing an impressive audition which Steve particularly admired.

(20

Phil Small and his brother Dave, Adelaide Motor Show. Photo courtesy of Phil Small.

JUNE 26	Countdown, The Mediterranean Hotel
JUNE 26	The Castle. The band plays a great show.

JUNE 28 - (SAT)

Shandon Hotel with Dalai Lama and Spare Change.

Following Spare Change, Cold Chisel play a professional one hour set. The first days of July are spent auditioning/working on songs with Phil Small. At various stages of this process different people are at different times convinced of Phil's suitability or otherwise. No decision is made.

JULY 3	Countdown, The Mediterranean, with Marcia Hines

The band play, a terrible show which includes a jam with Uncle. The only bright light is that the new PA built by Lee Conlan who would later found Revolver PA company, in Sydney. Despite blowing three JBL horns the PA sounds great.

JULY 4	Surf Club

The band again use the new PA, although not as loudly. On the 5th Don and Peter watch AC/DC at the Larg's Pier and returned the following night with Jim and party with Bon Scott after the show.

JULY 12 - (SAT) ADELAIDE UNIVERSITY

10 p.m. - 1 a.m. This was Les' last show, and a good one. John Swan, Uncle and bassist Michael Kiely jam with the band at various stages. A decision would be made within days. Phil Small was to be the new bass player with Cold Chisel.

Phil had played with Ian in a band which rarely left the bedroom in 1972, while Ian was still attending Marion High School. Phil worked as a display artist at John Martin's department store for four years, and still remembers the day Ian and Steve visited him at work to ask if he would audition for the band. Phil's initial response was along the lines of "What's wrong with your bass player?", as he had recently seen the band play and was not aware of any problems. But he did attend the audition and when he had heard nothing a few weeks later, forgot all about it.

Phil's grandfather, Leo, played piano around the traps in Adelaide before the Second World War in the Leo Fisher Band and his mother was also a singer. At the age of 11 Phil decided it was the life for him, when he saw his older brother David play the guitar in a garage band rehearsing at his house.

The bass was the obvious way to accompany his brother's guitar.

JULY 18	Elizabeth Hotel

The scene of some of the worst shows the band has played was not really the ideal venue to debut a new bass player, but both Phil and the new P.A. go well.

JULY 19 - (SAT) FLINDERS UNI

10 p.m. (supposed to start at 9 pm but running late) 12.30 a.m. A good show with Phil fitting in well. The evening is marred by the band's truck and car both getting bogged in the Uni car park.

JULY 23 - COUNTDOWN

The Mediterranean, with Freeway. *On The Road* returns to the set, the problems the band was having with it were sorted out at rehearsal the previous two days. The band put on a show that makes it difficult for Freeway, a Melbourne band with a record deal, to follow them.

JULY 24	Countdown, The Mediterranean, with Freeway . Another good night.
JULY 25	Countdown, The Mediterranean, with Freeway Another excellent show.
JULY 26	Countdown, The Mediterranean, with Freeway. Freeway must be wishing someone else was opening the show.
JULY 26	(Sat) Largs Pier. Cold Chisel get a late call to replace Split Enz. Tim Gayes, guitarist with Ariel joins them for a jam.
JULY 27	Largs Pier
JULY 28	Festival Theatre, Adelaide (Lou Reed support)
JULY 31	Countdown, The Mediterranean, with Ariel
AUGUST 1	Elizabeth Hotel
AUGUST 2	(Sat) Largs Pier, with Taxi and Johnny Wakelin

Phil Small's 21st birthday was celebrated at this show. Cold Chisel played first, till 10.30 p.m. After this show the band party with members of Fraternity, who are working on a reformation.

AUGUST 6	Countdown, with Stars
AUGUST 8	St.Peters Girls School

8 p.m.-11.30 p.m. A great show, the chemistry between Jim and Ian is really firing.

AUGUST 9	(Sat) Largs Pier, 8 p.m.-11.00 p.m. with Wildbush and The Joe Hooker Band

AUGUST 13	Countdown, The Mediterranean with The Hot City Bump Band
AUGUST 14	St Peters Boys College with Salvation Airforce.

Salvation Airforce included a brilliant guitarist called Steve Beleky who had played with Don and Swanee in Queen in 1973.

| AUGUST 15 | Elizabeth Hotel |

AUGUST 18 - GAWLER

After this show Jim announces that he's joining Fraternity. Ian and Don try talking Jim out of it at Fraternity's rehearsal the following night, but to no avail. Jim would fill in for the next few gigs, but after that he was gone. Both Jim and John now firmly agree that John talked him into making the move, and this wasn't the only time. As Jim has often said, "He could talk me into anything". Jim joins Fraternity, leaving Ian Moss to handle the vocal duties with Cold Chisel. Phil Small recalls that Don felt sure that Jim's flirtation with Fraternity would only be temporary and the singer would return to Cold Chisel soon.

Fraternity shot to fame in Adelaide in July of 1972 when the lineup of Bruce Howe (who would later feature in Jimmy's first solo band), Bon Scott, John Freeman and 'Uncle' won the National Battle Of The Sounds, becoming Adelaide's claim to fame in Australian rock'n'roll, and winning tickets to England, making them Adelaide's only international band. They changed their name to Fang in England, but soon found the going tough over there and split up before returning to Australia.

So when Fraternity decided to make a comeback, and with his brother John Swan on the drums, the offer was simply too good for Jim to resist. Although the first lineup had eventually fallen flat (Bon Scott had certainly landed on his feet with AC/DC) with the combined talents of John Swan (already a local legend) two original members in Howe and 'Uncle' a.k.a. John Ayers, along with Jimmy, the group seemed assured of success. The lineup also included Pete Bersee on violin and Maurice Burg on guitar, creating a combination rarely seen or heard before.

Apparently one highlight was the band's version of *All Along The Watchtower*, which featured a "triple lead with guitar, violin and harp," described in the press at the time as "mind-blowing." *All Along The Watchtower* was also a highlight of Cold Chisel sets.

Other songs Jim sang with Fraternity included Aerosmith's *Walk This Way* as well as Little Feat and J. Geils Band material. Fraternity also had quite a few originals, such as *Neanderthal Headbutt High*. Other musical influences included Frank Zappa and Captain Beefheart, whose *Clear Spot* album was a favourite.

(22

COLD CHISEL
Mt Erica Hotel, Melbourne
The name Cold Chisel conjures up images of heavy metal rockers in the Deep Purple, Black Sabbath, Led Zepplin mould.

The five piece Chisel outfit played a commercialised form of heavy pretentious, even though his voice handled the work satisfactorily.

The total sound of Cold Chisel on this Friday night was very muddy, and solos by lead guitarist Ian Moss, were often drowned by the other instruments.

Moss was also expert at feigning orgasm in true Hendrix tradition.

and aim their music at the hotel circuit. Unfortunately they are like so many other bands that play stultifying heavy beat music at high volumes.

The closest the band came to harmonies was in *The Backdoor Man*, a bluesy rocker.
Ross Owen.

Cold Chisel (left to right) Ian Moss, Steve Prestwick, Don Walker, Phil Small (singer Jim Barnes not pictured).

Stars, one of the hottest bands in Adelaide at the time had been signed to Mushroom Records, who had turned down Cold Chisel. Both bands were managed by Geoff Skewes who, for obvious reasons, tended to concentrate on the newly signed Stars more than Cold Chisel.

Don believes that Jim's time with Fraternity made him much more of a frontman. He was certainly much more at ease on a stage and confident of his abilities. Jim agrees wholeheartedly with this assessment.

During their time in England in 1972, Fraternity had seen and been suitably impressed by American acts such as the J. Geils Band, one of America's premier live acts - a high energy fusion of blues, rock'n'roll and R'n'B in a live show like nothing the Adelaide band had ever seen. They also apparently saw the Grateful Dead's PA and on their return to Adelaide the remaining members set about recreating both the energy of the J. Geils stage show, and the PA of the Grateful Dead. To achieve the desired stage show it was felt that Jimmy's reluctance before a crowd would have to change and they began to 'train' him. It had been a major blow to Fraternity when Bon Scott left (some sources suggest he got bored waiting for the PA to be built) as he was the one with the charisma and front required to achieve the stage act they desired, but they obviously also saw potential in Jimmy.

AUGUST 21   St Ignacious College. 8 p.m.-12 midnight

AUGUST 22   Shandon Hotel ("Powerhouse Disco") with Iron Knob. A good show with Jim.

AUGUST 23   (Sat) Countdown

The Mediterranean, with Pantha. Another good set. The band start trying out singers, including one promising prospect from Melbourne, but it doesn't work out.

AUGUST 29   Burnside Town Hall

Played as a 4-piece. Afterwards the band party with members of Fraternity, including Jim.

AUGUST 30   (Sat) Whyalla. Another 4-piece gig.

SEPTEMBER 2   Woodville Town Hall with James Wright Band. Another 4-piece show.

SEPTEMBER 5   Shandon Hotel, with Stars

Cold Chisel follow Stars and Jim joins them for their final set, which goes down a storm with the crowd.

SEPTEMBER 6   (Sat) Don catches The Dingoes and Stars at Countdown before jamming with members of Sherbet and the La De Das. The band continue to try out singers and work on new material - *Faust* and *Back Door Man*.

SEPTEMBER 11   Hotel Finsbury. A good response for the 4-piece band.

SEPTEMBER 13 - (SAT) COUNTDOWN

Cold Chisel play one of the best sets they've done at this venue, new songs such as *Faust* and *Back Door Man* are combined with *Letmenoforgetme* and *Jailhouse Rock*. Following this, the band head to the Largs Pier for the debut of the new Fraternity with Jim on vocals. The Fraternity gig had been given massive publicity for a local act and the band play well, gaining a good audience reaction. In the days after this Cold Chisel work on a new song called *I Met My Baby*, which would later become *Teenage Love Affair*.

SEPTEMBER 17   Arkaba Hotel, with Fraternity

Cold Chisel were advertised as playing at this gig but this did not eventuate although Don and Steve were in the audience.

SEPTEMBER 18   Tivoli Hotel, Cold Chisel now has a residency at this venue. The band play's well to a small but enthusiastic crowd of 100.

SEPTEMBER 19   Spruance Hall, East Elizabeth. An excellent night's playing.

SEPTEMBER 25   Tivoli Hotel. The crowd has dropped to 73 and the band's set is patchy.

SEPTEMBER 26 - COUNTDOWN

The Mediterranean, with Little River Band. A number of new songs are debuted in tonight's raging set, including *Goodbye To All That* and *I Met My Baby (Teenage Love)*, in addition to numbers such as *Faust*, *Letmenoforgetme* and *On The Road*. The band finish a powerful set with *Johnny B.Goode* and *I'm Gonna Roll Ya*, with Jim joining the band for the latter. Tonight's show, at almost 50% original material is a turning point for this lineup of the band.

OCTOBER 2   Tivoli Hotel

93 people turn up for tonight's show. The band jam with Dave Moys and members of Salvation Airforce, including Steve Beleky.

OCTOBER 4   (Sat) Merino

OCTOBER 5	Largs Pier, with Ariel. The band stays to watch Ariel after their 6.30 p.m.-9 p.m. set.
OCTOBER 9	Tivoli. The band plays well and gets a good reception.
OCTOBER 10	Shandon Hotel, with Railroad Gin, a Brisbane band who had released a couple of singles.
OCTOBER 12	(Sat) Countdown, with Captain Matchbox. The band plays three, mostly original sets, starting at 7.30 p.m. Another great gig which really confirms the band's self belief.
OCTOBER 15	Countdown, with Stylus. Not a good gig.

OCTOBER 17

Shandon Hotel, with Captain Matchbox Set List (probably complete): All Along The Watchtower / Lazy /Johnny B. Goode /The Ballad of Nick and Tiny /Faust / Goodbye To All That / Teenage Love / On The Road Again / I'm Gonna Roll Ya All Night Long

Although only a short set as they were one of three acts on the bill, this an amazing insight into the band's early development when they were a four - piece and Jim was with Fraternity. Phil Small had only been with the band a couple of months. At the time, Don described this show as "a sloppy night's playing but very ballsy".

The first thing that hits you is the drum sound - the drums are big, bold and central to the sound. *All Along The Watchtower* is full of guitar solos and a lot more driving than the Hendrix version it is probably based on. This was a popular cover song of the period, also being done by Fraternity and Kevin Borich and the La De Das. Ian asks Peter Moss for more foldback after this song, which was presumably the set opener. *Lazy* shows the band rearranging, adding improvised sections of both guitar and keyboards and like the previous *Watchtower*, it becomes quite a long song. Among the improvisations are snatches of sections which would appear in songs such as *Teenage Love*. Ian's vocals are smooth and soulful and he wisely makes no attempt to copy the higher register vocals of Deep Purple's Ian Gillian in *Lazy*. *Johnny B. Goode* is played fast, like the Hendrix version although it is not as guitar heavy. The first original in the set is one that has been lost (by that I mean there are no known recordings of it in existence), *The Ballad of Nick and Tiny*. It's a rocker, in the style of *Home and*

Broken Hearted which apparently spent little time in the set, despite the fact that a lot of work had obviously gone into the arrangement. *Faust* (Faust refers to a German legend of a magician or alchemist who sells his soul to the devil in exchange for knowledge and power) is next up, a Ron Carpenter song which dates back to Don's days with Bogislav. Much shorter than the previous songs, *Faust* is a melodic song with some smooth chordal textures in a medium paced rock song. *Goodbye To All That*, another melodic medium-paced rocker, has some most impressive sections and is the earliest of Ian's songs to be performed by the band. It climaxes with a powerful solo/bridge section adding to an already complex arrangement. *Teenage Love* is delayed as Steve makes some adjustments to his kit. The song is not played with quite the same frenetic pace as the first album demo (released on the album of the same name) and the arrangement differs in a few places, but otherwise it is the same song. During a quiet middle section Ian introduces Phil Small on bass, while Phil plays an impressive walking bass line. Surprisingly, *Teenage Love* is not the set closer. *On The Road* is very similar to the demo version recorded in November, a tight straightforward arrangement of a song which was an important one in the band's formative years. *Gonna Roll Ya All Night Long* is the title Ian gives the next song, an early version *I'm Gonna Roll Ya*. Aside from a few lyrical changes, this is pretty close to the version recorded nearly four years later! "See you later," is all Ian says to signal the end of the gig.

| OCTOBER 18 | (Sat) Pioneer Hall. 8 p.m.-11.30 p.m An excellent night's playing. |
| OCTOBER 19 | Largs Pier Hotel, with Renee Geyer |

The band plays a sloppy but powerful set, which is well received by the audience. Most of the band stay and watch Renee's new band. In the following days (Oct 21st) the band start work on a new song called *Open The Door Astrid*.

| OCTOBER 22 | Countdown. |

The band plays all night to a sparse crowd. Great playing. Don attends Ray Charles' gig the following night.

| OCTOBER 24 | Sonic Stairway Adult Disco opening night with James Wright Band. Ian and Don arrive late and the playing is sloppy. |
| OCTOBER 30 | Countdown, The Mediterranean, with Little River Band. Not a great show. |

OCTOBER 31 — Shandon Hotel, with Salvation Airforce. An average gig, the band stay to watch Salvation Airforce.

NOVEMBER 1 — (Sat) Apollo Stadium, Adelaide (Suzi Quatro support)

Following a 5.00 p.m. soundcheck, Cold Chisel play an excellent set starting at 8.15 p.m. Little River Band announces a plan to use Cold Chisel as their permanent support act.

NOVEMBER 1 — Largs Pier, with Fraternity & Roadwork

After the Quatro support the band play the first show with Fraternity and afterwards believe they have come out on top. The two bands party 'till after 5 a.m.

NOVEMBER 7 — Countdown, with Split Enz

The band plays a gutsy set. The highlight is Jim joining them for the last three numbers. They stay to watch Split Enz.

NOVEMBER 12 — Countdown

Cold Chisel plays all night. With only 60 people in attendance the band only play from 8.30 to 11.30. The following night Steve explains that he is considering leaving the band.

NOVEMBER 14 — Flamingo Hall, Christies Beach. A four-hour gig.

NOVEMBER 15 — (Sat) Largs Pier, with Fraternity & Roadwork. Cold Chisel play an impressive set and Don and Steve jam with Fraternity during their rather flat set.

NOVEMBER 16 - MAGGIES, WITH STARS

After this show Ian, Don and Steve go to the Largs Pier to watch Fraternity who play their most impressive set to date.

Cold Chisel manager Ray Hearn is in Melbourne talking to record companies. He returns on the Tuesday (18th) with news that Ross Wilson, Glen Wheatley and Fable Records are all interested in the band. As the band really didn't have a genuine demo tape at this stage, this interest would have stemmed from the recommendations of other bands such as The Little River Band, who were singing the praises of Cold Chisel in the Eastern states. The band respond with a meeting to discuss dress, advertising and image.

NOVEMBER 19

The four-piece Cold Chisel record demos at Slaters in Adelaide. Two songs, *On The Road* and *Letmenotforgetme* are recorded at a cost of $153.80. This is the band's first recording session. *On The*

Road was one of the regular original songs in the live set. *Letmenotforgetme*, as mentioned elsewhere was not always considered suitable for many of the band's live bookings, although the obviously better known *Georgia* was often performed. A new song being worked on at this time is *Northbound Train*.

NOVEMBER 23 — (Sat) Largs Pier, with Fraternity

7 p.m.-12 midnight. Cold Chisel are on first, their first two sets are lacklustre, the third opens with *Letmenotforgetme*, followed by the live debut of *Northbound Train* which have the crowd alight. The finale, *I'm Gonna Roll Ya* has Jim on vocals.

NOVEMBER 27 — Memorial Drive, Adelaide

(Deep Purple support) Cold Chisel get a terrible mix and play poorly, although many enjoy their set, including Deep Purple vocalist David Coverdale.

NOVEMBER 29 — (Sat) Glenelg Sailing Club

8p.m.-1a.m. After this show Steve Prestwich announces that he is leaving the band. The option of folding is raised, but Ian is keen to continue. Peter Moss blows up the band truck while driving to Port Lincoln.

DECEMBER 3 — The Octagon, a school show with Keystone Angels. The band play a great show, Steve still on the drums but planning to exit.

DECEMBER 4 — Countdown, with Ayers Rock.

Cold Chisel play three raging sets and watch Ayers Rock.

DECEMBER 5 — Elizabeth Hotel.

Steve announces that he will be staying with the band and they play a great show as a result.

DECEMBER 6 — Morning. Melbourne St. Fashion Parade.

DECEMBER 6 — Arvo, Largs Pier

Admission $1.00, 2.30 p.m. -5 p.m. Peter Moss feels that these sets were the best he'd seen the band play at that stage.

DECEMBER 6 — Evening, Largs Pier with Salvation Airforce and Boosey Hawke. The band continues from where they left off, watched by members of Salvation Airforce and having played three shows that day are ready to drop when they leave the stage.

DECEMBER 8

Morialta High School. 7.30 p.m.-11 p.m. One of those shows where everything seems to go wrong. Jim sings for most of the night and later tells the band that Skyhooks' Shirley Strachan had pronounced Cold Chisel "the second best band in Australia" on radio 5KA.

DECEMBER 9	Salisbury High School. An average show played as a 4-piece.

DECEMBER 11   Burnside Town Hall. Ray Hearn, the band's manager has brought Charles Fischer from Sydney's Trafalgar Studios to see the band. He is duly impressed and offers the band some studio time in March.

DECEMBER 12	Elizabeth Hotel
DECEMBER 13	Yankallila Community Hall. 9.pm-1 am

The band continue work on new songs, *Only A Fool* and *Fit To Bust Blues* as well as rearranging the start of *I Met My Baby (Teenage Love)*.

DECEMBER 20 - (SAT)

The band make an early start (they went to air at 9.30 a.m.) for their first television appearance, at a telethon at Adelaides Channel 9. They perform *Letmenotforgetme* and *On The Road* and Don does a short interview. Unfortunately, at that time many of the performances for television were not taped, or were later taped over, and this Cold Chisel performance has been lost.

DECEMBER 20	Countdown with Stylus.
DECEMBER 21	Largs Pier, with James Wright.
DECEMBER 31	Football Park. 6 pm-7 pm

DECEMBER 31/ JAN 1 LARGS PIER

12.45 a.m.-3.30 a.m. Despite the fact that Ian had made himself quite sick during celebrations earlier in the night (the party at the Pier that night included Bon and Malcolm from AC/DC, as well as Vince Lovegrove) Cold Chisel play a spirited set to see in the New Year.

Cold Chisel finished the year on a high note, according to RAM magazine:

"Ask anyone who has been Adelaide's top band over the year, and they'll tell you it's Cold Chisel. The band has a strong and ever-growing following, and have attracted the attention of several touring interstate bands. Their highlights for '75 include supporting gigs for Joe Cocker, Deep Purple, Lou Reed and Suzi Quatro. The band will start touring other states probably Feb-March next year."

[1975]

Cold Chisel as a four-piece, late '75/ early '76. Don, Phil, Ian (back) & Steve.

27)

[1976]

On the road

NINETEEN SEVENTY-SIX WOULD SEE THE BAND TOUR THE EAST AND WEST COASTS, SETTLING IN MELBOURNE AND THEN SYDNEY. THE RETURN OF JIM TO THE BAND IN MAY FINALIZES A LINE-UP WHICH WOULD REMAIN UNCHANGED FOR THE NEXT SEVEN YEARS. THE BAND ALSO RECORD SOME IMPORTANT DEMOS, ENSURING A CONTINUED FOCUS ON ORIGINAL MATERIAL, EVEN THOUGH THERE ARE STILL MANY COVERS IN THEIR LIVE SET.

JANUARY 3	Largs Pier Hotel, (Adelaide) with Roadwork and Boozey Hawke
JANUARY 8	Largs Pier Hotel, with strippers
JANUARY 9	Countdown, with Kevin Borich and the La De Das
JANUARY 10	Countdown, with Kevin Borich and the La De Das

JANUARY 16 - COUNTDOWN, WITH SAILOR

The Keystone Angels, who had worked steadily around Adelaide for the last 12-18 months, are signed to Alberts studios.

JANUARY 23	Largs Pier Hotel with Axe and strippers
JANUARY 24	Largs Pier Hotel with Powerhouse
JANUARY 25	Largs Pier Hotel with Phil Manning
JANUARY 31	Largs Pier Hotel with Fraternity & Stars
JANUARY 31	Countdown, with Powerhouse

FEBRUARY 5

Countdown, with Kevin Borich and the La De Das.

FEBRUARY 20	Largs Pier Hotel with Our Band
FEBRUARY 21	Largs Pier Hotel with Raven and Axe
FEBRUARY 25	Countdown, with Ol' 55

RAM magazine reports in a write up on the Adelaide music scene that "in March Cold Chisel will head for Melbourne, Sydney and Armidale."

MARCH 4

Arkaba Hotel with Rufus Red and Salvation Airforce

MARCH 5	Largs Pier Hotel, with Buffalo

MARCH 6 - COUNTDOWN, WITH ARIEL

Geoff Skewes was managing the band at this point although the band felt that he did not have the positive attitude they needed.

As a four piece the band come to Sydney and Melbourne to play. Photographs of the time show Don in the foreground although Ian was handling the vocal duties. The band had gone to Sydney first, but found work hard to get and only played a couple of shows there before heading down to Melbourne after just a week. The tour was a difficult one as they had troubles with their truck, money was extremely scarce, the band's usual following was absent and many gigs were blown out.

29)

As Cold Chisel made their first visit to Melbourne music press reports that Skyhooks' US tour is not going so well, a blow for the band who up until then could do no wrong. In '74-'75 Skyhooks had demonstrated that a local band could dominate the Australian market and compete successfully with any international artists. Skyhooks' failure to have any impact on the US market was a turning point in their career, even though they did enjoy some further success after this - events which were arguably paralleled by many other Australian bands. By 1980 Cold Chisel would be the ones who could do no wrong and Skyhooks would find themselves on an endless run of pub gigs, before splitting up.

On the road from Sydney to Melbourne the motor on the band's equipment truck blows and must be replaced in Melbourne, an expense the band could have done without to say the least.

| MARCH 13 | Nth Leagues Club, Woolongong. |
| MARCH 14 | Concord RSL |

MARCH 15

The band record demo tapes at Trafalgar Studios in Sydney. Songs demoed are *Only A Fool*, *Fit To Bust Blues*, *Northbound*, *Rosaline* and *One Long Day*. All songs are sung by Ian. None of the songs from this session have been issued in any form.

MARCH 16	Croxton Park
MARCH 17	Prospect Hill Hotel
MARCH 18	Martinis, Carlton (Melbourne)
MARCH 19	Southside Six (with Redhouse Roll Band)
MARCH 19	Matthew Flinders
MARCH 20	Goulburn Valley Hotel (Shepparton)
MARCH 23	Station Hotel
MARCH 26	Largs Pier Hotel
MARCH 27	Largs Pier Hotel

APRIL 2 - CROXTON PARK HOTEL

APRIL 3	Waltzing Matilda
APRIL 4	Tottenham Hotel
APRIL 5	Southside Six, Moorabbin-{Afternoon}
APRIL 5	Mt Erica Hotel (Prahran)
APRIL 7	Countdown Disco (Adelaide)
APRIL 9	Tea Tree Gully Hotel

APRIL 10	Largs Pier Hotel*
APRIL 14	Ros Trevor College
APRIL 17	Sundowner Hotel, Whyalla
APRIL 18	St.Augusta Football Club
APRIL 29	Urbrae Agricultural School (private function)
APRIL 30	Burnside Town Hall (private function)

The band part company with manager Geoff Skewes.

| MAY 1 | Countdown, The Mediterranean Hotel |
| MAY 1 | Largs Pier Hotel* ("Rock'n'roll Headquarters") |

During one of these Largs Pier shows Jimmy returns to see the band playing and, inspired by the new songs, asks if he can rejoin. Fraternity had completed another tour on the South Australian coast and despite the initial hype surrounding their return on the Adelaide scene, they had not lived up to expectations. With hardly a word being exchanged, the members simply didn't regroup after the break following the last tour.

Don recalls that one of the first new songs the band tried with Jim back was *Home and Broken Hearted*.

(30

MAY 14 - COUNTDOWN, THE MEDITERRANEAN

"Countdown has always been the most progressive (venue), often anticipating trends up to a year before they happen. Right now, (1976) Countdown is the only place you'll hear non-top 40 hits played between band brackets and it's the only place you can get to see top Oz bands for free on Wednesday and Thursday nights."

(TONY LEWIS, IN RAM MAGAZINE)

MAY 15	Port Adelaide Football Club
MAY 16	Largs Pier Hotel*
MAY 28	Largs Pier Hotel*
MAY 29	St.Michaels College

MAY 30 - LARGS PIER HOTEL*

RAM magazine runs a story by Adelaide writer Tony Lewis under the heading "Cold Chisel, Adelaide hot sizzle", which explains the situation behind Jim's leaving and returning as well as the affect this had on the band. I have included a couple of comments from the (slightly cynical) editor also:

"Of all the rock bands in Adelaide, none would command more respect from musicians and audience alike than Cold Chisel.

And as they have just completed a very successful maiden tour of Sydney and Melbourne, it appears that

it may not be too long before they command respect Australia-wide.

However, the Cold Chisel the Easterners saw was a four-piece band, as it had been since late last year their singer Jim Barnes left for (supposedly) greener pastures in the revamped Fraternity. After Jim left the vocals were taken over by guitarist Ian Moss, and although he handled them with great competence, he was never really happy with the situation, so the band searched on for another suitable singer, but without luck. Then just recently, Fraternity split again, so gigless Jim wandered back again and re-joined Cold Chisel soon after they returned from Melbourne.

One point about Chisel that had really worried yours truly was their presentation, or rather their lack of it- they had always seemed too introverted, and never really established a liaison with their audience. But Jim's re-instatement seems to have rectified the situation somewhat, and has given the band extra vitality.

Chisel's pianist, songwriter and spokesman, Don Walker, tells it like this: "Jim's about doubled our potential as far as what we can put out. Besides being a focal point himself, Jim puts out a certain spark to every one of us, and it makes us put out more than if we were just up there without him. Jim demands attention. If you put him on stage it's difficult to go on eating your dinner."

31)

Cold Chisel at the Mt. Eric Hotel. Ian, Steve, Phil (behind Jim) & Jim.

That certain spark is evident to anyone who has seen Chisel both before and after Jim joined. Ian Moss is much more comfortable playing guitar and taking only a share of the vocals. And bassist Phil Small and drummer Steve Prestwich seem more relaxed and confident, knowing that there's someone out front taking care of the visual side of the act. The whole band has gained (yes Tone tell us what the band has gained - ed) "CHARISMA", for want of a better word. (Golly Tone! Really! - ed) One thing you can definitely tell Sydney and Melbourne punters is that if they liked Cold Chisel last time around, they'll love 'em next time. (That's telling 'em - ed)"

JUNE

With Jim back on vocals the band record demos at Peppers Studio in Adelaide including *Fit To Bust, Daskarzine, Bunny's Blues, Drinkin' In Port Lincoln, Five Thirty E.T.A.* and *H-Hour Hotel,* all by Don Walker. *Drinking In Port Lincoln* and *H-Hour Hotel* from these sessions are released in 1994 on the *Teenage Love* album and *Hands Out Of My Pocket* single respectively.

JUNE 12

Festival Theatre, Adelaide (Little Feat support) Jimmy had been introduced to bands such as Little Feat by members of Fraternity during his stint with that band.

"Little Feat were one of the most enjoyable bands I've ever seen live. We supported them in Adelaide. We were terrible. I had the flu and could hardly sing a note, and they were real creeps. They hardly gave us any room to set up. No soundcheck. No matter how we played though it wouldn't have mattered. They were so hot."

(Jimmy, talking to Vince Lovegrove in December 1980.)

JUNE 18	Port Lincoln Hotel
JUNE 19	Largs Pier Hotel, with Stars
JUNE 24	Largs Pier Hotel, with Susan de Slade
JUNE 25	Largs Pier Hotel, with Our Band
JUNE 26	Largs Pier Hotel with Soldier
JUNE 27	Largs Pier Hotel, with Station
JULY 3	Largs Pier Hotel, with Soldier
JULY 4	Arkaba, with The Angels
JULY 8	Largs Pier Hotel, with Susan de Slade

JULY 9	Countdown, with Fullhouse

JULY 10 - LARGS PIER HOTEL, WITH DANGER DAN

During this period the band makes its first trip to Perth, playing Geraldton as well as Perth itself. While in Geraldton, Peter Moss recalls that Steve and Jim made themselves unpopular with the rest of the band when they spend much needed band funds on alcohol. The new motor put into the truck in Melbourne just a few months earlier also blows up.

JULY 14	Sandgroper Hotel
JULY 15	White Sands, Scarborough
JULY 18	Sandgroper Hotel
JULY 20	Scarborough Hotel
JULY 21	Sandgroper Hotel
JULY 22	Sandgroper Hotel
JULY 27	Perth
AUGUST 2	Morphett Vale High School
AUGUST 4	Plympton High School
AUGUST 6	Brighton High School

The band move to Melbourne, living in one room at the Hotel Majestic in St Kilda.

"When we first went to Melbourne we were staying at this little dive called the Majestic Hotel which was just one big long hall, just like a dormitory, until we totally ran out of money so we had to move out of the hotel - we were crashing out at friends places."

(Ian talking to the Centralian Advocate, 1981)

AUGUST 20	Croxton Park Hotel, Melbourne with Little River Band
AUGUST 21	Beaumaris Civic Centre with Stars
AUGUST 25	Croxton Park Hotel with Taste

(32

[1976]

Ian Moss, Mt. Erica Hotel

33)

AUGUST 26 - WALTZING MATILDA WITH SUPERNAUT

This gig is given a positive review in *Juke* magazine, particularly considering that they were a new, virtually unknown band.

"Adelaide, possibly Australia's answer to the British Isles, is the birthplace of this bunch of roughneck punk rockers. Most of the material they grind out on stage is original and seems to be inspired by their own life experiences. That being the case, what a wild existence! Drinkin' At Port Lincoln undoubtedly has this pub grovelling life in mind but these guys show no signs of being inebriated-quite the contrary, they are keyed up and work hard at pounding out that particular number.

"On-stage the band present themselves as a solid wall of hard hitting rock musos. The lineup is lead guitarist Ian Moss, then vocalist and Scotsman Jim Barnes, bass player Phil Small and keyboard man Don Walker. Together in their ripped denim and leather they belt out yet another gut rock number, Brisbane Daylight Express."

"As the name suggests, it's a fast moving song which stops for no one not even the many dancers determined to see the whole bracket through. The number slammed to an abrupt halt and I thought for a moment I'd been caught between the steel tracks and the wheels.

"On a sentimental note, Teenage Lover was the second last song for the night, bringing back fond memories of those years that passed by in a flash. Sentimental in content maybe, but far from placid in delivery. It was a punchy, electrifying number which was awkward to dance to but had your legs moving so fast you'd have thought Parkinson's disease had set in for good.

"After that little boogie the guys went to leave the stage. What's the deal? That was supposed to be second last on the list, where's the grand rock finale? A second look however, and guitarist Ian Moss and piano man Don Walker had remained. Two guys to finish with a big rock number! How can they make it? I soon found out it was not to be a big rock killer, rather a slow subtle life squeezer.

"Moss won my heart (believe me a hard thing to do) with his heart rending rendition of the old classic Georgia. The presentation was simple with guitar and piano alternating and merging. All those seated were

motionless, pinned in their chairs, melting at Moss's sensitivity. After that hard hitting rock what could be more unexpected? Music which has you on the edge of your seat, almost satisfied, and then leaves you frustrated when it finally ends.

"This number really marked the versatility of the band from scourging rock to mellow blues. Definitely a band that won't only be a support for long- a group to watch."

(REBECCA, JUKE)

AUGUST 27   Mt. Erica Hotel

AUGUST 28   Southside Six with *Ariel* and *Jets*

AUGUST 28 - MATTHEW FLINDERS HOTEL, CHADSTONE

At around this time Phil Coulson, an EMI promotions man had taken a liking to the band and, showing excellent judgement, was pushing for the company to sign them. Phil recalls that numbers such as *One Long Day* and *Georgia* particularly impressed him. Not having any power other than a little influence, he didn't approach the band at all, but he did convince EMI's Colin Peterson to fly down to Melbourne from Sydney to see the band play at the Station Hotel. (The band played often at this venue but as it was a non-agency venue that did its own advertising; dates for these shows are hard to find.) Phil recalls that, although the band played a great show that night to a packed house, Peterson was not impressed and flew back to Sydney without even speaking to the band.

OCTOBER 15 - MT ERICA

When pressed as to the possible reasons for this lack of interest, Coulson believes that the fact that he and Peterson had had a disagreement about the company's releasing a Mark Holden cover of a song just issued by EMI artist Eric Carmen (the two versions were in direct competition with each other) may have had something to do with it. Either way Cold Chisel had come very close to being signed, perhaps missing out through no fault of their own, without even knowing that anyone was looking at them!

Phil Coulson later went to WEA and, along with Steve Hands and Billy Pinnell was instrumental in getting the band signed there. From a musical point of view, Phil recalls that from '76 to '77 Jimmy had changed his vocal style from a more restrained delivery to a more screaming style (in Phil's words).

With the obvious benefit of hindsight, Don Walker feels that the band wasn't ready to be signed at this stage, although they certainly believed they were at the time.

This show is reviewed in *RAM* magazine by Ross Owen.

"The name Cold Chisel conjures up images of heavy metal rockers in the Deep Purple, Black Sabbath, Led Zepplin (sic) mould.

"The five piece Chisel outfit played a commercialised form of heavy metal rock, but unfortunately they seem to be a band living in the past, playing a music style that was popular on uni campuses several years ago.

"There's another side of course it's what the punters are used to.

"At the Mt Erica Hotel, Prahran, the Cold Chiselers showed they are fully aware of the rock formula that has seen so many heavy bands earn their bread and butter - long hair, loud music, a hotel dance beat, and plenty of bare arms and chests.

"Lead singer, Jim Barnes, wearing a leather vest over his bare, hairless chest performed many Paul Rogers inspired pelvic thrusts, pouts and symbolic fornication, but his act seemed a little pretentious, even though his voice handled the work satisfactorily.

"The total sound of Cold Chisel on this Friday night was very muddy, and solos by lead guitarist Ian Moss, were often drowned by the other instruments.

"Moss was also an expert at feigning orgasm in true Hendrix tradition, as he stroked the neck of his semi-acoustic Gibson.

A heavy rock version of Bob Dylan's All Along The Watchtower *didn't really come off, though Moss' guitar work began to shine towards the end.*

"Keyboard player Don Walker, barely visible as he squatted behind his keyboard banks, seemed to be a wasted member of the band. His work was purely rhythmical, no solos, and the instrument was used solely to fill the sound out.

"Titles of their songs summed up the basic dancin'/drinkin' music, Roll You All Night Long, Drinkin' At Port Lincoln, Keep Playin' That Rock'n'Roll.

"Cold Chisel obviously know on which side their bread is buttered and aim their music at the hotel circuit. Unfortunately they are like so many other bands that play stultifying heavy beat music at high volumes.

"The closest the band came to harmonies was in The Backdoor Man, *a bluesy rocker."*

OCTOBER 16 - SOUTHERN AURORA

Frustrated by their lack of progress in the Adelaide/Melbourne scene and the cold winters, the band move to Sydney figuring that they might as well go nowhere in a warmer climate. Don recalls that the move to Sydney was initiated by Sebastian Chase, who wanted to manage the band from Sydney, where he also managed Dragon and Rose Tattoo. Don also recalled that Sebastian was a good manager for the band, well liked by all, but that he eventually got too busy with his other acts and was virtually relieved when the band parted company with him.

"It got to the point where we couldn't afford a place to live, so we crashed on lounge floors of girlfriends and even people we didn't know all that well, and some of us were raiding their fridges behind their backs.

"When we decided we'd get out of Melbourne, four of us were on the back of a truck that was on its last legs, the rest hitch-hiked up. We met up in Sydney and put it together there."

(Don Walker talking to Christie Eliezer in 'Juke', May 1978)

"We knew that we were the best band in the world but we also knew what the climate was. We were in Australia, on the edge of the world. You could take Led Zeppelin and stick them in Sydney and they would go round and round and round for five years trying to get a record deal. That's the way it would work, no matter how good you were."

(Don Walker talking to Toby Creswell in 1994)

(36

OCTOBER 22	Bondi Lifesaver
OCTOBER 23	Grafton Racecourse
OCTOBER 25	Chequers
OCTOBER 26	Chequers
OCTOBER 27	Bondi Lifesaver
OCTOBER 29	St.Marys Band Club
OCTOBER 30	Bondi Lifesaver
NOVEMBER 12	Oceanic Hotel, Coogee
NOVEMBER 19	Bondi Lifesaver, with Aura
NOVEMBER 20	Bondi Lifesaver, with Stylus
NOVEMBER 25	Chrystal Palace, Gosford, with Buffalo
DECEMBER 1	Bondi Lifesaver

DECEMBER 4	Northern Suburbs Leagues Club, Wollongong
DECEMBER 8	George Hotel
DECEMBER 9	George Hotel
DECEMBER 10	George Hotel
DECEMBER 11	George Hotel
DECEMBER 17	St Mary's Hall
DECEMBER 18	Bennelong Restaurant, Opera House
DECEMBER 31	Parkes Community Centre (SA)

The band are joined on - stage by strippers during their set. Apparently Jimmy just couldn't resist the temptation to touch, only adding to the entertainment value for the audience.

(37)

Just how many times

THIS IS THE YEAR WHEN THE BAND GETS THE RECORD DEAL TO JUSTIFY ALL THE SACRIFICES THEY HAVE MADE. NATIONAL TOURS AND RECORDING DOMINATE THE LATTER PART OF THE YEAR, WHILE SMALLER SHOWS AROUND SYDNEY AND RETURN TRIPS TO ADELAIDE TAKE UP THE EARLIER PART, IN ADDITION TO SHOPPING THE DEMO TO RECORD COMPANIES AND HOOKING UP WITH THEIR FOURTH AND FINAL MANAGER, ROD WILLIS.

There are a couple of notable recordings from the band in the early part of 1977, which unfortunately appear to have gone missing. The first is a live-to-air performance for radio station JJ in Sydney from the Bondi Lifesaver. A couple of songs from this set have been located as the band used them on its early demo tape, (see July '77) namely *Rosaline, Four Walls* and *Home and Broken Hearted* and I have also heard *Georgia, 5.30 ETA,* and *Showtime* from the same show.

The other significant recordings were a demo session at Trafalgar Studios (on which a young Mark Opitz assisted) where *Bunny's Blues* was recorded (also included on the previously mentioned demo tape) and *Goodbye To All That* among others. The take of *Bunny's Blues* is the only song from this session to have surfaced.

JANUARY 28   Manly Vale

JANUARY 29 - MANLY VALE

The band consider changing their name to The Dogs, as Jimmy told Ross Stapleton in 1978, "I don't think anyone seriously considered keeping the name (Cold Chisel) when we first started. It took me years to get used to it. We were actually going to change our name about two years ago to The Dogs". Don then explained that by that time the band had built up a small following for Cold Chisel and the

agency said "You call yourselves The Dogs and you'll have to start all over again". Jimmy added, "It was just that we liked the idea of the name and it was before we had even heard of punk rock. It sounded good."

FEBRUARY 4   Blacktown Civic Centre

At this time Don was managing the band.

"We didn't have anybody who could get out and about and we needed a manager to get the band work because at the time Don was doing most of the managing - and while everyone slept till all hours of the afternoon, Don was up at nine in the morning out hassling work."

(Ian talking to the Centralian Advocate, 1981)

MARCH

The band does some recording for an ABC surf movie starring Beau Bridges, with the title *A Shimmering Light.* The song recorded is *Just How Many Times,* a regular in the band's live set at this time. Peter Moss recalls that the band recorded the song at an ABC studio in North Sydney and did the shoot at a beach house in Whale Beach (Northern Sydney) with the band dressed in Hawaiian shirts. Subsequently Don Walker was asked to surrender the copyright on the song, which he refused, effectively ending the band's movie career, or so he thought.

(38

e five brackets in
eing a little more
including a good
titled "Georgia On
the lead guitarist
is almost as good
playing. Certainly,
among the best
stralia has to offer
nt.

ns for an album
under way but the
refuse to name the
any at the present

el came together in
1973 in Adelaide,
jh now currently
dney, every four to

39)

The film was issued in 1978, almost all footage of the band removed and sound (from another artist) dubbed onto that footage. The dubbed sound is embarrassing and you'll miss the band if you blink. The film has not been rebroadcast since its initial release. It is now probably the most difficult to find Cold Chisel video footage.

MARCH 5	Stage Door Tavern
MARCH 19	Stage Door Tavern
MARCH 23	French's Tavern

MARCH - CHEQUERS

"Currently gaining deserved popularity and respect from other musicians is a band called Cold Chisel. Watching them perform at Chequers I couldn't fault them in any great detail.

...Vocals were exceptionally good and for a change, audibility was crystal clear....Without a great deal of movement or over abundance of lighting it was easy to watch this five member band give a good quality musical performance. Cold Chisel don't need the help of gimmicks to give good stage presentation - their own musical and vocal capabilities are

enough...Justice was given to The Doors' "Road House Blues" and a Jimi Hendrix number "Come On" completed the second bracket.

...Cold Chisel write and perform 95% of their own material, the remaining 5% being comprised of other artists songs such as Bob Dylan's "Tonight I'll Be Staying Here With You".

There were five brackets in all, the last being a little more laid back and including a solo number title "Georgia On My Mind" by the lead guitarist whose voice is almost as good as his guitar playing. Certainly, he must be among the best guitarists Australia has to offer at the moment.

...Main influences have been from Led Zeppelin to the Rolling Stones to Ray Charles, but I feel Cold Chisel themselves will soon be an influencing factor on many other groups starting out.

...My commendations to Cold Chisel for a good evening's worth of musical entertainment, and I for one will be looking forward to the release of their album."

(SUZANNE WILCOX, JUKE MAGAZINE)

APRIL 6 - CHEQUERS

It was at a Chequers show (probably on May 2) that Rod Willis first saw the band which would change his life, and he theirs. Unfortunately, it was also on one of these two shows that Jim let the many frustrations the band was going through get to him and went and joined his brother John in Feather.

"I was broke and disillusioned and they made me an offer I couldn't refuse," he explains. "I really wanted to play with John again (the brothers were in Fraternity together) but it was a different style of music to what I was used to, so I had to say no."

There are no bad feelings though: Barnes shares a house with the rest of Feather.

(Jimmy talking to Christie Eliezer in 'Juke' magazine)

While he was with Feather (which included the Frazer brothers, of whom Stewart later found success with Noiseworks, and more recently, John Farnham), John Swan had his brother sign a publishing contract with Rondor, whom John was signed to already. After Jim's return to Cold Chisel, Rondor head John Brommel worked at getting the band to sign publishing deals and eventually succeeded.

| APRIL 14 | It is announced in the press that Feather is signed to CBS. |
| MAY 2 | Chequers |

MAY 9

Don has dinner with Rod Willis at the Hilton. Following the gig, Rod ran into Don at a party after which Don rang Rod to discuss managing the band and the dinner at the Hilton was arranged.

Initially trained as a woolclasser, Rod became interested in live music when a friend living across the street began playing in a band. He was soon dabbling as a roadie with local bands before heading to the UK in 1966. Rod spent the next eleven years working as tour or road manager for acts such Fleetwood Mac, UFO, King Crimson, Emerson, Lake and Palmer, and Savoy Brown.

Rod had only been back in the country a matter of weeks when his brother took him to a gig Cold Chisel were playing at Chequers. Rod would be the fourth person to manage the band (not including Don), who had by this stage been turned down by every major record label in the country.

| MAY 13 | Newcastle University (Lunch) |

MAY 14 - BONDI LIFESAVERS

This show was to be Jimmy's farewell gig with the band as they had grown tired of looking for him every time he walked out. However the show went so well that all agreed he should stay.

The band head back to Adelaide to a show at Port Adelaide's Reapham Hotel where things suddenly fell into place.

"Something happened that night with the chemistry of the band. It just became more than the sum of its parts. When we looked at each other on stage there was amazement in our faces. It was like taking off in a 747. We'd been playing the same songs for years, but it was as though once that happened we knew how to do it."

(Don Walker talking to Toby Creswell)

"We had gone away for a long period and we came back. We had probably been playing like that for a while, but they hadn't seen us. The crowd went crazy and I think it was the first time we realised we'd improved that much. It had been a gradual process of getting more professional, playing better as a unit and then to come back to your home town, to people who knew you back to front, and they saw the difference in us. And we saw that reflected back."

(Jimmy Barnes talking to Toby Creswell)

MAY 24	Chequers
MAY 25	Chequers
MAY 28	Sydney University

JUNE

Frustrated with their lack of success here the band look at moving to America-

"We were planning to do some hard work, save up about $15,000, sell all of our equipment and just go to America and start from scratch. At that stage we couldn't have been any worse off playing dives there than we were here."

(Don Walker)

41)

JUST HOW MANY TIMES

"We always thought we had overseas potential but no-one else did. Everything we did we geared for what we thought might go well overseas.

We knew automatically that, if we did something that worked well in Australia, it would bomb overseas and that sort of philosophy was borne out by the first couple of local bands that went overseas."

(Don Walker)

JUNE 3	Dodds Hotel (Cooma)
JUNE 4	Dodds Hotel
JUNE 7	Croxton Park Hotel
JUNE 8	Beverley Crest Hotel (St Kilda)
JUNE 8	Be,Bop,& Loo Bar
JUNE 9	Tarmac Hotel
JUNE 10	Ferntree Gully Hotel
JUNE 11	Morwell Hotel

JUNE 15 - FRENCH'S TAVERN

It was at French's Tavern around this time that Warners A & R man, David Sinclair, who would soon make the decision to sign the band, first saw them. He recalls that the vibe about the band was really strong and their live following well established. On stage he recalls that they "took no prisoners, they were really keen to sit down and talk and the idea of making a record, they thought was just sensational."

JUNE 17	Bondi Lifesaver
JUNE 18	Bondi Lifesaver
JUNE 22	French's Tavern
JUNE 29	Chequers
JUNE 30	Chequers

JULY

Don Walker submits a demo tape to WEA Records. Already recognizing the band's strengths in the live situation much of the tape was recorded live, possibly at a Bondi Lifesaver show. Included are versions of *Rosaline*. *Four Walls, Home and Broken Hearted* and a song titled *Bunny's Blues*.

This take of *Rosaline* differs from the first album version in that it has a Jeff Beck-like guitar intro and a guitar solo after the piano solo (the album take has only a sax solo). *Four Walls* is a more uptempo version with almost completely different lyrics, drums on the whole track and a guitar solo. This

lyric is certainly not about a prison, as a double bed is mentioned instead of a single. This is probably the most interesting of the songs, as it was to be another three years before it would see the light of day. Of these three songs, *Home and Broken Hearted* is most like the released version.

Bunny's Blues is a Moss sung song in the style of *Georgia*, with only Don Walker's keyboards as accompaniment. That it never appeared on the first album or any subsequent releases (it was considered for Teenage Love but apparently left off due to the quality of the recording) makes it all the more interesting. The lyrics refer to many American locations and don't fit into the Don Walker mould at all. Don stated that he wrote the song when he was at university for a competition judged by Mike McClennan, which he won. When I recently asked Ian Moss about this song he could not even recall that the band had actually recorded it, although he did remember the song well enough to be able to hum a few bars.

The tape, like most recordings of the band at this time, reveals extremely competent playing and a distinctively Australian feel. The most striking aspect of it is the maturity in both the songwriting and performance-this is no bunch of kids yet to master their craft who show a little potential as one might expect. On listening to the tape it is hard to believe that this is an unsigned band! Warners signed the band. A number of Warners employees, Steve Hands and Phil Coulson had been fans of the band for some time (Phil trying to have then signed to EMI where he worked 12 months earlier).

Steve Hands would have a barbecue at his house whenever the band played in Melbourne and his wife, 'Von, recalls them always being ravenous, Ian Moss devouring twelve potatoes with one meal.

"We managed to get a few record companies interested, but they all wanted us to hang around and wait for a while. Then Warners came up and asked us to sign on the dotted line."

"They didn't seem concerned about singles, they just said 'let's do an album and see what happens."

(Jimmy Barnes, 'Juke' 1978)

John Brommel, head of Rondor Publishing at the time then desperately tried to get the band signed to a record company and found an interested party in WEA's David Sinclair, however David was concerned that the band's new manager Rod Willis did not have the experience required to handle the band at such an important time in their career. In order to rectify this situation Brommel hatched a plan whereby he called experienced band manager Peter Rix (Marcia Hines, Hush) and Rix agreed to manage Cold Chisel. The band then received the OK from David Sinclair and were signed by WEA without the actual management of the band altering at all. Sinclair himself says that "Rod hadn't proven himself as a manager and, as it turned out he had a really hot act and he grew with the band."

John Brommel gained Don Walker's signature on a publishing contract at Rondor during drinks after the record deal was signed at Warners offices.

JULY 1	Royal Antler
JULY 2	Northern Suburbs Leagues
JULY 4	Baccus Wine Bar, Bankstown
JULY 5	Bexley North
JULY 8	Meadowbank High School
JULY 9	Orana Hotel, Newcastle
JULY 11	French's Tavern
JULY 12	French's Tavern (the band is paid $70 for each of these shows)
JULY 15	Rooty Hill RSL (Cancelled) Blacktown RSL

"It seems Jim Barnes has decided not to join Feather and will be remaining in Cold Chisel. The latter have recently acquired a new manager in Rod Willis (who also handles Australia) and working steadily around Sydney."

(JUKE)

JULY 17	Parramatta Jail, 1.30 p.m.
JULY 19	Bexley Hotel
JULY 21	Bondi Lifesaver
JULY 22	Royal Antler
JULY 23	Orama (cancelled)
JULY 24	Icelands Prince Alfred Park
AUGUST 5	Drummond College, Armidale University (N.S.W.)

AUGUST 6 - BONDI LIFESAVER

"...among those catching the (Kevin Borich) Express' set at the Bondi Lifesaver last week were Daryl, Harvey and Chrissie from Sherbert, Rockwell T James, Warren Morgan, Dennis Wilson from Chariot, John Swan from Feather, Ted Mulry, Smiley from Hush, a couple of Dragons, Martin Ergman (ex-Bleeding Hearts), Donnie Sutherland from Sounds Unlimited, Mark Evans from Finch and Jim Barnes from Cold Chisel."

(JUKE)

AUGUST 11	Woollongong Town Hall (with Richard Clapton)
AUGUST 12	Swansea Workers Club
AUGUST 13	Royal Antler Hotel (cancelled)

Record demos for the first album. Songs recorded include Gonna Roll Ya, Northbound, Just How Many Times, Juliet, Home and Broken Hearted, Rosaline, It Aint Wrong, On The Road.

The band start demos for the first album, fitting in sessions in between live gigs often on the same day. The intention at this stage was to simply record all of the original songs the band felt should be considered for the debut release. The songs covered a broad range of styles, although the record company pressured producer Peter Walker to deliver as many fast paced, 3-minute songs as possible - a brief that he felt would not do the band justice.

Peter Walker had been the guitarist with Perth band Bakery, described by David Sinclair as "a sort of underground Doors." In trying to improve his knowledge of sound Peter Walker had been working at Trafalgar Studios, and although he was not the most experienced producer around, the band liked the idea that he too was a musician and would therefore be able to relate to their ideas more than a non-musician.

David Sinclair from WEA recalls doing a deal with Trafalgar Studios whereby a flat rate was paid for the band to record an album, rather than the usual hourly rate. This suited both the band and producer.

Peter recalls that there were many problems, which had to be overcome in the process of recording the album. Firstly, because the band were having to play so many live shows just to survive, it usually meant that Jim's voice was not in good shape for the sessions. The band was also virtually broke, meaning Ian and Phil could rarely afford new strings for each session and Steve had to use old drum skins. The band were also playing many of the songs at a tempo suited to the last set in a crowded hotel, and when viewed in the cold light of day, usually too fast. Peter recalls having to do a lot of work to ensure that the final, "meanwhile..." section of *One Long Day* did not speed up (as the band deliberately did live) as he felt that the passion should create the power, not the speed.

The record company also had strong feelings about Jim's vocals, particularly regarding his diction and Peter spent a lot of time ensuring that the takes he got were satisfactory in this area.

It was also a very experimental, primitive period in Australia's recording history, a time when most studios were switching from 16 to 24 track and most "effects" had to be produced manually. For instance the piano intro to *Northbound* has a chorus effect created by recording the section, altering the tape speed very slightly, then re-recording the part again and combining the two to create an effect which these days can be created by a $100 electronic effect.

AUGUST 13	Bondi Lifesaver (late)
AUGUST 17	Lidcombe Dancers
AUGUST 18	Ritz
AUGUST 19	Blacktown R.S.L.
AUGUST 20	Northern Suburbs Leagues Club
AUGUST 26	Morwell Hotel
AUGUST 27	Golfview Hotel, Geelong
AUGUST 28	Poynton's Carlton Club Hotel
AUGUST 31	Murray Teachers College (lunch)
AUGUST 31	Marryatville Hotel (Adelaide)
SEPTEMBER 1	Largs Pier Hotel
SEPTEMBER 2	Marryatville Hotel
SEPTEMBER 3	Sundowner Hotel (Whyalla)
SEPTEMBER 4	Elizabeth Rugby Club
SEPTEMBER 7	Bondi Lifesaver
SEPTEMBER 9	Cold Chisel sign to WEA records Australia.
SEPTEMBER 9	Coogee Bay Hotel
SEPTEMBER 10	Arama Hotel, Swansea
SEPTEMBER 12	War & Peace, Parramatta

MELBOURNE — This time last year, Adelaide's Cold Chisel were-bandied around as The Great White Hope of the local scene. A lot of things were promised from the band's admirers, a situation which even the best band can never live up to.

Inevitably, Cold Chisel couldn't satisfy the expectations (which was a bit tragic since the band members themselves had never shot off their mouths about how good they were and how they were gonna take over the country, etc.) and they soon drifted from favor.

"We were in no position to be a hope for anybody, least of all ourselves," laughs keyboardsman Don Walker. "Our songs weren't that strong enough, neither was our playing."

They fell into bad times, and vocalist Jim Barnes says that they made a lot of dumb mistakes. Earlier this year, the band's situation had become so bad they came close to splitting up. They had no manager, which meant little work and nil interest from record companies.

Then Barnes got an offer from Feather (whose vocalist John Swan is his brother) with whom he tried out for a week before returning to Chisel.

"I was broke and disillusioned and they made me an offer I couldn't refuse," he explains. "I really wanted to play with John again (the brothers were in Fraternity together) but it was a different style of music to what I was used to, so I had to say no."

There are no bad feelings, though: Barnes shares a house with the rest of Feather.

All of a sudden, things have fallen into place. They got themselves a manager, work load increased and suddenly, they were signed with WEA Records. The rest of the band are Ian Moss (guitar) Steve Trestwich (drums) and Phil Smallen (bass) and their music is a modernised R&B with recent overtones of country and swing.

Quite a unique blend, and their album which is to be released in January should open quite a few eyes. "We're aiming at the American market. That's where our type of bands are," says Jim.

Considering that Cold Chisel are a highly creative unit that could well be big time next year, we talk about Rabbit's Dave Evan's recent quote that Australian bands now are generally quite uninteresting because they basically sound the same.

"Your limitations are your own," says Jim disagreeing.

"If you have the patience to look for the right people, then you can find that creative unit. Look at bands like Jo Jo Zep & the Falcons, Dingoes, maybe Richard Clapton.

"The players are here, there is a lot of talent in this country. But a lot of bands try to do it unnaturally, they try to take a short cut and blow it. That's probably why it's taken so long for us, we've never gone the natural way."

—Christie Eliezer

SEPTEMBER 13

Record demos for the album. Songs recorded- *Gonna Roll Ya, Khe Sanh, Northbound, Juliet, Just How Many Times, Home and Broken Hearted, Rosaline, It Ain't Wrong, On The Road. On The Road* from this session will be issued as part of the *Hands Out Of My Pocket* CD single in 1994. *It Ain't Wrong* will be included on the Teenage Love CD.

SEPTEMBER 16	Bondi Lifesavers
SEPTEMBER 17	Basser College, University of New South Wales
SEPTEMBER 21	Macquarie University
SEPTEMBER 22	Avalon R.S.L.
SEPTEMBER 23	Manlyvale Hotel
SEPTEMBER 24	Mawson Hotel, Newcastle
SEPTEMBER 25	Bondi Lifesaver
SEPTEMBER 26	Rehearse

SEPTEMBER 28 - BONDI LIFESAVERS

Record demos for the album: The Door, Drinkin' In Port Lincoln, Teenage Love Affair, Hold Me Now, Mona and the Preacher, 5.30 E.T.A., Metho Blues, Daskarzine, Sorbonne Fender Chrome.

Teenage Love Affair, Mona and the Preacher and *Metho Blues* will be issued on the Teenage Love CD in 1994.

(44

OCTOBER 1	Northern Suburbs Leagues Club, 8-12.
OCTOBER 2	Redhead SLSC (Surf Life Saving Club)
OCTOBER 5	Illawara Catholic Club
OCTOBER 7	Bondi Lifesaver
OCTOBER 8	Royal Antler

OCTOBER

"Last night Jim Barnes clambered onstage to sing with Rose Tattoo. Angry Anderson stood in the corner by the amps and watched Barnes stomping around the boards and clapping his hands with those same exaggerated elbow-smashing movements that he employs with Cold Chisel. He looked positively mean.

Cold Chisel have just signed a recording contract with WEA and, hopefully they'll have an album out early in the new year. Hopefully, 'cos they're a good hard rock band.

...Onstage the band is strong. The majority of their material is original- maybe too many of those at the pub in West Wyalong, with the chick in Whyalla on the road songs, but they are balanced out by songs influenced by the keyboard player's experience of King's Cross. Songs like The Last Train Out Of Town about the Vietnam veterans capture some depressing moods with keyboards straight from the lonely depths of hell. And try the instrumental Because We End As Lovers (sic), with its weeping guitar. If you thought Since I've Been Loving You was Led Zep's greatest contribution then this masterpiece will kill you.

On a good night, Jim uses all the power of his wide-ranging vocals. When I first saw this band I liked the musicianship but passed Barnes off as one of the ten thousand Paul Rogers imitators. At subsequent gigs he's been good- there's something individual there, something much wider but I can't pinpoint it.

(ANDREW MCMILLAN)

Because We End As Lovers is in fact, *Cause We've Ended As Lovers*, a Stevie Wonder song recorded as an instrumental by Jeff Beck on the Blow By Blow album.

OCTOBER 13	Redhead S.L.S.C.
OCTOBER 14	Bondi Lifesaver
OCTOBER 17	Mt.Pleasant Sports Club -The band is paid $270.

OCTOBER 18	Station Hotel, Melbourne.

The venue is re-opened to live music and the ribbon is cut by Melbourne DJ Billy Pinnell.

The band play Khe Sanh, as well as Georgia, One Long Day and Led Zeppelin's Whole Lotta Love, among others in the set.

OCTOBER 19	South Side Six (with 'Stars')
OCTOBER 20	Sundowner Hotel
OCTOBER 21	Martinis
OCTOBER 22	The Be Bop & Loo Bar (Beverley Crest Hotel, St.Kilda)
OCTOBER 22	Matthew Flinders (arvo)
OCTOBER 23	Bull Bar
OCTOBER 26	Bondi Lifesaver. The band is paid $250 for this show.
OCTOBER 28	Stagedoor
OCTOBER 29	Mawson Hotel

This venue became a regular for the band and Don credits the money from this venue as really helping the band through hard times. It was at shows at the Mawson that *Wild Thing* started to develop as a live favourite.

OCTOBER 30	Swansea Workers Club
NOV/DEC	Gig around Sydney, Melbourne and Adelaide in between recording demos.
NOVEMBER 3	Studio demos.
NOVEMBER 3	Avalon R.S.L.
NOVEMBER 4	Bondi Lifesavers
NOVEMBER 5	Swansea Workers
NOVEMBER 8	Arkaba (Adelaide)
NOVEMBER 9	Arkaba
NOVEMBER 10	Waterloo Corner
NOVEMBER 11	Arkaba
NOVEMBER 12	Arkaba
NOVEMBER 13	Elizabeth Rugby Club
NOVEMBER 15	Station Hotel 8.00-10.00
NOVEMBER 16	The Be Bop & Loo Bar, Beverley Crest Hotel, St.Kilda. Free admittance.
NOVEMBER 17	Eureka Hotel, Geelong
NOVEMBER 18	Tottenham Hotel
NOVEMBER 19	Matthew Flinders (arvo) 2-5p.m.
NOVEMBER 19	Bananas (late) 1-3a.m.

45)

NOVEMBER 20	Rising Sun Hotel, Richmond 8.00-10.00
NOVEMBER 25	Stagedoor. The band is paid $250.
NOVEMBER 26	Alexander Club Revesby

'Juke' runs a short interview with the band under the heading 'Cold Chisel Fall Into Place'. Some of the more interesting parts of it:

"This time last year, Adelaide's Cold Chisel were bandied around as The Great White Hope of the local scene. A lot of things were promised from the band's admirers, a situation which even the best band can never live up to.

Inevitably, Cold Chisel couldn't satisfy the expectations (which was a bit tragic since the band members themselves had never shot their mouths off about how good they were and how they were gonna take over the country, etc.) and they soon drifted from favor.

"We were in no position to be a hope for anybody, least of all ourselves," laughs keyboardsman Don Walker. "Our songs weren't that strong enough, neither was our playing."

They fell into hard times and vocalist Jim Barnes says they made a lot of dumb mistakes. Earlier this year the band's situation had become so bad they came close to splitting up. They had no manager, which meant little work and nil interest from record companies.

Then Barnes got an offer from Feather (whose vocalist John Swan is his brother) with whom he tried out for a week before returning to Cold Chisel.

All of a sudden, things have fallen into place. They got themselves a manager, the workload increased and suddenly, they were signed to WEA records...

...their music is a modernised R & B with recent overtones of country and swing.

Quite a unique blend, and their album, which is to be released in January, should open quite a few eyes. "We're aiming at the American market. That's where our type of bands are." says Jim.

(CHRISTIE ELIEZER, JUKE)

NOVEMBER 27	Paris Theatre 10-11.30pm The band is paid $300.
NOVEMBER 28	Mt Pleasant Sports Club The band is paid $270.

NOVEMBER 29/30	Studio
DECEMBER 1	Bondi Lifesavers. The band are paid $350 for this show.
DECEMBER 2	Mawson Hotel, Newcastle. $300.
DECEMBER 3	Mawson Hotel
DECEMBER 6	Station Hotel
DECEMBER 7	Southside Six (Melb)
DECEMBER 9	Eureka Hotel, Geelong
DECEMBER 10	Matthew Flinders (early)
DECEMBER 10	Martinis (late)
DECEMBER 11	Be Bop & Loo Bar
DEC 12,13 & 14	Recording Studio
DECEMBER 15	Bondi Lifesaver
DECEMBER 16	Chequers
DECEMBER 17	Northern Suburbs Leagues Club
DEC 19,20,21	Recording Studio
DECEMBER 22	(Chequers was advertised but the band played the Broadway Ballroom.)
DECEMBER 23	Bondi Lifesavers
DECEMBER 23	Private 21st birthday party.
DECEMBER 24	Bondi Lifesavers

"Cold Chisel who were recording their album last week are enthusiastic about the results, in particular with the work of producer Peter Walker. The LP is due out Feb/March. This week the band are in Adelaide, their original hometown."

(JUKE)

DECEMBER 27	Arkaba Hotel (2 x 45 min sets at each night at the Arkaba)
DECEMBER 28	Arkaba Hotel
DECEMBER 29	Arkaba Hotel
DECEMBER 30	Arkaba Hotel
DECEMBER 31	Elizabeth Oval, 2-2.45pm
DECEMBER 31	Eel Trap Hotel, 8-10pm (2 x 45 min)
DECEMBER 31	Arkabe Hotel, 11.30- 2.00am (2 x 45 min)

(46

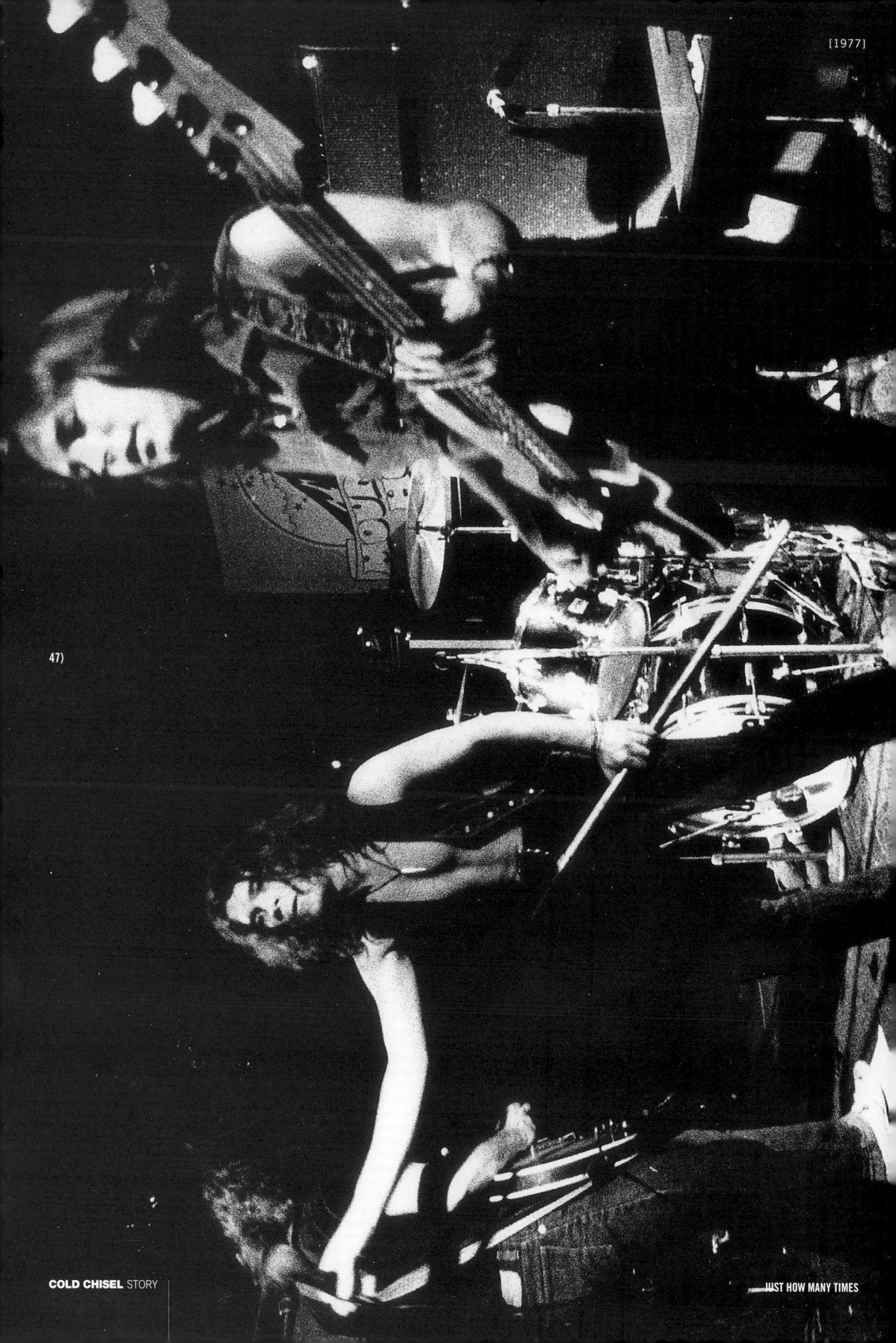

[1977]

47)

COLD CHISEL STORY

JUST HOW MANY TIMES

Living at the Plaza Hotel

THE RELEASE OF THE FIRST ALBUM AND THE RECORDING OF THEIR SECOND ARE FOLLOWED BY
MORE NATIONAL TOURING, A LIVE EP AND POSITIVE PRESS WHICH MARKS THE BEGINNING OF
THE COLD CHISEL 'LEGEND'. 1978 IS A YEAR OF MUCH EXPERIMENTATION IN THE LIVE SET, AS
THE BAND ROAD TEST NEW SONGS IN A SET WHICH IS NOW ALMOST COMPLETELY ORIGINAL.

JANUARY 1	Elizabeth Rugby Club, 8-9.30pm
JANUARY 1	Arkaba Hotel, 11-1 am
JANUARY 3,4, & 5	Recording Studio.
JANUARY 6	Sydney Festival, Opera House (lunch) ($250)
JANUARY 6	Coogee Bay Hotel (late) ($350)
JANUARY 7	Mawson Hotel
JANUARY 9	Recording of the first album commences at Trafalgar Studios with Peter Walker.
JANUARY 12	Bondi Lifesaver
JANUARY 15	Victoria Park, with Sherbet, ($100)
JANUARY 20	Martinis, (Melbourne)
JANUARY 21	Matthew Flinders
FEBRUARY 1	Belmont Community Centre (Sydney)
FEBRUARY 2	Pleasures Wine Bar, ($250)
FEBRUARY 3	Blacktown RSL
FEBRUARY 4	Northern Suburbs, Newcastle
FEBRUARY 5	Bondi Lifesaver
FEBRUARY 8	Western Suburbs Leagues Club, Newcastle

FEBRUARY 9 - BONDI LIFESAVER

"Since Christmas Cold Chisel have developed that hard edge that makes them one of the toughest rock'n'roll bands in the country. Pure balls...

Piano player Don Walker writes most of the band's material. Basically it's street music in the vein of Kings Cross Kid and The Smacko Queen, drawn from the experience of touring and living in the city. Walker's piano is cold and lonely, off-setting Ian Moss' guitar work. Jim Barnes stomps across the stage with elbow jarring claps and a strong voice. The rhythm section of Steve Prestwich's drums and Phil Small's bass is strong and punchy."

(ANDREW McMILLAN, 'RAM' MAGAZINE)

FEBRUARY 10	Stagedoor Tavern - WEA's David Sinclair recalls that the Stagedoor Tavern couldn't get enough of the band. "They would come on at 2 am and they were so loud, and the place was so alcoholic, so drunk, and they'd all fall out around 4 am totally drained."
FEBRUARY 11	Belmont Community Centre (cancelled-Studio)
FEBRUAR 12	Mt.Pleasant Sports Club (cancelled-Studio)

FEBRUARY 13	Mt.Pleasant Sports Club
FEBRUARY 14	Pleasures Wine Bar
FEBRUARY 15	Chequers ($200)
FEBRUARY 16	Chequers
FEBRUARY 17	Mawson Hotel
FEBRUARY 18	Stage Door Tavern
FEBRUARY 20	University of Woolongong
FEBRUARY 22	Mawson Hotel
FEBRUARY 23	Revesby Workers Club
FEBRUARY 24	Bondi Lifesaver with Jimmy and the Boys

FEBRUARY 25 - MANLY VALE HOTEL

With recording continuing, WEA announces to the band that they have slotted them onto the Foreigner tour and they want to have the album ready for release before it. Peter Walker started mixing the album on a Friday evening, sleeping on the floor in the studio through the weekend (the band assisting in between gigs) so as to have the album ready for the tapes to be collected on Monday morning.

From the beginning of the project Peter had insisted that the album would be mastered in America, as he had seen too many Australian albums virtually ruined because the dynamics of the tape had been lost in the mastering process when it had been done locally.

Unfortunately, in the rush to have the album released before the Foreigner tour, the record company felt that they didn't have time to master in the US, and so put the one and only master tape through an old machine which removed half of the oxide from the tape. The deal was that a local version would be printed, to cover the tour and a US mastered version would then take its place. Unfortunately, the tape sent to the US was the one damaged in Australia, and even though the US mastered version was still an improvement, it appears that very few of this version were circulated.

To Peter Walker's ears the current CD version is also from the Australian master. He felt that the US version was louder, with more bottom end.

MARCH 1	Waterloo Corner Hotel, Adelaide
MARCH 2	Waterloo Corner Hotel
MARCH 3	Abbey Road Disco Gawler

MARCH 4	Pooraka Hotel
MARCH 5	5KA Beach Concert (afternoon)
MARCH 5	Elizabeth Rugby Club
MARCH 7	Eureka Hotel, Geelong
MARCH 8	Croxton Park
MARCH 10	Frankston Teachers College
MARCH 10	London Tavern
MARCH 10	Bananas (late)
MARCH 11	Station Hotel (arvo)
MARCH 11	Tiger Lounge
MARCH 12	Poyntons Carlton Club Hotel
MARCH 15	Western Suburbs Leagues Club, Newcastle
MARCH 16	Bondi Lifesaver, Sydney
MARCH 17	Carringbarh Hotel
MARCH 18	Bondi Lifesaver ($400)
MARCH 19	War And Peace
MARCH 21	Collegians Rugby League
MARCH 23	Bondi Lifesaver with Skyhooks
MARCH 24	Swansea Workers Club
MARCH 25	Stagedoor Tavern
MARCH 26	Foster Concert ($280)
MARCH 27	Mt.Pleasant Sports Club (cancelled)
MARCH 29	Mawson Hotel

MARCH

Music press reports that Cold Chisel have almost completed their debut album to be released next month to coincide with their support gig on the upcoming Foreigner tour, adding that

> "The group have built up a strong reputation in the pubs and clubs as a hard rock band featuring lyrics from the usual "love-lost" guff to political and war themes."

APRIL 2

Bondi Lifesaver supporting Skyhooks, also on the bill: Rose Tattoo, Rococo, Agraphobia, Aleph, Kevin Borich, and Ray Burton.

> "Cold Chisel, usually headliners themselves, started their last set with a full head of steam. The first four songs were like playing tag with a runaway express train. Then, for some strange reason, they threw in the

slow Georgia, one of the all-time great, bluesy songs, but a sure hard-rock vibe killer if ever there was one...Best band of the day was Cold Chisel who disregarded the debris and played a full-tilt, extended hard set that had everyone jumping with life and joy.

They have a first album ready for release and have yet to make a major imprint on public consciousness. But they're fast reaching a standard where just about every show is hot. The temperature can only get higher."

(RAM MAGAZINE)

APRIL 4	Station Hotel (Melbourne)
APRIL 5	Council Club
APRIL 6	Croxton Park

APRIL 7	Eureka Hotel, Geelong
APRIL 8	London Tavern
APRIL 8	Bananas (late) with "The Angels"

APRIL 11 - FESTIVAL HALL ,BRISBANE (FOREIGNER SUPPORT)

The band was not all keen on the idea of doing support gigs for international artists. They had done it in Adelaide in 1975 and it didn't lead to anything. But Rod Willis felt that it was an excellent way to get them out of the usual venues and onto big stages in front of large audiences. It also took them around the country and they could play shows of their own while they were in town.

August 1978
Steve Prestwich, Mawson Hotel. Photo by Geoffrey Moore, from P. Small collection.

"The most pleasing aspect of Foreigner's tour opening gig was undoubtedly the performance of support band Cold Chisel. Relatively unknown in this city, the band burnt red hot. The reaction was so good that Brisbane radio has been plugging the hell out of 'em. Singer Jim Barnes sent shivers down the spine of everyone in the place-such was the power of his emotive vocalising. Even with sophisticated echo, phase, etc. used to prop his voice, Foreigner's Lou Graham (sic) had been out sung before he came on."

(BRISBANE DAILY)

APRIL 13	Hordern Pavilion, Sydney (Foreigner Support)

1978
Phil Small.
(P.Small collection.)

51)

APRIL 14 - FESTIVAL HALL, MELBOURNE (FOREIGNER SUPPORT)

Set list (probably complete): Juliet / Northbound / Khe Sanh / One Long Day / Home and Broken Hearted / Wild Thing

The band walks on to virtual silence and tear into the opening number with an energy reminiscent of early Led Zeppelin - the power of Jimmy's vocals hits you immediately, while just a couple of warm-up licks from Ian tell the audience they are in the presence of an exceptional guitar player.

The audience clap enthusiastically after the first numbers. It is obvious listening to these live versions that *Juliet* and *Northbound* both shine a lot brighter in the live situation than the album versions. It is unusual to imagine silence at the opening notes of *Khe Sanh*, but that's what happens here, as the album had not yet been released, and *Khe Sanh* was not issued as a single until May.

One Long Day is much like the version from the You're Thirteen... EP with Ian stretching out on the solo, while Jimmy pushes his voice so hard in the final section it almost fails. *Home and Broken Hearted* has Jimmy bringing the band down while he explains what the song is about to the audience before launching into a super-charged version. *Wild Thing* is complete with Jimmy telling the audience he doesn't want to see them sitting on their arses, in a rendition of the song comparable to that on the live EP.

John Hoffman, a Warners employee at the time, tells the story of how he went backstage after this performance to find the band sitting around in a dark little room "sharing a can of Coke or something like that." A little down the corridor Hoffy, as he was known, saw tables full of champagne, yoghurt, prawns and all sorts of luxury food and drink. Having had a few beers himself before the show, Hoffy brought a bucket of goodies back to the Cold Chisel room. Minutes later a member of the Foreigner road crew walked past and noticed the bucket, angrily blurting out something along the lines of, "You guys can't have this stuff now, maybe in a few years when you're stars." Hoffy quickly disappeared into the night.

Later in the night Hoffy bumped into someone else from Warners at a nearby bar who explained to him that their had been a lot of trouble at the gig and Foreigner wanted to have Cold Chisel removed from the tour. Fortunately, this did not eventuate.

Hoffy had first seen the band in 1977 when Steve Hands had taken him to one of their shows, and he recalls Jim giving a heartfelt rendition of Jimmy Webb's *The Moon is a Harsh Mistress*. He was quickly a fan and the band came to appreciate his calls of "It's me, Hoffy" which could be heard all through the venue during the quiet, "Someone's knocking at the kitchen door" part of *The Door*. He also recalls that in those early days the band were into music such as Springsteen, Randy Newman and Warren Zevon.

"They were really good guys. quiet, really nice. At the Melbourne show we were running short of time and we'd have only had 15 minutes to play. But Mick Jones (Foreigner guitarist) demanded (to the tour promoter) that we be allowed 30 minutes to play or there'd be no show."

(Don Walker)

APRIL 14	Bombay Rock (Late) with Ferrets and Daniel
APRIL 16	Festival Theatre, Adelaide (Foreigner Support)

"Cold Chisel, another Adelaide band that is on the brink of the big league, have been getting encores on the Foreigner tour, something rare for a support act that usually only get half P.A. power and the minimum of lights so as not to look too impressive before the main act. I've said it before, this band are going to be huge."

(Adelaide Daily)

APRIL 18	Tivoli, (Adelaide)
APRIL 19	St Leonards Inn - At this show Jimmy almost electrocutes himself after putting his finger in a light socket!
APRIL 20	Highway Inn
APRIL 21	Marryatville Hotel

APRIL 22

(This show may have been earlier in the year)-St. Leonards Park 2JJ Radio Broadcast with Midnight Oil, The Angels & Madder Lake. *Set list (complete ?)- Juliet / Northbound / F1-11/ I'm Gonna Roll Ya / One Long Day / Home And Broken Hearted / (encores?)*

Juliet is as usual, a blistering opener, followed by *Northbound*, Don Walker's piano cutting clearly through the mid-afternoon air as Ian tries some slide guitar over the introductory chords. A live version of this would have been a welcome addition to the You're Thirteen EP as the studio version lacks something present on these live renditions. After Jimmy complains about the time of day (it's obviously too early for him) the band play *F1-11*. This version differs significantly from the version issued on the Teenage Love CD- in fact the only similarity is the chorus and one section of the verse. The haunting organ lines present on the Teenage Love rendition are replaced with aggressive lead guitar in this version.

I'm Gonna Roll Ya is played at a furious pace showing why it has been a set favourite since 1975. "This is a song off our album - I've been dying to say that, also I've been dying to say 'three days'. It features Ian on some vocals, a thing called *One Long Day*." This is indeed another great rendition of a song which had also been a staple in live sets since 1975. If there is one song which encapsulated all the elements of Cold Chisel at this point it is this one, with Ian's controlled vocals and fiery guitar, the subtleties of Don's jazzy piano chordings and the bluesy energy of the whole band bringing the song to a climax.

Home And Broken Hearted has Jimmy telling the audience, "We'd like to see you up off your arses for a start." *Wild Thing* was almost certainly played to finish a shortened set.

APRIL 22	Marryatville Hotel
APRIL 23	Tivoli Hotel
APRIL 24	Bombay Rock, Melbourne, record launch.

APRIL 24

Self titled debut album released. Peaks at No. 38 on the national charts. The album contains 8 songs: Juliet /Khe Sanh /Home and Broken Hearted /One Long Day/ Northbound /Rosaline /Daskarzine/Just How Many Times.

Producer Peter Walker had been asked by the record company to deliver a rock'n'roll album suitable for radio airplay, but he strongly felt that this would not represent the band. While the album he gave them may not have impressed everyone at the record company, he felt comfortable with the selection of songs he and the band had settled upon.

"The album cover is a piece of Khe Sanh exotica that incorporates miniature band portraits and signatures, Daryl's old lady, Mickey Braithwaite is there too."

(Derek Johnson, RAM magazine)

The album contains at least two classics in *Khe Sanh* and *One Long Day*, both of which would remain as staples in the band's live sets to the very end. *One Long Day* was the closest the band came to an 'epic'. Clocking in at nearly seven and a half minutes, the song covers three different keys over four different sections, five with the blues intro added to live performances where the song would often go for ten minutes.

Ian Moss, Stagedoor Tavern.
Photo by John Swan, from Lorna Moss collection.

53)

Press reviews are positive:

"I honestly can't remember the last time an Australian album was released which impressed me as much as this one. It was probably Richard Clapton, or someone as long ago as that, because this really is a fine record, one that deserves a lot of listening to. Quite a few things strike you about it front up. Australian rock has never been blessed with great lyricists, but in Cold Chisel's Don Walker we find someone who has a lot to say, the songs crammed with a series of strong image building lines. The group's blues base is another striking feature of the group, surprisingly bluesy in the light of today's other music makers. And then there's the energy behind it all. Put these impressions together and you've got a small taste of what this album's about."

(Music Press)

"Featuring a lone John- Fogarty-eat-your-heart-out lead vocalist by the name of Jim Barnes, they systematically storm, coax, and push your emotions through the two sides of the album.

In the tradition of heavy rockers like Bad Company and Led Zeppelin, both of whom had their roots deep in the blues, Cold Chisel draw on similar roots and expand on them as far as the individual talents of the band members allow.

Juliet is a tough opening statement, a raging rocker that unfortunately lacks any real style, one of their weaker songs.

However, Khe Sanh the follower, is more to the point. With earthy lyrics that trace the itinerant travels of an ex-Vietnam war veteran, it recalls the hard-edged, rolling country rock that endeared The Dingoes to so many people.

One Long Day, Rosaline and Just How Many Times offer another side to Cold Chisel, this time slower and bluesy, with the odd touch of jazz phrasing from keyboard player Don Walker. Although the recorded version of One Long Day is slightly faster than their moving live version, they are classy pieces, spotlighting the band's strong blues sensitivity and their precision rhythm section.

Daskarzine sounds a little like Deep Purple revisited, unrelenting underneath the colorful on top.

It's just a pity that there is so much of a gap between Cold Chisel's fast and slow songs. Maybe a fast/slow side separation would have worked better. Whatever, it's still an album that comes from the heart. And the lead vocals are committed and convincing, refreshing in the Australian musical landscape, which has never had much of a history of authentic blues singers."

(AL WEBB, JUKE)

"On the evidence of their first album, Cold Chisel promise big things in the future. It's a very convincing debut simply because of the undeniable individual talents of the whole band and the fact that they are fortunate enough to have someone who can write solid and interesting songs. Don Walker on keyboards writes the songs and Jimmy Barnes provides the vocals proving himself more than able to handle any mood that the song calls for. Ian Moss is an exceptional guitarist and a strong enough vocalist to sing a number of songs on his own"

(DAILY PRESS)

"What has happened is that Cold Chisel turned out one of the finest Oz rock albums for a long time. It showcases the writing of Don Walker, who has a fine musical and lyrical sense, the wood-rasp voice of Jimmy Barnes and some fine flashes of guitar work from Ian Moss, perhaps one of the most expressive and hard-working guitarists currently playing in Oz.

(JUKE, JUNE 1978)

"When we released the album we didn't intend releasing a single because we're not a singles band. But when the radio stations asked for it...for something that most record companies and bands sweat months for...why not?"

"There's one song on the album that we specifically arranged so that it would be commercial- and it's not the one that radio stations played. So maybe we've got a hit single ('Khe Sanh') in spite of ourselves."

(Don Walker, June '78)

The song Don was referring to was *Home and Broken Hearted*. A single version of this song was actually recorded, but never released.

When asked by 'Juke' reporter Christie Eliezer what sort of feedback he'd got for the album, Don Walker said:

"I suppose it can all be covered by saying it's a bit more laid back than it should have been. That would have been OK if the 'up' songs had been a bit more energetic, like they are onstage. Until we figure out how to capture that onstage excitement on record, I guess we'll only be 90% happy."

"It's a very versatile album; another name for that would be commercial. There's something in there for everybody. When you have your first bash at an album, you've got all these tracks you've been saving for a year, some of them you can only play onstage once every three months. Every band tends to rush in there and try to do everything on a first album."

APRIL 25	Melbourne University (cancelled)
APRIL 25	Rusden (1.00-2.00pm)
APRIL 25	Prospect Hill (8.00-10.00pm)
APRIL 27	LaTrobe University
APRIL 27	Doyntons Carlton Club
APRIL 28	Deakin University
APRIL 28	Bombay Rock (late)
APRIL 29	Matthew Flinders

MAY

Single Khe Sanh/Just How Many Times released and the band tour the east coast to promote it.

Phil Coulson recalls that the video shoot for this song (he worked for WEA at the time) took place at a film studio in the Melbourne suburb of Oakleigh. The filming took one full day and the changing level of the contents of the whiskey bottle on Don's piano was due to continual drinking to help the band loosen up. Ian wore what he described as the 'Ritchie Blackmore shirt' for the clip, a favourite shirt in the style of that worn by one of his idols, the Deep Purple guitarist. A clip was also filmed for *One Long Day*, using the same set, a small segment of which can be seen in the Last Stand video.

"We've got to go back to Sydney this week. There seems to have been some problem with us releasing 'Khe Sanh' as a single. Some of the radio stations are objecting to lines like "and their legs were often opened' and 'or the growing need for speed and Novocain'.

"It was a strong belief in ourselves that kept us going, but it's not a unique one. Every band that's been through some success in Australia has been through that period. Right now there are bands going through it that will break through in 18 months."

(Don Walker, speaking with Christie Eliezer in 'Juke')

MAY 1	International Varieties, private party (Sydney)
MAY 3	Mawson Hotel
MAY 4	Bondi Lifesaver ($450)
MAY 5	Selinas, Coogie Bay
MAY 6	Bondi Lifesaver ($550)
MAY 7	War & Peace
MAY 9	Tamworth Workers Club
MAY 10	Mawson Hotel
MAY 12	Stage Door
MAY 13	Manly Vale
MAY 14	Bondi Lifesaver
MAY -16	Castle Hill RSL
MAY 17	Ambassador , Newcastle
MAY 18	Ambassador
MAY 20	Bondi Lifesaver ($600)
MAY 21	Belmont Sports Club
MAY 22	Mt Pleasant Sports Club

(54

MAY 23	Mt.Prichard Community Club
MAY 24	Comb'N'Cutter
MAY 25	Avalon RSL

MAY 26 - (FRI)

Swansea Workers Club (Newcastle) The band start this show as a four-piece without Don Walker, who, due to car troubles, arrived at 8.30 (the time he thought the show started) only to find it had been an 8.00 p.m. gig and the band had started without him!

This show is mentioned in a story on the band in RAM magazine:

"Cold Chisel have played Swansea Workers before. They're a popular band here and the auditorium is sold out solid. Halfway through the second set it's apparent why Chisel are popular down here. No muckin' about. These punters appreciate heavy, industrial-type energy and Cold Chisel were born in the steelworker mould. The punters especially like searing guitar solos with lotsa finger-flash and studied delivery and that's precisely what Ian Moss gave them.

They're the sort of band you probably have to see a few times before the full extent of their strengths comes through. That's because despite Barnes' and Moss' upfront strength and virtuosity, they still don't project anything particularly dramatic"

RAM's Anthony O'Grady went on to describe the party scenes that went on until the sun rose, demonstrating that Chisel had already established a very special rapport with Newcastle.

MAY 27	Stage Door Tavern
MAY 28	Penrith Leagues

(Some sources have Cold Chisel playing the Bondi Lifesaver with Midnight Oil, but I suspect that this was due to mistaken advertising for the Save The Whales benefit held a few days later, after being postponed from this date and venue.)

MAY 31 - FLOYDS, CANBERRA

The band are still looking at the overseas market:

"It's not as if we'll give Australia away, it's just that we've been working here for four years and after you do it for a while you can get overexposed really easy... we just want a bigger market, so America's the aim."

(Jimmy Barnes)

JUNE 2	Mawson Hotel, 8-12, 3x45min sets.

JUNE 3	Bondi Lifesaver , 2x45min sets.
JUNE 4	Stage Door Tavern, Save the Whales benefit with Midnight Oil and Jeff Oakes.
JUNE 6	Melbourne University (cancelled)
JUNE 6	Station Hotel 8-10pm
JUNE 7	Rusden (lunch, 1-2pm)
JUNE 8	Croxton Park, 9-11pm
JUNE 8	Bombay Rock (Late, 12.15-2.30am), with Teenage Radio Stars and Boys Next Door
JUNE 9	Tiger Lounge, 9-11pm.

JUNE 10 - COUNTDOWN

The band are booked to make their first appearance on Countdown, the ABC's high-rating pop music show. Following a rehearsal of the song (*Khe Sanh*) at the Ripponlea Studios Michael Shrimpton, the ABC's Head of Light Entertainment tells the band that they will have to alter the lyrics of the song if it is to be performed. The band has a quick discussion and decide that they will not alter the song and they will get opportunities to appear on Countdown on their own terms. As they are preparing to leave Shrimpton tells them:

"You've no idea how difficult you've made things for us, but by god I admire you for your principles and I wish you every success."

Although the band do appear on the show on many occasions in the future, it is the beginning of an often turbulent relationship between the two.

JUNE 10	Martinis. 9-11.30pm
JUNE 10	Bananas (late, 12.00-2.30am)
JUNE 11	Poyntons Carlton Club, 7.30-10.00
JUNE 14	Fiesta Villa, Findon Hotel, Adelaide
JUNE 15	Largs Pier
JUNE 16	Whyalla
JUNE 17	Paraka
JUNE 18	Elizabeth Bay Rugby Club
JUNE 20	Martinis (Melb)
JUNE 20	Martinis
JUNE 22	Village Green
JUNE 22	Bananas (late)

55)

JUNE 23 - BOMBAY ROCK WITH FINCH

"The place is crowded, biggest crowd for some weeks thanks to this relatively fresh band on the Melbourne scene. Their following is huge in Adelaide and Sydney but they're just beginning to break here due to LP release and increased touring...The band appeal to the boys from the docks because they exude pure energy. Jim Barnes spits, sweats and swears like an old tomcat. He speaks to the angry and frustrated in a voice which is rough, yet full of emotion. And he drinks like a fish...

A regimented line of girls stand in the frontline. Actually the band appeal to just about anyone, their music is just so tight, original and gutsy. Ian Moss plays guitar like a holy man, producing reverential silences throughout his solos. Don Walker's piano playing is melodic in an old-fashioned way, yet always pushing; he makes me think of blues players in sleazy late night bar.

The atmosphere begins to heat up (literally); people in the VIP lounge look out onto the horizon and pull out their binoculars. Some even start to walk towards the front, an unheard of act in this haven of the cool.

Up front, Jim hurls himself into the audience who stand aside, slightly awed by this seething mass of energy in their midst's. Everybody's dancing and sweating hot. The raw light of the stage is turned off the stage and onto the audience by the singer. The band turn into silhouettes, the dancers are burning gold.

The songs that standout in this set are F-111, their new single with a good catchy hook and lots of speedy rhythm, a bluesy instrumental and a song which will be appearing on their next LP (to be recorded in the next two months). This song has a line 'somebody's knocking at my kitchen door' which builds up from a husky whisper, to a pounding jolt, to a full throttle rocky scream- the structure of the song is amazing.

When the band finish after an encore, I walk towards the back to wash off the beer thrown all over me during the performance.

To my amazement, the VIP lounge and back half of the hall have been nearly completely emptied during the performance, the usually lacksadasical (sic) occupants have all moved towards the stage. I leave with a temperature."

(MIRANDA BROWN, JUKE MAGAZINE)

JUNE 24	Station Hotel
JUNE 24	Manhattan (late)
JUNE 25	Bombay Rock with Sweet Jayne
JUNE 26	Mt.Pleasant Sports Club
JUNE 27	Doyalson RSL*
JUNE 28	Civic Hotel, Sydney*
JUNE 29	Kings Cross Rex*
JUNE 30	Royal Antler Hotel*

*These dates (27th-30th) are cancelled as the band record their next single, F-111, which was never issued as a single then, or in any form until 1994's Teenage Love album. The version recorded on these dates is never issued.

JULY 1	Mawson Hotel
JULY 2	Bondi Lifesaver
JULY 3	Sundowner Hotel
JULY 4	Castle Hill RSL
JULY 7	Blackheath
JULY 8	Stagedoor Tavern

(56

Ian Moss, "Georgia" Mawson Hotel, 1978. Photo by Geoffrey Moore, from the P. Small collection.

JULY 9 - BONDI LIFESAVER

Hair tumbling down his face, Jimmy Barnes leaned into the mic stand screaming from the crotch while Ian Moss matched Barnes' scotch-hardened vocal coarseness with finely attuned lead guitar that bit, spat and wailed simultaneously.

Behind them Steve Prestwich and Phil Small ploughed on, enhancing their reputation as one of the tightest rhythm sections in the land. Prestwich, y'see isn't one of those drummers who is content to sit back and hold the sound down. Hell no! Through hard rockers like Kings Cross Kid and the new Conversation he drives the band off the podium.

Don Walker's cold, lonesome piano stalks through the early morning sleaze of Breakfast At Sweethearts and Barnes stammers through The Door with frightened urgency, his voice cutting through the smoke screen of the Midnight Rambler- style chiller like a blade of ice.

And then it's back to hard rock and the screaming hook of their next single F111. It's this sort of uncompromising hard rock feel that has established Cold Chisel as one of the country's most popular pub bands over the last twelve months. Except on Sunday night, it didn't look like that at all. 'Cos the only rage goin' down was on stage. And rather than rocking the walls with calls for mare, the crowd just applauded politely.

What the hell! Cold Chisel came back anyway with Barnes yelling 'Well that was a pretty fucked attempt at an encore. But we're back 'cos we wanna keep playing.!'

Maybe that's their secret. They just keep ragin' and playing, 'cos they're enjoying themselves. Audiences have no excuse not to do the same."

('RAM's ANDREW MCMILLAN)

JULY 10	Melbourne Hotel, Brisbane
JULY 11	Queens Hotel
JULY 12	Exchange Hotel
JULY 13	Jindalee
JULY 15	Queens Hotel
JULY 16	East Coast Leagues

JULY 18

The band head to Byron Bay to rehearse for the second album, the recording of which starts at the end of the month. Also working with the band in Byron Bay is producer Richard Batchens. Richard had been recently named 'Producer of the Year' for his work with Richard Clapton and his other credits include work with artists such as Johnny O'Keefe, Billy Thorpe, Sherbet and Chain. Richard had previously seen the band play on a couple of occasions in Melbourne.

Richard recalls that although the band had very few songs ready for their about-to-be-recorded second album, the time at Byron Bay was not particularly productive and was virtually treated as a holiday for the road crew.

JULY 28	Swansea Workers Club
JULY 29	Countdown/ Jam Disco

JULY 30

Begin recording second album with producer Richard Batchens at Alberts Studios. According to a group spokesman the new album will have "a tougher sound than the last one."

The second album sessions were not easy. Richard Batchens was going through a difficult period in his life - in his own words he wasn't as together as he could have been, and the band had few songs ready. Richard recalls that it was an effort to find an album's worth of material. There are very few leftover songs from these sessions, *Mona and the Preacher* is probably the only one.

Both producer and band also felt the weight of high expectations apon them. While the first album had sold respectably, it was now time for the band to repay the record company's faith (and financial outlay) in them. Richard believed that the band was still looking for an identity and was different from the previous artists he had worked with as producer.

The band was still relatively inexperienced in the studio. The sessions were spread over six months, during which the band gigged as heavily as they ever had. The songs were often written and arranged in the studio. Richard was very critical of many of the individual performances of band members and spent a lot of time re-doing parts, to the point where he felt it became mechanical. Richard felt that,

"There were a few moments of magic, but most of it had the life sucked out of it through repetition."

The same tapes that were used for the extensive demo/rehearsal sessions were used for the actual recording and it was during the actual mixing that Richard realised that the oxides had been worn off the tape surface and much of the top end was lost.

"I was aware that the tape was dead sounding and I didn't know what to do. I took it upon myself that I'd fucked up."

Despite the problems in the studio, the band continued playing impressive live shows and the 'vibe' about the band was growing all the time.

"Yeah, it was just one of those things we couldn't bring out 'cos we were green. None of us had ever been in a recording studio before and we had to learn a lot."

(Jimmy Barnes)

"The next album will be much more a guitar album. That in itself will make it a very much more intense, live album 'cos Ian's a very intense, live player- he doesn't have a session player's temperament."

(Don Walker)

AUGUST

Khe-Sanh given "A" classification (not suitable for airplay) due to lyric content. However the song charts at No.4 in Adelaide. It is astounding now to think that this song, which has become a true classic of Australian rock and possibly the most recognised Cold Chisel song only attained a national chart position of 43.

Music press reports at the time state that the band has signed with the Elektra/Asylum label in America and that there is a "scheduled" release in January/February (1979) of a compilation album with material from the group's first and second albums, and that some of the songs from the first album will be re-recorded. Another source reported that the self-titled LP had just been released in Canada! This may have been a deliberately leaked rumour from Chisel management.

These reports were later (March '79) denied by the band, "It's all bullshit. We're not signed with anybody" said a matter-of-fact Don Walker.

"A few companies have expressed interest and think we're good. We're with WEA in Australia, but the label in America has seperate companies. They get the choice of whether to pick you up and release you or not...they just have to decide whether they can make a good proposition of the Cold Chisel album in America. Now until they hear the second album they can't give us any indication at all except that they already really like the first one. They know they want to take Khe Sanh and One Long Day and there's a couple of other tracks they're looking at depending on how many hot tracks there are on the second album. Then they'll just work out the mixture, they know their own markets best."

AUGUST 1- RECORD DEMOS AT THE MUSIC FARM

The band rarely did work of any great value here as it was generally treated as something of a holiday for the road crew, who seemed to know all the best places to get supplies of exotic substances.

AUGUST 2	Swansea Workers Club
AUGUST 3	Maxies
AUGUST 4	Bondi Life Savers
AUGUST 5	Mawson Hotel
AUGUST 9	Civic Hotel
AUGUST 10	Revesby Workers Club
AUGUST 11	Ocean Beach Hotel
AUGUST 12	Local Inn
AUGUST 16	Stagedoor Tavern
AUGUST 17	Kings Cross Rex
AUGUST 19	Stagedoor Tavern
AUGUST 18	Macquarie University
AUGUST 20	Marconi Club
AUGUST 21	Sundowner Hotel
AUGUST 22	Castle Hill RSL
AUGUST 23	Local Inn
AUGUST 24	Picnic Point High School
AUGUST 24	Bondi Lifesaver
AUGUST 25	Swansea Workers
AUGUST 26	Northern Suburbs Leagues Club

(58

AUGUST 27

The band are filmed playing live at the Sydney ABC studios in Forbes St. *Songs broadcast are Khe Sanh / One Long Day / Goodbye / Conversations / Dresden / The Door / I'm Gonna Roll Ya / Shipping Steel / Breakfast At Sweethearts / Georgia*

Part of this video was released on the Seeing Is Believing video (the one song *Breakfast At Sweethearts*). The footage shows the band in a pub environment, doing the type of gig that was standard for them at the time.

For the technically minded, Ian is playing a red Stratocaster through a Fender amplifier, (he would soon change to Marshall) rigged through a quad box. *Conversations* has Ian improvising different parts to those recorded on the album, while *Dresden* shows itself to be a much better live song than the album would suggest. A powerful version of *The Door* sees Jimmy completely lost in the passion of the song at the climax and *Breakfast...* features a very tasty guitar intro. The lyrics of *Shipping Steel* are different, Jimmy sings "sometimes little girls get hot yeah" instead of "hikers on the edge of town" as well as a couple of other lines which are indecipherable. Perhaps the highlights of this performance are the only 'released' footage of *Georgia* and *One Long Day*, which are not available (in Australia) on video in any other form..

Overall this is an impressive document of the live shows the band was giving in late '78. A raw and unpolished gem.

Much of this performance has been screened on cable television in Australia soon after that medium's introduction.

AUGUST 28	Kuringhi College (arvo)
AUGUST 28	Mt.Pleasant Leagues Club
AUGUST 29	Floyds, Canberra
AUGUST 31	Largs Pier with Everest

Five hundred and forty people cram into the Largs Pier to see the local boys made good.

SEPTEMBER 1	Pooraka Hotel
SEPTEMBER 2	Old Mariner (attendance- 900 people)
SEPTEMBER 3	Elizabeth Rugby Club with Everest
SEPTEMBER 6	La Trobe University
SEPTEMBER 7	Commodure Hotel

SEPTEMBER 8	Bombay Rock with Madder Lake & Stealer
SEPTEMBER 9	Countdown, ABC (arvo)
SEPTEMBER 9	Manhattan
SEPTEMBER 10	Bombay Rock with Texas

SEPTEMBER 11

Release Goodbye (Astrid Goodbye) / Georgia single. The single reaches No. 65 nationally.

Georgia had been a staple of the Chisel live set for years already and it is an excellent example of the type of sensitive jazz/blues renderings Moss and Walker were capable of, providing a perfect foil for the band's generally more aggressive style. Where *Georgia* was a perfect showcase for the more sensitive side of the band, *Goodbye* was an example of the more aggressive side of the band and became a regular in every Chisel live show.

Georgia comes from the first album sessions at Trafalgar studios, while *Goodbye* is a preview of the upcoming second album, although this take is a different one to that which appears on the album. The single take has a stereo affect on the intro riff, a different guitar solo and a fade out ending being the more obvious differences, in addition to the piano being more prominent in the mix of the album version.

The lyrics have also been altered, as Jimmy explained: "On the album version it says 'no more pissin' around' whereas on the single version it says 'no more messing around'. When we recorded the single it was a different version completely. We recorded that even before we had done the album. We actually did it when we were doing demos for the album because it was actually a demo"

SEPTEMBER 12	Tamworth Workers Club
SEPTEMBER 13	Mawson Hotel
SEPTEMBER 14	Maitland RSL
SEPTEMBER 15	Stagedoor Tavern with Teenage Radio Stars (11.30-1.00am, 2x45min sets)
SEPTEMBER 16	Selinas
SEPTEMBER 17	Belmont Sports Club
SEPTEMBER 19	Stagedoor Tavern
SEPTEMBER 20	Lidcombe Dancers
SEPTEMBER 22	Floyds, Canberra
SEPTEMBER 23	Floyds, Canberra

59)

SEPT 25-28	Recording second album.
SEPTEMBER 29	Manly Flicks
SEPTEMBER 30	Bombay Rock
OCTOBER 1	Bondi Lifesaver
OCTOBER 2-3	Recording second album.

OCTOBER 4 - REGENT THEATRE, SYDNEY

Set (complete ?): God Save The Queen / One Long Day / Home and Broken Hearted / The Door / Georgia / Merry Go Round / Khe Sanh / Wild Thing / Shipping Steel / Northbound / Conversations / I'm Gonna Roll Ya / Mona and the Preacher / Breakfast At Sweethearts / Dresden.

This show was recorded and part of it issued as the You're Thirteen, You're Beautiful and You're Mine EP. Peter Moss recalls that this was a great show and a significant turning point for the band. It was also the second time that the band played *Merry Go Round*. Peter recalls the band rehearsing the song the preceding week and being quite happy with it.

Cold Chisel are advertised on the bill for the Australian Rocktober Tour 1978, featuring Thin Lizzy, Wha Koo, Cold Chisel and Jon English. These shows never eventuate when Cold Chisel pulls out, apparently unhappy about being billed below Jon English. Cold Chisel are replaced by The Sports, although some advertisements do carry their name.

OCTOBER 6	Ocean Beach Hotel
OCTOBER 7	Stagedoor Tavern
OCT 9-12	Studio, recording second album.
OCTOBER 13	Swansea Workers Club
OCTOBER 14	Selinas
OCTOBER 15	Guilford Leagues Club
OCTOBER 16	Sundowner Hotel
OCTOBER 17	Civic Hotel
OCTOBER 19	Comb' n' Cutter
OCTOBER 20	Local Inn
OCTOBER 21	Cave Beach Surf Club
OCTOBER 22	War & Peace, Parramatta

OCTOBER - ?

Set List-(probably complete but lacking encores)- Juliet/ Northbound /Conversations/ I'm Gonna Roll Ya/ Breakfast At Sweethearts/ Georgia/Shippin' Steel/ Khe Sanh/Idleness (a.k.a. When The Sun Goes Down)/ Call Me/Merry-Go-Round/Plaza /One Long Day/ Never Gonna Make You Cry/ Dresden/ Showtime/ Home and Broken Hearted/ The Door / Wild Thing

This show comes from an unknown venue and date (possibly Queensland) and by the arrangements of some of the songs my guess is it was recorded in late '78, sometime after You're 13... . After the first two numbers, Ian can be heard tuning his guitar to Don's piano and Jimmy comments that this won't be a very laid back night, despite the fact that there's not exactly 4000 people here. This show has the band shaping songs for the new album, which they were in the process of recording at the time. *Conversations* is almost complete in its arrangement, this version includes a descending piano glissando which falls into the bridge section in dramatic style. *Gonna Roll Ya* and *Breakfast...* are true to the album versions and *Georgia* is part of the main set (it would soon be an encore number), showing that even at this early stage they were not afraid to mix up musical styles in the set list.

(60

Khe Sanh features a guitar solo instead of the organ solo on the album. Considering that the first album was obviously the current one at the time and the *Breakfast.* album was still five months away, this set features very little of the first album and is very dependent on new material making few concessions for those who may have come to hear the first album songs. What really makes this show interesting is a number of songs which did not make it onto the *Breakfast...* album, and in some cases didn't make it onto any album!

The first of these is *Idleness*, a song which was bandied around quite a bit in the next few years (see Oct '79 & Jan '83) but was never officially released until 1994 (under the title *When The Sun Goes Down*), a very strong medium-paced Don Walker song, which must have came close to being included on the second album, and was also demoed for both *East* and *Twentieth Century*. The next is *Why Don't You Call Me*, rumoured to be a Jimmy Barnes song. This one is a revelation- virtually a disco song, (the

band certainly was experimenting with disco at this time as Don later revealed that *Showtime* was originally meant to be a disco song, adding that the band didn't play disco very well-and here's the proof!) reminiscent of the more commercial dance tunes of the time. It is not one of the band's more memorable numbers and was never to be heard of again.

The transformation of the band for the next number, *Merry-Go-Round*, is astounding . They suddenly sound focused and dangerous again. Plaza segues into One Long Day with a fluid blues section (see April 27 1979 3XY broadcast). These last three songs are the types of performances that earned the band their live reputation. The next surprise is a full tilt rocker, which could be called *Never Say Goodbye*, but certainly never saw the light of day officially. *Wild Thing* has a reggae middle section, which leads me to believe (along with the *One Long Day* arrangement) that this performance is some time after the *You're 13...* recording was done.

The Chisels come in from the cold

"Well, they did suggest his name, but we certainly didn't kick up because we'd known him for quite a while. He turned out really well."
I've been living with the album for the past week

"Oh yeah, somebody said that to me last week. There was an article in an Adelaide paper yesterday which said I was a cynic."
Are you?
"Well, he quoted me as saying that I was, when

OCTOBER 24	Floyds, Canberra
OCTOBER 26	Commodore Hotel
OCTOBER 27	Croxton Park Hotel
OCTOBER 28	Mathew Flinders
OCTOBER 29	Bombay Rock

In an interview, Jimmy's brother John Swan mentions that he has Don Walker on the lookout for good songs for him while Jimmy helped by giving him a list of musicians to audition for his band. However, Swan didn't use any of those suggested by his brother as he thought they were all tired and out of fresh ideas.

NOVEMBER 3	Armidale University, (arvo)
NOVEMBER 3	Playroom, Tallebudgera with The Ferrets
NOVEMBER 4	Cold Queens Hotel, Brisbane with The Ferrets. The band play to a full house of more than 800 punters.

"...they howled and screamed and contorted a blast of sound, way past any civilised sonic barrier, into the inflamed brains of over 800 punters."

(RAM MAGAZINE)

NOVEMBER 5 - (PETER FRAMPTON TOUR)

Brisbane, Festival Hall. Embark on a national tour with Sherbet supporting Peter Frampton.

"Chisel wander on stage just like they do in pubs and package the impact of their usual two sets per night into about three quarters of an hour. The crowd are receptive, quite a few cheering recognition on the opening bars of most songs. They don't actually get out of the seats and headbang down the aisles. But they demand an encore, loudly. Another loud cheer when the piano intro for Wild Thing rolls out. The ending comes crashing in a shower of sweat, like a Malibu dumper. Barnes leaps at the microphone, jabs a clenched fist power salute at the audience. "Fuck the pope!" he screams. He could have said "See you at the Casbah" for all the shock, horror, outrage it caused. And Chisel wandered off stage."

(ANTHONY O'GRADY, RAM MAGAZINE)

NOVEMBER 9 - (PETER FRAMPTON TOUR)

Perth Entertainment Centre with Sherbet. The Kinks were also advertised on this bill but apparently pulled out at the last moment as they were not keen to do a support spot for Frampton as they had just finished a successful headlining tour of the US. It is announced that they will headline their own tour next year.

NOVEMBER 10	(Peter Frampton Tour)
Perth Entertainment Centre with Sherbet	
NOVEMBER 13	(Peter Frampton Tour)
Adelaide Oval with Sherbet	

NOVEMBER 15 - (PETER FRAMPTON TOUR)

Myer Music Bowl Melbourne with Sherbet

The press reports that due to further delays of the Breakfast at Sweetheart's album, the band will release an "interim" E.P. Speaking from his hotel room before the Music Bowl show on the Peter Frampton tour, guitarist Ian Moss said

"Apart from the touring there were also mishaps like the fire breaking out at Alberts Studios. I went to the studio one day and there were all these fire engines everywhere.

Speaking about the forthcoming LP he continued,

"Less overdubs and more full on rock'n'roll. The first one had a fair bit of variation, like Khe Sanh for example."

Moss also mentioned that he had put down a track with Don Walker called *The Dummy* for a Razzle Records Guitarist album as well as working with Daryl Braithwaithe on his solo project.

Asked his opinion of Peter Frampton he replied,

"Oh...average I guess." How have Frampton's audiences responded to Cold Chisel ?

"Well in Brisbane and Perth there were a lot of 12-year old female fans in front, and I guess the older ones were somewhere in the back. Adelaide was the best one. It was great because there was such a mixture of ages. There were a lot more of those Zeppelin/Deep Purple freaks. That's the people that would come to see us, that's our audience."

NOVEMBER 18 - (PETER FRAMPTON TOUR)

Sydney Sports Ground with Sherbet

Set list: Guitar intro / Home And Broken Hearted / Northbound / The Door / Georgia / Breakfast At Sweethearts / Khe Sanh / Merry Go Round / Wild Thing

After a brief introduction for "Australia's hard rockin' Cold Chisel", a guitar solo precedes *Home And Broken Hearted*, replacing usual opener *Juliet* for this tour. *Northbound* is next. A song which was obviously very important to the band, live renditions reveal qualities not apparent on the album cut. The show is an afternoon event as Jimmy comments on how nice it is to see so many people enjoying the sun before introducing *The Door*. This is the first of a number of songs to be previewed in this shortened set from the upcoming second album. Like much of that album, this live version of *The Door* reveals an energy not captured on the studio version and is indicative of the band's intention to make the second album a much more rock'n'roll album than the first one was.

Georgia is next up. The band seemed to delight in taking audiences from the most frenetic pace possible, as in *The Door* to the other end of the scale, in this case with *Georgia*. It's difficult to understand why *Georgia* was included in these shortened support sets, when the band had an album out and material for a new album to test on audiences (and *Georgia* was not on either of these). Obviously the band were determined not to be easily pigeon holed by new audiences, and of course, the additional media usually present at these shows.

Breakfast At Sweethearts is introduced as a reggae song. *Khe Sanh* receives cheers of recognition from the audience and things are really rolling again after the restrained mood of the previous couple of songs. Rousing renditions of *Merry Go Round* and *Wild Thing* complete as good a support set as you'll ever see. Before *Wild Thing* Jimmy plugs the band's late show that night - "if you feel like kickin' on afterwards, after the show, The Lifesaver's the place to go. We're gonna be kickin' some goals there." The guitar solo in *Wild Thing* is even more inspired that that on the *You're Thirteen...* EP and the band lifts the last half of it to a ferocious level, leaving the Frampton crowd suitably impressed and ensuring the headlining act had to work hard to successfully follow Cold Chisel.

The Frampton tour continued to New Zealand, without Cold Chisel.

| NOVEMBER 18 | Bondi Lifesaver with Finch (Cold Chisel's fee:$1750) |
| NOVEMBER 19 | Bondi Lifesaver |

NOVEMBER 20

Release You're 13, You're Beautiful and You're Mine limited edition live EP featuring five tracks recorded at Sydney's Regent Theatre. It peaks at No.36 on the national charts.

The full track listing runs:

One Long Day/Home and Broken Hearted/Merry Go Round/ Mona and The Preacher/Wild Thing. All were Don Walker songs with the exception of "Wild Thing". Interestingly, the German pressing (released in 1983) is more like a traditional single, with "Wild Thing" on Side A and Side B containing Merry-Go-Round/Mona and The Preacher/One Long Day/Home and Broken Hearted.

The EP contains four songs which would become Cold Chisel classics, and one which would become something of a rarity in *Mona and the Preacher*. This version of *Wild Thing* would ensure that the song became a Chisel classic while the renditions of songs from the first album, particularly *One Long Day* were more energetic and inspired than the previously released cuts. These performances were the first indication to the record buying public of the intensity and energy the band was capable of generating, even though they were still some time away from recreating this in the studio. As a live band, Cold Chisel could match it with anyone and some of the performances on this record still rate with their best. *Wild Thing* was to receive some airplay from radio and although it was not a huge 'hit', it served as warning to audiences who had not yet witnessed Cold Chisel live.

You're 13, You're Beautiful and You're Mine was only a limited release and very soon became a collectors item. It was re-released, again in limited form on CD in 1995.

When asked in early 1979 about the title for the EP Jimmy Barnes recalled

"Oh we were just sitting around trying to think of a name in the studio and it was one of those days. We were in a funny mood, cracking jokes and laughing and Rod's (Willis) coming up with these stupid names for the album. I remember one was I Got the Jack from A Queen. (laughs) We were all coming up with

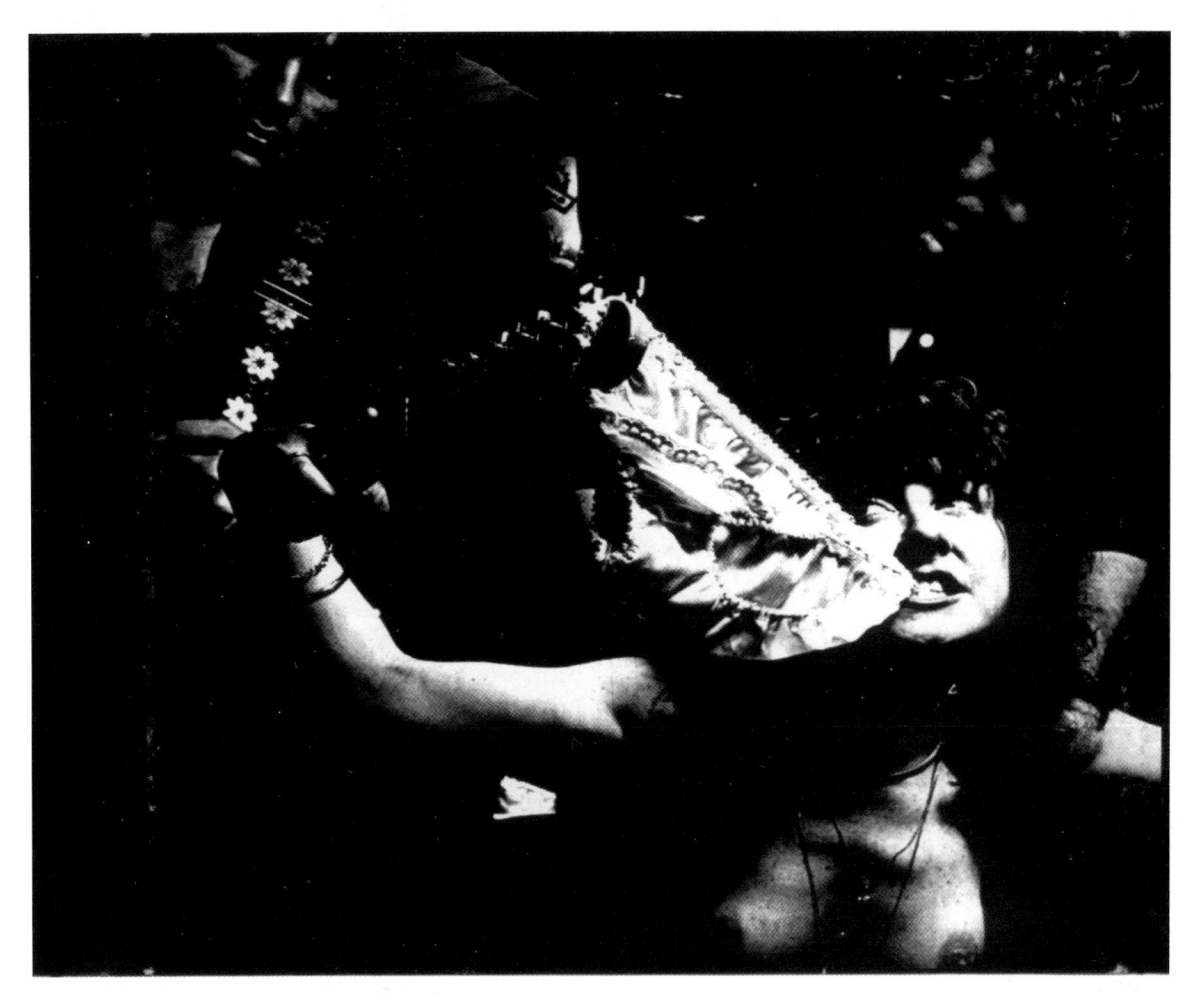

names like that, and David Sinclair, the A & R guy at WEA came up with What about You're 13, You're Beautiful and You're Mine and we all just started pissing ourselves laughing. We said 'yeah, yeah, that'll do.'

Barnes added that he thought the EP was "a fine testament to the band live ,particularly a smokin' version of One Long Day, Merry Go Round and Goodbye, they're my preferences. That's the style of song that I like, I prefer them, although I really like the others too. Unfortunately, Goodbye wasn't included on the EP. Other references to this EP include Walker discussing Jimmy's mumbling of the lyrics to the new Merry Go Round, "Before the new album (Breakfast At Sweethearts) we used to do gigs and get all these chicks lined up against the front and they obviously tried to learn the lyrics of Merry Go Round off the EP and they would be trying to sing along with him and they would be just about breaking their jaws". Jimmy says that this was because on the EP there are places where there just aren't any lyrics, while Don states that Jimmy just mumbles some of the vocals.

"Comparing the scintillating version here of One Long Day with the dour studio version on their debut album is like comparing the real thing with a cover version. Recorded live, Cold Chisel have real fire, an awesome momentum and a bright sound, all of which were completely stifled by the inhibiting surroundings of the studio and psychological strain of multiple takes. They hit bets when they hit once, and hard.

Guitarist Ian Moss shows how inspired he can be with the reins off, and the rest of the band do likewise, including vocalist Jim Barnes, who uses his voice more effectively when singing to an audience and having to communicate gut feeling to real people.

(AL WEBB, 'JUKE' MAGAZINE)

NOVEMBER 24	Stagedoor Tavern
NOV 25/26	Recording the second album.
NOVEMBER 27	Civic Hotel
NOVEMBER 28	Recording
NOVEMBER 29	Floyds, Canberra
NOVEMBER 30	Bananas
DECEMBER 1	Ritchies (attendence-533 people)

DECEMBER 1	Tiger Lounge, Richmond
DECEMBER 2	Broadfoard

DECEMBER 3- SARAH SANDS HOTEL, BRUNSWICK

...Don Walker's songs are, of course the band's winning cards. His piano may have been largely inaudible in the mix, but he was present in spirit as Jim Barnes howled out his excellent lyrics and four-square melodies. Walker may not be a musical adventurer (have you heard the album - (Ed)(the band probably wouldn't allow it even if he was so inclined) but he works within conventional forms like the twelve bar rocker (Goodbye Astrid) or the dingoes' style ballad (Khe Sanh) with real freshness. And his lyrics are outstanding; not just by the abysmal standards of your average Oz songwriter but by those of the wide world.

There are occasional flowery excesses but most of the images of urban sleaze and long roads are exactly right and he has the rare ability to climb unsentimentally into a character's mind on numbers such as One Long Day and Shipping Steel. And perhaps he is becoming slightly braver musically if the rolling reggae swing of Breakfast at Sweethearts is an indication.

Ian Moss has mastered most of the known Stratocaster cliches and puts them all in exactly the right places, while the rhythm section play as firmly as a rugby backline. The band pace their set faultlessly and deliver the most fervent version of Wild Thing you can ever hope to hear. (Their live EP is worth the money just for that track).

(ADRIAN RYAN, 'JUKE' MAGAZINE)

DECEMBER 6	Warnambool
DECEMBER 7	Sth. Gambier Football Club
DECEMBER 8	Countdown
DECEMBER 9	Countdown
DECEMBER 14	Lidcombe Dancers
DECEMBER 15	Coogee Bay Hotel, Selinas
DECEMBER 16	Mawson Hotel
DECEMBER 17	Northern Suburbs Leagues Club
DECEMBER 19	Civic Hotel
DECEMBER 20	Gymea Hotel, Jam Disco
DECEMBER 21	Cronulla Leagues Club

DECEMBER 22	Coogee Bay Hotel
DECEMBER 23	Local Inn
DECEMBER 25	Bondi Lifesaver
DECEMBER 27	New Albury Hotel
DECEMBER 28	Richies, Melbourne
DECEMBER 29	Tiger Lounge
DECEMBER 30	Manhattan Hotel

DECEMBER 31 - COUNTDOWN, ADELAIDE

Press reports suggest that Rod Willis is negotiating on several offers, which could see Cold Chisel in America sometime in March. It also confirms (incorrectly) that they've already set up a release deal in the U.S. with Elektra, which will see the release of a compilation album of tracks from their debut album and their second album. Their first U.S. single is to be *Khe Sanh*, which will go out under the title *The Last Train Out Of Sydney*.

It was also reported that Willis had found a lot of interest in the band in South America and Europe and that he was hoping to organise a tour for the band taking in these places.

The band finish the year by taking out 2nd in the Top Oz LPs in the RAM rock poll, as well as 2nd in the Best Guitarist, 1st for Best Oz Keyboards, 3rd in the Top Oz Group, and 2nd for Best New Group.

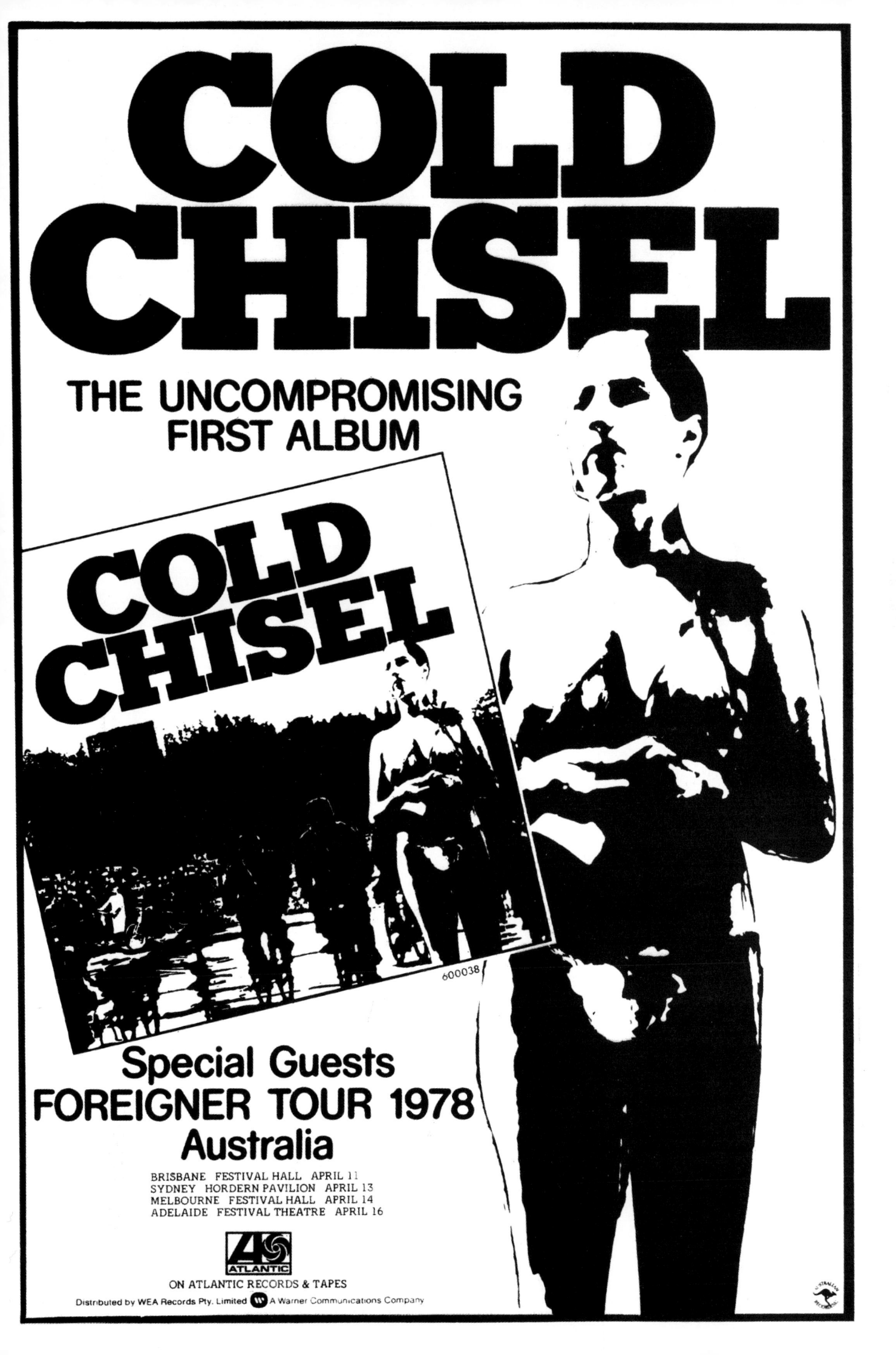

Breakfast at Sweethearts

IAN MOSS RECALLS 1979 AS JUST A BLUR OF LIVE GIGS AS THE BAND WORKED HARDER THAN EVER, CONSOLIDATING ITS POSITION AS ONE OF THE COUNTRIE'S MAJOR LIVE ACTS. THIS WOULD ALSO BE HELPED BY THEIR BREAKTHROUGH INTO MAINSTREAM RADIO WITH THE FIRST SINGLE RECORDED WITH THE PRODUCER WHO WOULD HELP THEM RECORD THE ALBUM WHICH TOOK COLD CHISEL TO SUPERSTAR STATUS.

67)

JANUARY 3	Adelaide Boy Scouts Convention

This was to be the last time that Peter Moss worked with the band. Peter recalls the arrangement that had been struck between he and the band back in 1975 was simply not appropriate anymore.

JANUARY 4-10	Recording the second album continues.
JANUARY 11	Croxton Park, Melbourne
JANUARY 13	Southside Six

JANUARY 15 The band shoots the cover for the second album at the Marble Bar of the Hilton Hotel in Sydney, a room notorious at the time for its "unconventional" clientele.

JANUARY 16	Jam Disco
JANUARY 17	Local Inn
JANUARY 18	Belmont Sailing Club
JANUARY 19	Royal Antler
JANUARY 20	Stagedoor Tavern
JANUARY 21	Sth. Sydney Juniors
JANUARY 21	South Sydney Leagues Club
JANUARY 22	Sundowner Hotel

JANUARY 23 - CAPTAIN COOK HOTEL

The band has already established a loyal live following, prompting Angels' manager John Woodruff to comment, "the thing about Cold Chisel audiences is they're independent of the usual rock crowd. Honestly, every time they play, all these people who just aren't regulars at the venue turn up. It's like 'clear the room, the Chisel army are about to hit.' Then you never see them at the venue again 'till Chisel play next time."

JANUARY 26	Marryatville Hotel, Adelaide
JANUARY 27	Marryatville Hotel, Adelaide
JANUARY 28	Glenelg Pier Rod Stewart Tour

JANUARY 31 - PERTH ENTERTAINMENT CENTRE

Cold Chisel tour Australia and New Zealand as Special Guests of Rod Stewart. The band play to 40,000 people in one show (Auckland) and 30,000 (Melbourne), giving them valuable experience with bigger crowds on large stages. Phil Small is pursued enthusiastically by a gay member of Stewart's entourage who apparently insisted that he shouldn't knock it until he tried it, while Jimmy got some advice on soul singing from Stewart (he told Jim to listen to Sam and Dave, which he did).

One (unconfirmed) report has Stewart and Barnes apprehended by the police in New Zealand pushing a piano down a hotel corridor towards a window !

There was however a great deal of tension between the two camps, as Stewart's band, who were number one on the charts around the world, were therefore confident that they were the best in the world, an attitude which the members of Cold Chisel were not prepared to accept as willingly as the Stewart entourage thought they should. Things came to a head in Brisbane when at the hotel bar after the show, Steve asked one of the Stewart band guitarists what it was like to play in a girl's blouse band, or words to that effect!

Attempts were made to have Cold Chisel removed from the tour until Steve apologised to Rod and his wife Alana, who insisted that she had been married to her husband for some time and he was very much a man!

FEBRUARY 1	Perth Entertainment Centre
FEBRUARY 2	Perth Entertainment Centre (cancelled)
FEBRUARY 3	Parker-Villa Ampitheatre
FEBRUARY 5	Adelaide

FEBRUARY 9 - VFL PARK

"For openers Australia's Cold Chisel had the audience on it's feet dancing and chanting 'More' when most support acts would get booed off the stage in anticipation of the star."

(DAILY PRESS)

FEBRUARY 12	Sydney Sports Ground
FEBRUARY 13	Sydney Sports Ground (cancelled)
FEBRUARY 16	Festival Hall Brisbane
FEBRUARY 17	Festival Hall Brisbane
FEBRUARY 17	Queens Hotel
FEBRUARY 18	Festival Hall Brisbane

FEBRUARY 23 - AUCKLAND, WESTERN SPRINGS

Breakfast at Sweethearts is released. The album sells 12,000 copies in its first two weeks of release and becomes a Top 5 hit.

The album contains 10 songs, all written or co-written by Don Walker- Conversations /Merry-Go-Round /Dresden/ Goodbye (Astrid Goodbye) /Plaza /Shipping Steel /I'm Gonna Roll Ya /Showtime / Breakfast At Sweethearts /The Door

It can be a frustrating album to listen to (the production would be best described as dull) despite a last minute remix being ordered by Don Walker. The album did spawn at least two radio classics *Shipping Steel*, and the title track. A couple of others, *Merry-Go-Round* and *Goodbye*, became regulars in the live set for the next four years. The songs reflect a much more straightforward rock style, although the production lacks the dynamics and colour required to showcase the songs effectively. At times the band themselves sound uninspired, in glaring contrast to live performances at the time. The song *Breakfast At Sweethearts* shows the band extending themselves musically with it's blues/reggae (quite new at the time) feel, while the other slowy, *Plaza* is a nod to the almost jazz flavour of some first album cuts, although not nearly as complex. Lyrically the songs reflect the band's situation, professionally and personally at the time.

Reviews for the album are positive although the band themselves later reveal some dissatisfaction with the production. "I'm sort of reasonably happy with it", Jimmy told Juke's Ross Stapleton in March 1979.

In the same interview Don Walker, obviously reluctant to be too specific about the entire album stated that he was happy with the way *Showtime* came out, to which Jimmy muttered that it was something of a miracle. Obviously the song required a lot of work and Jim described it as basically a matter of trial and error with a lot of help from their producer Richard Batchens.

Apparently Batchens criticized Jimmy's singing, which did not make for a good working relationship, along with the producer's "you just play the songs, I'll worry about the sound" attitude. Later Jimmy was less tactful and in May 1980 he told Rolling Stone's Sam Bendigo *"Breakfast at Sweetheart's stunk and you can spell that f-u-c-k-e-d."* He continued:

"Christ, we were happy with the sales but it wasn't a Cold Chisel album. We wanted a strong rock'n'roll album but we ended up with a wishy washy sound and weak arrangements from a great bunch of songs."

(68

Steve Prestwich added in the same interview,

"Imagine our position: our first album sells well, the record company is happy, and we can't wait to make a second record. So we allowed ourselves to be led. I believe the only reason that album sold well at all was because we toured like crazy after it was released."

Don Walker added that he believed the second album to be the product of frustration,

"It was a very bad low point for the band. We were constantly touring and when we got a weekend off we were thrown into the studio and expected to be creative. The whole business had got to be a drag and you can hear that on the album. We laid down the rhythm tracks one month and then went back into the studio a month later for a few overdubs and wondered why nothing had any fire or spontaneity. To finish Breakfast at Sweethearts we had to go out and find members of the band and drag them into the studio- nobody cared at all."

For more on the recording of Breakfast At Sweethearts see July 30 1978.

In order to really understand what the album could have sounded like, one should listen to the live take of *Conversations*, recorded a few months later which appears as the b-side of the *Choirgirl* single.

"Breakfast at Sweethearts was a good description of young people leaving a secure background and getting into city living. It was a good picture of what life was like with no money in King's Cross, Darlinghust, St. Kilda or Fortitude Valley around 1978."

(Don Walker talking to Glenn A. Baker in 1988)

"I don't forget sequences of music. If I don't jot down words straight away I just forget them. But I can remember large amounts of music in patterns. Then I have to rack my brains for something worthwhile to say which hasn't been said a million times before.

At the moment I have about three or four songs and can't think of anything worthwhile to write about. When I do I generally hammer it all together pretty quickly."

(Don on songwriting, late 1978)

"Breakfast is a good album but we're only still

scratching the surface. As you know, this album was all Don's songs. For the next one I've got four or five of mine, Ian and Steve have a couple, and Phil is getting into it too."

(Jimmy Barnes)

"Chisel are a strong band who play fine, gut-wrenching music and who, seemingly, have only just started to stretch their capabilities. Any band who can produce both the roar of something like Goodbye and the intricate complexity of Dresden has got to be a new future for Australian rock'n'roll."

(ANTHONY O'GRADY, RAM MAGAZINE)

"Breakfast is not just a collection of songs, it exudes a conceptual aura at street level, cleverly indigenous. (you see, King's Cross can be cool too!) The main vehicle for this is Don Walker's lyrics. Reading the lyric sheet is an education, more spice than Willessee's program content -copulation, hotels, truckies, love, hate (but no used car rip-offs).

"...Predictably the album is predominantly rock & roll with the highs and ebbs perfectly placed.

The track placing can not be faulted. Most cuts feature guitar and few do it better than Ian Moss whose feel for inflection is superb. He is in fact my hero - nonetheless my appraisal stands as objective, just listen. I can't wait for number three.

In lieu of bacon and eggs, I'll Breakfast at Sweethearts anytime, try it, I think you'll like the menu."
                                    (JEAN HUNTRE, 'JUKE' MAGAZINE)

FEBRUARY 25	Wellington
FEBRUARY 26	Christchurch, QE2 Park (Rod Stewart support)
FEBRUARY 28	Christchurch, QE2 Park (Rod Stewart support)
MARCH 2	Sydney Uni
MARCH 3	Sydney Cove Tavern
MARCH 5	Sundowner Hotel-(N.S.W.) 520 people
MARCH 6	Captain Cook Hotel
MARCH 8	Village Green, Melbourne, 604 people
MARCH 9	Bombay Rock with Aliens and Secret Police 1150 people
MARCH 10	Sentimental Bloke, 650 people

MARCH 13	Ambassador, Sydney
MARCH 14	Maraoubra Seals
MARCH 15	Sylvania Hotel
MARCH 16	Stagedoor Tavern
MARCH 17	Manly Vale

MARCH 17

Cold Chisel are on the cover of national music magazine *Juke* and a three page story shows that the media are taking the band very seriously.

The band themselves are also taking things a lot more seriously too, updating their PA and lighting systems to something twice as powerful.

"You become aware of how professional you should be. Six months ago, out of five shows two would be good and the other three would be how's-your-father. Now every show has to be just spot on."

(Jimmy Barnes)

MARCH 19	The band begins a three-month national tour.

Breakfast At Sweetheart's/Plaza is released as a single.

MARCH 21	Queen's Hotel (Brisbane) (cancelled)
MARCH 21	Armidale University, 450 people
MARCH 22	Darling Downs Institute, Toowoomba, 450 people
MARCH 23	Patch
MARCH 24	Queens (cancelled)
MARCH 25	Brisbane University
MARCH 27	Wollongong
MARCH 28	Comb'n'Cutter
MARCH 29	Manly Flicks
MARCH 30	Newcastle, Redheads Surf Club
MARCH 31	Stagedoor Tavern
APRIL 1	Penrith Leagues
APRIL 2	Canberra, 737 people
APRIL 3	Armadale Hotel Melbourne, 478 people
APRIL 4	Tattersalls Hotel Warnambool, 400 people
APRIL 5	Sth Gambier Football Club
APRIL 6	Arkaba Hotel, Adelaide
APRIL 7	Arkaba Hotel, Adelaide
APRIL 8	Arkaba Hotel, Adelaide

APRIL 11	Herdsman Hotel, Perth
APRIL 12	White Sands
APRIL 14	Lilac Hotel
APRIL 15	Charles Hotel
APRIL 18	Herdsman Hotel, 261 people
APRIL 19	Raffles, 650 people
APRIL 20	Rafferty's
APRIL 21	White Sands
APRIL 22	Charles Hotel, 589 people
APRIL 25	Melbourne
APRIL 26	Sandown Park

APRIL 27 - BOMBAY ROCK WITH AUSTRALIAN CRAWL

Fee: $2500. This show is broadcast live on east coast radio (3XY Melbourne, 4IP Brisbane, 2NX Newcastle and 2SM Sydney, Adelaide radio apparently declined the offer to be involved), reflecting the band's confidence in its live performances and has become a popular item among Chisel fans. One suspects that as the entire album is performed, apart from the obvious promotional advantages, this broadcast also allowed the band to showcase songs from the new album the way that they believed they should sound.

The songs broadcast were: Shipping Steel/Home and Broken Hearted /Dresden /Conversations/ Showtime/The Door/ Breakfast At Sweetheart's/ Plaza/One Long Day /Merry-Go-Round /Wild Thing /Goodbye Astrid.

The introduction tells us that the band is planning a big night, with Jimmy having his birthday later in the night and this is truly an extraordinary performance, considering the risks involved with going live to such a large radio audience! All of the second album tracks are played with more power and feel than the recorded versions and the cut of *One Long Day* is superb. Linked to *Plaza*, Walker initiates a clever key change leading to a blues intro, allowing Moss to trade some magical guitar licks, building the tension before falling into the main body of the song. *One Long Day* also showcased the skills of the rhythm section of Phil and particularly Steve as they negotiate all the feel and tempo changes, particularly on the arrangement played at this time.

Wild Thing is a manic version- like that on the EP, with a reggae interlude in the middle. The band is brought back for one encore, *Goodbye (Astrid)*. After the radio broadcast the band played yet another set, going to well after midnight (it was Jimmy's birthday on the 28th). This set included at least one new song (perhaps the band were keen to put their second album behind them) which ground to a close after a minute or so to which Barnes responded "this one's so new even we don't know it" before the band restarted and successfully completed the song.

71)

APRIL 28	Manhattan Hotel, $1500

APRIL 29 - SOVEREIGN HOTEL.

$1500, 500 people

Rod Stewart drummer Carmine Appice, (also of Vanilla Fudge and Beck, Bogart and Appice fame) offers Jimmy a spot in his newly formed solo band.

Other reports suggest that the band's *Breakfast at Sweethearts* album has been released in America where it has disappeared without a trace. However, apparently an LA station using the call sign K-SAN has been playing the band's first album, in particular the *Khe Sanh* track, for obvious reasons. This is reportedly giving the band sales through imports.

MAY 2	Fraternity RSL, 856 people
MAY 3	Local Inn
MAY 4	Bondi Lifesaver
MAY 5	Royal Antler, 833 people
MAY 7	Ambassador Hotel (NSW), 476 people
MAY 9	Surfair, Noosa, 665 people
MAY 10	Homestead, Sydney
MAY 11	Playroom
MAY 12	Waterloo Hotel
MAY 13	Easts Leagues Club
MAY 16	Comb'n'Cutter
MAY 17	Sylvania Hotel, 655 people
MAY 18	Marconi Club, 1150 people
MAY 19	Bondi Lifesaver
MAY 21	Sundowner Hotel, 920 people, $2000
MAY 23	Local Inn, $2000
MAY 24	Fairfield Hotel
MAY 25	Royal Antler Hotel
MAY 26	Stagedoor Tavern
MAY 28	Mt Pleasant Sports Club
MAY 29	Canberra ANU
MAY 30	Eureka Hotel, Geelong, $2000
MAY 31	Village Green
JUNE	*Shipping Steel/Showtime* is released as a single and goes on to sell just 186 copies , making it their least successful single.
JUNE 1	Bombay Rock with The Aliens and Fast Buck, 1000 people

JUNE 2	Manhattan Hotel
JUNE 3	Sovereign Hotel
JUNE 5	Victoria Hotel, Ballarat
JUNE 6	Goulburn Valley Hotel, Shepparton
JUNE 8	Sweethearts, Adelaide
JUNE 9	Sweethearts, Adelaide
JUNE 10	Sweethearts, Adelaide

JUNE 11 - 30

The band take a well earned break, with Don returning to family in Armidale where he works on new songs, Ian heads back to Alice Springs where he is joined by Steve for a camping holiday while Phil and Jim return home to Adelaide.

JULY

The band spend three weeks rehearsing (and doing the odd gig) at Nowra, on the southern New South Wales coast. Manager Rod Willis says that he felt the band needed to get out of Sydney to work on material in a more professional manner instead of constantly trying to find Jimmy or whoever had gone missing, as always seemed to be the case in Sydney. Both band and management are said to be very enthusiastic about their new material, which includes contributions from all members. Rod Willis added "I'm really excited. When I hear the new songs I hear American radio."

Producer Richard Batchens also accompanies the band to Nowra and he is extremely enthusiastic about the new songs which he felt were incredibly commercial. Batchens' presence was due more to record company's wishes than the band's. Some band members had lost confidence in him by this time.

In Nowra the band stay in three holiday houses (plain weatherboards going cheap in the off-season) and set up their gear in a literary society hall (Pyree Hall), running through new songs including Steve's *Best Kept Lies*.

JULY 6

Nowra Roller-skate rink with local band Jackal

Set list (probably complete): Shipping Steel / Show Me / Khe Sanh / Merry-Go-Round/ Choirgirl / Blue Movies (Never Make Me Cry) / Standing On The Outside /Best Kept Lies/ Idleness / Tomorrow / My Turn To Cry / The Door / One Long Day / Wild Thing

One of the gigs they did play was an unannounced show at the Nowra roller-skate rink as Jimmy and the Sweethearts. They play to about 200 skaters, none of whom are there because they like the band (the gig was kept secret, support band Jackal didn't even know that Chisel were on after them!). The audience soon stops skating and crowd around the front of the stage. *Tomorrow* included out of tune backing vocals from Don Walker. It is really a chance for the band to test new songs and a good warm-up for the Brisbane show in two days time.

The band also played at the nearby Bomaderry RSL earlier in the year and Ian sung the first half hour or so when Jim was late and missed the start of the show.

JULY 8

Brisbane River, 4IP gig with The Sports, Jo Jo Zep and the Falcons and Air Supply.

By the time Chisel come on, the show is running way behind schedule (10 minutes is not enough time to change over each band's equipment) and the show organisers (4IP) are trying to convince Chisel connections to play a shorter set, as the Navy boat used to construct the stage has to be back at the dock by 5.30 p.m. Despite some equipment problems (no tune-up, faulty piano and no organ) the band play a spirited set, joined by Wilbur Wilde on saxophone for *Breakfast at Sweethearts*. Jimmy (sporting a stubble which was almost a beard), had been annoyed at the number of sailors venturing onto the stage whenever an excited member of the crowd approached the stage (they were swimming to get there!). He stopped the show and said "There's a lot more to do but we're not doin' any because we don't like uniforms of any description on stage," which gained the expected response from the audience. This did nothing for the backstage atmosphere as angry sailors were everywhere, mixing with Chisel crew.

The band played more than their allotted 45 minutes (originally 75 minutes was allotted) and had their four hire cars towed away, despite leaving notes under the windscreens.

Breakfast at Sweethearts

COLD CHISEL STORY

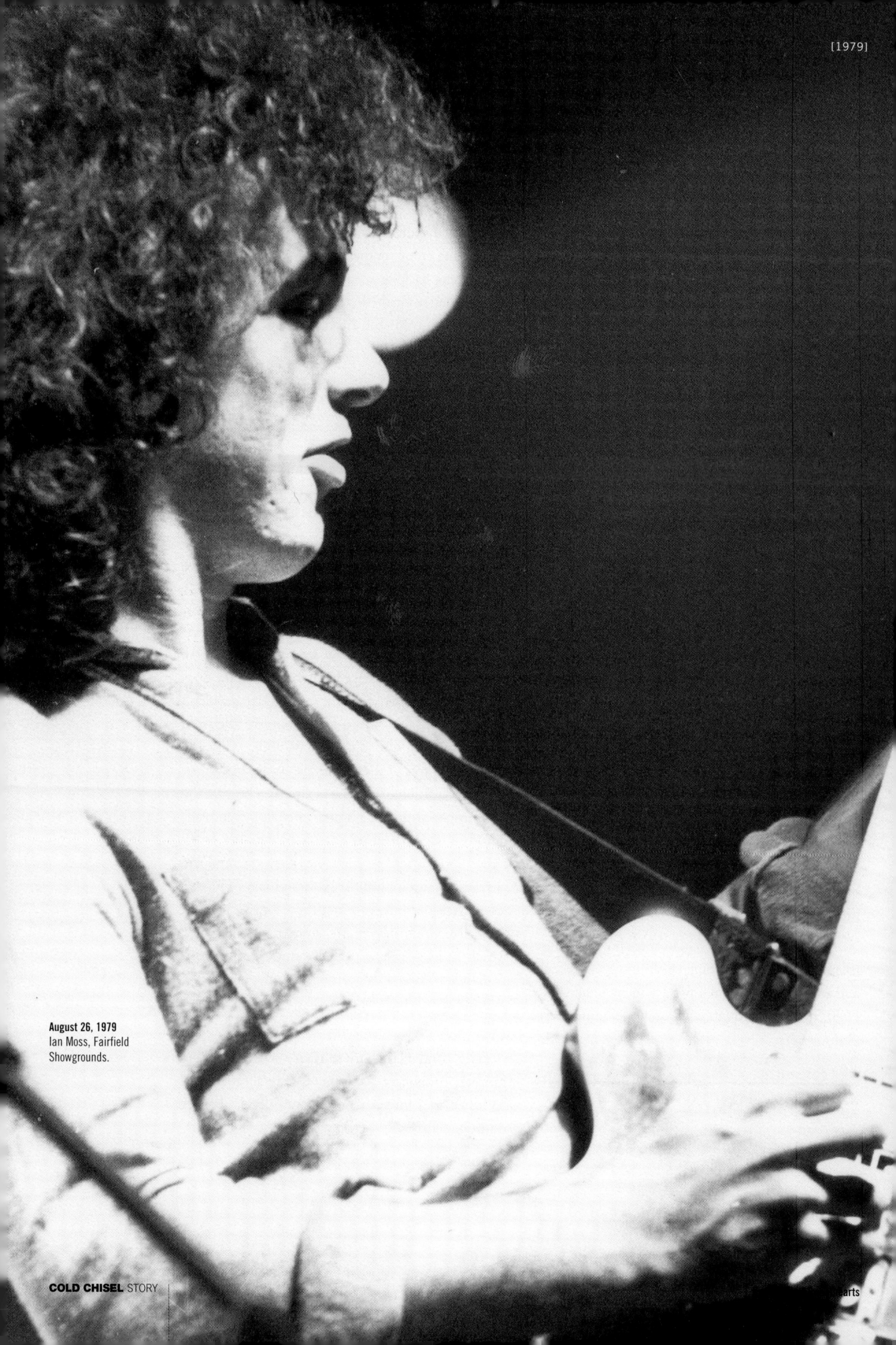

August 26, 1979
Ian Moss, Fairfield
Showgrounds.

JULY 23 - 27

Cold Chisel begin recording sessions at Paradise Studios with the intention of recording a single with Richard Batchens. However the band and producer do not have the required chemistry and, now wary of situations like this, the sessions are put on hold. The band is introduced to Mark Opitz.

JULY 28	Sydney Cove
AUG - OCT	Set Fire To The Town tour.
AUGUST 1	Surfriders Ball, St.Kilda (Melb), $3000
AUGUST 2	Council Club Hotel, (Melb), $2500

AUGUST 3 - TOTTENHAM HOTEL (MELB)

At this show Jimmy is able to catch up with family living in Braybrook. Don Walker wore his executioner hood (seen in some group photos of the time) for the entire show. The band opened the show with a powerful *Shipping Steel* and finish two hours later with a thunderous *Wild Thing* which includes *Purple Haze*, played by request for those kids leaning on the monitors in the front (including this particular writer !).

AUGUST 4	Crystal Ballroom, (Melb)
AUGUST 7	Granada Hotel, (Tas)

Chisel's arrival in Tasmania is reported on the six o'clock news and while the band only averaged 600 people per show it was still quite an event. At one show where the punters were a little too polite, Barnes ran across the tables, knocking jugs of beer flying, which had the desired effect.

AUGUST 8	Granada Hotel, (Tas)
AUGUST 9	Menai Hotel, Burnie (Tas)
AUGUST 10	Old Tudor Inn, Launceston (Tas)
AUGUST 11	Hotel Tasmania, Launceston
AUGUST 14	Eureka Hotel, Geelong (Vic)
AUGUST 15	Lady Bay Hotel, Warnambool
AUGUST 17	Marryatville Hotel, (SA)
AUGUST 18	Woodville Town Hall
AUGUST 21	The Headquarters, Canberra
AUGUST 22	Comb and Cutter, Blacktown
AUGUST 23	The Sylvania Hotel (NSW)
AUGUST 24	The Royal Antler Hotel
AUGUST 25	Stagedoor Tavern

AUGUST 26

Fairfield Showground - Along with Jo Jo Zep and The Falcons. Sports, Aliens, Mental as Anything and The Radiators, Cold Chisel draw 15,000 people to this show. Ian causes some concern when he shows up just 30 seconds before the band is due on - the band had Sports' Andrew Pendlebury ready to play with them ! ("I was on another planet" was his only excuse !) Press reports suggest that the band will start working on the new album next month with a top US producer.

AUGUST 27	Mt Pleasant Sports Ground, Wollongong
AUGUST 29	The Castle Hill RSL
AUGUST 30	Fairfield Hotel */ Marconi Club* (*both venues were advertised but the band actually played at the Local Inn)
AUGUST 31	Florida Hotel, Terrigal

During the Queensland leg of the tour, Gold Coast press slams the band over its publicity posters, which feature a burning monk. In a typical case of 'any publicity is good publicity', punters flocked to the bands shows in record numbers and Cold Chisel begin to define their image as a band with something to say - not a common trait with Australian acts of the time.

SEPTEMBER 1	Coogee Bay Hotel
SEPTEMBER 2	Penrith Leagues Club
SEPTEMBER 3	Strata Motor Inn

SEPTEMBER 5 - SURF AIR HOTEL (Q'LAND)

Jimmy asks if there are any women's libbers in the audience and, if so, to wave their bras. On establishing that there are no women's libbers in the audience he adds, "Good, well here's a song for the rest of you, *Blue Movies*." Unfortunately, the band's hire car is sprayed with Sexist Shits after the show. Jimmy told *Juke's* Ross Stapleton,

"There's only one thing worse than women's libbers, and that's women's libbers without a sense of humour!"

The band is also in trouble with Queensland press, the *Gold Coast Bulletin* really putting the boots in:

"If there were showbiz awards made for bad taste, I wouldn't hesitate to nominate rock band Cold Chisel for first prize. In one of the sickest publicity gimmicks ever dreamed up, Cold Chisel's promoters have been busy distributing posters of a monk burning himself to death. The photo of the monk is also repeated on a Cold Chisel tour programme. The programme also shows sketches of a hand flicking lighted matches. Near that is a headline, which says Set Fire to the Town. If that isn't an invitation or an incitement to pyromania (arson) I don't know what is.

"Members of Cold Chisel are pictured smirking and laughing under the picture of the burning monk. It's sick, sick, sick ! On another page of the programme there is a picture of one of the band members with his shorts pulled down and his bare behind pointing up. And as well as that kind of unsavoury behaviour, it seems Cold Chisel revels in booze, sex and aggression."

Their official record company biography states:

"They care little for the peripherals of the rock business, much preferring to drink more, fight harder, f...crazier than any other band in Australia." The biography continues "They are traditional, definitive rock'n'rollers with excesses being a key word to their lifestyle. Yet a more unassuming group of musicians or a more charming collection of individuals one would rarely expect to encounter."

SEPTEMBER 6	Toowoomba Institute (arvo?)
SEPTEMBER 6	Homestead Hotel (Bris)

SEPTEMBER 7 - 4ZZZ

Joint Effort Cloudland - Prior to this show Jimmy and Steve do a 15-minute radio spot to promote the show. Chisel draw 1500 people. The band are playing many new songs, including *My Turn to Cry* and *Blue Movies* from Jimmy, while Don's *Choirgirl* is a change of pace. Juke's Ross Stapleton felt that the high point of the show was Prestwich's *Best Kept Lies*, although he added that Moss' extended guitar solo detracted from the overall affect, and adds that he firmly believes "that the day of the guitar hero has passed."

Stapleton, who went on the road with the band at this stage noted that listening material on the bus at that point consisted of Peter Cook and a track from the latest Sex Pistols album *Big Tits Across America*, which Jimmy played all weekend.

SEPTEMBER 8 - JET CLUB, COOLANGATTA

"A converted cinema that combines live bands with disco records played by some wimp with a really fake American accent" is how Ross Stapleton described this venue. The crowd are lethargic and it is not until set closer *Wild Thing* that they really warm to the band. They encore with *Georgia* before retiring. The suddenly enthusiastic audience demand another encore and the band oblige with a version of *Goodbye* which includes Jimmy climbing the PA stack to the balcony and running the length of it before going through the crowd in a display which apparently left the audience most impressed.

Stapleton witnesses a shouting match between Jimmy and a roadie (does anyone shout louder than Jimmy ?) about the use of the roadies' room for a party. The dispute is settled when Jimmy calms a little and offers to let the roadies sleep in his room.

SEPTEMBER 9	East Leagues Club, Brisbane

This show is hampered by the fact that about two-thirds of the venue is occupied by long tables and chairs. During the trip back to Newcastle the band check out the Music Farm recording studio where they are considering recording their next album.

SEPTEMBER 11	Ambassador Club, Newcastle
SEPTEMBER 12	Fairfield Hotel Sydney
SEPTEMBER 13	Macquarie University
SEPTEMBER 14	St.John's College, Sydney University
SEPTEMBER 15	Manly Vale
SEPTEMBER 16	Parramatta Leagues Club
SEPTEMBER 17	Sundowner Hotel
SEPTEMBER 18	A.N.V.Canberra
SEPTEMBER 19	Riverina College, Wagga
SEPTEMBER 19	The Star Hotel in Newcastle closes its doors for the last time and a riot ensues.
SEPTEMBER 21	Countdown, Adelaide
SEPTEMBER 22	Countdown, Adelaide
SEPTEMBER 23	Countdown, Adelaide
SEPTEMBER 26	La Trobe University (Melb)

SEPTEMBER 27   Sandown Park Hotel* / or Mt. Pleasant Sports Club* / Geelong West Town Hall*

*(*all three venues were advertised for this date, but it appears that the band played at the Eureka Hotel in Geelong.)*

SEPTEMBER 28 - BOMBAY ROCK

"Cold Chisel are one band whose long nights on the road have served them well on the album charts...even if their records are but a pale reflection of their powerhouse live rituals. This time around there are a few changes to what was becoming very much an onstage formula... On Walker has had some of the burden of writing new material lifted from his shoulders, though the songs provided by Ian Moss, Phil Small and Jim Barnes are mostly remarkable.

"Exceptions are the chunky ballad Choirboy *(sic) and the engaging reggae-styled* Best Kept Lies, *which features democratic five piece harmonies and an overlong guitar solo that unfortunately dilutes the song's impact..."*

(ADRIAN RYAN, JUKE MAGAZINE)

SEPTEMBER 29	South Side Six / Castle Hill RSL*(cancelled)
SEPTEMBER 30	Ferntree Gully Hotel /or Marconi Club / Local Inn*

*(*These venues were also advertised for the same dates although the Melbourne dates were the ones actually played.)*

OCTOBER 2	Family Inn, $3000

OCTOBER 3 - 14

Choirgirl is recorded among demo sessions at Paradise Studios with Mark Opitz for the *East* album. Other songs demoed at this time (the band demoed all the new material they had) including *Star Hotel , Idleness, Standing on the Outside, F111, Best Kept Lies,* and *The Party's Over. Star Hotel* is slightly slower, revealing the reggae feel and the lyrics are almost completely different except for the chorus. The first verse is:

Standing just off the bitumen

Suitcase my only load

I spent last night selling everything

And the sun found me on the road

Three long years at the wishing well

I drank each jack as they came

I crashed last night at the Star Hotel

It'll never be quite the same

Idleness is a song which had been around since the time of the second album as it was in the live sets at that time (and was also in the late '79 sets) , and was obviously being considered for the East album.

Perhaps due to the quantity and quality of the songs submitted by the other band members, Idleness did not appear on the album. It was again demoed in '83 and eventually surfaced as *When The Sun Goes Down* on the Teenage Love Affair album.

Don later said that Mark Opitz was responsible for helping the band arrange their songs, or

"taking the raw song and saying 'well this might work live but if you do a bit of editing here and cut a few things out then you'll have a nice packaged radio single', he really brought that Albert Productions' intelligence over on how to do a real punchy hit single".

"Mark's the first guy that we've worked with that all of us in the band have been totally confident of his abilities."

(Don Walker talking to B. Pinnell, June 1982)

NOVEMBER 1979

Choirgirl / Conversations (live) single released, charts nationally at No. 14. A 12" version of this single is also released with a live cut of *Khe Sanh* on the B-side, giving fans three more tracks to add to the collection. To promote the single the band mime the song on Countdown, Jimmy and Ian sporting very trendy short hair cuts. *Choirgirl* gives a preview of the more three dimensional sound Mark Opitz was getting for the band while the two live cuts are excellent examples of how the band had progressed onstage since the recording of the *You're 13...* EP. *Conversations* in particular is a powerful performance, a huge improvement on the album track and an example of how the band may have wanted the second album to sound. Well worth seeking out!

"Great sound on this studio single, which comes as a 12 inch, 33-rpm package. Flip is a live take of Khe Sanh. Choirgirl is a slower Chisel song that's just brimming with bluesy feel and soulful vocals. Excellent."

(JUKE MAGAZINE)

NOVEMBER 13	Wollongong Leagues Club
NOVEMBER 14	Florida Hotel
NOVEMBER 16	Coolangatta

NOVEMBER 17 - COOLANGATTA

On the way to these shows Steve Prestwich is injured when the band's bus is involved in an accident just outside Taree, hitting a ditch and rolling. Everyone was asleep at the time and Prestwich, who was on a bunk, fell onto a handrail hurting his back and ribs. It took almost an hour to get him out and he spent the night in hospital before being flown back to Sydney. Jimmy Barnes and Don Walker were not on board at the time as they were doing press interviews in Sydney. Ray Arnott filled the drum stool for the two shows.

Ray recalls getting a call one late one afternoon asking what he was doing for the next few days.

The next morning he was on a plane. Rehearsal was that afternoon's soundcheck. Ray had occasionally run into the band in the studio and been to a couple of shows but didn't own their records. He just took his cues from Jim and Phil. (For background information on Ray Arnott, see July 1983.)

NOVEMBER 18	Lismore RSL

NOVEMBER 23 - DECEMBER 2

"Pooled Resources" tour. Others on the bill for these shows include The Angels, Flowers with other acts joining the bill in each city.

During press interviews for this tour, Ian Moss mentions that the band have a one-off deal with Elektra who will be releasing an album made up of songs from both of the Australian albums (Cold Chisel and *Breakfast...*).

"We've remixed some of the songs and we decided what was on the American release."

NOVEMBER 23	Adelaide

At this show The Angels go on before Cold Chisel and Jimmy sprains his ankle.

NOVEMBER 25 - MELBOURNE FESTIVAL HALL WITH THE BOYS NEXT DOOR

At this show Cold Chisel play their set before The Angels. The standard '79 opener *Shipping Steel* is followed by the new arrangement of *Home and Broken Hearted* which has a new intro and an extra chorus coda - this arrangement would remain throughout 1980 also. A slightly shortened set is finished with *Goodbye* before an encore of *Choirgirl* which segued straight into *Wild Thing*. Also included early in the set was a cover of *Shakin' All Over* which had been given a 'rave up' in the middle. It's another Chisel cover which never saw official release.

NOVEMBER 29	Canberra Showgrounds pavilion with The Royal Family.

Steve is sick and is replaced by Trevor Young (ex Buster Brown, Coloured Balls & Blackfeather). It was after this show that Jimmy met his wife-to-be, Jane Mahoney.

DECEMBER 1 - SYDNEY, MARCONI STADIUM

With Dave Warner, Rose Tattoo and The Hitmen. Soaring Sydney temperatures keep attendances down at this show.

Set list (probably complete): Shipping Steel/ Shakin' All Over/My Turn To Cry/ Conversations/ Khe Sanh/ Breakfast At Sweethearts/ Tomorrow/ Juliet/ Best Kept Lies/ Standing On The Outside/ The Door/ Merry-Go-Round/ Four Walls/ One Long Day/ Goodbye Astrid/ Choirgirl/ Wild Thing.

This set features a number of new songs. The usual opener, *Shipping Steel* is followed by a pause before Jimmy can be heard telling the band Shakin', as the usual second song, *Home And Broken Hearted* is left out. *Shakin' All Over* is finished with a reference to the heat: "in this fuck'n' god-damned heat how I'm shaking".

My Turn To Cry is the first of the newies, the arrangement as that which would appear on the recorded version, although the backing vocals are not as smooth. *Conversations* and *Khe Sanh* are typically powerful renditions. *Tomorrow* has a different intro and minor lyrical alterations to the final recorded take. *Juliet* brings the audience back to familiar territory while *Best Kept Lies* does not have lyrics for the second verse (those from the first are repeated) and the solo section in the middle is a completely different arrangement.

Standing On The Outside is the same arrangement as the demo version mentioned, with a number of lyrical variations, although musically similar to the final version. *The Door* has some superb guitar in a re-arranged ending. By *Merry-Go-Round* they're literally flying, fighting for supremecy over the heat. *Four Walls*, like the demo, features backing vocals, creating a solemn atmosphere behind Jim's voice. *One Long Day* has Ian doing some Van Halen - style tapping on the blues intro.

The encores are the current single, *Choirgirl*, and *Wild Thing*. A solid hour in almost 40 degrees temperatures leaving band and audience exhausted.

DECEMBER 2	Newcastle International Motordrome

(with The Motels and Dave Warner) Torrential rain falls as the gates open for this show.

DECEMBER 12	Sylvania Hotel, 810 people
DECEMBER 13	Local Inn
DECEMBER 14	Royal Antler
DECEMBER 15	Stagedoor Tavern
DECEMBER 19	Shorland Caberet Rock
DECEMBER 20	Comb'N'Cutter
DECEMBER 21	Fairfield Hotel
DECEMBER 22	Nowra & Bombaderri RSL
DECEMBER 23	Milton Showground Hall
DECEMBER 24	Batemans Bay Youth Hall

DECEMBER 25 - MARUYA MEMORIAL RSL

Set List (incomplete) Conversations / The Dummy / Shakin' All Over / Breakfast At Sweethearts / Home and Broken Hearted / My Turn To Cry / Best Kept Lies / Standing On The Outside / Knocking On Heaven's Door / Star Hotel / Mona and the Preacher / Merry-Go-Round / Four Walls / One Long Day / I'm Gonna Roll Ya / Shipping Steel / Khe Sanh

The incredibly arduous work rate of 1979 did not halt for Christmas. The set contains a number of previews from the yet-to-be recorded third album, and is evidence of an enormous improvement in the performance of the remaining older songs. The heavy work schedule was probably a contributing factor in this transformation, the band playing as tight as possible and arrangements being honed to maximise tension and excitement.

Conversations has Ian joining in on the last four choruses, an idea not used on the later tours. *The Dummy* is the first surprise, only remaining in the live sets for a matter of weeks. Its vocal arrangement is given extra power with Jim joining in on choruses and a few other parts. The rhythm section speeds up and add subtle variations under the long guitar solo at the end of the song. While perhaps not as commercial a song as many others in the set, *The Dummy* is a very worthy addition to the set at this point.

Shakin' All Over is similar to the version mentioned at the Pooled Resources shows, the bridge rave-up being a highlight of a song which has never been released by the band. *Home and Broken Hearted* has a new intro and coda and Ian is playing with great speed and dexterity. *Best Kept Lies* is still loose, both lyrically and melodically. *Standing On the Outside* has lots of lyrics which will not make it onto the final recorded version, such as "no amount of work's gonna buy me an invitation" and "rich man poor man got the same destination".

Knockin' On Heaven's Door is much like the version included with early pressings of the third album. This is probably among the first performances of *Knocking On Heaven's Door*, and it has a freshness like the *East* rendition. *Star Hotel* still features the lyrics from the early demo (see Appendix One), although it is at about the same speed as the third album version. *Mona and the Preacher* sounds as good as it's ever sounded, but it will soon be dropped from the set. *Merry Go Round* is as always, powerful and exciting, much like the version on the Manly Vale video of early 1980. *Four Walls* features almost a cappella backing vocals in this new arrangement of a song which hasn't been played since 1977. A part from this and a few minor lyric changes, it is almost the same as the third album version.

One Long Day now has a blues intro, during which Ian tries out some Van Halen-like tapping techniques in another superb version of a song which just keeps growing in stature. *I'm Gonna Roll Ya* makes it two from 1975 in a row, although it is starting to sound a little pale beside the new songs.

Overall, an important period in the band's development as the six months on either side of this show represent perhaps the greatest growth period in the band's career.

DECEMBER 26	Bega Town Hall
DECEMBER 28	Ferntree Gully Hotel
DECEMBER 29	Bombay Rock, 1056 people
DECEMBER 30	Calledonian Hotel, 701 people

The 1979 RAM magazine's rock poll has Cold Chisel as the Top Oz Group in a tie with The Angels. Chisel also take out second in the Best Male Singer (behind Doc Neeson), second in the Best Oz Guitarist (behind Kevin Borich), Best Oz Keyboards (1st), Best Oz Bass (4th) and Best Oz Songwriter (1st).

Breakfast at Sweethearts

4IP Concert, Brisbane

79)

Breakfast at Sweethearts

1974, Armidale Jim in make-up, photo courtesy of Gary Skinner.

1974 The backyard of the house at Kentucky, Steve the van and dog. Photo courtesy of Gary Skinner.

August, 1980 Capitol Theatre, Sydney

81)

Tour 1981 Don, Jane & Jim

January, 1981 Tasmania, photo Phil Small collection.

(82

US Tour 1981 Ian Moss Rhode Island

83)

April, 1982 Circus Animals, Wentworth Park

(84

New Years Day, 1981 Myer Music Bowl, Melbourne.

85)

UK Tour, 1982 Relaxing with Tour Manager Mark Pope.

1982 Paris Underground

1982 On tour in Paris

1982 At the hotel, London.

87)

(88

London, 1982   Jim tries his hand at interior decorating. From Left Gerry Georgettis, Jim, Mark Pope & Harry Parsons.

Backstage Sweetwater Festival, New Zealand

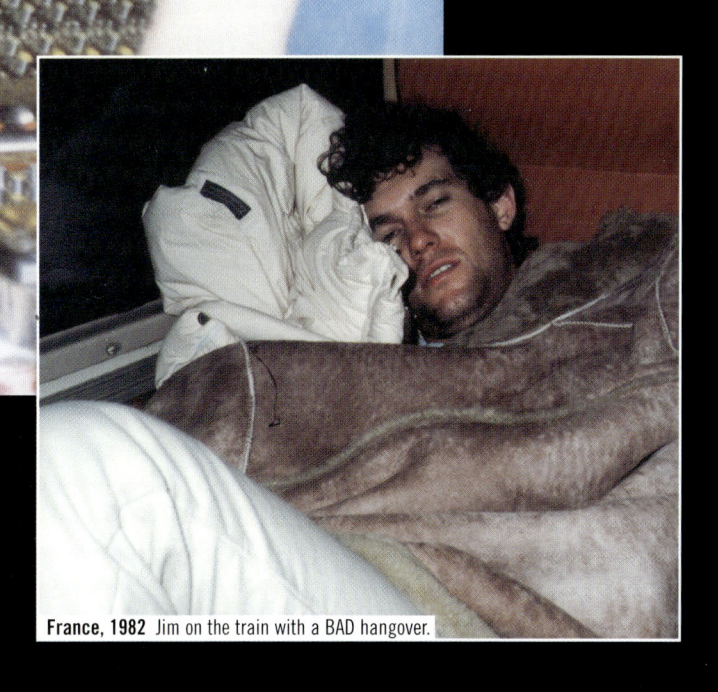

Backstage Sweetwater Festival, New Zealand

(90

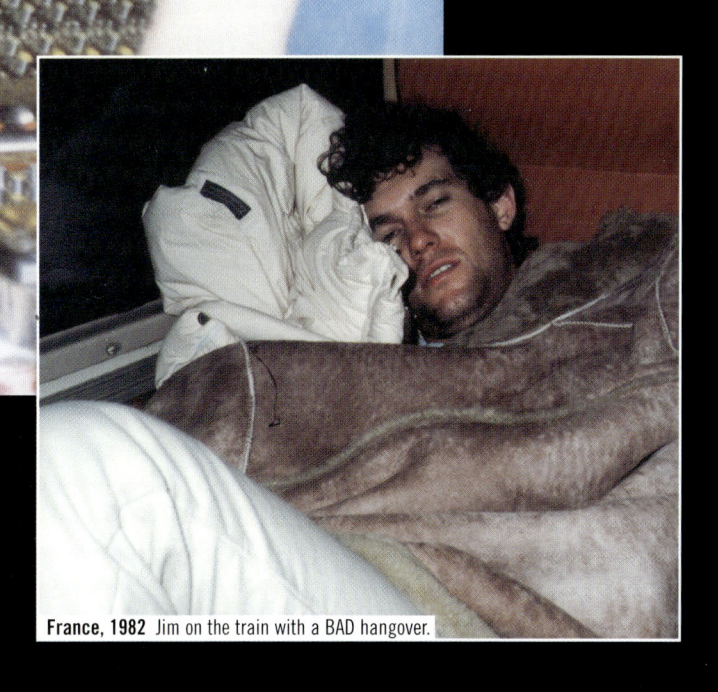

France, 1982 Jim on the train with a BAD hangover.

1983 Ian, Germany

Norway, 1982 Ferry, Copenhagen

91)

Norway, 1982 From left, Rod Willis, Jim, Steve & Phil.

Germany, 1983 It can get lonely on the road.

93)

Germany, 1983 Checking the finances.

Paris, 1982 On the Underground

(94

Sydney, 1983 Jim with Renee Geyer, Last Stand Tour.

U.K. Tour, 1982 Hammersmith, Odeon Slade Tour.

95)

Wyong N.S.W, 1998 Photo shoot

[1980]

East

THE YEAR BEGINS WITH THE BAND PLANNING THEIR THIRD ALBUM, THEIR LIVE REPUTATION IMMENSE, AND THE COUNTRY'S RECORD BUYERS AND RADIO PROGRAMMERS WAITING WITH EAGER ANTICIPATION FOR THE BAND'S NEXT RECORD.

(96

That album is a huge success and the band quickly record their follow-up, a live album which provides evidence of the band's legendary onstage reputation. This is undoubtedly the greatest year in the band's development, both on stage and record, creating standards by which they would be measured for the rest of their days.

JANUARY 1980

The band is presented with a gold disc for their debut album and a platinum disc for *Breakfast At Sweethearts.*

The Australian Guitar Album, featuring Ian is at last released, on the Razzle label. The album also includes songs from Kevin Borich, Mario Millo, Lobby Loyd, Mick Elliott, Ian Miller, Phil Manning, Russell Smith, Harvey James, among others. The Ian Moss track *The Dummy* was recorded more than 12 months earlier and was written by Ian with Don. It's a complex song, sung by Ian and featuring a variety of guitar textures, showing a strong Jeff Beck influence. With the exception of Jimmy, the other members of Cold Chisel also play on the track. This song was also released as a B-side to Ian's Mr Rain solo single in the late '80s.

"...So the standout track for me is Ian Moss' The Dummy, very much a Cold Chisel number but with Ian really exploring the different tonal capabilities of his guitar, in first a muted solo, then his typical rip-roaring Chisel style."

(RAM MAGAZINE'S MICHAEL SMITH)

Jimmy makes an appearance on the Rude Dudes album by Ray Arnott, along with his brother John.

JANUARY 4	Arkaba Hotel, Adelaide, 940 people
JANUARY 5	Arkaba Hotel, Adelaide, 1245 people
JANUARY 9	Blacktown RSL, 984 people
JANUARY 10	Shortland Rock
JANUARY 11	Bondi Lifesaver, 1113 people.

This was most likely the show at which the live version of *Knocking On Heaven's Door* included on the bonus single with early copies of the East album was recorded.

JANUARY 12	Family Inn, 1007 people
JANUARY 12	Choirgirl is No. 13 on the national chart. (No. 10 last week)
JANUARY 13	Penrith Leagues, 742 people
JANUARY 14	Sundowner Hotel, 825 people
JANUARY 15	Bellevue Hotel, Tuncurry, 850 people
JANUARY 17	Pips, Brisbane, 517 people
JANUARY 18	Surfair, 1039 people
JANUARY 19	Patch, Coolangatta, 1416 people
JANUARY 20	Lismore RSL, 619 people
JANUARY 21	Sth. Grafton RSL, 850 people
JANUARY 22	Doyalson RSL, 760 people
JANUARY 23	Ocean Beach Hotel, 350 people
JANUARY 24	Sylvania Hotel, 849 people
JANUARY 25	Manly Vale with Matt Finish, 812 people
JANUARY 26	Selinas, 1175 people
JANUARY 27	Wollongong Leagues Club, 990 people
JANUARY 30	Captain Cook Hotel, 750 people
JANUARY 31	Council Club, (Victoria), 800 people
FEBRUARY 1	Village Green, 700 people
FEBRUARY 2	Kingston Rock

FEBRUARY 3	Soveriegn Hotel, 631 people
FEBRUARY 4	Caledonian Hotel, Wonthaggi
FEBRUARY 5	Colendina Hotel, 415 people
FEBRUARY 6	Bendigo Surround, 581 people
FEBRUARY 7	Wagga Australian Rules Club, 595 people
FEBRUARY 8	Albury Civic Hall
FEBRUARY 9	Lilac Town Hall, Goulburn
FEBRUARY 10	Nowra RSL
FEBRUARY 12	Jolly Frog Hotel, Sydney, 700 people
FEBRUARY 13	Shortland Rock Concert (cancelled)

FEBRUARY 15 - MANLY VALE

When venue management announce that punters were not to climb on the tables, Jimmy tells the audience that this is to be the last time the band will ever play here again (obviously confident that the band is moving to bigger and better things !) so "why the hell don't you get up on the tables and enjoy yourselves ?"

The band did play there again in April.

FEBRUARY 16	Highway Hotel, Parramatta
FEBRUARY 20	Westlands Hotel, Whyalla
FEBRUARY 22	Arkaba Hotel

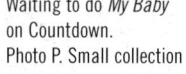

97)

Waiting to do *My Baby* on Countdown.
Photo P. Small collection

FEBRUARY 23	Arkaba Hotel
FEBRUARY 25	Bexley North Hotel
FEBRUARY 26	Doyalson RSL
FEBRUARY 27	Comb'n' Cutter
FEBRUARY 29	Bondi Lifesaver

MARCH

Continue recording *East* album at Paradise Studios, including Jimmy's *Payday in a Pub* and *Hands Out Of My Pocket*. Don explained later that this song was only ever played once - the take that was released eventually on the *Teenage Love* album - and that Jimmy could be heard calling out the arrangement on the original master tape. The song is about a cousin of Jimmy's who committed suicide after being forcibly returned to her family from a religious cult.

"Well there were no demos, it was pretty much hashed in the studio. Once we'd got on a roll with the writing we knew we were onto something really special for the sake of ourselves, I don't think it occurred to anybody whether that would translate to sales or not."

(Don talking to Billy Pinnell in 1991)

The last song recorded was Ian's *Never Before*, after which the band heads overseas for holidays, leaving Mark Opitz to work on the sequencing of the album. Particularly effective was the way many of the songs appear to flow into each other, unifying the many diverse styles present on the album.

Also recorded at this time was *The Party's Over*, one of the first songs written by Don, and eventually issued on a bonus single with the early pressings of *East*. This song would also pop up occasionally in the live sets, showing up in the German '82 shows as well as being included on the live *Swingshift* album and later on *Teenage Love*.

Interestingly, a different version of this song was released on a German-only compilation album *Northbound Train* in 1982 (hence it's return to the set at that time). This 'new' version was produced by Peter Walker, not Mark Opitz (who produced the March '80 version) and although never released in Australia the 'German' version has some very nice touches from the guitar and drums and a very atmospheric feel. Well worth seeking out if you are a fan of what Don calls Chisel's "pseudo sophisticated" stylings.

MARCH 1	Fairfield Hotel, 856 people
MARCH 3 - 14	Recording third album
MARCH 15	La Trobe Valley Festival, with Mother Goose, The Saints, Mondo Rock OR Australian Crawl, OL' 55 and local band Academy Harvest. The show costs $8 for advance tickets or $10 at the door, starts at noon and runs until midnight.
MARCH 16	Woolongong Leagues Club
MARCH 17-28	Recording
MARCH 27	Comb 'n' Cutters
MARCH 29	Bondi Lifesavers
MARCH 29	Family Inn (Afternoon)
MARCH 30-31	Recording

August 1980
John Swan with Cold Chisel, Capitol Theatre

APRIL

The band continues recording at Paradise Studios where for four weeks they have exclusive use of the studio 24 hours a day. Mark Opitz has arranged this (previously unknown for an Australian band) luxury.

In the Sydney suburb at Woolloomooloo, Paradise Studios is a double story ex-warehouse renovated with elegant wood panelling. It features (aside from recording facilities) a recreation room with pool table, pinball machine and TV and abathroom with showers, a sauna and a giant Jacuzzi spa bath.

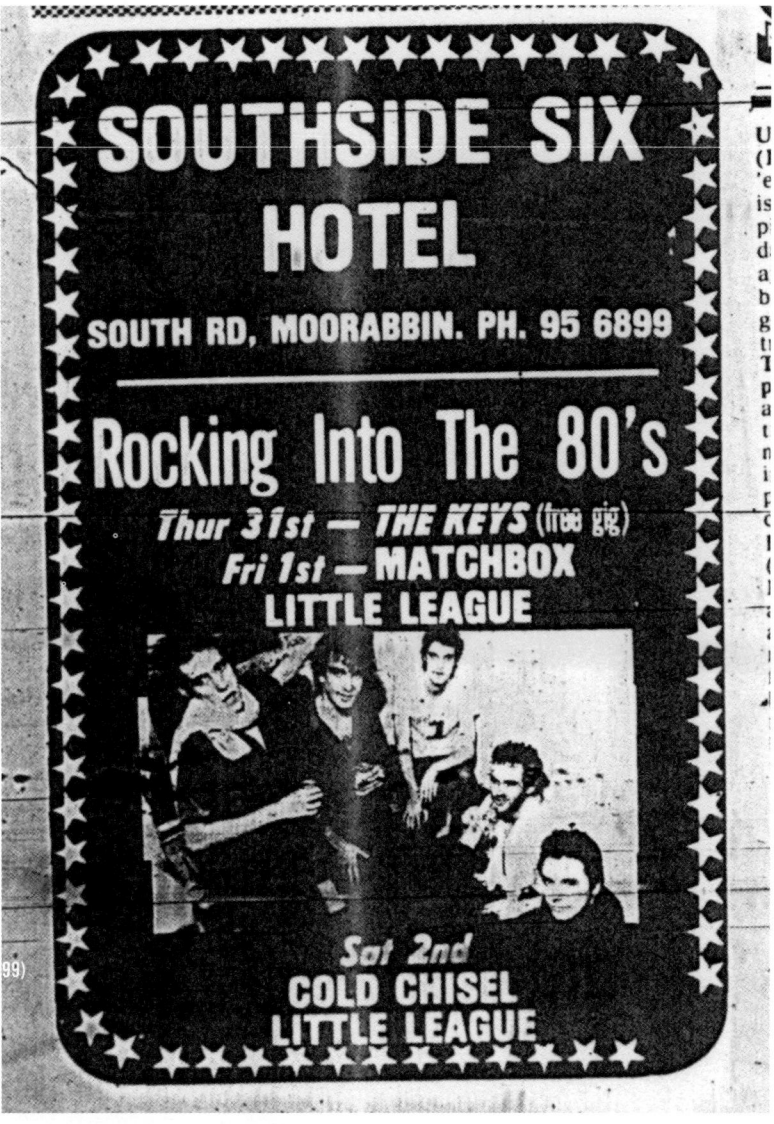

The studio was off-limits for four weeks to anybody not directly involved with the band. Reports suggest that the band's enthusiasm in the studio was infectious and the Jacuzzi was used for many a late night frolic.

APRIL 5   Bondi Lifesavers, 1,300 people

APRIL 12 - MANLY VALE

960 people

This show is filmed as a live promo for the album. The footage shows the band during a very exciting point in its development, having enjoyed success with its second album and about to release a new album they knew was by far the best thing they had done. Even the way the older songs are played shows that it's not just the new songs. The band had grown in so many ways in the previous 18 months they are almost unrecognisable musically. The live versions of the new songs such as *Star Hotel* have something special, a raw power and intensity, which

could not be captured on the album. This show is a wonderful document of the point when Cold Chisel became the best band in the country, but had not yet enjoyed the mass success that would follow almost immediately after the release of *East*. A still from the *Goodbye* clip from this show was used for the cover of *Swingshift*.

Video set list: Cheap Wine/ Rising Sun/ Best Kept Lies/ Shipping Steel/ Choirgirl/ Star Hotel/ Merry-Go-Round/ Knocking On Heaven's Door/ Goodbye Astrid

APRIL 12

On the day that the album is completed long time Chisel roadies and friends, Alan Dallow and Billy Rowe, were killed when the equipment van they were driving while working for Swanee smashed into a tree and burst into flames. Dallow was engaged to Jimmy's sister Linda and lived with her and their young son. Jimmy had met Dallow years earlier when he had jumped in to help him in a fight in the Larg's Pier days. Immediately after the accident the conscious Dallow refused assistance until his unconscious friend Rowe was freed. Both burned to death.

APRIL 13   Brighton Hotel, support Dirty Alice featuring former Cold Chisel bassist Les Kaczmarek. Don Walker leaves for the USA.

APRIL 18   Ian, Phil and Steve leave for the UK.

MAY

The band set up a trust fund for the children of their two former roadies Bill Rowe and Alan Dallow.

"It's been a very emotional time for the band", said manager Rod Willis.

"They were not paid employees by any means, they were part of the Chisel family. They starved with the band in the early days. We could never pay them properly for their sacrifices because it's only now that we're making money.

"All we can do for them now is set up funds for their children." (Rowe had a 12-month-old daughter and Dallow a two-year-old boy.)

The band members are holidaying overseas, Jim in Tokyo, while Ian, Phil and Steve are travelling together through South-East Asia and planning to meet up with Jimmy in London.

Don Walker is in America, where he met and chatted with Bruce Springsteen (they were both staying in the same hotel) in addition to visiting Hugh Hefner's Playboy mansion where he played pinball, and checked out Hefner's bedroom full of sexual devices. Later reports had Don heading towards New Orleans.

At the end of April Don flew to Paris from New York and booked into a small hotel on the Isle St Louise. A couple of days later he returned to the hotel after an afternoon's sightseeing and beer drinking in the sidewalk cafes to find Ian Moss walking out of the hotel door. Ian, Phil and Steve had caught a train from London to Paris, Ian leaving the other two with luggage at the station while he scouted for accommodation. Ian had walked a half a mile or so with no luck and was just leaving the hotel having been told there were no vacancies there either when Don walked in the door. Don had not told the others of his intention to go to Paris.

MAY 8	Don Walker returns from the USA.

MAY 9

Cheap Wine / Rising Sun single is released.

The A-side is undoubtedly one of Don Walker's finest commercial songs and it is added to radio playlists around the country. *Rising Sun*, one of Jimmy's better songs, tells of his desire to find Jane in Japan and "steal her right back again". The single is a national Top 10 hit and represents a new standard of both songwriting and recording for the band.

"...Another excellent song from Mr. Walker, a stunning vocal performance from Jimmie (sic) Barnes, the band cooks and the production is good. This track may not please some of the die-hard head-bashers but will certainly broaden their appeal via the airwaves."

(RAM MAGAZINE, JUNE 13)

JUNE/JULY/AUG	Youth In Asia Tour - 64 dates in 15 major cities in 88 days playing to 120,000 people.
JUNE 2	Bexley Nth Hotel, 983 people

JUNE 2

East, the band's third studio LP is released. The first 10,000 copies come with a bonus live single of *Knocking' On Heaven's Door/The Party's Over* (studio version). The album debuts at No. 44 in the national charts. Jim Barnes said that the album name was aimed at the American market, "Relating Australia to South East Asia makes the place sound a bit more mysterious and appealing."

The album features twelve songs, written by all members of the band as pre-release reports had suggested. In contrast to the previous album (nearly everything on this album is in contrast to the previous one!) the band had plenty of time to experiment in the studio and it is obvious that this is a well thought-out album with a lot of depth, both musically and lyrically. It set new standards for an Australian recording. The attention to detail and variety of styles is what hits you immediately. In the '70s Australian records had been about the artist capturing their live set on record. This was an album that stood alone with no concession given to the live show.

(100

STUNNING CHISEL!

COLD CHISEL

East
(Elektra)

So maybe it comes down to your definition of hope. Just something that politicians and second hand car selesmen deal in? Something only hippies hold for the human race? The man who co-starred in all those *Road To . . . .* movies? Cold Chisel's songs have a double spirit theme of shattered idealism and desperate hope. The whole world might collapse but as Bruce Springsteen put it: "it ain't no sin to be glad you're alive."

And so life goes on:
Once I smoked a Danneman cigar,
drove a foreign car,
baby that was years ago.
I left it all behind.
Had a friend, I heard she died, on a needle she was crucified,
baby that was years ago.

Dutch Record Sleve
Courtesy of Phil Shoppee

The next thing that hits you is the songs - the simple pleasure of hearing such well-crafted songs that you can't wait to hear again. The only thing that stops you from playing one song again is the anticipation that the next track might be even better! It's that kind of an album. No wonder the band was just brimming with confidence when they did return to the road.

Don Walker described it thus:

"This may sound silly but what you are looking at is the sudden magical involvement of the band in our music."

East was the only album where all members of the band wrote and contributed songs. In 1991 Billy Pinnell asked Don if the number of songwriters in the band had ever been a problem.

"No I don't think so. My view was that if there are five songwriters in the band, everyone should get a look in to the extent that they want to. I hadn't

noticed that that was the only one that all five got on."

Reviews were predictably gushing:

"...Anyway you look at it it's a stunning album, the sort of album that Cold Chisel have promised since their first...

"Walker has a strong street corner sensibility and romanticism which mirrors those that live the rock'n'roll lifestyle, documenting it with cockiness, comedy, sadness and quixotic. Characters and scenarios come alive. You can feel the grey loneliness of a prisoner in Four Walls and Tomorrow, the bleak worry of those forced onto the dole queues, or the average Joe Citizen's love/hate relationship with Ita Buttrose, the nation's most admired woman.

...It's exhilirating how Chisel have matured since Breakfast. Bravado is something they've never lacked, but now that audacity is supplemented by controlled dynamics with majesty in their concentrated attack.

The way Moss and Barnes have finally started to relax within the studio to exercise more authority is probably the strongest asset of the LP."

(CHRISTIE ELIEZER, JUKE MAGAZINE)

"The playing on the album is mind-boggling - Barnes singing like never before, Moss playing like never before, and Walker, Small and Prestwich all achieving better and better results from their instruments.

"...East has something quite different, quite unique in Australian music. In taking the diverse influences of Otis Redding, Elvis Presley, Sam Cooke, the Who, the Faces and the Shadows and applying this sensibility to an Australian context Cold Chisel have done something remarkable. With East Cold Chisel have soul."

(ED ST. JOHN, ROLLING STONE)

The cover of the album was a collaboration, according to Don Walker in Roadrunner magazine;

"I got the idea of the bathtub and the Marat-Sade rip off. I knew I wanted to fill the whole thing up with certain flavoured bric-a-brac. Jenny (from Chisel's management agency, Dirty Pool) spent about a week getting all the bric-a-brac together out of the antique shops and second hand book shops. There was a certain list of books I wanted and I gave her a list, but once she was on the case and knew the area I was looking at she came back with some wonderful stuff that I would never have thought of."

The album cover was shot at Roger Langford's apartment in Elizabeth Bay, Sydney, the same apartment where the *Cheap Wine* film clip was shot. The back cover was shot on the balcony.

JUNE 3	Family Inn Hotel, 1150 people

JUNE 5 - PARRAMATTA JAIL

(90 min show, 3.30 pm start)

The Willessee current affairs show send a crew to film the band playing *Four Walls* and ask that the band change the set so that is the first song played. The band say they don't mind but tour manager, Chris Bastick is unwilling, as the lighting and sound people were not prepared. This means the TV cameras and lights are there for the first half dozen songs, creating a bizarre atmosphere with their lights and the constant presence of the guards. No one is allowed to stand.

The band, with Jim in headband, open the set with *Standing On The Outside* and play most of the *East* album as well as *Khe Sanh, Shakin' All Over, Home* and *Broken Hearted, Juliet, Conversations, One Long Day, Shipping Steel, Goodbye, Wild Thing*, and *Breakfast At Sweethearts*.

"...It's tighter, more precise, more desperate than ever before...the response this day was by far the best given by the prisoners to any visiting band.

"Who cares about the future of rock'n'roll when we've got Cold Chisel."

(VINCE LOVEGROVE, RAM MAGAZINE)

JUNE 6 - SELINAS, WITH WARD 13

Full house- capacity 2500 people.

"The band powered into the music from Chisel's album East, and everyone knew the words and sang along against the wall of sound from the sound system. There was no contest after the first few songs, the crowd were right up there with the band, urging them on and giving back everything they gave."

JUNE 7	Manly Vale
JUNE 8	Wollongong Leagues
JUNE 9	Captain Cook Hotel, Canberra

Attendance: 960 people. The *East* album goes gold, debuting at No. 44, it was No. 2 the following week and stays in the Top 10 for 26 weeks.

Capitol Theatre, 1980

(102

JUNE 11	Waurn Ponds, Geelong, 525 people
JUNE 12	Village Green, 849 people
JUNE 13	Bombay Rock, 1420 people
JUNE 14	Sentimental Bloke, 600 people- full house
JUNE 15	Queensbury Leagues Club (Cancelled), replaced by the Pier Hotel
JUNE 16	Armidale Hotel
JUNE 18	Melbourne Town Hall, Trinity College Ball
JUNE 20	Arkaba Hotel
JUNE 21	Arkaba Hotel, Adelaide
JUNE 25	Maroubra Seals
JUNE 26	Vicar Of Wakefield
JUNE 27	Sydney University
JUNE 28	Highway Hotel

Waiting to do *My Baby* on Countdown.
Photo P. Small collection.

103)

JUNE 29	Brighton Hotel
JULY 1	Doyalson R.S.L.
JULY 2	Cardiff Workers Club
JULY 3	Kempsey Workers Club
JULY 4	Plantation Hotel (Coffs Harbor)
JULY 5	Playroom, Gold Coast, 1500 people

JULY 7 - FEDERAL HOTEL, BUNDABERG QLD

525 people

"Last Monday night Bundaberg raged to the most exciting rock show ever to explode in the town. Chisel broke out at 10 p.m. with the first track from their current album, East, Standing On The Outside. They were immediately met with raging reactions from the Bundaberg crowd. The audience were immediately blown out by the thunderous, awesome power of the group. I have not heard a tighter rhythm section, crunchier lead guitar and powerful vocal works all rolled into one unified outfit for eons...

"...I have never seen a Bundaberg audience react in such a positive form as last Monday night, as rockers fell over each other bopping and gyrating throughout the venue. After several encores, Cold Chisel finished the gig with a surging, power packed version of Goodbye Astrid. The audience was reluctant to go but after 100 minutes of unadulterated ecstasy the people eventually sifted out completely satisfied that they had got more than their money's worth."

(BUNDABERG NEWS-MAIL)

JULY 8	Park Hall Hotel, Rockhampton, 811 people
JULY 10	House on the Hill ,Cairns
JULY 11	House on the Hill, Cairns

JULY 12 - TOWNSVILLE

Set List- (complete) Standing On The Outside/ Home and Broken Hearted/ Shipping Steel/ I'm Gonna Roll Ya/ Best Kept Lies/ Shakin' All Over/ Never Before/ My Turn To Cry/ Choirgirl/ Juliet/ My Baby/ Rising Sun/ Breakfast At Sweetheart's/ One Long Day/ Cheap Wine/ Khe Sanh/ Conversations/ Star Hotel/ Merry-Go-Round/ Georgia/ Tomorrow/ Knocking On Heaven's Door/ Wild Thing/ Goodbye Astrid

The show opens with an announcement that tonight is the biggest crowd to see an Australian rock act in Townsville. The crowd stands as the band walk on, Jimmy wearing the headband from the *East* album cover. *Standing On The Outside* is the opener

SONIC STORM AS...
Chisel cut into Perth

SOME bozo with a tea-towel wrapped around his head is probably what most people expected, but after watching Cold Chisel perform at The Raffles last Tuesday night, forget the band on the Titanic, this lot should've been playing at Hiroshima.

Chisel are currently the radio and TV darlings with three LPs, and epee in the shops and *East* selling better than the Stones.

for this tour, played with extraordinary power. The sound is immediately balanced and the band falls straight into a tight groove - no signs of first song nerves here! Second song (since 1978!) is still *Home and Broken Hearted*, with its new arrangement (see 'Pooled Resources' tour). *Shipping Steel* has been given a reggae treatment, as heard on *Swingshift*, while *I'm Gonna Roll Ya* is played at a frantic pace, sounding a little basic beside some of the new songs and fresh arrangements of older numbers. Jimmy's announcement that its "fucking nice to play here" receives the expected response before the band leaps into one of the more experimental new songs, *Best Kept Lies*.

Shakin' All Over continues an amazingly diverse opening batch of songs - songs from every album, a '50s cover, reggae and an Ian Moss vocal! The rarely played *Never Before* follows with an extended guitar break - a stunning performance of a song which was never released in live form. *My Turn To Cry* is as powerful as you'd expect. This is Cold Chisel arguably at their prime, and despite the 'pop' overtones of the *East* album, the live performances are still as brutal as ever. If there is a break from the onslaught it's *Choirgirl*- but this doesn't last long as Jimmy yells "come on you fuckers, make some noise" during the intro to *Juliet* which stands up

surprisingly well in this set. More songs from the new album follow, before the band play *Breakfast At Sweethearts*, which is an improved version from those heard in the previous year. The next installment of *One Long Day* follows. Long the centrepiece of Chisel shows, this version features some truly virtuoso playing from Ian in the blues intro and this epic arrangement is similar to that which appears on *Swingshift*.

Cheap Wine is introduced as the new single and quickly followed by *Khe Sanh*, while *Conversations* gets the same guitar intro as on *Swingshift* - another song which seems to have grown another leg when played with the band's new confidence. "I don't know how many people in this audience are out of work and how many are just generally pissed off. Here's one for yous" is the intro for perhaps the most important of the new songs, *Star Hotel*. *Merry-Go-Round* follows, this is one of the songs which will stay in the live set until the end, and powerful performances like this one is the reason why. Here it closes the main set, although there is never any doubt about an encore as the audience claps loudly and call for more from the moment the band walk off the stage.

(104

The encore begins with a passionate *Georgia* from Ian and Don, after which Jimmy tells the over-enthusiastic audience "one thing first, the next cunt that throws another thing up here is gonna get fuckin' a mic stand down their throat". *Tomorrow* restores the pace and the show is completed with the multi vocals of *Knocking' On Heaven's Door* (Ian, Don, Jim), the excess of *Wild Thing* (which includes "just give it to me on the PA stack here" and reggae interlude) and finally *Goodbye Astrid*. In any discussion about when Cold Chisel were at their prime, this period must be right up there.

JULY 14	Mackay. Theatre Royal
JULY 16	Hervey Bay, 'The Place'
JULY 17	Surfair
JULY 18	Toowoomba Institute
JULY 19	Cloudlands

Recording Swingshift Capitol Theatre, August 1980.

105)

JULY 20

This is a day off and as the band travel down the coast from Brisbane to Lismore they stop in at the Music Farm recording studio where Midnight Oil are recording their *Bird Noises* E.P. As related by Peter Garrett in the *Last Stand* film, members of both bands jam into the early hours of the morning, despite the heavy schedules of both.

JULY 21 - BUNGALOO BOWLING CLUB (LISMORE)

Rod Willis and WEA's David Sinclair leave for America carrying the band's albums to seek a US record deal. Sinclair recalls that the general response (from US record companies) was a desire to record the band over there as they felt they could do it better, although Sinclair also put this down to the fact that the American A&R guys received a lot more credit if they could be seen to be developing an act for the American market, as opposed to simply finding a band ready to go.

JULY 23	Dapto Leagues Club, 1150 people
JULY 24	Sylvania Hotel
JULY 25	Family Inn
JULY 26	Chequers, 1750 people
JULY 28	Sundowner Hotel, 1300 people
JULY 29	Record the *Misfits* track at Paradise studios for use in a documentary about unemployed youth.

JULY 31 - BOMBAY ROCK   W/SNEAK PREVIEW

"...Barnes is the rock voice. No-one sings Heartbreak Hotel like Elvis. Barnes does the definite update. And Shaking All Over. Hang in there with your own personalised sixties hook line... Khe Sanh, Cheap Wine. Goodbye... Ian Moss still spattering Hendrix, Page impressions and all that late sixties earth shake any self-respecting metal lead recalls...Lyrical keyboard, lyrical vocal, and Choirgirl that bit special. Barnes of the asbestos throat cools it out. Choirgirl and My Baby. Rare moments in the endless mix of heavy metal R & B spilling a power that rips through eighty minutes and encores harder than it started out. And Barnes is magical. Knocking at Heaven's door.

Flashing a spirit one part Jim Morrison, one part tequila soaked bandicoot. Maybe words don't make sound and vision. Maybe you shoulda been there. Or were. Or will be. Chisel make great rock."

(JON OSSHER, JUKE MAGAZINE)

AUGUST 1   Ferntree Gully Hotel

AUGUST 2 - SOUTH SIDE SIX WITH LITTLE LEAGUE

The band also perform *My Baby* on Countdown.

"To me the most exciting rock'n'roll always went far beyond entertainment. As soon as rock'n'roll becomes just entertainment, it's going to die.

"But I think it should be entertainment too, I'd hate to ever become a 'whinging issues' band."

(Don Walker, Talking to Melbourne Age, Aug 2)

AUGUST 3	Pier Hotel (Frankston)
AUGUST 4	Horsham Theatre
AUGUST 6	Argent Hotel (Broken Hill)
AUGUST 7	Westlands Inn (Whyalla)
AUGUST 8	Thebarton Town Hall (Adelaide)
AUGUST 8	

East is No. 3 on the chart, (No. 2 previous week) after 8 weeks in the chart. Cheap Wine is at No.36 after 11 weeks.

AUGUST 11 - PERTH CONCERT HALL

"Cold Chisel put on a sweaty, unconventional performance at the Concert Hall on last Monday night and thrilled the capacity audience of mostly very young fans to the hilt...

"It wasn't till the two genuine encores, lasting half an hour, that Cold Chisel really showed they have what it takes to be one of the hottest bands in the country.

"In this section emerged the shows unexpected highlights - guitarist Ian Moss' vocal rendition of Georgia to Don Walker's keyboard and Billy Rogers' sax accompaniment, and the whole band's Knocking On Heaven's Door..."

(JULIE ZILKO, WEEKEND NEWS, PERTH)

AUGUST 12	Perth Concert Hall
AUGUST 13	Perth Concert Hall
AUGUST 14	Perth Concert Hall

AUGUST 16 - PALAIS THEATRE, MELBOURNE

(with Australian Crawl & Matt Finish) sold out: 2600 people

"...They put everything they have into their music and the result is sensational. With occasional help from a brilliant saxophonist and a raging harmonica player, the set just got better and better.

"...The concert lasted five hours, Cold Chisel played two and a half hours and in my opinion that's value for money.

"Molly reckons Cold Chisel are Australia's best act. For once I have to agree with him."

(TOORAK TIMES)

AUGUST 18	Caulfield Institute

(106

(107)

Solitaire, which is given the *Georgia* treatment from Ian, Don and Billy Rogers.

A double album is released in late February of the following year and receives excellent reviews:

"...Last of the Riverboats is given a classic treatment from Jim Barnes. He gives the song more gut level passion than the original ever hinted at...Solitaire is one of the sets highpoints. A dirge that is given an admirable treatment by Ian Moss (vocal, guitar), Don Walker (piano), and Bill Rogers bittersweet sax."

(JOHN DI MASE, JUKE)

A video has also been issued of this show.

AUGUST 20	Riverina College, Wagga
AUGUST 21	Hellenic Club, Canberra

AUGUST 22 - COMB'N'CUTTER

The standard set list for this part of the tour ran: Conversations / Juliet / Shipping Steel / Rising Sun / Never Before / Choirgirl / My Turn To Cry / Best Kept Lies / I'm Gonna Roll Ya / Breakfast At Sweethearts / Don't Let Go / My Baby / Star Hotel / Daskarzine / Four Walls / One Long Day / Standing On The Outside / Cheap Wine / Khe Sanh / The Door / Merry Go Round / Long As I Can See The Light / Ita / Knocking On Heavens Door / Tomorrow / Goodbye / The Party's Over / Wild Thing

AUGUST 23	Stardust Hotel

Rod Willis returns from the US.

AUGUST 26	Florida Hotel
AUGUST 27	Cardiff Workers Club
AUGUST 29	Capitol Theatre. Second last gig of the tour, *East* has gone double platinum, selling 100,600 copies.

AUGUST 30

Capitol Theatre, with Mental As Anything and INXS. Attendance: 2483 people. Much of the *Swingshift* album was recorded at this show. (A poster for this show can be found inside the Chisel CD)

Set list- Conversations / Juliet / Shipping Steel / Rising Sun/ Never Before / Choirgirl / My Baby / Misfits / Star Hotel / Daskarzine / Four Walls / One Long Day / Standing On The Outside / Khe Sanh / Don't Let Go / Merry Go Round / Long As I Can See The Light / Ita / Knocking On Heavens Door / Tomorrow / Goodbye / The Party's Over / Wild Thing

AUGUST 19

Andrew Durant Memorial Concert, Jimmy, Don and Ian perform at this show for fellow Adelaide musician Andy Durant who died of cancer in May. Between them they appear on no less than 11 songs on the album (extra songs are on the CD and video versions).

Vocally Jimmy is impressive on *Goodtimes* and *Last of the Riverboats*, during which he smokes a cigarette as he sings. Ian plays some lovely guitar on *Wasted Words* and *Song For the Road*. *Mighty Rock* has Jimmy really firing and the night is completed with an extended jam on the Chisel arrangement of *Knocking' On Heaven's Door*. One of the highlights is

The band was joined onstage by saxophonist Billy Rogers (ex-Dragon) and harmonica player David Blight (who played in a blues band called Nightflyers with Phil Small's brother David on guitar). Both were close friends of the band and played on a number of their studio recordings.

"Talk about rare moments of joy with the right crowd...by their own admission and the audiences this was one of Cold Chisel's best nights on the current tour. A long set that started way up and miraculously just kept on building. Part of it was the skilful addition of outside elements: the guest solos from David Blight's harmonica and Billy Roger's (sic) sax, and the incredible rendition of Star Hotel complete with adrenalin-pumping newsreel footage of that Riot-Of-The-Year...But the heart of it was the band. Five parts of one incredibly fit musical body, tour-hardened and album confident that never faltered, never slackened the intensity."

(GREG TAYLOR, RAM MAGAZINE)

"Most of the album (Swingshift) was recorded at Sydney's Capitol Theatre on the last night of our Youth In Asia Tour. It was a really hot night. Everything just happened, you know? Everyone fired."

(Jimmy, talking to Vince Lovegrove, Dec 1980)

AUGUST 31 - HOADLEYS BATTLE OF THE SOUNDS

East has sold a staggering 100,600 copies earning it double platinum status.

SEPTEMBER	*Cheap Wine /My Turn To Cry* single released in the U.K. *My Baby/Misfits* is released in Australia.
SEPTEMBER 19	*East* sits at No.1 after 14 weeks in the chart, ahead of AC/DC's *Back In Black* which had only been out for 8 weeks.

SEPTEMBER 25 - MELBOURNE

3XY Under 18's concert: 6,000 teenagers.

"It's been a long time since I've seen Chisel perform and they have certainly progressed. Seeing them in a concert situation is ideal because it gives the band the opportunity to flex its muscles in a conductive atmosphere.

"In the hour and a half they pulled all their best moves. Good song after good song came tumbling forth. It was a reminder to me (of) just how many good songs this band have composed.

"Most of the set comprised of material from East understandably. Upfront, Jim Barnes stalks the stage with a menacing look on his face. His army pants and Asian headband give the boy a guerrilla image that suits his delivery. Behind him the band is firing. The rhythm section of Phil Small and Steve Prestwich is always exquisite. Surprisingly the man tickling the ivories, Don Walker, took a comparatively low-key stance. On guitar there is the old master, Ian Moss. Moss' performance was superlative. His prowess continues to grow. His fluid lines were sheer joy.

"The songs? They belt through Star Hotel, Standing On The Outside, Khe Sanh, Ita, and My Baby. Each receives thunderous applause from the crowd. The highlights? I'd have to say their version of the old standard Don't Let Go was a joyful surprise. Choirgirl and Cheap Wine were the high points though. These are songs that set the spine tingling for sure."

(JUKE'S JOHN DIMASE)

SEPTEMBER 30   Civic Hotel

OCTOBER 5 - DARWIN AMPITHEATRE

The biggest live performance in Darwin's history (previous record held by Rolf Harris!) and members of the 6,000 audience climb on stage to bow to Ian and Jimmy. The band has to stop the show when the stage is bombarded with flowers and ferns, returning to complete their set when the crowd had settled a little.

While in Darwin the band take the opportunity to put in a few surprise appearances at some of the local hotels. Peter Moss recalls that one favourite 'trick' was to wait until the resident band was taking a break, then walk on and play on their instruments, quickly impressing the audience and making the remainder of the evening much more difficult for the other band.

OCTOBER 8   Mt Isa Civic Centre

"Wednesday's concert, which started with a reserved and unresponsive Mt Isan audience, ended in drunken ecstasy for the majority."

ARREST AFTER ROCK RAMPAGE

● From Page 1

A 19-year-old youth was charged with causing malicious damage and was bailed to appear in Newcastle Court on January 5.

Police said the girl, who was taken to hospitl by ambulance, broke her arm accidentally.

The crowd of about 1,500 went on a wild rampage at the rock concert.

A youth suffering lacerations to the head was taken by ambulance to hospital.

He is believed to have hit his head on the footpath outside the concert hall after being knocked to the ground in a brawl.

During the concert five cars were stolen from the Palais Royale's car park and nearby streets.

Two of the cars

OCTOBER 9 - MT ISA CIVIC CENTRE

"The band is dynamic live and with material supplied by the classic East album, plays only superb songs. The encore set includes several classic numbers from the late 60s and early 70s period which whipped the crowd into a frenzy. Among those were the timeless Hendrix master pieces Wild Thing and Purple Haze which gave guitarist Ian Moss ample room to demonstrate his enormous talents.

"Also included was Bob Dylan's immortal Knockin' On Heaven's Door and Creedence Clearwater's As Long As I Can See The Light - sure to be favourites wherever this band plays..."

(DAILY PRESS, MT. ISA)

OCTOBER 18

Tickets go on sale for the Perth show and sell out in four and a half-hours. An estimated 5,500 people turn up on the first day of ticket sales.

OCTOBER 21   Princess Theatre Melbourne, 3XY Concert

OCTOBER 24 - PERTH

Entertainment Centre (capacity audience of 8,000)

"Cold Chisel proved that it was Australia's premier rock band at its Entertainment Centre performance last night...

"...Many of the crowd were on their feet from the start. But by the end of the concert the ushers seemed to have lost control of the enthusiastic audience and their frantic hand-waving and torch-flashing seemed to be in vain."

(WEST AUSTRALIAN)

OCTOBER 26   Don Walker goes to the U.S. to finalise details of the band's overseas record deal.

NOVEMBER

"Cold Chisel's live album Swing Shift, which was due for release in November has been pushed back to February/March 1981. The rescheduling is due to the success of East which has now sold more than 150,000 copies in this country and is still selling six thousand copies a week...

"Obviously the thing most on the minds of the Chisel camp is the long awaited overseas deal. They're very close to signing it; keyboardsman Don Walker is in America at the moment to finish off negotiations."

(MUSIC PRESS)

SUMMER OFFENSIVE TOUR
SUPPORT NO FIXED ADDRESS
NOVEMBER 30 ROUNDHOUSE, SYDNEY

The band play to a full house of 3500 people - previous house record, 1700.

"Our support band, No Fixed Address, were nearly kicked out of the Roundhouse for being Aborigines, soon after they walked offstage - after wiping out three and a half thousand people."

(Don Walker)

The band's overseas deal is finally signed (after more than two years of false reports and rumours). The band signed with Elektra for the US and Canada, with *East* to be released there on 14 February, 1981. The U.S version is to include *Khe Sanh*, at the expense of Ita and *Four Walls*. The back cover photograph will be replaced with an alternative group shot.

Rod Willis also announced that the band had signed with LA booking agency ICM and was expected to make its first tour there in March-April 1981. It was reported that Elektra would decide which track should be lifted as a single, but this would "obviously be a toss up between *Choirgirl* and *Cheap Wine*."

PALAIS ROYALE RAMPAGE: YOUTHS DANCE ON TABLES AT COLD CHISEL CONCERT

● Cold Chisel singer . . . Jimmy Burns.

GIRL HURT AT WILD ROCK SHOW

By DICK SWANTON

A GIRL broke an arm and a youth was arrested in wild scenes at a concert by top rock band Cold Chisel last night.

Police were called to the Palais Royale after the ceiling of the 1,000-seat hall was damaged.

Broken glass and empty bottles littered the floor.

● Continued Page 2

Concert Rampage . . . the Palais Royale.

DECEMBER 2 - NEWCASTLE PALAIS, CABERAT

1700 people

Cold Chisel almost double the house record with a crowd that had queued around the block all day. The venue is closed down after the gig, with one girl breaking her arm in the crush and much bad publicity surrounding the whole event.

The band also announces that they have signed a recording deal with WEA's Elektra Records for the USA and Canada. The band is signed for the release of its next six albums.

DECEMBER 3 - TAMWORTH TOWN HALL

1035 people

"On Wednesday night they filled the Tamworth Town Hall, an ancient echo chamber with 900 plus fans who had started to queue long before the doors opened at 7pm.

Chisel was the first major act to perform in the Town hall for about two years and the kids, starved of live music, eagerly paid $5 a piece to see them.

It was no doubt a little nostalgic for Chisel's keyboard player and main songwriter, Don Walker.

Bogislav won the local Battle of the Sounds competition in 1970 at Tamworth Town Hall."

(Peter Cochrane)

In other news, the band's plans to stage a New Year's Eve concert on the grounds of the Cronulla Rugby League Club are turned down by liquor licensing authorities.

DECEMBER 4   Glenn Innes Town Hall

DECEMBER 5 - INVERELL TOWN HALL

After this show Jim and Don fly back to Sydney to re-record parts of *Khe Sanh* for the American version of the *East* album. Walker told the local papers after the Inverell show:

"The Americans have liked our two previous albums but they claimed the production was below par, or at least, below their standard. But they finally approved of East- and that's going to be our first release in America."

DECEMBER 8   South Grafton R.S.L. 947 people

(110

DECEMBER 9 - PALAIS HOTEL IPSWITCH

716 people.

While waiting for the show that night the band heard the news of John Lennon's death.

"It hit the whole band in the gut", said Don Walker.

"He was an inspiration to everybody-quite apart from his music, just what he represented."

"The band went a bit crazy."

"We threw the normal set out and started with Imagine, which we'd never played before and finished with Twist and Shout."

| DECEMBER 10 | Homestead Hotel Brisbane, 1000 people |
| DECEMBER 11 | Playroom, Gold Coast |

They are a three piece band featuring Budd Judd (guitar), good thinking man's music. — ROBBIE COATES

ARTIST MANAGEMENT
69 Oxford St., Bondi Junction
P.O Box 196 Woollahra NSW 2025

EXCLUSIVE MANAGEMENT REPRESENTATION OF FINE AUSTRALIAN ROCK 'N' ROLL

THE ANGELS COLD CHISEL FLOWERS MENTAL AS ANYTHING

BOOK DIRECT - 02·389 2100

| DECEMBER 12 | Playroom, Gold Coast |
| DECEMBER 13 | Lismore City Hall, 2004 people |

DECEMBER 15

The band are presented with a triple platinum disc for sales of over 150,000 and the band re-signs to WEA Australia. *East* is still in the Top 10 after nearly 25 weeks - it has sold more than 160,000 copies and is still selling 4,000 copies a week.

The band starts doing demos for their next record at Paradise Studios.

DECEMBER 16 - FAMILY INN

1435 people   (There is a poster for this show inside the sleeve of the Chisel CD)

The Governor of Bathurst Goal invites the band to play there at a family day in February. Also, the film clip for *Star Hotel* runs into censorship problems for supposedly giving too one sided a view of the violence between punters and police at the Star Hotel riots, and the clip can't be shown on some shows such as Countdown.

DECEMBER 18 - WOODFULL PAVILION, MELBOURNE SHOWGROUNDS

3910 people

"A recent gig at Melbourne Showgrounds' Centennial Hall saw a stream of fainting boppers hauled from the crowd."

(JENNY HUNTER BROWN)

DECEMBER 20	University of Adelaide, 2800 people
DECEMBER 27	Wollongong Leagues Club
DECEMBER 28	Brighton Hotel
DECEMBER 29	Comb & Cutter (There is a poster for this show inside the sleeve of the Chisel CD.)
DECEMBER 30	Royal Antler
DECEMBER 31	Endeavor Hotel Cronulla

Steve Prestwich, Capitol
Theatre, 1980

(112

UNDERSTANDABLY TURNING THEIR ATTENTIONS TO THE OVERSEAS MARKETS. IN MANY WAYS, THE US TOUR WOULD BE A PIVOTAL POINT IN THE BAND'S CAREER. FOLLOWING A PERIOD OF A NUMBER OF YEARS WHERE THEY HAD TAKEN ALL BEFORE THEM, IT CAUSED MUCH RE-EVALUATION AND EXAMINING OF THEIR POSITION. MEANWHILE, AS FAR AS AUSTRALIAN AUDIENCES WERE CONCERNED, THE BAND COULD DO NO WRONG.

In December of 1980, the band's former manager Vince Lovegrove interviewed Jimmy for Juke magazine and talked about the band's current position:

"At the moment Cold Chisel are sitting precariously on that narrow edge of success that many Australian bands reach after years of hot rocking it around the country.

"The main difference between Cold Chisel and the rest, is that these rough house rockers have taken a slower, steadier, less compromising path.

"The group has never wilted to pressures. It has remained rock steady!

"Mostly, they've remained aloof from the media. There's been the odd occasion when they've agreed to a Countdown debacle, even been pinup stars, , but in the main Chisel have been the anti-pop stars."

The **Summer Offensive** tour continues as the band play to over 102,000 people at 54 shows.

JANUARY 1	Launceston (Tasmania)
JANUARY 3	Geraldton, (WA)
JANUARY 4	Belmont Racecourse
JANUARY 5	Centennial Oval Hall, Albany
JANUARY 8	Bunbury Hotel
JANUARY 9	Belmont Hotel
JANUARY 10	Old Melbourne Hotel
JANUARY 11	Charles Hotel
JANUARY 16	Riverwood Hotel
JANUARY 17	Manly Vale
JANUARY 18	Bruce Stadium, Canberra

Triple 7, Rockbuster Program with Mi-Sex, Mental As Anything, The Reels, True Confessions, Caress Of Steel and Once Cheated.

JANUARY 20	Sandown Park
JANUARY 21	Council Club
JANUARY 22	Pier Hotel
JANUARY 23	Tarmac Hotel
JANUARY 26	Sweetwaters Festival, New Zealand

The band play to 40,000 people and reports suggest they steal the show from Roxy Music.

JANUARY 30	Cloudlands (support by Mr Meaner)

JANUARY

Set List (probably complete) : Standing On The Outside / I'm Gonna Roll Ya / Ita / Shipping Steel / Choir Girl / My Turn To Cry / Misfits/ Merry Go Round / Red House / Best Kept Lies / Juliet / My Baby/ Khe Sanh / Four Walls / One Long Day / Don't Let Go / Cheap Wine / Star Hotel / Rising Sun /Goodbye Astrid /Just How Many Times / Tomorrow / Twist and Shout / Long As I Can See The Light

Although I cannot trace the exact date or venue of this show, it is certainly from the latter part of this tour, and of great interest due to the incredible number of rarities in the set. The band did not have an album to promote. *East* was more than six months behind them and *Swingshift* was not yet released, so they experimented with the set to keep things interesting.

Standing On The Outside is still the show opener, followed by *I'm Gonna Roll Ya* and then we're treated to *Ita*, not played during the Youth In Asia Tour, and not played after this tour. *Shipping Steel* is another song which is being played for the last time on this tour, and it has returned to its more muscular form, without the reggae feel. The next surprise is the very rare *Misfits*, a song I never thought would have been played live. After *Merry Go Round* Jimmy announces the next song as one that they've only played at soundcheck, Jimi Hendrix's *Red House*. By this point it's obvious that you are witnessing a special show, although Moss does have some guitar troubles during *One Long Day* and these are not completely rectified until a few songs later- much to Jimmy's annoyance. He appears to absolutely hate any kind of equipment trouble and can be reduced to anger at simply tuning on stage!

The remainder of the show lacks the special spark present in the early part, until the encores, when all equipment problems are obviously rectified. *Just How Many Times* is played, possibly for the first time since 1978, this version featuring a most impressive extended solo from Ian, with Jimmy showing a side of his vocals rarely seen. Following *Tomorrow* is another surprise, *Twist & Shout*, creating a real party atmosphere. Cold Chisel as a dance band. *As Long As I Can See The Light* rounds off a most entertaining night and leaves this audience knowing that they have witnessed a great band refusing to just go through the motions.

FEBRUARY 16	East is No. 16 on the national chart after 37 weeks.

FEBRUARY 19	Bathurst Jail
FEBRUARY 20	Amoco Hall, Orange
FEBRUARY 21	Griffith
FEBRUARY 27	Apollo (Adelaide)
MARCH 1	Hordern Pavilion
MARCH 5	Wagga

MARCH 7 - FESTIVAL HALL (MELBOURNE)

"I caught the band on stage at Festival Hall Melbourne about two weeks ago and it was without doubt, one of the best live performances I've seen.

"And that's a pretty big statement when you take into account that I've seen AC/DC and Police a couple of times each just since the start of the year.

"It would have been a miracle of modern science to have fitted one more person into Festival Hall and, from the moment Chisel came on stage, everyone was on their feet.

"...The frantic build-up never stopped throughout the whole time Chisel was on stage and the finale - a couple of old rock standards such as Twist and Shout *was stunning.*

"If America has been knocked out by the live gigs AC/DC and Police have staged across the States these past few months, they'll probably never recover from a full-scale Cold Chisel tour."

(TV WEEK)

MARCH 11

Jimmy Barnes and Friends play at Selinas with Heaven, Radiators and Jimmy and the Boys. Jimmy and Friends play a 90 minute set, tickets are $4. This show was not a secret gig, as press releases went out asking to "please hype all media."

MARCH 22 - REGENT THEATRE, COUNTDOWN

Rock Awards. The band play *My Turn To Cry* but at the halfway point of the song they move away from the rehearsed version and into an angry comment on the show, asking where were *Countdown* when the band needed them - "I never saw you at the Largs Pier Hotel, I never saw you in Fitzroy Street" - referring to the period when they were struggling in the pubs and the verse finishes with the comment, "And now you're tryin' to use my face to sell *TV Week*". The performance had by this point reached a standard of intensity never before seen on live TV in this country and finishes with the

(114

115)

band smashing their instruments, giving the impression that vandals have just struck in a well planned hit and run attack!

A stunned and stuck for words Molly Meldrum returns to the podium mumbling something about, "I told you they were a great band live".

For the record, the band took out seven of the 11 categories at the awards. Most Outstanding Achievement In Australian Rock Music, Most Popular Australian Group, Best Australian Album, Most Popular Australian Record (for *East*), Best Australian Recorded Songwriter, as well as Best Australian Producer for Mark Opitz, and Best Australian Record Cover - but failed to appear to collect any, before surprising all with their live appearance. Looking at footage of the performance today, the band's aggressive, full-bodied rock sound displays a tightness and a cohesiveness simply not seen in these days of instant stars and bands with big hits before they have played live. The sound is remarkably good for TV. Ian's guitar sound, even on television is one that most guitarists would kill for, all the more impressive considering that this is a cheap guitar bought specifically for this performance!

In 1991 Billy Pinnell asked Don why the band responded as they did:

"We felt we were in an awkward situation in that these awards had always been a very sort of King Of Pop thing, which was right at the...you know it was an area of music that really had nothing to do with us. And yet we were tipped to win a whole swag of them, so we had the choice of going on and becoming,... you know going on and smiling for the TV cameras and becoming the Kings Of Pop or whatever. Or just ignoring the whole thing which would be like a snub to the voters because I think at that stage the awards were by popular vote so that'd be sort of a snub to people out there who'd put the vote in.

"So we thought we'd go on and do a performance that held something of the violence that people could expect in a live show from time to time. Rather than conforming to the restrictions that generally occur in a huge television production like that. I mean in a huge television production like that you get assistant camera men saying, "Hey scruff, stand over there and don't move" you know? And you get five seconds to do this and that and it's all very carefully scripted and there was a certain amount of enjoyment in blowing all of that apart."

Ian Moss explained the events this way:

"TV Week is a small, almost offensive TV magazine that decided to jump on the bandwagon of rock and roll. We saw the whole thing as genuinely phony.

"Moss added that this was the band's way of telling them "to shove it."

(Monitor, Detroit, Michigan)

COLD CHISEL RUN HOT

AS WE'VE told you before, Cold Chisel's album East is due out in America any day now and I couldn't think of a better time for it to be happening.

I caught the band on stage at Festival Hall in Melbourne about two weeks ago and it was, without a doubt, one of the best live performances I've seen.

And that's a pretty big statement when you take into account that I've seen AC/DC and Police a couple of times each just since the start of this year.

It would have been a miracle of modern science to have fitted one more person into Festival Hall and, from the moment Chisel came on stage, everyone was on their feet.

And the crowd knew every word and beat of every song, not just the tracks Chisel has released as singles.

There were even a few scenes which reminded me of the old days — young girls invading the stage and making a dash for Jimmy Barnes or Ian Moss and, while that might even be a bit abhorrent to the Chisel guys, it was all taken as part of a night that turned out to be good fun and even better rock 'n' roll.

The frantic build-up never stopped throughout the whole time Chisel was on stage and the finale — a couple of old rock standards such as Twist And Shout — was stunning.

If America has been knocked out by the live gigs AC/DC and Police have staged across the States these past few months, they'll probably never recover from a full-scale Cold Chisel tour.

I believe the band is off to the States around May and, in my opinion, there is no way they won't succeed in a big, big way.

Group has big music success

A CAPACITY crowd watched the Australian rock group, Cold Chisel, make almost a clean sweep last night in eight categories of rock music awards at Sydney's Regent Theatre.

Cold Chisel stole the night's major award for most out-

The aftermath of this event led to something of a war of words between the band (Rod Willis) and Countdown host Ian Meldrum, who gave the group a serve during the following week's show, the details of which I won't get into here as it has more to do with politics than music. Apparently, ill feeling between the two parties lasted many years.

The band had in the past been a little more generous to Countdown, aware of the marketing potential the show offered,

"Countdown lets us play to an extra two million potential fans and gives people in the country places a glimpse of us performing. Then, hopefully, they'll try to see us when we come to their town.

"The only drawback is doing the miming. Still, I can do the vocals live, usually, which helps a bit."

Jimmy, TV Week in September 1980.

Jim did refuse to mime *The Time Warp* (can't think why?) with a bunch of other rock personalities on the show.

It is also announced that the band is working on a film soundtrack for the Matt Carroll film *Freedom*, and Ian Moss is planning to work on Richard Clapton's upcoming solo album.

Another project the band was considering at this point involved a documentary - type film, which may have seen the band filmed playing a show in a desert location well known to Ian, about twenty kilometres outside of Alice Springs. It was hoped

that this would coincide with the camel festival, which draws large crowds from all around the centre. One of the reasons for this never taking place may have been Don Walker's concerns about whether the band's music would work in a desert setting, although he even considered having the band play some of the music recorded for the *Speed* soundtrack.

MARCH 23

Swingshift is released locally and *East* is released in the USA.

"Most of the album was recorded at Sydney's Capitol Theatre on the last night of our Youth In Asia Tour. It was a really hot night. Everything just happened, you know? Everyone fired."

(Jimmy, talking to Vince Lovegrove, December 1980)

Reviews are excellent:

"You'd expect a live album from this lot to be an unchained demolition derby, and hang the subtleties, and Chisel don't fail you, right from the start, the live rendition of utterly charming Conversations is an entity of its own. Ian Moss crunches out some classic heavy metal doodlings, a roaring monster scratching to escape. Walker's familiar tinkly piano riff emerges from the mix somewhere, the rhythm section charges in and Barnes mad dog vocals send the song spinning.

"Swingshift is one of the finest live albums you will find- it's a live album that makes an actual statement about a particular facet of a band, without the characteristic ego stroking or contractual tokenism or facadising to jaded creativity. Simply, it's superbly handled rock'n'roll.

"Cold Chisel have been creaking around the pubs long enough not to play bad gigs; they remain spontaneous enough to play gigs that range from so-so, to hey that was good, to nights of magical brilliance. But when they do hit their stride, there's not a band around that can catch them. There's a strength and integrity that comes from the way they keep feeding from their roots, but the powerfully simplistic rhythms and surging adrenaline drive forgo any signs of outdatedness...

"But basically, if this LP doesn't get you off your ass, you are obviously three days dead and what the heck are you doing reading a magazine anyway?

(CHRISTIE ELIEZER JUKE)

117)

"It's exciting, barrel house music, with all the immediacy of live performance, without sacrifice of musicianship... In all a fine album from a sensational band."

(DAVID BENTLEY, WEEKLY SUN, QLD)

"Cold Chisel's new double live album Swingshift is the best live album I have ever heard.

"That's a sweeping statement but Swingshift is just the album to back such a description. It surpasses even such old standards as Lou Reed's Rock'n'Roll Animal album.

"Swingshift marks Cold Chisel as one of the world's great rock bands and it would be a bargain at twice the price."

(THE BULLETIN, TOWNSVILLE, QLD)

"As live albums go, Swingshift is a beauty. It avoids the pitfalls so many successful bands slip into when doing a live LP, notably playing up to their adoring fans and turning the whole thing into a huge ego trip...A superb album. Now if they can only keep Barnes off the bottle until things break for them in the states."

(SATURDAY EVENING MERCURY, HOBART, TAS.)

MARCH 28

American industry magazine Cashbox gives the East album a good review:

"A little more mainstream rock that (sic) land of Oz mates The Little River Band, Cold Chisel is every bit as accomplished. East is the band's dramatic US debut, and it should have no trouble finding a home with American AOR stations. Most of the tough rocking tunes are centred around the strong melodies of pianist Don Walker and the dynamic vocals of Jim Barnes. No second LP needed here as this aussie fivesome is already there. Top tracks are Cheap Wine and Tomorrow. An AOR must. "

Billboard magazine was also impressed:

"A superstar attraction in its native Australia, Cold Chisel plays meaty yet accessible rock along the lines of Bob Seger or early Rod Stewart. Lead singer Jim Barnes possesses the same kind of smoky delivery as these singers although the songs themselves have their own distinct personality. Ian Moss is talented guitarist whose piercing style animates several tracks. The ballads and slower numbers are especially well done. Joe Camilleri's saxophone work is also noteworthy."

Record World saw it this way:

"These Australian hit makers have several points in their favor, including three competent songwriters. One of them, Jim Barnes is an aggressive lead vocalist, whose more intense moments scream for attention, recalling Burton Cummings in the Guess Who days. Their down-under hits, especially Choirgirl, have US AOR/pop potential."

(118

The US version of *East* came with a couple of changes, Ita and *Four Walls* being replaced with a remixed version of *Khe Sanh*. The back cover photo was also changed, "The back cover shot looks like what the Americans would see as a bunch of cowboys." The quality of the printing on the US cover is also most impressive.

Chisel off to wow America

TELE BEAT

COLD Chisel's current series of Sydney performances look like being their last in this country for at least six months.

In late June, Chisel, arguably the most powerful live rock'n'roll band in the country, will be embarking on their first

For more than seven years they've been slogging it out in Australia, working in .pubs and halls right across the country on some of the most gruelling tours

broaden their horizons to avoid turning stale and losing ground. '

Says vocalist Jimmy Barnes: "We've got to go to America, anywhere really, to get better. to

APRIL 6

Swingshift debuts at No.1 in Sydney, Canberra, Adelaide and Newcastle while filling the No.2 spot in Melbourne, Brisbane and Perth. Nationally No.2.

APRIL 7

Press reports:

"The NSW Health Commission has stopped the commercial release of a film documentary about adolescence in Sydney's Western suburbs, according to its producer. Pam Scott, an independent film producer, said yesterday that the commission had suppressed the 47 minute documentary entitled Kids because it was too "politically sensitive...

"The film also features footage of a special under-18s concert at Cabramatta youth centre by the award-winning rock group Cold Chisel."

APRIL 13

Swingshift is No.1 nationally, already achieving platinum sales while East has sales of over 200,000.

APRIL 21 - MY BABY US RELEASE

"Australia's Cold Chisel scored Down Under with the top selling LP East last year, but judging from the first domestic single release from the album, it could have been called West. Jim Barnes lead vocal has a

decided Midwest American quality to it, while the guitars ring with US rock."

(US INDUSTRY MAGAZINE, "CASHBOX")

MARCH - APRIL

The band, minus Jimmy, work on the soundtrack to the Australian film *Freedom*. All of the music was composed and produced by Don Walker and the album was mixed by Mark Opitz. Peter Walker, who produced the first Cold Chisel album, plays guitar and engineers the sessions. INXS' Michael Hutchence handles the vocals on two songs while others feature Don Walker, Ian Moss or guest vocalists. The album also includes Billy Rogers (saxophone), David Blight (harmonica).

The songs themselves are distinctively Walker, echoing Cold Chisel but more importantly, uniquely Australian, as all of Don's work is. This record is worth hunting out for the great songs (check out the Hutchence sung *Speed Kills*) and the guitar playing of Moss, who was particularly inspired at this point. The Chisel song *Ita* can also be heard in the film, but not on the soundtrack album. See May 1982 for a review of the soundtrack album.

119)

During the filming of the "Forever Now" clip.

APRL 28	Melbourne State College
APRIL 29	Swinburne Institute Of Technology

APRIL 30 - BOMBAY ROCK

James Manning reviewed this show for Juke and after listing many reasons why he thought he would not like the band - "Acting like prats on Countdown", "The mountain of Cold Chisel publicity was having a negative effect", "If Jimmy Barnes needs bottles of vodka to get him going, then that's his problem." Manning saw the show:

"But once the band were into their first number, no-one could have denied their talent. It is probably a dangerous thing to say, but going by the performance I saw, Cold Chisel must be nearly above criticism...

"Guitarist Ian Moss stands right in front of Walker. I have never had any lack of respect for his guitar ability after seeing him playing with Kevin Borich on this stage twelve months ago. Tonight he is equally deft. His vocals are now an important ingredient in the band...

"And centre stage is Jimmy Barnes. Australia's No. 1 'over the top' hero. Younger brother of hard rocker John Swan. With the familiar bottle of vodka in hand, leaning on his microphone stand. Despite the legends, he was looking remarkably fit. He has a voice and stage presence to make most would-be front men envious.

"He plunged into the crowd and headed up to the VIP lounge where he sang a chorus. He also sang from atop of Don Walker's keyboards, and as he left the stage he flung the remains of a bucket of water over the audience. A quiet evening for Jim? But he still worked up a hell of a sweat.

"The band played most of Swingshift. Breakfast At Sweethearts, Rising Sun, Choir Girl, Khe Sanh, Four Walls, My Baby, Cheap Wine, and Star Hotel.

"After teasing the crowd with a long break they came back with a powerful encore. This started with only Ian Moss and Don Walker onstage doing a version of Georgia On My Mind. This song can be corny at the best of times, but with Moss' voice they pulled it off beautifully.

"For those still wanting more there was a girl at the front of the stage lifting her jumper to a desirable height."

MAY 1 - TARMAC HOTEL, LAVERTON

Fans have formed queues hundreds of metres long by late afternoon outside the venue before this show. When a fight erupts in the crowd, Jim stops the band and points out the offending punter to security who promptly eject him while the band continue from where they left off.

MAY 2 - PIER HOTEL, FRANKSTON

"Police had to be called to break up a mini-riot following a Cold Chisel performance at Melbourne's Pier Hotel.

"As usual there were long queues to get in, and after some time the hotel closed its doors. A fan who had driven 50 miles to see the band approached the bouncers and begged to be allowed in. He was sent away and kept coming back two more times, begging to be let in 'because I've driven all this way.'

"The third time, a skirmish started. A friend of the fan who was punched up ran to the stage to tell Cold Chisel what was happening. Jimmy Barnes immediately stopped the show and allowed the kid to come up on-stage and explain to everyone what had happened.

"The band then launched into Star Hotel, changing the name of the song to Pier Hotel. Chisel then stormed off stage and refused to return for their encore. This resulted in hotel patrons throwing glasses at the stage. Bouncers moved in and shifted the crowd outside.

"Things began to look ugly outside the hotel. There were skirmishes in the car park while others stood chanting anti-Pier Hotel slogans.

"Someone set off the fire alarm which resulted in engines clanging to the scene. Finally the police came and cleared everyone away."

(BRIAN JONES IN 'JUKE' MAGAZINE)

MAY 3	Ferntree Gully
APRIL/MAY	East debuts on the Cashbox charts (US) at No.193.
MAY 24	Band signs US/Canada deal with Elektra/Asylum.
MAY	My Baby single released in the USA
MAY 16	Paramatta Leagues Club
MAY 17	Brighton Hotel
MAY 18	Doyalson RSL

(120

121)

MAY 19	Doyalson RSL
MAY 20	Selinas, Coogee Bay Hotel
MAY 21	Wollongong Leagues Club

MAY 22 - COMB & CUTTER

Jimmy and Jane were married earlier in the day and guests including members of The Angels, Flowers, Mental As Anything and the cream of the Sydney music industry attend this show after the post-wedding party at the new Mr and Mrs Barnes' house.

| MAY 25 | Sundowner Hotel |
| MAY 26 | Cronulla Leagues Club |

JUNE

The *East* album receives a positive review in England's *Melody Maker*, a magazine which can often be scathing in its reviews.

"This is simply the sort of record you can play and enjoy for what it is - a collection of strong rock songs, well played and presented with variety and confidence and a large glimmer of life.

"Vocalist Jim Barnes is a joy to hear, his voice throaty in the manner of the old blues rockers and convincing with it.

"This is a set that appeals for its melodies, arrangements and wit. Even if it never makes the charts."

JUNE 5 - AUSTRALIAN ALBUM SALES

| Cold Chisel: 31,500 |
| Breakfast At Sweethearts: 65,800 |
| East: 207, 648 |
| Swingshift: 67,781 |

JUNE

Hopes are high for the US tour, the band has been working towards this for seven years and their level of success in Australia has virtually forced them to look for other markets or face over-exposure at home. The band is booked to do support stints with Joe Walsh, Rush, Jefferson Starship, and 38 Special. After seeing the band play in Sydney their American agent reportedly said, "their only problem will be to find bands not scared enough to go on after them." On the eve of the release of *East*, Don Walker told *Juke* magazine that the band had gone through some paranoia over the lack of response from America to

their work but, "we remembered we'd got together as a band because we enjoyed playing together and we'd continue doing that, regardless of worrying about what other countries thought of us."

"We've got to go to America, anywhere really, to get better, to gather more experience, more things to write about, more inspiration. The motivation for the trip is partly ego, and that is what drives you to get better. We've probably reached a peak as a band in Australia.

"I'm not saying that we can't get any bigger in Australia, but at the moment we have to expand our market for the band's sake, and for the sake of business as well. There's a lot of money to be made there. With that we can do the things we want to do production-wise. And show-wise it takes a lot of money.

"So we want to keep getting bigger so we can do better things with it. It will be used to improve the show."

(Jimmy talking to the Sunday Telegraph, Sydney, May 25, 1981)

Publisher Rondor Music's John Brommel recalled that the band always had trouble communicating with American ears due to Jimmy's diction. As with many Australian singers, Americans simply couldn't understand him.

The band do shows in New Zealand en route to the states.

"I figure New Zealand will be a good testing ground for Chisel. And when they hit the septic tanks (yanks) next year, one of the greatest rock'n'roll bands in the world will begin the second phase of their career. Only this phase will reap them the financial rewards they so richly deserve."

(Vince Lovegrove, December 1980)

"It probably won't make a great deal of difference to the actual approach or performance. Maybe it'll put an edge to it. A nervous edge. We'll know that they haven't seen us before, so in the back of our heads we'll know we have to hit them hard! The adrenalin'll be pushing hard, just like in a concert situation."

(Jimmy talking to Vince Lovegrove in December 1980)

(122

U.S./Canada border
Mark Pope & Phil Small

JUNE 25   This was originally going to be the band's first US date at the Milwaukee Music Festival but this did not eventuate.

JUNE 25-26   Band tours New Zealand, setting a house record in Auckland.

JUNE 27 - MAINSTREET, AUCKLAND, WITH THE FAMOUS FIVE AND BLIND DATE

"...it had quickly become apparent that Cold Chisel's reputation as Australia's premier live rock band was more than just some eager publicists dream.

"Hitting the stage just after midnight in the giant, sweating sardine can Mainstreet had transformed itself into, they seized the crowd by the throat with their opening number, Conversations - and never let go.

"With the volume wound up to brain boiling level, the five-piece roared through a set of originals and selected covers that must have set a new record for sheer emotive rock and roll energy...

"...Star Hotel, Shipping Steel, Cheap Wine, Long As I Can See The Light, Don't Let Go and One Long Day, with Moss really impressing on lead vocals were just some of the highlights.

"But there were far too many to list.

"Just stunning."

(Colin Hogg, Auckland Daily)

At the news conference in Auckland, Don Walker hints at possible difficulties with the US record company even at this stage,

"We are definitely dealing with a record company that doesn't quite know what the hell it's signed, and that doesn't have any great urge to find out. Hopefully, when they hear us live, individuals will become fanatical and we'll start making some headway."

JUNE 28 - US TOUR

The band arrives in the US with *East* sitting at No. 173 on the *Billboard* charts and 180 on the Cashbox chart. Reports suggest that 105 stations are playing the album across the country and although reviews are good, *East* does not chart any higher.

JULY 5

San Diego, USA supporting Heart with Jimmy Buffet. Phil Small recalls that at this show the band only played about twenty minutes, through hired amplifiers which they didn't even have an opportunity to soundcheck.

Soon after arriving the band are cancelled from the Allman Brothers, Tom Scott and other shows because they are branded a heavy metal band!

The band then join Joe Walsh in Phoenix, and later Ted Nugent in Dayton, Ohio.

They also do support shows for Joe Ely, and the Fabulous Thunderbirds, who Don described as one of the most inspiring bands he'd seen in years. Not all shows were supports, for one show at a bar in Tucson, Arizona (a venue which was so decrepit that they hoped a fire which had started in the wreckers yard next door that afternoon would burn down the venue before the gig started!) they found another band, Spider, who thought that Cold Chisel were supposed to be supporting them! Somehow, ugly scenes were avoided and Cold Chisel played, to have members of Spider wanting to buy them drinks and literally falling over themselves to do anything for Cold Chisel.

"We were pretty well looked after, especially after the first gig in each tour. The first gig we did with Joe Walsh was in Houston, and setting up for that I think we had half an hour or forty-five minutes to play, and we were being treated very much as the low man on the totem pole.

But as they saw that we could play and that we were worth working with a bit, conditions for us got better and better at each gig until we had the PA companies and the promoters and people like that really showing all the symptoms of being fans of the band. And the same with...we did a stint with Ted Nugent. In general I'd have to say that we got treated really well."

(Don Walker talking with B. Pinnell, June '82.)

JULY 6

Night Train, Tucson, & radio interview with KWFM Tucson:

"Playing a warm-up date at the Night Train last Monday to prepare for a national tour was the Australian quintet Cold Chisel. This band is a tenacious group determined to play middle-of-the-road rock'n'roll harder than anyone else.

"Even so the veteran rock audience wasn't paying much attention to the first several songs. But Cold Chisel pushed on and filled the dance floor before two-thirds of the show had passed. Lead singer Jimmy Barnes and guitarist-vocalist Ian Moss project the image of nice boys gone bad. They also provide a rascally sexual focus for the music."

(Tucson Ⅽ ᴢᴇɴ, Aʀɪᴢᴏɴᴀ)

JULY 8	Radio interview with KZEW Dallas
JULY 9	Houstin Summit

JULY 10

Dallas Reunion Arena with Joe Walsh

"The 11 original songs and the instrumental performances are usually quite good and occasionally inspired, but what really sets East apart from the sludge of vinyl oozing out of record factories is singer Jim Barnes.

"He's a smoky, expressive vocalist with great range and the ability to put a lot of feeling into a song without turning it ridiculous, melodramatic farce. He roams from depressed to hunted and desperate to intoxicated to joyful and does it all with a refreshingly tough vitality."

(Jɪᴍ Rᴜᴛʜ, Nᴇᴡs-Fʀᴇᴇ Pʀᴇss, Cʜᴀᴛᴛᴀɴᴏᴏɢᴀ)

JULY 11

Tornado Jam, Austin. Also: Fabulous Thunderbirds, Joe Ely, Stevie Ray Vaughan and Debert McClinton.

Set List: Conversations / Khe Sanh / Rising Sun / Houndog / My Baby / Star Hotel / Merry-Go-Round / One Long Day / Standing On the Outside / Goodbye Astrid / Wild Thing

The band are introduced by road manager Mark Pope who adopts a fake American accent to ensure he is understood: "Good evening. Would you please welcome, from Sydney, Australia. Cold Chisel." This is only the band's fifth show in the US and is a good example of the type of shortened sets they were playing on the tour.

(124

Managers Secretary
Denise Sharp

U.S. 1981
Tornado Jam with Joe Ely
& Jimmy Vaughan. Ian
on the right and Jim's
head far left.

125)

The opening *Conversations* quickly kicks the band into top gear after Ian's tense opening blaze, played over military style drum rolls from Steve. *Khe Sanh* quickly follows, both sounding no different to what one would expect from the band at this point.

"Do yas like rockabilly down here or what? I think these people think they came to the pictures. It's a fuckin' rock'n'roll show, not the fuckin' movies. Get off your arses you cunts. This is called The Rising Sun Just Stole My Girl Away."

Jimmy speaks so fast it's sometimes difficult even for an Australian to understand him. This audience of Southern Americans would have had no hope. At least nobody would be offended.

Rising Sun has Ian taking rockabilly back to its home in fine style. *Houndog*, introduced as "a heavy metal song", is a real surprise. Why the band were playing songs which they had not yet even recorded or even finalised the arrangement for, as part of short sets on this tour is hard to understand. They can certainly never be accused of taking the easy option.

"I don't know how big the unemployment problem is in America, but it's pretty bad in Australia and a lot of people aren't gonna sit around and take it. This one's about a riot we had in Australia, it's called Star Hotel."

This is spoken a little more clearly. Jimmy really pushes his voice on this one, although at times it sounds a little thin. Perhaps he has thrown himself a little too wholeheartedly into this tour, his voice is showing signs of overuse. *Merry-Go-Round* is superb. Ian told me that he felt that, at 26 years old, he was at his peak as a guitarist on this tour and this performance is evidence of this.

"We hope youse people here like some blues. We hear you do, so it's cool. This one here features our guitar player on some vocals. It's called One Long Day."

Once again Ian's playing in the blues intro to this piece is exceptional, and he sings his heart out, "and be a little fuckin' strange" being an uncharacteristic lyrical addition. What the audience were making of all this is hard to know, but they certainly seemed impressed. *Standing On the Outside* also sounds as good as it's ever sounded. Cold Chisel really were on fire and it's hard to imagine any audience which could not be moved by them.

Jim admonishes those people up the front who have been fighting for their seats, telling them that when the main band comes on they're just going to get trampled to death anyway. *Goodbye* and *Wild Thing* complete a set which rivals any of the live recordings you'll ever hear of the band. *Wild Thing* has a reggae interlude in the middle and some Zeppelinish call and response guitar/vocal 'moans' before the intro.

Cold Chisel followed Stevie Ray Vaughan and later Jim and Ian joined Jimmy Vaughan, Joe Ely and others for a jam, which was a highlight of the tour for them both.

JULY 12 - RED ROCKS, DENVER COLORADO

With Joe Walsh

"The rain fell hardest during Cold Chisel's set, and the Australian band made quite a favorable impression by refusing to cut their set. The group is on their first American tour since becoming big sensations Down Under, but no new band should be so desperate for publicity that they would get electrocuted onstage.

"Nevertheless, singer Jim Barnes screamed, 'Bleep this rain!' while the band knocked out some frantic versions of songs culled from East, their first internationally released album. Khe Sanh, My Baby and Cheap Wine highlighted their excellent set - look for them to get invited back to town for their own show late this summer."

(G.Brown, Denver Post)

"The warm-up band, Australia's Cold Chisel, had a relatively hard time breaking the crowd in for the show.

"It wasn't because of a poor performance, as Cold Chisel hammered out a high quality 45 minute warm-up show. Rather it was because the crowd quickly grew restless waiting for Walsh.

"Strong showings were turned in by keyboardist Don Walker and lead vocalist Jimmy Barnes, who spent much of the set jumping on and off Walker's piano.

"But Cold Chisel, still relatively unknown in this country, will eventually win over its share of fans - if the group can secure a few headline dates."

(Phoenix Daily News)

"The album is an excellent, varied collection of rock styles - and though the rest of the country has been slow to pick up on the record, the Colorado market has been extremely supportive, especially to the single, My Baby.

"I would have preferred one of the Australian singles to have been released first," Barnes admitted. "I'm the front man, but I don't sing "My Baby." I would

have liked something like "Choir Girl" or "Cheap Wine." Apparently "Cheap Wine" had a drug reference in it - not pro or con, just a reference and we were advised heavily against making it our first single."

(The Denver Post)

JULY 14 - PHOENIX WITH JOE WALSH

Fly to New York City

Album review:

"Inadvertently, I have once again placed the best album in the column in the last position. Cold Chisel is a five-man group that has some of the classiest vocals I've heard in a while. All five sing, that's why.

"They are like a hybrid of two other famous Aussie bands: AC/DC and the Little River Band. A strange mixture, true, but follow my rationale: They have a hard rocking edge, but they don't let it dominate the entire sound like AC/DC; they can be very melodic with rich harmonies and pop charm, like LRB, but that sharp steel core keeps the sound from becoming too saccharine. (sic) In short an exciting group that comes across like the best of both worlds...this disc receives a high recommendation."

(Sentinel, Waterville, Maine)

| JULY 22 | Dayton Ohio, with Ted Nugent |
| JULY 23 | Springfield, Illinois with Ted Nugent |

JULY 24 - DUBUQUE, IOWA

The *East* album was given a good review in Iowa, but unfortunately this was on May 10, as were most of the record reviews and much of the momentum created by these was lost by the time the band arrived in the country.

"In no way is this a clone of other rock bands that have crossed the ocean from Australia. It's kinda hard to crank out crunch chords with only one guitarist, except if that guitarist is as flexible and intelligent in style as Ian Moss..."

(Mike Kutcha, Quad City Times, Davenport, Iowa)

| JULY 25 | Riverside Arena, Austin, Minn. |

JULY 26 - DULUTH, MINN.

"Cold Chisel is a popular Australian outfit and a controversial one, with 'punk' overtones in some of its music and in its somewhat rebellious lifestyle. All the image building falderol aside, East shows them as

(126

capable heavy rockers with a deft songwriting touch that gives their music an appealing quality.

"The better songs are penned by keyboard player Don Walker, who contributed Standing On The Outside, Choirgirl and Khe Sanh, all noteworthy. Khe Sanh, the group's first single in Australia, was a hit despite being kept off the radio due to its controversial nature. It concerns a Vietnam veteran, his memories of the war and his problems at home. It serves to remind us that Australia had its share of Vietnam casualties too...If Cold Chisel maintain this level or better yet, improves it, then it will definitely be heard from again."

(BOB.R. QUALLS, CONWAY, ARKANSAS)

"Their effect on me has been two-fold. On one hand, Cold Chisel exhibits all the traits of a straightforward good times rock band on tunes such as Rising Sun (with its Jerry Lee Lewis hooks) and Cheap Wine (with all due apologies to swaggering rock stars who used to drink nothing but the best). The other side of Cold Chisel illuminates the effectiveness of social statement through music, as in Choirgirl, Standing On The Outside and Khe Sanh, the latter being a musical equivalent to Martin Sheen's opening monologue in Apocalypse Now. In this respect Cold Chisel have had just as much impact at home as the Police and the Clash have, although on a worldwide basis the Aussies still suffer from a lack of exposure. With Jim Barnes and his searing approach to the singing of each song, the lyrical stance of Don Walker and the tight instrumentation of Ian Moss' guitar, Phil Small's bass, and Steve Prestwich's drums, Cold Chisel has created a most satisfying release in East.

Here's hoping the record company will treat us to their earlier recordings real soon."

(JIM MCDONALD, THE TELEGRAM, BRIDGEPORT)

Not all reviews were positive however, to the point where you sometimes wondered whether they were talking about the same album! J.D.Considine of The News American was one:

"Upon hearing that Cold Chisel had taken the AC/DC's place as Australia's favorite rock band, I expected nothing less than ear-splitting, hyperactive rock'n'roll. What a disappointment. Cold Chisel is more along the lines of the Little River Band before it went senile. Pleasant listening if you like country-style tear jerkers about Aussie Vietnamese War veterans (Khe Sanh), but somehow, that's a taste I've never managed to acquire."

Another less than glowing review, from The Daily Collegian in Pennsylvania, proves that the reason some critics loved the album (vocals, songs etc.) was the same reason others didn't:

"...Both the instrumentals and vocals are hopelessly forced, the latter sounding like Robert Plant without lungs. It's all so predictable and dull; all the sorrowful stock that forms the foundation of AM radio. We've heard it before, and much to often. So much for Kangaroo Rock!"

Bill Duchan, of the 34th Street Magazine at the University of Pennsylvania (again) was even less impressed!:

Although virtually unknown in the United States, Cold Chisel has managed to earn quadruple platinum status in their native Australia with East, their third album. However, after a listening, the question one asks is not "Why haven't I heard of them?", but "Has everybody Down Under lost their musical taste?" A recent press release boasts that East features songs "which match urgent themes with aggressive playing." Nothing could be further from the truth. The Chiselers dabble in many modes (reggae, rockabilly, rhythm and blues) but never seem to say anything of any importance. On the few occasions when they attack relevant issues, the results never rise above MOR musical mash."

(Well, he did admit that he only listened to the record once!)

127)

"After listening to Cold Chisel's American debut album East, record fans may recommend the group head back west to their homeland...

"...The group's first single Khe Sanh also is featured on East. This country - rock ballad about the soldiers who went to Vietnam is highly overrated. Australian radio stations wisely refused to play it because of its controversial lyrics...

"...If this record is any indication, the interest of American listeners in the album may be short-lived."

(SUE SIMON, THE MISSOURIAN, COLUMBIA, MISSOURI)

JULY 27	Fort Williams Garden, Ontario (Thunder Bay)

At this point in the tour East had sold 12, 630 copies in the USA

JULY 31

Pine Knob, Detroit, with the Marshall Tucker Band.

In what was something of a mismatching of acts, Cold Chisel does this leg of the tour supporting the cowboy kings of South Carolina, the Marshall Tucker Band. "Maybe we can stretch to those people who are more into rock than the country." The band includes *Georgia* in the set.

Don Walker reflects on the current state of American music in an interview with Detroit's Monitor, a weekly paper.

"I think it's a real shame that the very best musicians and rock and roll bands play in carnival clubs in America, and the very worst bands are playing to millions.

"It's incomprehensible. Jerry Lee Lewis, Ray Charles, Miles Davis - it seems these people are intrinsically better."

AUGUST 1	Pine Knob, Detroit

AUGUST 3 - RALEIGH, NTH CAROLINA

"Why did it take an Australian rock band to write the first tune to really get at the experience of many Vietnam veterans?

"The Aussies were in Southeast Asia, too, of course, but I think the Vietnam subject matter of the song has more to do with the particular skills of Don Walker, the main writer for Cold Chisel.

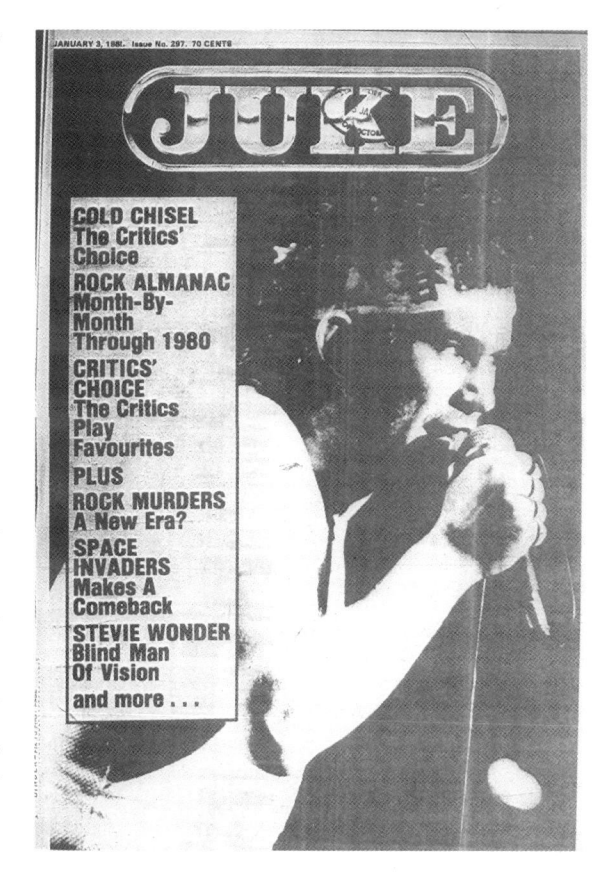

"Walker just may be the most evocative new songwriter in rock. His talents, as well as those of the rest of the band - and those talents are many - are excellently displayed in this album which boasts more than just Khe Sanh, the aforementioned song about a Viet vet's attempts to cope with civilian life...

"Cold Chisel can play blistering hard rock and intricate, mood evoking ballads with equal dexterity. And the band offers wit, intelligence and freshness to boot.

"Cheap Wine, another Walker song is a minor classic. It offers an apology for the hobo life with an affable snarl. Sitting on the beach drinking his cheap wine the singer exults:

Mending every minute of the day before

Watching the ocean, watching the shore

Watching the sunrise, and thinking there could never be more.

(five paragraphs later...)

The bottom line is this: Cold Chisel is the best 'new' (in terms of being heard in America) band of 1981."

(DAVID PRATHER, OBSERVER AND TIMES, FAYETVILLE, NTH. CAROLINA)

(128

AUGUST 5 - CIVIC FESTIVAL, CHICAGO

With Cheap Trick

> *"Combining literate, often thought-provoking lyrics
> with stylistically varied music, Cold Chisel has become
> quite a success in their homeland... "*
>
> (ILLINOIS ENTERTAINER, AUG, 1981)

AUGUST 7 - PROVIDENCE, CENTRE STAGE

> *"Cold Chisel is a new band from Australia that stands
> a good chance of finding an American audience. Their
> debut album, "East" is full of well written, tightly
> performed rock and roll tunes. Solid vocals should
> help get this some airplay. Not bad at all."*
>
> (HERALD-LANTERN, NEW JERSEY)

AUGUST 10 - CASA BOOGIE, UTICA

This show is broadcast live to air on radio W.O.U.R.

*Set list: Conversations / Shipping Steel / Best Kept Lies /
Merry Go Round / Choir Girl / My Turn To Cry / Khe Sanh /
Don't Let Go / Forever Now / My Baby /Houndog/ Rising
Sun / Four Walls / One Long Day / Standing On The
Outside / Tomorrow / Goodbye Astrid -encores- Breakfast
At Sweethearts / Cheap Wine / Wild Thing*

Following a brief introduction from the station
who say that they've been playing the band since
February, they launch into a *Swingshift*-like

Conversations. The first minute or so is a little hazy
as sound engineers mix the sound for radio, but it is
as powerful as Australians have come to expect and
the audience respond loudly before *Shipping Steel*,
which is back to its rock'n'roll feel, unlike the live
album version. "Here's one off the East album", is
Jim's intro for *Best Kept Lies*, with a most impressive
guitar solo from Ian, who played so well on this tour
that Joe Walsh said he was the best guitarist he'd
seen. *Merry Go Round* has Don doing a false "tender
ballad" start before a particularly aggressive
performance from all.

Despite the fact that the band are on the other
side of the world and playing to an audience that has
never seen them before, the atmosphere is no
different to that of an Australian show. The audience
just as enthusiastic, proving indeed that the band
were very successful in the live situation over there,
even if they failed to make an impact on the sales
charts.

My Turn To Cry is as powerful as ever and *Khe
Sanh* is obviously recognised by many in the
audience who cheer in the intro. "Here's a song we'd
like to do for any Jerry Lee Lewis fans in the
audience, he was sick but apparently he's gettin'
better. You can't kill the killer," is the intro for *Don't*

US.1981
Elvis Presley's tour bus,
Cold Chisel and crew.

Let Go. "This song's a new song, this is one that'll probably be on our new album which comes out here... when we get back to Australia and record it. It's written by the skinny one with the buck teeth, our drummer" - a preview of what would become *Forever Now.* The intro, first verse and chorus are as on the finished version, however the quiet bridge section is replaced with improvised guitar and then keyboard sections and the song ends with the same guitar phrase as in the intro. This song had been played in some of the shows immediately before the band left Australia, but would not have been included in many US sets as most were only 20-30 minute support slots.

My Baby is followed by another new song, *Houndog,* lyrical variations in which included, "fuck the waitress, and hit the road again." And "the Greyhound bus is an early bird, the budget girl's just been transferred." The quieter bridge section is missing and the song ends with a solo guitar run. *Rising Sun* and *Four Walls* follow, before *One Long Day,* which is introduced as a blues song and has a blues intro like that on the *Swingshift* album which features some truly breathtaking guitar from Ian. Ian mixes up the last line of the verse singing, "I'm gonna find myself a busted jetty and some mangrove landscape" before more fluid guitar.

Standing On The Outside has Jim forcing his voice to the point where it starts to crack - he has been pushing it all night. But the audience is oblivious, in fact delirious in their response. *Star Hotel* follows with an introduction about the unemployment problems in Australia and how they are caused by the government, which has led to a lot of riots. Jim's voice seems to be holding up, although he is a little more measured in his delivery. *Tomorrow* has more inspired playing from Ian and there is no break before *Goodbye Astrid.* Jim's voice is struggling on the chorus, this is probably the most singing he's had to do for the last six weeks. This doesn't seem to affect him though and he still attacks the song as though it's his last.

The band leaves the stage and radio listeners are treated to a pre-recorded station promo from Jimmy as the ecstatic audience scream for more. They are given *Breakfast At Sweethearts* and *Cheap Wine,* the intro of which is also obviously recognised by the audience. *Wild Thing* seems a little unsure in the intro, probably having not been played for some

time, but quickly becomes a driving version, which leaves the crowd chanting loudly for more. The chanting continues for some time before the DJ, when it's obvious that they aren't returning, gives the band an enthusiastic rap before returning to normal programming.

AUGUST 14   Country Club, LA

"If groups like Journey and Jefferson Starship can shoot up the charts on the strength of some of the uninspiring trash they continue to produce, then Cold Chisel - who're tougher, more intelligent and equally macho - will eventually make it into the same commercial bracket, if not with this album, then definitely with another one. Cold Chisel can headbang with the best of 'em, if need be, but are versatile enough to avoid being typecast. A band to watch out for."

(SENTINEL, SAN FRANCISCO, CAL)

AUGUST

Juke reports that the band are currently touring (in the US) with the Rossington Collins Band and that their party pranks have made them popular with headliners such as Ted Nugent and Joe Walsh. It was also reported that at some shows Nugent and Walsh dragged members of the band onstage to jam.

AUGUST 17 - COLD CHISEL RETURNS TO AUS

On returning to Australia, Rod Willis described the tour as a qualified success.

"The album had already died in the charts before we even got over there. But we had a really good agent we were getting really good money and really good billing. We actually turned down two months work to get back here."

Apparently another problem was the variety of styles on the album;

"It has to be made easy for them. The industry over there feels it has to formulate. If you're doing more than one style of music they get confused."

"The record company also did not throw its weight behind the album. Because they didn't have an investment in the album (it was paid for by WEA Australia) they didn't push it as much as they might have - and we didn't have the say that we have in this country when we deal with the record company." Rod told Roadrunner's Donald Robertson.

"Obviously next time we go, we'll have a much better idea of what to expect. We were learning all the time on this one. But we now have a reputation as a shit-hot support act. Promoters are asking for the band. We got an encore every time we played."

"Obviously we didn't sell many albums, obviously there are problems over there with our behind the scenes set up. The things I believe we achieved were all in the live playing line. We didn't make a big impression on radio over there, because I don't think at that stage we had the songs. I believe we might have one or two songs now that American radio programmers can probably relate to....the big gains we made were live in front of every audience we played to. That's a slow way to do it in America. The fast way to do it is, as you know, get something big happening on the radio, or if you're not that kind of band, then you just have to do the live slog because it's such a big place and that takes quite a few years."

Q: Are the band prepared to go back (to the United States) another time?

A: Oh yeah.

Q: What would stop you from going back?

A: Lack of money would be one reason.

Q: So the record company are prepared to subsidise you again over there?

A: Oh, yeah, there's no problem with that.

Q: Were you disappointed the album didn't do better, sales - wise?

A: I was, but at the time I was pretty mad about it, because I thought that the album had everything at the time to do well over there and I thought it was just people along the line letting us down. I think in retrospect that the album wasn't as well suited for over there as I thought at the time.

Q: Is Circus Animals better than East would have been for airplay now?

A: It's hard to judge. I think it would. We're told from over there that it's better suited to American ears, so that's about all I can go on.

(Don Walker talking to Billy Pinnell, June 1982)

In the mid '80s Don would tell Rolling Stone Magazine,

"We had these childish fantasies about America. Because there were all these people I admired, like Elvis, Jerry Lee Lewis, Jim Morrison, Ray Charles as well as other Americans not necessarily involved in music. Sitting in Australia I thought that was what America was all about. The reality, of course, is that Jim and Elvis are dead. Jerry Lee is having a stomach operation and Ray Charles is playing to 200 people in seedy little clubs. Rock and roll to the average young American, is Rush or Styx. It's Entertainment This Week. They've never heard of the Sex Pistols, or what we might consider the classic New York groups. Everywhere we went we found hundreds of people who genuinely thought that Styx were the best band in the world."

AUGUST 24	Khe Sanh released as second US single.

SEPTEMBER 14

Record demos for Circus Animals album at Trafalgar Studios including Jimmy's Suicide Sal, a track later released on the Teenage Love album. Other tracks demoed include: Numbers Fall, You Got Nothin' I Want, Bow River (Any Time You Want as it was then titled), All In Trouble, Work My Fingers, Sharp Shooter (one of Steve's), Yesterdays, Rock My Soul (another of Steve's), Nothing's Forever (an early Forever Now) , Taipan, Don't Make Sense, Still The One (Steve's), Sit On My Face, Jeff Who (one of Ian's), Wild Colonial Boy, Misadventure (an early version of Phil's "The Game"), Daylight, Houndog, F1-11, and When The War Is Over.

Producer Mark Opitz recalls that he was personally not happy with the progress being made on the album until Steve's songs (*Forever Now* and *When The War Is Over*) were included. Unlike Don, who was determined to ensure that *Circus Animals* was not a pop album, as some quarters had perceived *East*, Opitz was looking for the single to ensure the album's success. Opitz felt that Steve's songs, both of which he thought were potential hits, enabled him to "let Don be Don", meaning that he was able to produce Don's songs the way Don wanted them, without concerns about 'hooks' or radio potential.

Cold Chisel are rumoured to be appearing at next months Tanelorn Festival but this does not eventuate. Christie Eliezer reported that the decision was made after Rod Willis picked up a hitch-hiker and during a discussion about music (without revealing who he was) Rod asked what he thought of Cold Chisel.

"They're a great band but they're getting so exposed now its beginning to shit me" was his answer.

This convinced Willis, but apparently the promoters claimed that Chisel were asking an outrageous fee and encouraged rumours that the band might actually play. A woman apparently paid a visit to two members, promising all sorts of exotic drugs and delights, including a helicopter flight. She was sent to a fictitious studio in Hornsby to talk to Jimmy about it!

It is announced that the band will be returning to the US in March where management felt that while the band did well in the live situation, record sales were disappointing and they think it was because the band went over there too long after the release of *East*.

OCTOBER 11 - DARWIN

This show is scheduled for October because Jan/Feb, when the rest of the tour takes place, is right in the middle of the wet season and they are playing outdoors. The band play to 6500 people (over 10% of the population, a statistic not heard of in this country since Led Zeppelin played Perth - in 1972) at the Darwin Ampitheatre, testing out many new songs from the next album and opening the show with *You Got Nothing I Want*. Another surprise inclusion was Sam and Dave's *When Something Is Wrong With My Baby* done as a duet between Moss and Barnes.

Moss had some amplifier problems while a couple of other band members and crew suffered gastric problems during their stay in the Territory. Spare time was filled jamming at the Old Vic Hotel and cooling off around the pool. Steve Prestwich also found time to investigate aboriginal rhythms with the locals. The tentative title for the new album is Tunnel Cunts and the word is that the band will return to America in April/May of '83.

OCTOBER

Recording of demos moves to Paradise Studios, among the songs demoed is Phil's *Notion For You* and Don's *F-111* as part of sessions which would eventually become the *Circus Animals* album. There was another song of Phil's that was worked on for this album but which never saw the light of day. This was an early version of *The Game*, titled *Misadventure* which showed up on the Twentieth Century album, completed by Don's lyrics. Don would later state that the only reason *F-111* did not make the album was due to the comic book content of the lyrics which did not fit into the overall direction of the rest of the album. Both *Notion For You* and *F-111* are certainly very strong songs but one also suspects that their absence from the final album may have had something to do with Don's desire to move the band away from the more commercial direction it found itself in with *East*, a position he felt quite uncomfortable with.

Another song, which also was recorded at this time, is Jimmy's *A Little Bit Of Daylight* a song which would see daylight on Jimmy's first solo album. Another song demoed with the working title

Acapulco Piranha was Steve's *Forever Now*, a song which had been in the live set since before the US tour, this live exposure enabling the band to ensure the best possible arrangement for the recorded version. Letter To Alan was demoed with the working title Billy and Alan.

DECEMBER 8 - 13 Mixing

DECEMBER 14

You Got Nothing I Want is released and picked up by radio stations across the country, charting at No. 47 nationally first week in (it will peak at No. 12). The band announces a 12 week national tour beginning in Melbourne on New Year's Day. Fly to Lake Eyre salt lake to shoot the Circus Animals album cover.

DECEMBER

The band play low key shows around Sydney pubs billed as the Barking Frogs.

133)

[1981]

L.A. Country Club
From the left, Bryn Bridenthal, Marty Schwartz, Jim, Phil, Mel Poener. Marty was the inspiration for "You Got Nothing I Want".

(134

THE GAME

COLD CHISEL STORY

Circus Animals

HAVING RE-EVALUATED THEIR POSITION FOLLOWING THE US TOUR, COLD CHISEL RETURNED WITH A VENGEANCE, THE NEW SONGS HAVING AN AGGRESSIVE EDGE NOT PRESENT ON THE EAST ALBUM. IN THEIR HOMELAND THEY COULD DO NO WRONG, GOING FROM STRENGTH TO STRENGTH ON EVERY FRONT. THE LIVE GIGS, PARTICULARLY THE 'CIRCUS' SHOWS, WERE AMONG THE FINEST THE BAND EVER PLAYED. OUTSIDE OF AUSTRALIA THEY LOOKED ELSEWHERE WHEN THEY PARTED COMPANY WITH THEIR AMERICAN LABEL DUE TO A POSITION OF DISINTEREST FROM BOTH PARTIES. THE U.K AND GERMANY BECKONED.

JANUARY 1

Myer Music Bowl, Melbourne, with Moving Pictures and the Rock Doctors: 6000 people attend. This was a triumphant return to Melbourne with the band shying away from the usual pubs (the 'Bowl' was quite popular with rock acts at the time) and an audience keen to taste post - *East* Cold Chisel. They were not disappointed.

"Right from the opening chords of Conversations which had the crowd up on their feet, Cold Chisel proved that despite the conventional restrictions of their material, they could still put in an exhilarating and at times, flamboyant performance that built right from the first song to the last notes of the encore.

A number of songs (introduced by old growler Barnes) previewed from the late-February due Circus Animals album... their appeal is tailor made for the casual as well as the committed fan: accept them for what they are without probing into the sociological or musicological aspects and just allow yourself to drift away in the exhilarating rush. Even somewhere as large as the Bowl, the music came over as human and vigorous.

"The evening before I'd gone jogging in the gardens by the Bowl and heard the band doing a soundcheck. They were goofing off, but they sounded great. Steve Prestwich thrashed out a drum solo and Moss did some Hendrix neato tricks, even a Purple Haze blues workout from the Woodstock triple set. But when they did stop fooling around and launched into Star Hotel, the effect was stupendous to say the least.

"Cold Chisel right now are the hardest rocking band in the land. A great pop/rock band in anyone's book."

(EVAN GROVE, JUKE)

"From the first bars of their introductory Conversations the Chisel gave the audience its savor of belted, uncompromising rock'n'roll. And from that time the entire Music Bowl was on its feet. The focal point was undoubtedly the much emulated lead singer, Jimmy Barnes. Deliberately disheveled, Barnes was ceaseless energy. His vocals, both raucous and vitriolic, were contrasted by the smoother, occasional vocals of guitarist Ian Moss.

"Phil Small played a relentless bass guitar and Don Walker, keyboards while Steven Prestwich bore responsibility for the driving percussion..."

(JANE HOWARD, THE AUSTRALIAN)

| JANUARY 3 | Newcastle International Motordrome: 8,000 people attend. |
| JANUARY 5 | Taree, Manning River |

JANUARY 6 - COFFS HARBOR CIVIC CENTRE

"Cold Chisel were very, very, very loud. They were also very, very rawedged. Rock cranked up and out, interspersed with blues-root ballads, and blessed by the very lived-in voice of Jimmy Barnes..."

(TERRY BYRNES, JUKE MAGAZINE)

JANUARY 7	Playroom, Gold Coast
JANUARY 8	Playroom, Gold Coast
JANUARY 9	Noosa, Football Ground: 12,000 people attend.
JANUARY 10	Coolangatta, Grand Hotel
JANUARY 11	Grand Hotel
JANUARY 12	Italo Club Lismore
JANUARY 13	South Grafton R.S.L.
JANUARY 14	Manning River Hotel
JANUARY 15	Entrance District Sports & Community Centre
JANUARY 16	Vista Theatre, Woolongong

1982 - NEW ZEALAND

The band commence a seven date tour of New Zealand with support from INXS, including the Sweetwater Festival where they band headline with Ultravox and play to 60,000 people.

| JANUARY 19 | Hamilton Civic Centre with INXS |
| JANUARY 20 | Tauranga Soundshell with INXS |

JANUARY 21 - NAPIER, NOFIEW SOUNDSHELL

With INXS

Although INXS were only a shadow of the band they would become, the members of Cold Chisel became aware that their tour partners were bound for success when the Cold Chisel wives and girlfriends started commenting on the performance and charisma of frontman Michael Hutchence.

JAN 22 - PALMERSTON NTH SPORTS STADIUM

With INXS

"...Cold Chisel hammered -whittling away the skeptics and critics. And, a special tribute to guitarist Don Walker (sic). His voice is as good as his riffs.

"The band's last song, Twist and Shout - a worthy tribute to the Beatles, released the catch. The seething crowd turned into chaos. And the first song of the encore - Willy Nelson's Georgia - a duo from (sic) Don Walker and the keyboardist, soothed. It was a truly rousing rendition...

"...Cold Chisel came, conquered and left people with resolutions to get more at Sweetwaters..."

(EVENING STANDARD)

| JANUARY 23 | New Plymouth, Bowl of Brooklands With INXS |

JANUARY 24 - WELLINGTON TOWN HALL

With INXS

"Cold Chisel came on half an hour after the departure of INXS and tore straight into Standing On The Outside, the first track off their East album. How Jim Barnes' vocal chords have lasted this long with the treatment he gives them is a wonder. Perhaps it's due to the water and beer he constantly sucks on during his performance.

(136

137)

[1981]

"It's a great rock'n'roll voice and Ian Moss on lead guitar was the other strength of the band, which ripped into every song. The audience loved it...

"...When Cold Chisel left the stage for the first time, the audience yelled and clapped for more - and more is what they got. The band, joined by a couple of members of INXS, played a string of classics including Knocking On Heaven's Door, Honky Tonk Woman, and Twist and Shout.

The encore was more enjoyable than the concert. Those going to see Cold Chisel at Sweetwaters will not be disappointed."

(WELLINGTON EVENING POST)

| JANUARY 25 | Nelson, Trafalgar Centre with INXS |
| JANUARY 27 | Christchurch Town Hall with INXS |

JANUARY 31 - SWEETWATER FESTIVAL

"Chisel tore on in typical no-nonsense fashion.

"If there's a better hard-nosed rock and blues band in the world, I'd like to see it.

"Expectations were high - maybe too high - and the band certainly delivered the goods. But the scenes of frenzy normally associated with Chisel shows weren't in evidence.

"Standing On The Outside, Star Hotel, Don't Let Go, Shipping Steel, and the new single You Got Nothing I Need (sic) got the full-throttle treatment from the amazing Jimmy Barnes lungs. While on the bluesy end, Red House in particular served as a showcase for guitarist Ian Moss' daunting skill and taste.

"Barnes climbed the stages thirty foot scaffolding for a blistering Twist and Shout and even plunged into the jam-packed crowd, singing and waving his vodka bottle aloft in the sort of act of bravado he's cut his reputation on.

"The fairly high proportion of new, unfamiliar songs might have thrown a few in the crowd, but no-one could say Chisel didn't deliver the goods."

(LOCAL PRESS)

FEBRUARY 3	Castle Hill RSL
FEBRUARY 5	Manly Vale
FEBRUARY 6	Cronulla Workers
FEBRUARY 7	Maroubra Seals
FEBRUARY 9	Wagga, Plaza Theatre

FEBRUARY 10	Albury Cinema Centre
FEBRUARY 11	Shepparton Civic Centre
FEBRUARY 12	Bendigo Showgrounds
FEBRUARY 13	Horsham Town Hall
FEBRUARY 16	Collendina Hotel
FEBRUARY 17	Ballarat Civic Centre

April, 1982
Wentworth Park

(138

FEBRUARY 18 - THEBARTON TOWN HALL

(Adelaide) with the Divinyls

"First night and the crowd was rapt before the first note. No revelations, sure, but this band has matured out of sight. It now stands beside or above the world's best heavy rockers, AC/DC included. Years have moulded the rhythm section as solid as Gibraltar. Don Walker, whose writing contributions are so enormous he really doesn't need to play a note, is bouncing his keyboards along now too.

"But it's singer Jimmy Barnes and guitarist/second singer, Ian Moss who provide the fireworks. Jimmy just keeps screeching that amazing voice out. Guitar heroes are outdated, but Moss is something else. His singing also continues to mature...It seemed to go on and on: loud and punishing, but never boring (as such music can become) and often absolutely exhilarating."

(STEPHEN HUNTER, THE ADVERTISER)

"Most of the crowd would have stayed all night, but Cold Chisel is smart enough to leave them wanting more. Coincidentally, their final encore was the Beatles standard Twist and Shout, performed as an encore on that same stage by the Kinks last week.

"The Kinks were lucky to get there first - Cold Chisel would have blown them off stage."

(THE NEWS, ADELAIDE)

FEBRUARY 19   Thebarton Town Hall with the Divinyls

FEBRUARY 20 - THEBARTON TOWN HALL

With the Divinyls

"Cold Chisel have signed an exclusive worldwide deal with Polydor International. This will cover all territories excluding Australia, New Zealand, the United States and Canada, where the band are contracted to WEA.

"The first overseas releases under the deal will be the forthcoming Circus Animals. Polydor will release the LP at the end of March to coincide with its US/Canadian release through Electra.

"Chisel's manager, Rod Willis is flying to Germany at the end of this month to deliver the master tapes and have discussions with various record companies there about the way Chisel want to be marketed in Europe."

(JUKE MAGAZINE)

It is also announced that INXS will accompany Cold Chisel on their upcoming New Zealand tour.

FEBRUARY 22	Doyalson RSL (NSW)
FEBRUARY 23	Doyalson RSL
FEBRUARY 25	Plantation Hotel, Coffs Harbor
FEBRUARY 26	Cloudland Ballroom (Bris)
FEBRUARY 27	Lismore City Hall
MARCH 3	Armidale
MARCH 4	Tamworth
MARCH 5	Dubbo

MARCH

The *Circus Animals* album is released. Don Walker:

"The songs that the other guys are writing are getting so good these days you know, like Steve has written a couple of excellent songs for radio, while this time none of mine were suitable for singles or anything like that. Same with Jim and even if Steve's songs hadn't been there, Ian's written a couple in that direction a little bit."

139)

France, 1982
Jimmy with a bad hangover.

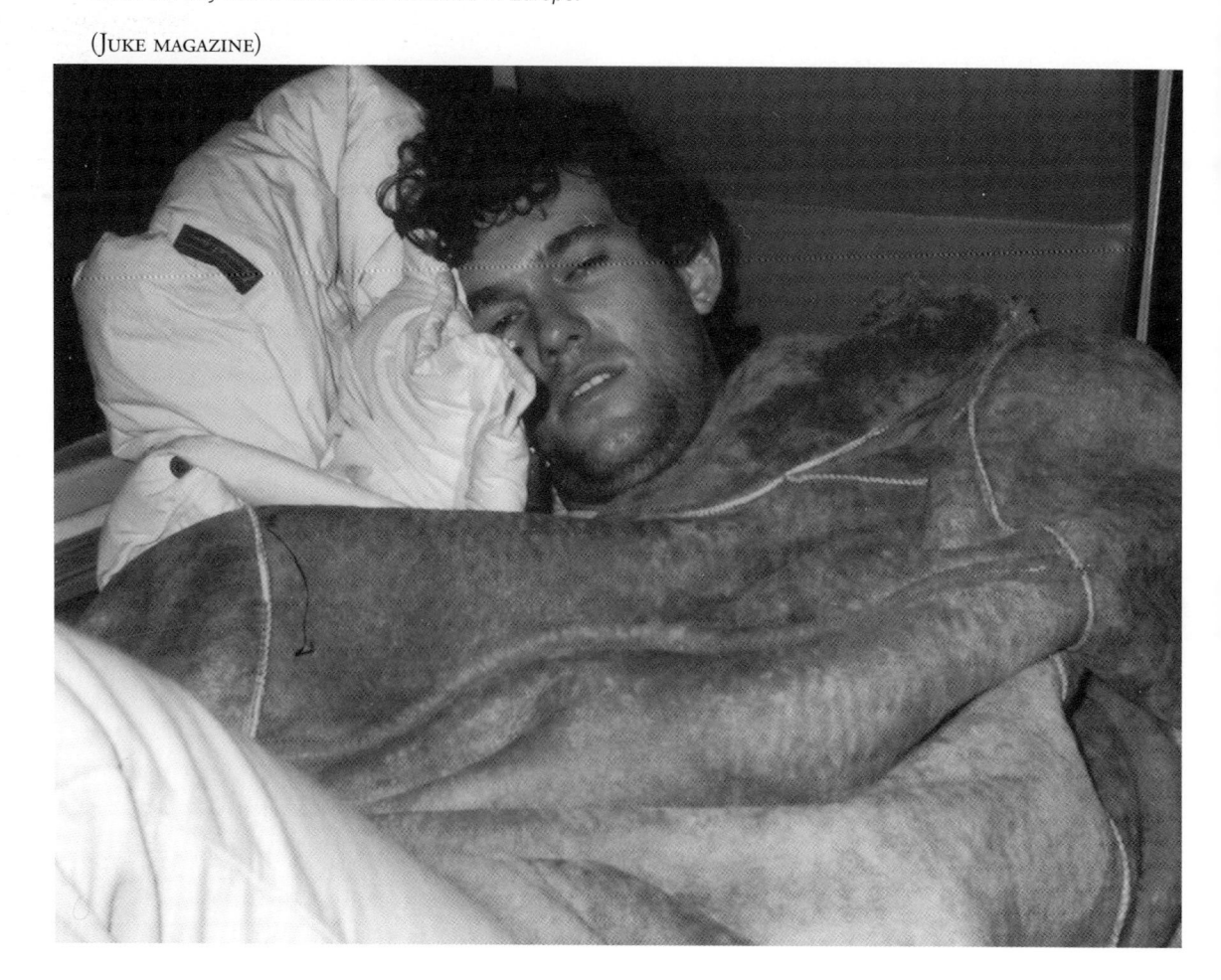

Billy Pinnell:

Q: *"Sometimes that can be a bad thing for bands, when there are too many songwriters vying for a spot on two sides of an album, like the Beatles would be a prime example I suppose. Is that going to cause any problems with your band?"*

A: *"No, we're quite aware of the pitfalls of a lot of writers in the band starting to fight for space and we make sure it doesn't happen just by being quite...you just have to be professional about it. Like I would have loved to have seen Phil get a song on the last album and he worked his heart out for the six weeks we were in the studio, he had two songs, both of which are potentially beauties and will probably turn up in the future. But in that six weeks, despite help from some of the rest of us just the last 10% of those songs couldn't come together so they had to be held over. That's a shame in some ways, but on the other hand you're trying to produce the best album that you can out of what's available at that moment and that's what everybody's aim is, not to see how many notches they can get on their gun for that album.*

"Everybody realises the commonsense of that situation when you start out with twenty songs or so for an album and you know there's only going to be ten get on there. It's up to the whole band to choose the best ten regardless of who wrote them. I don't mind if I've only got two songs on an album provided they're my best two songs and provided that that makes the best album that can be put out at the moment.

"I wanted the album to have more; I don't know what the word is for it, when you achieve swing in the studio. We always found it pretty hard to get that kind of thing happening that we can get happening live on good nights, we found it pretty hard to get that happening in the studio. But, with this album we really wanted to try and do it, so I was writing songs probably more with that in mind than even melody or anything like that. Steve with his own songs will always be more experimental with the beats behind it, like Best Kept Lies and Forever Now are not standard rock'n'roll rhythms."

"The music, in the main, is as coarse as battered sandpaper. The lead singer, perennially in search of rock's most decadent decibels, is known to rarely give prime time manners.

"And the band in elaborate defiance of all things sacred, makes little effort to entertain the establishment or pay its dues to the haute couture. Yet Cold Chisel manages to reel out some of the most articulate rock'n'roll around...Brash, forceful, full on it's what rock once was and what Chisel still are."

(ROBERT VELLA, JUKE MAGAZINE)

MARCH 3	New England University Armidale
MARCH 4	West Tamworth Leagues Club
MARCH 5	Dubbo Civic Centre
MARCH 6	Comb & Cutter
MARCH 7	Canterbury &Bankstown League
MARCH 8	Sundowner Hotel

No kinks in Cold Chisel

By Tim Parker

Ray Davies, of the legendary Kinks, would have been envious.

(140

REVIEW

There he was at Thebarton Town Hall, just a week or so ago, forced to cajole the audience into standing up.

When one-time Adelaide band Cold Chisel hit the same stage last night, the crowd bounced to its collective feet and showed no

the virtuosity of Aussie axe hero Ian Moss and the intelligent, driving songs of Don Walker make Chisel one of the best rock outfits anywhere.

MARCH 8

Circus Animals is released in New Zealand where it debuts at No. 11. Forever Now is released as the second single in Australia.

"The song that he (Steve) got on East (Best Kept Lies) was the first song he ever wrote and I just don't think it had occurred to him before that he could write songs that would get on albums. That song broke the log jam so he spent a lot of time sitting at home with a bass writing. And he came up with about five or six different ideas for the last album and two of them ended up on it. He's probably the most prolific of all of us these days."

(Don Walker talking to Billy Pinnell, June 1982)

MARCH 9	Family Inn
MARCH 11	Cardiff Workers Club
MARCH 12	Royal Antler
MARCH 13	Sylvania Hotel
MARCH 17	ANU Refectory Canberra (A.C.T.)
MARCH 18	Melbourne Ball, Crystals Disco
MARCH 19	Hobart University Building (Tasmania)
MARCH 19	Circus Animals debuts at No.4 on the 3XY music chart.
MARCH 20	Earl's Court, "The Venue", St.Kilda. with INXS (presented by 3XY and Dirty Pool)

(141)

April, 1982
Wentworth Park

MARCH 21	Frankston
MARCH 22	Memorial Club Alice Springs (Northern Territory)
MARCH 23	Memorial Club
MARCH 24	Memorial Club
MARCH 26	Perth

MARCH 27 - PERTH

Despite such a gruelling tour schedule, and after so many years, Ian still sees it positively:

"I must admit, I really enjoy it when we hit the road- pardon the term - when we're back together I still really enjoy it. It's just good fun, a good time clowning around."

(April 1982)

APRIL 5	Circus Animals is No. 10 in New Zealand.

APRIL 13	*Embassy Ball Room (Perth)
APRIL 14	*Embassy Ball Room
APRIL 15	*Embassy Ball Room
APRIL 16	*Embassy Ball Room

These shows are cancelled and the band instead play the Parramatta Leagues Club on April 15 as a warm-up for the circus shows.

APRIL 17

Wentworth Park, Sydney, "An Evening With The Circus Animals." These shows see the band performing along with circus acts in a circus tent setting, an idea conceived and set up by Mark Pope.

Set includes: Standing On The Outside / Merry-Go-Round/ Conversations/ Four Walls /Rising Sun/ Khe Sanh/ One Long Day/Letter To Alan/Wild Colonial Boy/ Choirgirl/ Breafast at Sweethearts/Cheap Wine/ Bow River/ Taipan/ Numbers Fall/ Forever Now/ You Got Nothin' I Want/ The Party's Over/ Daskarzine / Shake Rattle And Roll

"The big top filled to capacity, trapeze artists, dancing elephants, stunt motor cyclists...all the aspects of the circus at its best. Without intermission, Standing On The Outside flooded the marquee to enthusiastic applause and any doubts I had were quickly quelled. The sound close to perfect and a stage superior to many in some of Sydney's so called rock venues.

"With front man Jimmy Barnes providing some excellent vocal acrobatics, Chisel pumped their way through numbers from the earlier Breakfast At Sweethearts (Merry-Go-Round, Conversations), East, (Four Walls, Rising Sun), and Circus Animals in toto.

"Interfused with the classics Khe Sanh, Choirgirl, Cheap Wine, and highlighted with superbly crafted lighting effects, demonstrated most clearly in the venomous Taipan, Numbers Fall, (accompanied by caberet style dancing girls keeping up the tone of the circus), and the latest single Forever Now.

"The more than enthusiastic audience reaching fever pitch to the frantic You Got Nothing I Want. Pure, unadulterated power. Exemplifying just how diverse a band Cold Chisel are, a total mood change with the Claptonesque guitar work and poignant vocals of Ian Moss on the Walker penned The Party's Over.

"Then back up with a raucous finale. Will there be an encore? There had best be if the tent is to remain standing...band back on stage but where is Barnesy? Suspended from a bike on the highwire, a shower of balloons and 'Shake Rattle and Roll'.

(142

CIRCUS ANIMALS

DIRTY POOL CONGRATULATES
COLD CHISEL

on being voted best consistent
live act for the second year
in succession at the recent
1981 countdown awards

143)

we would also like to congratulate
the other nominees in this category

THE ANGELS

MIDNIGHT OIL

MENTAL AS ANYTHING

MONDO ROCK

To quote Angry Anderson
who presented the award
"It's consistently very
difficult to be
consistently good
live"

COLD CHISEL STORY

CIRCUS ANIMALS

"Raunchy, articulate and ultra-professional, Chisel with guest backing vocalists and brass section truly performed. Working together as a tight adept unit yet still allowing each member to promote his individual musicianship.

"In two invigorating hours Cold Chisel proved once and for all they are one of the finest live bands this country has produced for many years."

(ANNE HODGSON, JUKE)

APRIL 18

Wentworth Park, Sydney, "An Evening With The Circus Animals" Set List: Standing On The Outside / I'm Gonna Roll Ya / No Good For You / Taipan / Letter To Alan / Daskarzine / When The War Is Over / Four Walls / Khe Sanh (harp) / Wild Colonial Boy (harp) / My Baby or Ita / Numbers Fall (with dancers) / Forever Now / Houndog / Rising Sun / One Long Day / Choirgirl / Bow River / You Got Nothing I Want / The Party's Over / Cheap Wine / Merry Go Round / Star Hotel / Goodbye

"The show began with a Grand parade, naturally. Elephants, camels, horses and some of Australia's best circus acts marched around the ring and then the drama and spectacle commenced. There was a motorcyclist on a tight rope suspending a lady on a trapeze. A trampolinist who attempted to break his own world record for triple somersaults, (he got to eight and it wasn't announced whether he was successful or not). A daring young girl twirling on a rope by her ankle that induced dizziness just watching. Two lunatics who rode the 'Globe of Death' on motorcycles...

"If you weren't there well I'm sorry, but the whole show was brilliant."

(KENT GODDARD, RAM MAGAZINE)

These shows are the band's first live appearances in Sydney in over a year and are considered by some to be the best shows they ever did. The band plays to 10,000 people over the two nights. Phil Small recalls that the first night was the better of the two as he felt that the band had put so much work into the event that by the time the first night was over they were totally exhausted.

"This was at a time when the band was at their peak -one of the best live bands on the planet! The brilliant repertoire of songs begins at the first album with One Long Day and Daskarzine through to my favourite album, Circus Animals. With guest musos Dave Blight, a horn section and female

vocalists...We all know the kudos that have been thrown to Jim, Ian and Don through the performing years and after the party was over. A band is a band and it is rounded out by probably one of the all time great rhythm sections. Phil Small was probably the most underrated musician ever in the history of Australian music but his tone and ability to sit in the groove - there was none better. Steve Prestwich had the dynamics of Ian Paice and the feel of Bernard Purdie. Steve could have played with anyone from Duke Ellington to Iggy Pop. An outstanding natural musician."

(Sound mixer, Gerry Georgettis, 1996)

Although filmed and recorded, very little material from these has seen the light of day. A live take of *Taipan* surfaced on video (live footage AND live sound), as did a clip of *Bow River*, while a number of clips which surfaced on the Seeing Is Believing video featured footage, but not sound from these shows. Rumours abound of video and audio tapes from these shows, but as yet none are in circulation.

Almost immediately after these shows' the band take a well earned break, Jimmy and Jane heading to Japan.

APRIL 19 - FOREVER NOW IS NO. 17 NATIONALLY

Plans are announced for *Circus Animals* release in America, Japan and Europe in the second week of May, while a three-song EP is planned for Britain. The band also announce that they will tour wherever the record breaks first.

MAY

Freedom Soundtrack album is released.

"From medieval dance music to Oriental chants - from Harlem blues to wild colonial folk. Maybe it's not going to please the gut-rocking rage-at-all-costs Chisel fans, but no mind. Its unique, mystical manner will surely freak out those with a more classical upbringing.

"The two haunting tunes that demand the price of the album on their own are Port Adelaide II and the title theme. Running one into the other, Walker wallows in solitaire cocktail piano and coat and tails acoustics, moulding a dusky, solemn mood. Yet just when you think the guy has made one too many concessions to the bow-tie brigade in slams the gutter-drenched saxophone of Billy Rodgers, bringing some welcome dirt into the penthouse.

(144

"Port Adelaide I is not far behind in urgency with its languishing slow style. Don Walker has always hinted at a love of the blues and this morbid affair delivers it in liberal doses of decadence. The pitch-black, pitch-perfect harmonica and Walker's gravelled vocals definitely belong amidst the pool-halls and cigar smoke. Rougher than cue-chalk yet smoother than a snookerball.

"Of all the songs on Freedom, the one that most closely resembles the Chisel sound is the highway bully, Speed Kills. The most commercially alert track here, it brings forth the crazed beautifully deviate vocals of INXS' Michael Hutchence. So reminiscent of early Stones, about the time they were hot-footing it down Route 66.

"Yet rock and roll is not what this soundtrack is all about. It's back to traditional values with the boisterous hillbilly bash Sedan Hoot and onto Oriental pomposity with the placid intro and blistering extro of Eleuptheria.

"The introduction is especially haunting with its echoing chants ricocheting off the doomsday drumming.

"Finally Last Stretch and Forest Theme seal this rather morbid disc with plucky acoustics and inverted rhythms that go back to medieval days for their inspiration.

"If nothing else, they prove that there's a future in delving into the dark, distant past. Freedom of choice, I guess."

(ROBERT VELLA, 'JUKE')

MAY 3

Circus Animals is released in Germany and Holland. The album is still at No. 5 nationally in Australia. It receives rave reviews in Germany, which leads to a rethinking of their overseas strategy.

MAY 10

Circus Animals is No. 1 nationally while the Forever Now single is No. 5, it will peak at No. 4 the following week. The album has dropped to No. 43 in New Zealand, however this situation would soon be rectified (see June 7)

MAY 17

US release of Circus Animals and the Forever Now single. It is also released in Japan.

One reviewer for America's Billboard magazine compared the band's sound on *Circus Animals* to that of Bob Seger !

To make matters worse the US record company appear to be trying to keep the band a secret, whereas Men At Work's Business As Usual album receives immense press advertising, radio promos etc.- all the things needed to ensure that the appropriate people are aware of the album. The fortunes of the two records in the US could not be more contrasting.

JUNE 2 - PENTRIDGE GOAL, MELBOURNE

The band play to a mixed (male and female) audience for the first time in a jail, doing a shortened set in the middle of the day. Also present was Melbourne DJ Billy Pinnell who described the experience as one of the most memorable gigs he'd ever attended. Having not played for about six weeks in this case, the band would often do a show in a jail or under an assumed name in a small venue.

2 NIGHTS TO REMEMBER

WENTWORTH PARK
APRIL 17 & 18

145)

wea
Record 600113
(Cassette M6600113)

JUNE 3 - MACYS

The band play this show as the Barking Spiders, in what was supposed to be a secret gig, more than 1000 people turn up for the gig meaning 600 had to be turned away due to the limitations of the venue.

JUNE 4	Bombay Rock (Melbourne)

Circus Animals at No.3 (No.2 previous week) on the 3XY chart after 12 weeks in the chart. Forever Now sits at No.16, (No.6 the previous week) after 10 weeks in the chart.

JUNE 5	Tarmac Hotel
JUNE 6	Festival Hall, Melbourne , with Wendy and the Rockets and The Runners.
JUNE 7	

The band commence a four week pub and club tour of Melbourne and Sydney.

Forever Now is released as a single in New Zealand and the album turns around to head back up the charts there.

"*We never worked out five year plans and stuff like that, so I didn't have a real expectation of where I wanted to be in 1982. As far as the music we're producing, I think East was a sort of a culmination of a few albums - the product of working on a certain thing for a few years. I think the new album is a long way ahead of that, but it's not together in that I think the next album, or maybe the one after, the direction we're going will sort of peak again. So you get these two album or three album peaks...I think a lot can be done along the lines of what we started out with on Circus Animals.*

Q: Are you planning already songs for the new album?

Yes, I think we'll go into the studios and do some demos when we get back to Sydney. Everybody is writing at the moment.

(Don Walker talking to Billy Pinnell, June 1982)

JUNE 8	St Kilda Town Hall
JUNE 9	Waltzing Matilda
JUNE 10	La Trobe University
JUNE 11	Ritchies, Council Club Hotel
JUNE 12	Club Chevron
JUNE 13	Collendina Hotel
JUNE 15	Family Inn (NSW)
JUNE 16	Sefton
JUNE 17	Newcastle Workers
JUNE 18	Bruce Stadium, Canberra
JUNE 19	Manly Vale
JUNE 20	Penrith Leagues

(146

1974
On the set of the *Forever
Now* Film Clip

147)

| JUNE 21 | Newcastle Workers |
| JUNE 21 | |

Forever Now is released in Germany. The album is at No. 8 in Australia and No. 17 in New Zealand while the single is No. 23 in New Zealand.

JUNE 24	Marconi Club
JUNE 25	Vicar Of Inake Field
JUNE 26	Sydney Cove
JUNE 27	Astra
JUNE 30	Cronulla
JULY 1	Musos Club
JULY 16	Jindabyne
JULY 17	Jindabyne

JULY/AUGUST

The band tour New Zealand with stories filtering back to Australia of boxing matches and rugby games (in a pub). The tour is a sellout and the album goes to No .1, the single to No. 2.

JULY 28	Dunedin
JULY 29	Dunedin
JULY 30	Christchurch
AUGUST 1	Palmerstone Nth

AUGUST 3 - WELLINGTON, WITH ROSE BAYONET

"Barnes belted out a string of songs which were over-loud and therefore the sound was distorted. Any intensity which presumably, material of this calibre would have, was spoilt by a lack of emotion. It was a monotonous performance. The sound was blurred because of its volume, the style unoriginal and the material unvaried."

(Tracey Strange, The Dominion)

| AUGUST 4 | Hastings |

AUGUST 7

Auckland, Logan Campbell Centre. Parts of this show and its soundcheck are shown in an interview on New Zealand television, including portions of *Twist And Shout* and a new instrumental piece being worked on in the soundcheck. In answer to a question about the future, Jimmy replies, "Well just keep playing and hopefully get better and make better albums and try and crack it big overseas."

AUGUST 8 - HAMILTON

The Adelaide News reports that former Cold Chisel member, Les Kasmarek has started Adelaide Recording Studios, a studio specializing in demos for young bands and advertising.

AUGUST

Jim Barnes and brother John Swan jam with the Foster Brothers at the Strata Motor Inn, Swan shouting the entire 250 strong crowd a free drink, while Marcia Hines danced the night away on the dance floor.

SEPTEMBER 3	Grange, Campbelltown
SEPTEMBER 4	Amoco Hall, Orange
SEPTEMBER 8	Civic Centre, Broken Hill

SEPTEMBER 11

Memorial Drive, Adelaide. with Swanee and Mickey Finn, Radio SA FM 2nd Anniversary Concert. The band play to 14,000 people over two nights at this venue. Also on the bill are Mickey Finn featuring members of Fraternity, Jimmy's one time band.

"Barnes' stage antics became more defiant as the level in his vodka bottle, always close at hand, lowered. They culminated in a swift climb to the top of the scaffolding at the side of the stage, to dangle precariously from a steel pole to deliver the band's final number, a version of the Beatles' Twist and Shout.

(148

● *It has been said that Cold Chisel should be locked up, but never by us. It therefore came as a surprise to us to see them outside Pentridge prison in Melbourne, but we were so relieved to learn they were just there to entertain. So too was Melbourne's EON-FM announcer Bill Pennell who taped an interview with the boys from airing.*

"Moss, immersed in his own music and seemingly oblivious to the crowd, had the audience mesmerised with his easy manipulation of the guitar, and effortless singing which probably rivaled Barnes' voice once too often for the fiery vocalist's liking."

(KATHY NASH, ADELAIDE ADVERTISER)

SEPTEMBER 12   Memorial Drive, Adelaide.

Tickets : $10.70. (as above)

"For the girls, there was of course Barnes and guitarist Ian Moss, the black curled Adonises who opitimised the light and shade, the hostility and subtlety of Chisel's music. One banged about the stage demanding attention like a party show-off, the other mesmerised through his gentleness and obliviousness to the crowd. These days Moss's steady but slow rise in confidence makes him as much a potent force onstage as Barnes' near legendary antics...

"Like England's Clash or America's Band, Chisel have revitalised their music with a skillful assimilation of old traditions whereby they can leap from pop to rockabilly to blues to R & B without glaring cultural gaps showing. How they will face where they take their music is over-ridden by their killer punch- passion. It glosses over errors and Barnes' slurred and breathless mutterings; they filled our lives with a rare exhilaration which makes you forget everything else."

(JON FORSYTHE, 'JUKE' MAGAZINE)

UK 1982
Phil Small & Rod Willis
sample an ale.

TROPICAL TOUR

SEPTEMBER 15   Memorial Club, Alice Springs

SEPTEMBER 18 - DARWIN

The band play an open air gig to 8,000 people.

"Darwin had been blitzed with six weeks of intense promotion and they came in all sizes and colors. Anglo-Saxons, Aborigines, Asians, Air Force boys with fashionable short back and sides and an esky. Dads with little girls sitting on shoulders. Girlfriends obligingly carrying the extra baggage, a spare carton of stubbies.

"At 8pm Cold Chisel were onstage and blasted Darwin for two hours, including the almost obligatory two encores of three numbers."

(GREGG BORSCHMANN, THE AUSTRALIAN)

SEPTEMBER 21	Mt Isa
SEPTEMBER 24	Cairns
SEPTEMBER 25	Townsville
SEPTEMBER 26	Mackay Showgrounds
OCTOBER 1	Rockhampton Showgrounds
OCTOBER 2	Gladstone Skate Centre
OCTOBER 3	Maryborough Showgrounds
OCTOBER 8	Her Majesty's Theatre, Brisbane.

These shows coincide with the Commonwealth Games in Brisbane.

OCTOBER 9	Her Majesty's Theatre, Brisbane

With Aboriginal band, No Fixed Address and Goanna Band. These shows are called the Black and White Parity Ball. (A poster for this show is inside the sleeve of the Chisel album)

OCTOBER

The band record demos at Paradise studios with Steve Smith producing, including Steve Prestwich's *Nothing But You* and *Monica*, a Latin influenced track which had been a jam at soundchecks for some time.

Also recorded was Don's *Yesterdays*, possibly one of his finest songs. A true gem which unfortunately was not released until 1994, this version was not as well developed as the released cut. Other songs demoed were *A Way That I Know, A Week Away From Paradise, No Sense, Ghost Town, Yeah That One* (working title for *Nothing But You*), *Take A Shower, Five Five, Spend All My Life, Daylight, Anytime* and *Temptation*.

149)

Ian told the Perth Independent that songwriting had been a problem,

"It's hard work and it's not flowing like it used to in the old days when we recorded East. Back then we went in to write five songs and at the end of the week we had twenty to choose from. That hasn't happened again and I don't think it happens very often for anyone. I suppose it's mainly lack of inspiration...that's definitely been a bit of a problem lately. Everyone in the band has been going through a bit of a slow period.

"We went into the studio too soon. We ended up trying to write songs in the studio which is a good way to lose money. No-one had had enough time to get their ideas together and it was hopeless. We were trying out a new producer - a guy called Steve Smith (best known for his production on Robert Palmer's Sneakin' Sally Through The Alley), who we brought over from America and it just didn't work out. We're certainly going to think very carefully about producers in the future, and even see if we can handle the job ourselves."

OCTOBER 22   US record contract with Elektra is officially terminated.

EUROPE 1982

The positive response to the band's work in Europe, particularly Germany, combined with their US labels best efforts to ensure the band remain a well kept secret brings about a change in focus for the band's overseas attack. This tour sees the band play shows in Paris, Germany, Holland, Denmark and London.

"We haven't toured there (Europe) yet and we're really looking forward to doing something like that because it's new ground, a new environment." Jimmy continued, *"It's brand new ground for us 'cause we haven't had that much released in Europe and we've just done a new deal with Polydor and they did all of the rest of Europe and Britain and Japan, it's virtually new ground for us so it's exciting."*

(Jimmy and Steve on New Zealand television, August 1982)

One set list from the German tour, (probably Bremen) ran : Merry Go Round/ Khe Sanh/ Taipan/ Wild Colonial Boy/ Bow River/ One Long Day/ You Got Nothing I Want/ Rising Sun/ Forever Now/ Wild Thing/ Choirgirl/ Standing On The Outside/ Don't Let Go/ Star Hotel/ Goodbye Astrid/ ~ The Party's Over/ Cheap Wine/ Houndog

NOVEMBER 16   Hamburg

NOVEMBER 17 - HAMBURG

Reviews in Germany had been particularly impressive:

"Believe me, Cold Chisel are hot! They could even give AC/DC a run for their money."

(GERMAN MUSIC PRESS REVIEW)

"Friends don't be mistaken. Read carefully what I'm telling you here, O.K? Sentence by sentence, 'till the end, then nothing can go wrong. This is not one of the usual attempts to bring good music by unknown artist's home to you. This is a request and it is going to be successful. It must be. The group is called Cold Chisel. Never heard of, of course. Long forgotten is my unobtrusive review of their last LP East. That album is however a HYPERGREAT ALBUM.

"Got it? So further on. The group is far more famous elsewhere than here in Germany. Namely in Australia, where they come from and are at least as popular as Peter Muffig (A parody on the name of a German rockstar) is over here. Therefore they have recorded this live double album, Swingshift. Have you got it so far? The only thing missing now is a description of the music. Wild, powerful rock music, hard and raw, intelligent, imaginative, and very individual (really!). Let's say FULL HOUSE* by the J.Geils Band for now and today. Not a bit old fashioned, despite blues, reggae and rock'n'roll, despite Dylan's Knockin' On Heaven's Door and Long As I Can See The Light by CCR. Drummer Steve Prestwich has two toms, three cymbals but nevertheless the necessary murdering sound. Jim Barnes doesn't bother about his vocal cords but he can do more than just screaming. He proves that often enough.

"Who else is playing? You can see that on your own copy of the album. You will overlook The Party's Over like me, even if they should have included Standing On The Outside or Ita from East instead, or even Dresden from Breakfast At Sweethearts. Nevertheless, here are Cold Chisel. Friends, you are going to make them big over here as well aren't you? If you disagree with me, okay, then the six stars are just my opinion."***

(GERMAN MUSIC PRESS REVIEW)

*Highly praised live album from the J.Geils Band in 1972.

(150

[1982]

151)

Photo by Ian Green

NOVEMBER 18   Paris

"Our show in Paris late last year was a disaster", Ian Moss told Perth press in May 1983 in a reference to this date.

NOVEMBER 23   Marquee, London

* A poster for the above shows can be found inside the sleeve of the Chisel CD.

"...every expatriate Aussie and Kiwi in London packed in to see one of Down Under's hottest

"...Cold Chisel are hard rock; subtle and versatile on record, incredibly powerful live. They're seasoned troopers by now, with years of gigging behind them, and it shows. They know all about pacing a set, from the thunderous power chords of the wonderful "Taipan" through the down home rhythm'n'blues of "Merry Go Round", to the Latin tinged, Forever Now and the headbangers delight, You Got Nothing I Want.

"...Ian Moss' guitar work is much more in evidence live than on record, he plays lightning fast solos like they're going out of fashion.

"...Then they came in with a great raunchy, grinding version of the great Wild Thing, at which point your reviewer stopped reviewing and got down to some serious headbanging.

"For my money, Cold Chisel are the best thing to come out of Oz since AC/DC. For god's sake don't let them escape unheard!"

(Jill Eckersley, Kerrang)

NOVEMBER 24 - MARQUEE, LONDON

When Melody Maker's Brian Harrigan showed up late to interview the band, his small talk began with "What have you been doing since you've been in Britain?" to which Jimmy replied, "Waiting for you mainly." This perhaps emphasised the cynical attitude the band had towards Britain.

"We were doing some European dates and we thought that while we were around this way we might as well do some in Britain. We'd like to do well here but it's not like a major aim of ours, to be honest. It's probably more likely that we'd do better in Europe and in America than Britain anyway. People here seem to be more concerned with what you wear than what you play."

Jim also revealed in the interview that the band were planning to record their next album overseas, perhaps in Britain and that this is the one they're hoping will break them in America.

Following the Marquee shows the band embark on a short tour of England as support act for Slade.

A review for one of these shows gives some idea of the difficulties the band had to overcome at times. The reviewer had arrived late at the gig, believed the band to be the "new Rose Tattoo" and had made up his mind before the end of the first song (which was not the band's first!) Here's a small sample:

"Cold Chisel are huge, I'm assured, in the land of Paul Hogan and Norman Gunston, but they aint a tenth as funny. The crowd bayed lustily - but with me they were about as popular as a rattlesnake in a lucky dip!...The promise of a 'very long' set stretched before me. A cribbed song list offered only 16 titles, but if each one lasted as long as the epic before my ears at point of entry..."

(Sandy Robertson, unfortunately reprinted in Juke)

NOVEMBER 26   Paris

NOVEMBER 29 - ZECHE, BOCHUM

Set list-Merry-Go-Round/Khe Sanh/Taipan/Wild Colonial Boy/Bow River/One Long Day/You Got Nothin' I Want/Rising Sun/Forever Now/Letter To Alan/Wild Thing/When Something Is Wrong With My Baby/Standing' On The Outside/My Turn To Cry/Star Hotel/Goodbye Astrid/The Party's Over/Cheap Wine/Hound Dog/Four Walls/Breakfast At Sweethearts/Don't Let Go

This show is a great performance and a marvellous document of the band's progress in Germany. It gives you a special feeling to hear the band doing to a foreign audience what Australian audiences always took for granted. The old standard *Merry-Go-Round* is a great opening and there is loud applause at the opening notes of *Khe-Sanh* - surely Zeche Bochum can't be full of Australians!

Taipan and *Wild Colonial Boy* are ferocious, Jimmy improvising in every gap and Ian giving his all. By this point the audience have realised that this band is something very special and people are already yelling out loudly to Jimmy between songs. *Bow River* has the audience clapping along from the start and Ian gives an enthusiastic delivery. *One Long Day* is given a very different intro to that which it had on the '80 tour which segues smoothly into the main riff of the first, Moss sung section. Ian now doubles the melody of some phrases ("could not stand the pace" and "sometimes I get that gypsy urge to travel far") on the guitar as he would often do

(152

1982
Paris

during '83 also. *You Got Nothin' I Want* and *Rising Sun* are delivered flawlessly and the audience seem to be clapping along to current single *Forever Now* even before it has started.

Following an impressive *Letter To Alan* the band surprisingly launch into *Wild Thing!* This is the only occasion on which I have heard this song done in the main set instead of as an encore or set closer. It sounds as fresh and vigorous as it did in 1978, unlike some later '83 versions. Jimmy is already experimenting with some of the improvisations that would feature in the *Last Stand* versions. Many in the audience call out for *My Turn To Cry* while another asks for *Star Hotel*, but in another surprise *Something Is Wrong With My Baby* is played. Just when you think you can work out some rhyme or reason for the song choice- the early inclusion of *Wild Thing* seeming to suggest the intention to really charge up the pace right away. *Something Is Wrong...* is given a superb treatment. One gets the impression that the German audiences are not used to such great variety from a band. Cold Chisel were never ones to follow the accepted rules of rock.

Standing' On The Outside restores the pace and the audience are clapping along again. *My Turn To Cry* follows, as requested, while *Star Hotel* has an extended improvised intro which Ian is all over, in exciting fashion. Ian underlines Jimmy's melody for "uncontrolled youth in Asia" and this leads us to *Goodbye* and the conclusion of the main set.

On returning for the second encore, Barnes 'apologises' for the absent Moss, "We've lost half the band, Mossy's still wanking in the back room. He's dutch." *Four Walls* and a very restrained *Breakfast at Sweethearts* follow along with *Don't Let Go* to complete another successful German gig. Many reports suggested that the band was very close to breaking it really big in Germany (pop. 90 million) and this gig certainly suggests that this was the case.

NOVEMBER 30   Kiel

DECEMBER 1 - COPENHAGEN

Review: What's On, Dec 2: "Cold Chisel: Forever Now. Soporific - been done much better before and I thought this weeks batch of singles couldn't have got any worse."

Review: Newcastle Journal: "Cold Chisel: Forever Now. Superb, emotion packed effort."

Review: Music Week: "Cold Chisel, Forever Now : How Dire Straits might sound if they rocked harder. Tight vocal choruses, and for all the guitar derivations, it has an attractive air."

Review: Kerrang "Cold Chisel, Forever Now: A lacklustre cut from the generally impressive Circus Animals LP. Don't be fooled by the faceless Dire Straits/Police/Journey style of this ditty, for Chisel are, in point of fact, an excellent Aussie rock combo, as the aforementioned Circus Animals set amply proves."

153)

On the set of the
"Forever Now" filmclip.

(154

Germany 1982
Backstage

DECEMBER 3 - MARKTHALLE, HAMBURG

Attendance: 850 people

"In a few minutes Lionel Hampton will be onstage as well", joked someone as drummer Steven Prestwich used his brush for a good swing. Indeed, this encore sounded a bit unusual for the Australian quintet that had produced steelhard rock and boogie as well as soft blues and reggae- infected pop over the previous 90 minutes.

"Two figures in particular fascinate on this live expedition through the varied repertoire of Cold Chisel [In the German review an expression is used to translate the band name, which in English means "Corn Chisel"! : guitarist Ian Moss and lead singer Jimmy Barnes. It's not that their three fellow band members are doing only background work - on the contrary. But Moss and Barnes are the characters who give Cold Chisel the real, hard rock image, without compromise.

"Ian Moss never fiddles, like many of his string colleagues, like a precision engineer on his guitar. Every move is precise and results in full riff or the start of an ecstatic solo. Here lives the old style guitar-hero. And the Scottish rough-voiced Jimmy Barnes

never bothers with slushy vocal-purring. This rock'n'roll animal spits rasped clear sounds. It isn't always clean singing, sometimes it sounds more like the noise of a motor saw or orgiastic yelling. But it's in this way that Jimmy Barnes belongs in the same category as Bob Seger, Mitch Ryder, Elmer Gentry and Chappo."

(WILLIAM TRESEN [WILLI ON THE BAR], GERMAN MUSIC PRESS)

Set List: Merry-Go-Round/Khe Sanh/Wild Colonial Boy/Taipan/Bow River/One Long Day/You Got Nothin' I Want/My Turn To Cry/Forever Now/Letter To Alan/Hound Dog/Four Walls/Standing On The Outside/Don't Let Go/Star Hotel/Goodbye Astrid/The Party's Over/Rising Sun/Conversations

This show was filmed and broadcast on German television as part of the Rockpalast show, a show that each week featured a band playing live. Other bands to play this show in the early eighties included a very young U2 ('81 and '84) as well as Cheap Trick. Cold Chisel's performance was initially broadcast as a 45 minute special in April 1983, but a longer version was re-broadcast in 1993. The set list above is from the latter broadcast.

(156

U.K. 1982
Hammersmith Odeon,
Slade Tour

The band opens with a powerful *Merry-Go-Round* before going straight into *Khe Sanh*. *Wild Colonial Boy* and *Taipan* are blistering, with both Jimmy's voice and Ian's playing in fine shape. By *Bow River* any doubters in the audience know that this is the real thing, and the applause is generous. *One Long Day* has a blues intro, a little faster than that on *Swingshift* although the song itself is played at a slower speed like the first album version. *You Got Nothing I Want* has Moss really wringing molten notes from his guitar, and receives a very warm response from the audience.

The remainder of this gig is full of absolute killer performances, the band really giving their all for such a large TV audience, even playing *Conversations* and *The Party's Over* in the encores.

A fine show with a lot of rare numbers. If you are seeking a copy of this fine show beware that many of the copies in circulation are of inferior quality, due to repeat copying. There are also two versions of the broadcast; one is not as complete as the other, lacking some songs (i.e. *Merry-Go-Round* and *Conversations*).

DECEMBER 4	Berlin, Quartier Latin
DECEMBER 5	Darmsladt, Lopo's Werkstatt

DECEMBER 6 - MUNICH, ALABAMAHALLE

"This Australian band have given themselves the traditionally ugly name that most heavy metal outfits boast, and their music also is that of the old school - Gillan, Rainbow, etc. This should appeal to UK heavy metal fans who have adopted Rose Tattoo and AC/DC without a trace of xenophobia. Grinding vocals give way to softer ones on the occasional slowie, but for the most part the pace is frenetic. Well worth recommending to heavy metal fans among your clientele."

(CIRCUS ANIMALS REVIEW, MUSIC MAGAZINE, UK 1982)

DECEMBER 9	The Venue, London. This show is a sellout.
DECEMBER 10	Nottingham, with Slade

DECEMBER 13

Chippenham, with Slade "Metal" magazine reports:

"December 1982 - 700 or so Chippenham hairies are watching in puzzled immobility at five scruffy lads who are spraying forth a particularly infectious blend of

rock'n'roll from the stage. As one leather jacket remarked: "I don't usually listen to the support band, but this lot are dynamite! Er - who are they?"

"It really doesn't bother us that we have to start all over again. Just because we're big in Australia, it doesn't mean we automatically assume the rest of the world are going to kiss our feet. We'll never be pretentious. How ever far a band's got, there's still a long way to go." Steve Prestwich told a reporter after the show.

Back in Australia, rumours are rife that Cold Chisel are to split up, as Ian Meldrum reported in TV Week magazine:

"Apparently there was a fairly major argument among the guys in the band and their management had to be called in to cool things off.

"But, fortunately, everything did cool down after a while and everybody is happy again. Unfortunately, because I was one of the first to hear the rumor, a lot of people started accusing me of inventing it.

"Well that's not true... and I have confirmed with a top ranking executive from the Chisel's record company, WEA, that something really did go on.

"This year they've really only done one big tour.

"I hope to see a lot more output from the band in early 1983."

DECEMBER 14	St Austell, Cornwell
DECEMBER 15	Winter Garden, Bournemouth
DECEMBER 17	Hammersmith
DECEMBER 18	Hammersmith
DECEMBER 19	Birmingham Odeon

DECEMBER 20

Birmingham Odeon, last date on the tour with Slade

The band had certainly impressed a few people on this tour, with members of Motorhead and Girlschool gushing about them while Gary Moore in an interview said that they were his favourite new band. Magazines such as Melody Maker, Record Mirror, Kerrang and Fury were all eager to interview the band. There were also offers to do the European festival circuit in summer.

CIRCUS ANIMALS

(158

[1983]
Don't Let Go

THIS WAS GOING TO A BIG YEAR FOR THE BAND'S CONTINUED DEVELOPMENT. 1982 HAD BEEN A GOOD YEAR AND PLANS PENCILLED IN FOR 1983 INCLUDED A NEW SINGLE FOR JANUARY, A RETURN TO THE USA IN APRIL, AN ALBUM TO BE RECORDED IN MAY/JUNE FOR RELEASE IN THE FIRST WEEK OF AUGUST IN ADDITION TO THE EUROPEAN FESTIVALS, ALSO IN AUGUST. A MAJOR AUSTRALIAN TOUR WAS PLANNED FOR OCTOBER TO DECEMBER.

JANUARY

Recording demos at Rhinosaurus including *When The Sun Goes Down*, a song which had been around since 1978 when it was called *Idleness*. It was also demoed in around September of 1979 for possible inclusion on the East album. Other songs demoed were *Keep On Knockin'*, *No Sense, Only One, Fire,* and *Yeah That One (Nothin' But You)* and a new song of Ian's which has yet to see the light of day.

JANUARY 30	Narara Festival

30,000 people attend the three day festival. Having not played anywhere near Sydney or released anything in over 12 months, this gig is a big one for the band. In what many believe was one of their finest performances Cold Chisel are onstage for three and a half hours!

FEBRUARY	Juke magazine reports that Cold Chisel had considered calling it quits last year.
FEBRUARY 4	Blue Gum Hotel, (secret gig)
FEBRUARY 5	Moss Vale
FEBRUARY 7	Newcastle Workers
FEBRUARY 8	Wauchpoe RSL
FEBRUARY 10	Sth Grafton RSL

MARCH	Two dates are played as The Barking Spiders as warm-ups for the shows with Gary Young, Gary recalls one being at a hotel near Bowral.

MARCH 11 - THE PLAYROOM, GOLD COAST

These shows coincide with the Stubbies International Surf Classic. Gary Young (formerly of Daddy Cool and Jo Jo Zep and The Falcons, among others) fills in on drums during these shows while Steve has an operation on a back problem. A day was put aside for rehearsals in Sydney, which Gary recalls was mainly taken up with socialising as the guys saw each other for the first time in a month. Despite the small amount of rehearsal time, Gary describes his time with the band as "A real blast" and Don speaks highly of the shows they did with him. Gary later went on to play with the Phil Manning Trio, The Renee Geyer Band, The Black Sorrows and Cattletruck, among others.

Rod Willis: "There are offers and we would like to do the festival circuit during the European summer, but everything depends on when the next album is finished. We intend to take as long as we want to, and the guys are just writing the songs for it at the moment."

MARCH 12 - THE PLAYROOM, GOLD COAST

Set List: Merry- Go- Round / Khe Sanh / Forever Now / Standing On The Outside / I'm Gonna Roll Ya / When Something Is Wrong With My Baby / Wild Colonial Boy / Cheap Wine / Taipan / Letter To Alan / Rip It Up / Four Walls / Houndog / Rising Sun / Goodbye Astrid encores: Choir Girl / Ubangi Stomp / Wild Thing

This is only Gary Young's third show with the band and despite this and a few drum patterns that aren't what we're used to, the band still play a very impressive show. It's as though the chalange provided by the situation inspires them all to work just a little harder. The first couple of numbers sound as good as they've ever sounded and although *Forever Now* has a different drum arrangement, it still works.

At times Jim or Don turn to Gary and indicate what the drums should be doing at various points in songs and at other times they smile at each other as a different beat still seems to work in a song. This is definitely an 'on' night for Ian, I've never seen him move about the stage so much, at times jumping or executing little dance steps as he gets lost in the music.

"We'd like to take this opportunity to let you know that our usual drummer - for those who couldn't make it last night, our usual drummer Steve has done his back in - in a car accident - and can't play. He's in traction. Gary Young, of various bands, has come along, he doesn't know the songs and he's learnt 'em this week and he's done a fuckin' great job don't you reckon?"

I'm Gonna Roll Ya flies along, probably returning to the set for the reason that it's a straight forward rocker with an uncomplicated arrangement. *When Something Is Wrong With My Baby* allows the band to display another side, a soulful and tender duet between Ian and Jim. While this show is similar to the Sawtell RSL show a few days later, it is a little more inspired and the better of the two.

Wild Colonial Boy, Letter To Alan and *Taipan* are now the backbone of the set, demonstrating the band's ability to create intensity and power without depending on an increase in the speed. All are songs which, in the live environment, eclipse their studio counterparts. Ian cmploys some Van Halen - style tapping sequences to the final solo of *Letter To Alan*, a technique he has employed since the late seventies

but which has only been captured on record once on the live *You Got Nothing I Want* from the *Last Stand* album. More of this technique is in evidence in the intro to *Houndog*. This really was an 'on' night for Ian!

A powerful *Goodbye Astrid* finishes the set, complete with some improvisation on the intro, this part hadn't yet become too formularised, as it would later. The only surprise in the encores is the inclusion of *Ubangi Stomp*, sung by Gary Young, which he introduces as "probably the heaviest version ever played." *Wild Thing* includes snatches of *Voodoo Chile* in the guitar solo and some beautiful interplay between Jim and Ian in the interlude.

As in the Sawtell show, *Star Hotel, One Long Day* and *My Turn To Cry* are absent from the set, as are the new songs the band was working on at the time.

MARCH 13 - THE PLAYROOM, GOLD COAST.

All Gary Young knew about Cold Chisel, apart from the songs he'd heard on the radio was that they had a reputation for being real ragers. He was a little disappointed to find that this reputation didn't always apply to the band in 1983. He recalls returning to the hotel at a very late hour following some heavy partying after one show to find Ian and Phil swimming laps in the pool, Jim having a quiet night with his family and Don planning to checkout an impressive sunrise from a favourite location.

MARCH 15   Lismore RSL

MARCH 16 - SAWTELL RSL

Set List- Merry Go Round / Khe Sanh / Cheap Wine / Letter To Alan / I'm Gonna Roll Ya / Breakfast At Sweethearts / Wild Colonial Boy / Forever Now/ Standing On The Outside/ Rising Sun / When Something Is Wrong With My Baby/ Houndog / Bow River / Rip It Up / You Got Nothin' I Want / Goodbye Astrid - encores- Choirgirl / Ubangi Stomp / Wild Thing

Playing a slightly revised set with Gary Young on drums, the band open with a spirited *Merry Go Round* and move straight into *Khe Sanh*, which features both a keyboard and a guitar solo tonight. "For anybody who doesn't know it, our drummer has done himself an injury and is in hospital. Well, he's actually out of hospital now, but he was very sick. And so, he can't play drums. Gary Young is playing drums with us, he doesn't know the songs and he's doin' a fantastic job learning them." Jimmy announces to the audience.

(160

			COLD CHISEL SCHEDULE	
SATURDAY	MAY	7th	FREIHEITSHALLE	HOF
SUNDAY	MAY	8th	KONGRESSHALLE	AUGSBURG
MONDAY	MAY	9th	DAY OFF	
TUESDAY	MAY	10th	MUSICHALL	WUERZBURG
WEDNESDAY	MAY	11th	AUSSTELLUNGSHALLE	STUTTGART
THURSDAY	MAY	12th	AULA DER UNIVERSITAET	SAARBRUECKEN
FRIDAY	MAY	13th	DAY OFF	
SATURDAY	MAY	14th	HALL POLYVALENT	LUXEMBOURG
SUNDAY	MAY	15th	GARTENHALLE	KARLSRUHE
MONDAY	MAY	16th	DAY OFF	
TUESDAY	MAY	17th	STADTHALLE	ROSENHEIM
WEDNESDAY	MAY	18th	NIBELUNGEN_HALLE	PASSAU
THURSDAY	MAY	19th	DEUTSCHES MUSEUM	MUNICH
FRIDAY	MAY	20th	DAY OFF	
SATURDAY	MAY	21st	STADTHALLE	ERLANGER
SUNDAY	MAY	22nd	ELZER HOF	MAINZ
MONDAY	MAY	23rd	DAY OFF	
TUESDAY	MAY	24th	RHEIN-MOSEL-HALLE	KOBLENZ
WEDNESDAY	MAY	25th	MUSENSAAL	MANNHEIM
THURSDAY	MAY	26th	PHILIPSHALLE	DUSSELDORF
FRIDAY	MAY	27th	DAY OFF	
SATURDAY	MAY	28th	KLEINE STADTHALLE	BREMEN
SUNDAY	MAY	29th	KONGRESSAAL	MUENSTER
MONDAY	MAY	30th	DAY OFF	
TUESDAY	MAY	31st	SARTORY SAAL	KOLN
WEDNESDAY	JUNE	1st	STADTHALLE	BONN-
THURSDAY	JUNE	2nd	DAY OFF	
FRIDAY	JUNE	3rd	STADTHALLE	OSNABRUECK.
SATURDAY	JUNE	4th	STADTPARK (OPEN AIR)	HAMBURG
SUNDAY	JUNE	5th	MARKTHALLE	HAMBURG
MONDAY	JUNE	6th	DAY OFF	
TUESDAY	JUNE	7th	METROPOL	BERLIN
WEDNESDAY	JUNE	8th	SPORTHALLE	HANNOVER
THURSDAY	JUNE	9th	OSTSEEHALLE	KIEL

161)

song. *Breakfast At Sweethearts* features some superb guitar from Ian and some different drum fills from Gary, which work quite nicely.

Wild Colonial Boy is a chance for Jimmy to really stretch the vocal chords - as usual, stunningly powerful. Other bands could write hits like Cold Chisel, but this style of 'swamp' Australian blues rock is an area where no-one else could touch them.

Forever Now at times misses Steve's drum patterns, though the combined efforts of the rest of the band ensure that an impressive performance is the result. *Standing On The Outside*, like many of the songs in this set, retains a freshness one would not expect in a song which has been played so many times. *When Something Is Wrong With My Baby* changes the atmosphere in the room as people realise that an unfamiliar (most probably think it's a new Cold Chisel song) song is being played. This is a superb performance, done as a duet between Ian and Jim, with a piano solo and an inspired solo from Ian. Gary's feel for this type of song is apparent. This is another of those superb Cold Chisel performances which has never made it onto record.

Jimmy loudly cries "*Houndog*"and the band play an edited version of that song, lacking the slower bridge section as it does for the remainder of 1983. This is one of the first times this arrangement has been played, as the bridge was present in the first couple of shows Gary did with the band. *Bow River* is still fresh and inspired - Ray Arnott recalls Ian being reluctant to perform it later that year. It appears that the set is being made up as they go along, as cries of "*Rip It Up*" are heard from various band members as they work out what to play next.

You Got Nothing I Want and *Goodbye* (complete with blues intro, sped up ending and improvised coda led by Don) completes a most enjoyable main set.

Choir Girl has a lazy feel and Jimmy taunts the audience with "This is Countdown", nearly cracking up with laughter during the final choruses. "We'd like to take this opportunity to re-introduce Gary Young on drums, and I still think he's doing a fucking great job and he's gonna sing you a song." For the first time we have a Cold Chisel drummer singing lead vocal. *Ubangi Stomp* is a rockabilly number from an early Jerry Lee Lewis album, in this performance complete with yodels at the end!

Cheap Wine is next up, a powerful version (How many times have I said that?). One thing that becomes obvious when hearing Cold Chisel with a different drummer are the many subtleties of the drum arrangements in the songs - Steve is not a showy drummer in the style of Bonham or Moon, but a lot of thought went into his drum patterns and arrangements. Like the best bass players, their true contribution is not always apparent until they are absent. The band sound great with Gary, particularly on the more uptempo, less complex arrangements, which sound as good as they've ever sounded and allow him to just play rather than worrying about the unusual turns some of the other songs make.

I'm Gonna Roll Ya is a surprise inclusion, and one of the highlights of the set. It hasn't been played for some time and sounds fresher than ever for the break. Some versions at this time included choruses of *You Keep On Knockin'* towards the end of the

Wild Thing features a long three way improvised section in the bridge between Ian's guitar and his and Jim's vocals, not unlike that on the Last Stand version.

Notable omissions from this set are *One Long Day, Star Hotel, Taipan* (played at other shows with Gary) *My Turn To Cry*, and some of the new numbers the band had been working into the set.

MARCH 17	Newcastle Workers Club

APRIL 2 - SKYLINE

Ampitheatre, Bathurst Motorcycle Grand Prix with Choirboys and Boss. This cost the band at least $20,000 as the crowds did not have the money to pay the admission with the concert coming after three days of heavy partying and they had already spent the money on alcohol. The NSW Police Tactical Response Group were called to attend a riot which erupted as hundreds of drunk bikies tried to smash down the fences surrounding the ampitheatre at the site. (A poster for this show can be found in the sleeve of the Chisel CD.)

APRIL 6	Fraternity Bowling Club
APRIL 8	Fraternity Bowling Club
APRIL 19	Castle Hill RSL

"Rough as a shearers brawl, because they haven't played regularly for a while - but, despite some new arrangements and a handful of untried songs, reassuringly their usual self."

APRIL 20	Castle Hill RSL (NSW)
APRIL 22	Maroubra Seals

* These shows were to raise money for the upcoming second German tour.

APRIL 23	Maroubra Seals German tour.
APRIL 24	Maroubra Seals

APRIL 27 - OLD MELBOURNE HOTEL, PERTH

Set List (probably complete)-Taipan/ Standing On The Outside/ Rip It Up/ Letter To Alan/ Hold Me Tight/ Flame Trees/ Merry-Go-Round/ My Turn To Cry/ Khe Sanh/ River Deep Mountain High/ Rising Sun/ Four Walls/ Forever Now/ Wild Colonial Boy/ Bow River/ Ghost Town/ You Got Nothin' I Want/ Goodbye Astrid/ Georgia (inc. This Guy's In Love With You intro!)/ Temptation/ Home and Broken Hearted/ Breakfast At Sweethearts/ Wild Thing

This show is another gem, and a fascinating period in the band's history. The band is really firing, having recently blown away the crowds at Narara

and Bathurst, completed a successful tour of Germany, and with swag of great new songs the band had every reason to be feeling pretty good.

Taipan has some almost scary shrieks from Jimmy in the intro - his voice on this night is brutal.

How anyone can sing with such aggression night after night is a mystery to anyone who has ever tried to sing. However this is not just Jimmy's show, the whole band is on song tonight, experimenting with new songs and inspired improvisation in older songs. *Standing On The Outside* is followed by the Little Richard/Elvis standard *Rip It Up*, a frenetic rendition of a song which was a regular of almost all '83 sets. This version features extended solos which would be absent in later renditions. Yet another cover version to add to the list.

The ballad intro to *Letter To Alan* is an uncomfortable contrast to the pace set thus far. Moss takes all the solos as on the recorded version, unlike later in '83 when these would be shared with Walker for reasons we can only speculate upon. Tonight Moss is particularly creative, coaxing squealing harmonics from the guitar and fast octave phrases which were a trademark of his at this time. Things really get interesting with an early rendition of *Hold Me Tight* which starts with a descending abrasive guitar run, not unlike the chorus part of *Whole Lotta Love*. Jimmy is not certain of many of the lyrics and he comes in a bar late after the guitar solo, but the overall effect is most impressive and a lot more inspired than the versions which would be released more than six months later- with another drummer. *Flame Trees* is played next, some twelve months before its eventual release. Jimmy mentions that it was written by Steve and he is reminded by Don that he has a hand in it too.

What does become obvious in this show is that the band was ready to record a new album now. Four new songs are played and we know that many others had been demoed for a new record (Idleness a.k.a. *When The Sun Goes Down* in January for instance. *Build This Love* was another). Only four songs from *East* are played in the set and a number of covers are included, suggesting that the band was eager for fresh new material.

The set continues with a return to the more familiar *Merry Go Round*, a song that always seemed to be a guarantee of a powerful performance. *My Turn To Cry* recalls that Countdown appearance in '81 and *Khe Sanh* is always an audience favourite. *River Deep Mountain High* is an astonishing performance and a song which would be brought back later in the year for the *Last Stand* tour. Another of those covers. This was released (twice!) as a B-side and is well worth seeking out.

Wild Colonial Boy is another song that seemed to bring out an inspired performance from the band. It is apparent that the band appears to relate to the *Circus Animals* material much more than to the more pop oriented *East* material. The new material (to eventually be released on *Twentieth Century*) signalled another phase which would not ever be as clearly defined, due to the problems which would eventually lead to the band's split. This period is particularly interesting as it documents the early part of that next phase before any of these problems had arisen and blurred the natural musical development of the band.

Ghost Town is one of these songs and it too seems to make a lot more sense and sounds a lot fresher than the recorded version, even if Jimmy really does struggle with the lyric- the enthusiasm is apparent.

Goodbye already has the improvised blues intro used in Last Stand shows, with Jimmy commenting that "anybody can play guitar" when Moss threatens to steal the show from his intro.

The encores really make this show special with Walker and Moss including snippets from Burt Bacarach's *This Guy's In Love With You* into the intro of a beautiful rendition of *Georgia*. *Temptation* is a surprise inclusion here also as the song was not a regular in later '83 sets. Jimmy next asks if anyone has any requests and (not played for some) *Home and Broken Hearted* is done. There is some hesitation before the lines "went to a party tried to drink myself happy" which are sung together by Jimmy and Ian, possibly as they try to remember how it goes! *Breakfast At Sweethearts* and *Wild Thing* complete a very enjoyable night, for both band and audience.

| APRIL 28 | Perth |
| APRIL 29 | Perth |

EUROPE 1983

"Germans are very rock orientated. They are probably more into hard rock bands than people in Australia", Ian Moss told local press in Perth before leaving for the band's second tour of Germany.

| MAY 1 | Fly to Germany |

GERMANY 1983 (SUPPORTING ROGER CHAPMAN)

Review: NORTHBOUND (THE BEST OF COLD CHISEL)

"Included on this sampler are the eleven best known titles from the first three LPs, which are largely unknown here, of this Australian band. Following the excellent double live LP Swingshift there should be a lot of interest now for the old songs from the LPs Cold Chisel, Breakfast At Sweethearts and East.

Northbound documents the time span between 1978 and 1981, wherein the quintet from the fifth continent didn't act as hard-core (as on the latest LP Circus Animals) but looked for success with a wide spectrum of mid-tempo styles: rock, blues and folk elements were used to create an excellent mixture.

Seven of the songs are, however included in extended versions on the live double LP.

***Uli Clef

(GERMAN MUSIC PRESS REVIEW)

| MAY 7 | Freiheitshalle, Hof (Sat) |

Attendance: 900 people, the band receive a good reaction.

| MAY 8 | Kongresshalle, Ausberg (Sun) |

Attendance: 1000 people, another good reaction

| MAY 10 | Musichall, Wuerzburg (Tues) |

Attendance: 1200 people, the band's set gets a poor response from the audience.

| MAY 11 | Ausstellungshalle, Stuttgart (Wed) |

Attendance: 1500 people, the reaction here is only 'medium'.

| MAY 12 | Aule Der Universitaet, Saarbrucken (Thur) |

Attendance: 1800 people, this is a younger crowd who give the band a great reaction.

| MAY 14 | Hall Polyvalent, Luxembourg (Sat) |

Attendance: 1000 people

MAY 15   Gartenhalle, Karlsruhe (Sun)

Attendance: 1800 people, a good crowd reaction.

MAY 17 - STADHALLE, ROSENHEIM (TUES)

Attendance: 800 people, the band performance is 'slack', the hall echo is bad and the audience response is poor.

The shows were not going well. The German promoter even went as far as suggesting the band's drummer was letting them down. Steve, if he was playing poorly, has no idea why, and certainly did not intend to do so. The band themselves were totally perplexed and changed the set around from one night to the next, hoping to improve the situation.

At around this time Jim calls Melbourne drummer Gary Young, who had filled in for Steve just a few months previous and asks him to come to Germany on the next flight, that Steve was not playing well and that the tickets (to Germany) would be waiting at the airport. Gary had just committed himself to Renee Geyer's band and was about to embark on a tour with them, something he felt he could not back out of at such short notice.

Matters were exacerbated when members of the Roger Chapman entourage took exception to the presence of Jim's wife, Jane, and baby daughter on the bus, and asked them to make other travel arrangements.

Jim now believes that much of the frustration was taken out on Steve, because he tended to get his back up and be stubborn when criticized, and this made him a target. Jim also felt that he was working his butt off while others were not and it was at this time that the seeds for a solo career were sown.

The worst moment was when Jim actually left the band, leaving Rod Willis and the band with a tour to complete and no vocalist. Jim was soon back in the ranks, but it was a significant moment.

MAY 18   Nibelungen Halle, Passau (Wed)

Attendance: 1000 people, the band give an excellent performance in a good venue and receive a good response.

MAY 19   Deutsches Museum, Munich (Thur)

Attendance: 1800 people, the band play well however the audience are not allowed to stand, restricting their response.

MAY 21   Stadthalle, Erlangen (Sat)

Attendance: 1200 people, the band play a good gig and receive a good response.

MAY 22   Elzer Hof, Mainz (Sun)

Attendance: 1800 people, the band receive a reasonable reaction for a fair performance.

MAY 24   Rhein-Mosel-Halle, Koblenz (Tues)

Attendance: 1800 people, the band play a bad gig although the audience reaction is good.

MAY 25   Musensaal, Mannheim (Wed)

Attendance: 1800 people, good audience reaction.

MAY 26   Philipshalle, Dusseldorf (Thur)

Attendance: 1800 people, best audience reaction of the entire tour (so far)

MAY 28   Kleine Stadthalle, Bremen (Sat)

Attendance: 1500 people, reasonable audience reaction.

MAY 29   Kongressaal, Munster (Sun)

Attendance: 2000 people, the band play a good gig and receive a very good reaction.

MAY 31   Sartory Saal, Koln (Tues)

Attendance: 1600 people, an excellent performance from the band and a great reaction from the audience.

JUNE 1   Stadthalle, Bonn (Wed)

Attendance: 1600 people, a great reaction from the audience.

Germany, 1983
Ian tuning up backstage

(164

JUNE 3   Stadthalle, Osnabruck (Fri)

Attendance: 1000 people, good audience reaction.

JUNE 4   Stadpark, Hamburg (Sat)

Attendance: 3200 people in an open air venue who give the band a great reaction.

JUNE 5   Hamburg, Marktellier (Sun)

The band play poorly and the audience reaction is poor.

JUNE 7   Metropol, Berlin (Tues)

Another open air show to 3500 people, the band performance is only OK, the sound is bad and the audience response OK.

JUNE 8 - SPORTHALLE, HILDESHEIM, HANNOVER (WED)

Attendance: 500 people, an excellent audience reaction to a good gig.

Set list (probably complete) - Wild Colonial Boy/ Forever Now/ Hound Dog/ Painted Doll /Breakfast At Sweethearts/ Khe Sanh/ Hold Me Tight/ Taipan/ Merry-Go-Round/ Rip It Up/ Four Walls/ Bow River/ You Got Nothin' I Want / Goodbye Astrid

This was the period when the band was falling apart internally, reportedly due to problems with Steve. This was Steve's second last show with the band (apart from the Last Stand tour). One would expect this show to document any musical problems in the band - Don stated in interviews that the band had played some 18 shows without a good one and that the set list had been decimated in an attempt to solve the problem. There is little evidence of this in this gig, apart from the fact that Jimmy appears agitated by a few things during the show.

Cold Chisel

26.5.	Düsseldorf
28.5.	Bremen
29.5.	Münster
31.5.	Köln
1.6.	Bonn
3.6.	Osnabrück
4.6.	Hamburg
5.6.	Hamburg
7.6.	Berlin
8.6.	Hildesheim
9.6.	Kiel

The show is off to a fine start, there is no noticeable problem- it's not the best Cold Chisel gig, but their standards were very high. *Houndog* is missing the slow bridge section, as it would for the remainder of '83. *Painted Doll* has a few lyric changes and Jimmy is really pushing his voice (as usual). *Khe Sanh* is not recognised by the audience (no response to the intro) and features a quite different guitar solo from Ian. *Hold Me Tight* is the second new song and it is given a powerful delivery. *Taipan* is introduced as "a song about a snake, one that is only found in Queensland, Australia". *Taipan* and *Merry-Go-Round* are both powerful performances, as is *Rip It Up*.

It's hard to find fault with these performances, even when you know that the band was not happy with them. By this point in the show the audience is applauding enthusiastically, but Jimmy comments on the piano sound, "Can you hear that? Fuckin' horrible". As Ian commented in an interview with Donny Sutherland, the drop in the intensity of the shows would not be apparent to the audience, but it was to the band. The other factor to consider is that the band was never one to air dirty laundry in public and 'musical differences' has long been given as an excuse to cover other problems.

During the bluesy intro to *Goodbye* someone obviously annoys Jimmy, his response being "go and get fucked cunt", obviously not a good day for Jimmy. The band leave the stage to a very enthusiastic audience, obviously won over by the band's performance even though all was obviously not well behind the scenes.

JUNE 9 - OSTSEEHALLE, KIEL (THUR)

Described as a good gig and a good audience response.

The tour had not been a good one. Jimmy described it to Scott Howlett in *Playboy* magazine:

"We couldn't play during the German tour. I was up there singing like a fuckin' arsehole. We were playing like shit, we weren't concentrating, we were making mistakes, and I remember one night during the last song, Don Walker, totally out of character, just put his hands under his CP70 keyboard and tipped the whole lot up and walked off in disgust. I knew that we were finished.

Germany
Chapman roadie, Jim &
Tour poster.

(166

"The band was just playing like a load of shit. It was the worst tour we'd ever done." At this point Howlett reminded him that this was when Steve left and Jimmy's voice dropped to a whisper.

"I don't know what happened. I don't know. It was really weird. Steve had problems and we'd tell him every night. : 'You played like shit, and he'd say [mocks a Liverpool accent]: 'No I was perfectly in time, you four were fucking out of time'.

"I think he was the first one to be bored. He was the first to be sick of it basically and he didn't give a fucking shit when it came to quitting time. He was quite happy about it. I think the only reason I sang good some of the time was because I was the one out front and I was the bugger who was gonna be copping bottles in the head. The others could afford to lose concentration and I guess Steve just saw the writing on the wall and just didn't give a fuck.

"So he was the first to go and then when that happened the band was slowly fading." Rod Willis saw it thus: "I think we all anticipated a split was going to happen. Germany was a pretty unbearable situation. I didn't think they played as badly as they thought they did but there were definitely problems within the band at the time. Things were not happening for them outside Australia and they were also getting frustrated with each other and it manifested itself to a great degree during that German tour."

Don recalls the tour this way:

"In about June or July of that year we did a tour of Germany. The band was going well up until then. On the tour of Germany the band fell apart solely because the band played so badly and we couldn't fix it. We'd come across situations before where we'd maybe play one bad gig or two bad nights in a row would drive everybody insane and we would have to fix it. Heads would roll, we'd be stuck into each other, all that kind of thing until we fixed the problem. Because great shows had become like a drug. When we reached Germany, from the first show we played unbelievably bad, sloppy and we couldn't get it together. After five or six bad shows the feeling within the band and on the tour was, we couldn't fix it. We tried everything.

Germany, 1983
Lyor, Jim, Don, Mark
Pope, Ian, Ray Hearn &
Steve

167)

"In the end, halfway through the tour we decided collectively that the problem was that Steve was not holding up his end- because he didn't really want to do that tour. So we decided to make a change there which was a radical move seeing Steve had been with us at that stage for ten years. But that was really, that really meant the end. You couldn't eject such an important element as Steve without the rest of the chemistry falling apart."

Steve Prestwich told Toby Creswell:

"It's probably safe to say that if I wasn't playing to my fullest ability, it was as a result of something, rather than the thing itself. I really did give it one hundred percent but one hundred percent was not being witnessed. I certainly didn't go with the intention of playing badly or trying to wreck the band. I knew, in my heart, there was more to it than copping it sweet. Whatever is happening in the band is going to manifest itself in the band's performance, myself as well. To me, it seemed like a symptom that the band was coming to its natural end. It had been ten years after all. The band was a different band. It was now five individuals."

| JUNE 12 | Arrive back in Sydney |
| JUNE 15 | Band manager Rod Willis has a meeting with Don Walker. |

JUNE 17

"STEVE PRESTWICH LEAVES COLD CHISEL", was what the headlines said, but in fact Steve had been sacked. Rod Willis said in the press that Steve would probably concentrate on his songwriting, as a number of people had expressed interest in his songs,"He's laying rather low at the moment because everyone's trying to ask him questions." Press releases at the time suggest that the band is looking to the future and Rod Willis talks in excited tones about plans to celebrate the band's tenth anniversary in October. They were hoping for a big jam session featuring past band members (one presumes they are referring to those who have jammed with them over the years as there has really only been one other band member, bass player Les Kaczmarek who had departed eight years previous).

| JUNE 21 | Band meeting. |
| JUNE 23 | Rehearsal & band meeting RAY ARNOTT |

JULY 2

The band begins rehearsals at the Manly Vale Hotel with Ray Arnott on drums, before launching themselves on yet another tour. Former Spectrum and Dingoes drummer Ray Arnott had filled in for the band in late 1979 and recalls that he was in good shape for the tour as he was preparing his second solo album for release at the time, and knowing that he was soon to shoot the cover and promo photos, had been working out and improving his fitness. Ray had been doing sessions for the Vanda & Young stable, including work with John Paul Young, Cheetah, The Choirboys and three Flash'n' The Pan albums. Ray's first solo album (1980's *Rude Dudes*) featured both Jimmy Barnes and John Swan singing backing vocals on a couple of songs.

Ray had enjoyed his earlier brief stint with the band and felt an affinity with Don's writing, which he likened to that of Vanda & Young in its Motown influence. Ray's status with the band was always only temporary, although he thought it might have lasted a little longer than it did.

Ray noted that one of the ways in which the band had changed since he last played with them was that "The band was much more in tune with contemporary sounds - there was more of an urgency of being professional. Don, in particular was much more conscious of that. Jimmy's efforts had not changed, He always works 175%. It's a bit like Here we go, keep up or hang on."

Germany
Bowling with the record
company.

(168

STEVE PRESTWICH LEAVES COLD CHISEL

After nine years STEVE PRESTWICH becomes the first founding member of Cold Chisel to exit. Predictably, no one in the band wants to say anything; "Prestwich's departure is totally amicable" according to the band's manager, ROD WILLIS.

"He's laying rather low at the moment because everyone's trying to ask him questions. . . He hasn't divulged any ideas for joining a band again; I believe he's more interested in songwriting."

Since Prestwich penned two of Chisel's most successful recent singles — *Forever Now* and *When The War Is Over* — this could be a sensible move.

"He's got a lot of songs that haven't been able to be used by Cold Chisel," continues Willis, "and he's got a real commercial end to his writing." (Make of this what you will.)

"I know there's a lot of interest from a lot of parties: I don't think he's going to have much problem getting them recorded."

Meanwhile his former playing partners are being fairly leisurely about *their* next vinyl venture. "I wish I could say 'Yes, there will be a new Chisel album before Christmas,'" sighs Willis, "but I'm not going to set any time limits. We won't be going into the studio as such, but rather recording sporadically as the songs are road-tested and we feel they're ready.

"We've had a big re-think on musical direction, and that's not just since Steve's left the band. Over the last few months a lot of thought has gone into what we're going to perform on stage, what direction we're going in.

"I'm not saying that we're changing dramatically in any area

WANTED: one hard rock and roll drummer. No syndrums. Must have own vodka supply.

bring synthesers in!" (A million heartseat easier!) "If we're emphsising any direction it's not we've been from the start: a *hard* rock and roll and, as opposed to a heavy' rock and roll band.

So. . . WANTED: One Hard Drummer. At press time Willis couldn't give any clues, even though the band starts n interstate tour on July 8. Apparently at least three stickmen are under consideration; in any case no decision will be made about anything more than temporary status till later in the year. After two weeks in

made about New South Wales and Queensland gigs. And there won't be any more overseas jaunt until a new album is read The significant point her is that while Cold Chisel remain with WEA in Australia, their worldwid contract with Elektra ha ended: obviously Willis wants to know what his new product is before auctioning it to the many interested international record companies.

(Footnote: the first two gigs with the new-look Chisel *are* in Sydney, bu don't count on getting tickets. The first is at

JULY 8	Silverwater Women's Prison (Ray Arnott's first gig)
JULY 9	Long Bay Jail

JULY 12

The band commence a 20 date tour of Melbourne and Adelaide, culminating in 3 shows at Jindabyne snow resort. Scott Howlett, who worked with the band on that tour, recalled that it was clear that the band members were keeping to themselves. They were staying in separate accommodation and the camaraderie that had existed between the band was gone. Howlett does believe though that despite this the band did put in three of their best performances on this tour.

JULY 12 - LA TROBE UNIVERSITY (MELB)

Set list (complete) -Wild Colonial Boy /Rip It Up /Painted Doll /Rising Sun /Breakfast At Sweetheart's/ Letter to Alan/ Hold Me Tight /Numbers Fall/ Juliet/Star Hotel/ Taipan/ Merry-Go-Round/ Sing To Me / Only Make Believe/ Bow River/ Got Nothin' I Want/ Goodbye Astrid/ Something's Wrong With My Baby/ Standing On The Outside/ Hound Dog/ Your Cheatin' Heart/ My Turn To Cry/ Tomorrow

This is the public debut of the 'new' Cold Chisel, without Steve Prestwich. At this stage there was no talk (publicly) of the group disbanding and the intention was to do this tour to recoup expenses from the German tour and then to do the now overdue next album. Prestwich songs are absent, although all of Don's newies are still present as well as a large serve of 'different' cover tunes.

The venue, a large hall is absolutely packed to the rafters as it seems that at this period in the band's history they appear to underestimate their own drawing power. From within the band things may have been in disarray, but from a public perception, the legend was as great as ever. *Wild Colonial Boy* opens proceedings and although the performance sounds a little sluggish, there is no obvious difference to be detected by the audience. The band immediately move into *Rip It Up*, with new drummer Ray Arnott pausing on the intro a couple of times for fear of interrupting Jimmy's "thank yous". *Painted Doll* is next, at a more relaxed pace than it is usually played - perhaps Arnott sticks to the pace the songs were rehearsed at rather than the pace Jimmy pushed them to in performance.

"I'd like to take this opportunity to ah, introduce Ray Arnott playing drums here. And he's had a week's rehearsal. He's doing' pretty fuckin' well don't you think so eh?" is Ray's introduction to the audience before the band launches into *Rising Sun*. The show begins to warm up as Moss hits some magical notes in *Breakfast At Sweethearts*. He really takes the intro and solo to places they haven't been before and assures the audience that the magic is still there - its just not conjured as readily as it once was.

Letter To Alan has Walker taking some of the (previously) guitar solos although Moss is responsible for some lovely volume swells in the slow bridge section, and his solos sound quite inspired in the sections he does play. This arrangement would stay with this song for the remainder of the year.

"Having' a good time or what?" Jimmy asks after *Hold Me Tight*, "we're starting to find our stride you know? This is the third gig we've done with Ray by the way. We've done a few in Sydney, they were both in goals and so the audience has no chance to fuck off if they wanted to." *Numbers Fall* has been recalled to the set, it hasn't been played for a while and is gone by next week's Geelong gig. Still it's good to hear this bluesy song done live.

"We've got to relearn all these songs you see?" Jimmy explains. "Here's one that we haven't done for a while" is the introduction for *Juliet*. Moss tunes his guitar to Don's piano and Jimmy comments on how "we've got a piano tuner we'd like to kick to death out the back". *Star Hotel* features more aggressive inspired playing from Ian, whether mimicking Jimmy's melody part or doing call and response - he really shines here. This show really does have some great moments as Ian is definitely 'on' tonight.

Merry-Go-Round has Jimmy's guitar unusually loud (you can actually hear it!) and more fluid guitar lines from Moss in the bridge (it really is his night). *Sing To Me* makes its public debut and both Jimmy and Ian are a little uncertain of their cues as Jimmy cuts off Ian's solo with "taking care of business" before he has completed it.

Only Make Believe is a new cover and is followed by a spirited *Bow River* which has some of the guitar solo parts taken by the keyboards. *You Got Nothin' I Want* sounds a little unrehearsed and starts with an awkward sounding (aloud) count in. It's another which appears to be lumbering along, the only

inspiration being in some Van Halen - style tapping sequences Ian tries in the solo. *Goodbye Astrid* has reverted to the intro riff start as on the studio version and is a spirited, enjoyable performance to end the main set.

Six songs are played in the encores, starting with *When Something Is Wrong With My Baby*, a heartfelt rendition from Ian and Jimmy, and another for the covers list - if only there had been guitar playing like this on the solo Barnes version! *Houndog* is missing the bridge (the slow middle section sung by Ian) as it would for the remainder of '83. As everyone is preparing to leave, and the band has put tape music through the PA, the band return for another encore, obviously keen to try as many songs as possible with Arnott before an audience. An audience calling for *Khe-Sanh* and *One Long Day* are a little surprised when they are given *Your Cheatin' Heart*, but sensing that they are getting something unique, there are no complaints. *My Turn To Cry* and *Tomorrow* see the audience more than satisfied with the new Cold Chisel.

"The huge La Trobe university auditorium was filled to capacity on Tuesday night by avid Cold Chisel fans anxious for a glimpse of these wild men of rock'n'roll. From the first screaming note of Wild Colonial Boy, Chisel had the crowd in their hands.

"Chisel have a presence onstage, a subtle power that the audience can feel even before the music starts. The power of the music is distinctly Chisel; raw rock with that ever present blues flavour.

"Ray Arnott is only the temporary drummer and he will be a bit nervous for the first couple of gigs," tour manager Mark Pope said."

(BRIAN ADAMS, MELBOURNE HERALD)

| JULY 14 | The Venue, St.Kilda |
| JULY 15 | The Venue, St.Kilda |

JULY 16 - PALAIS THEATRE, GEELONG

Set list (probably complete)-Wild Colonial Boy/ Khe Sanh/ Letter To Alan/ Tomorrow/ Four Walls/ Standing On The Outside/ Painted Doll/ Cheap Wine/ Taipan/ Bow River/ Hold Me Tight/ Sing To Me/ Rising Sun/ Only Make Believe/ You Got Nothin' I Want/ Goodbye Astrid/ Breakfast At Sweethearts/ My Turn To Cry/ Merry-Go-Round/ Let's Go Get Stoned

One of the most interesting things about this show is the set list, quite different to that done on other dates in this tour, not so much in the content but in the sequence. *Wild Colonial Boy* is an intense, powerful version complete with all the tricks Ian Moss could muster into one final solo and audience participation on the vocals. The audience becomes the sixth member at this show, singing along to everything except the yet unreleased material. *Khe Sanh* is an even better excuse to sing along and a stunning *Letter To Alan* shows that this lineup could create magic.

Star Hotel increases the frantic pace in a set, which just seems to be building and building. This is an exciting version featuring all the interplay between Barnes and Moss, which made live versions of this song unique. *Tomorrow* continues the building before *Four Walls* eventually releases some of the tension. Ray Arnott has altered the drum pattern in the quiet bridge section of Tomorrow creating an interesting variation, which certainly took nothing away from the song. *Four Walls* could have been left to the audience alone to sing, such is their enthusiasm to join in. *Standing On The Outside* continues what must be one of the most exciting sets the band has ever done. This show just exudes a great party atmosphere. Great playing, a great set of songs and a great audience all combines to create something special. *Painted Doll* brings a stop to the singing as the audience is unfamiliar with it but the frenetic delivery from the band ensures that the atmosphere is maintained. Live versions of this song always eclipsed the studio version.

Cheap Wine, *Taipan* and *Bow River* are all exceptional performances and anyone attending this show would have had no idea that there were any problems within the band. On the contrary the band appeared to be going from strength to strength. *Hold Me Tight* has the audience clapping faster than they've ever clapped. *Sing To Me* brings the pace right back, but nothing can stop the band or the audience now.

Now on the home strait, the band play the most inspired *Only Make Believe I've heard*, although the start of *You Got Nothing I Want* is messed up. This song was never quite the same with Ray Arnott on drums. A frenetic (as usual) *Goodbye Astrid* closes the main set.

The first encore is *Breakfast At Sweethearts*, with a lovely unaccompanied guitar intro before the band joins in for the real intro. This song always sounded great during this period, due in part to Moss' inventiveness on the guitar, which makes early versions sound tame. A couple more full-tilt rockers and *Let's Go Get Stoned* complete a night, which is still talked about in Geelong, and the band's last show there.

JULY 17	Pier Hotel

JULY 19 - ADELAIDE UNIVERSITY

Mayo Refectory. An interesting addition to the set on this night was *Georgia*.

"Gone was the self-indulgent confidence they exuded at Memorial Drive last September in drawn out songs and drawn out solos. Returned, gloriously was the Cold Chisel of '77, tormented by the urge to make it, whatever it is. They were driven and driven hard, trying for something, I don't know what, They had returned to their inheritance of gut pumping blues rock with an energy and eagerness which indicated just how long, after all they had been away. And didn't the crowd just love it.

"Cold Chisel were in great form from the first note, but Goodbye Astrid lodged them a level higher into some sort of musical overdrive. Unfortunately this was their last song, but they were called back in for one great encore."

(JAMES WILLIAMSON)

JULY 20	Old Lion Hotel
JULY 21	Old Lion Hotel
JULY 22	Bridgeway Hotel, South Australia. Tickets for this show spell the band's name "Cold Chisle"
JULY 23	Bridgeway Hotel, South Australia
JULY 26	St.Kilda Town Hall, Uni Ball.
JULY 27	Club Chevron
JULY 28	Club Chevron
JULY 29	Bombay Rock, with Swanee

JULY 30 - BOMBAY ROCK, WITH SWANEE

Set list (incomplete) *Merry-Go-Round/ Star Hotel/ Wild Colonial Boy/ Letter To Alan/ Rip It Up/ Bow River/ Painted Doll/ Goodbye/ Standing On The Outside/ Rising Sun/ Houndog*

Juke's Dennis Twilight saw the gig like this:

"When a disturbingly clean guitar sound rendition of Merry-Go-Round heralded the Chisel set, the worry beads were openly passed a round. It was hard to believe that this was the same song. Heck, it was hard to believe that this was the same band. Only Mossie's impish porkchops Blackmore-on-heat series of solos saved this one. Star Hotel was thin, as was Wild Colonial Boy, although Mossie's one-handed trickery again pulled the bands fat out of the sandwich-maker. Letter To Alan, another favourite from Circus Animals actually caught the moody reflectiveness of the studio mix. Mere technical accident or game-ball for a winning service? By the time of Elvis Presley's Rip It Up, the problems began to crystalise into a disease festival. First, when it came to rhythm, Mossie's guitar was mixed off the sound spectrum. For instance on Bow River, you couldn't hear the rhythm guitar! Second, Don Walker was on several occasions adding a previously unheard Kymball organ sound for no apparent, logical or comical reason. Third new jungle-beater Ray Arnott is not Steve Prestwich. Fourth the song-list had too many balloons in it and not enough firecrackers. Fifth and finally the only thing that was carrying the songs on many an occasion was Jimmy Barnes' power tonsilling. Which is a credit to Jim as he's such a unique vocalist, but I wanted to see the whole band perform, not just the man who has thankfully grown his hair back over his ears."

He did see some positives:

"On the new tactics front, the only original new song I could pick up was something called I Got A Bead On You or Painted Dog (he must have been asleep for Hold Me Tight and Sing To Me - Mic) *Mercifully, this one hit home, so I figure there's hope on the new Chisel disc. The band's standout song was their closing number Goodbye Astrid. Suddenly it was the Chisel of old, with their aggression dangling out and their attitude set on Burn. Mossie's guitar became a wand of mystical power as it split the entombed air with more electro- dynamic blasts than a geiger counter reading of Rob Halford's brain. Don Walker's hi-tech tinkling was something on this too. What a rocker! - Oh guys, why not more like this ?"*

"Dennis went on to refer to their "current dishwashing liquid sound" and prayed that they "don't do a Midnight Oil on us and lose their hard rock soul."

"If the band were sounding tired, it's probably because I couldn't keep up."

(Ray Arnott, 1997)

AUGUST 2   Tarmac Hotel, Laverton, with Swanee

AUGUST 3 - TARMAC HOTEL, LAVERTON

With Swanee

Set list (complete) - Houndog/ My Turn To Cry/ Star Hotel/ Merry-Go-Round/ Rip It Up/ Flame Trees/ Wild Colonial Boy/ Letter For Alan/ My Baby/ Hold Me Tight/ Taipan/ Painted Doll/ Bow River/ Let's Go Get Stoned/ One Long Day/ You Got Nothin' I Want/ Rising Sun/ Only Make Believe/ Goodbye Astrid/ Sing To Me/ Khe Sanh/ Tomorrow/ Don't Let Go

The Tarmac (later known as 'Westside') is one of the venues Chisel played during their first Melbourne visits in 1976 and they must have played there close to 20 times. The venue by the early '80s takes over a thousand people. This is one of the last gigs before the meeting which resolved to finish the band, and so is a valuable document of the musical state of the band at this time. Less than three weeks after this show the final tour would be announced. The opening number is *Houndog*, followed by *My Turn To Cry*, a lumbering version compared to earlier performances. *Star Hotel* has some inspired lines from Ian and *Merry-Go-Round* lifts the mood, although it does lack a certain 'freshness'. *Rip It Up* is a little more inspired. The next song is something of a surprise as they play Steve's (and Don's) *Flame Trees*, as initially all Steve Prestwich songs were dropped from the live set after Ray Arnott joined the band. Perhaps they had decided that it should be on the new album and therefore should be played. *Wild Colonial Boy* is impressive, as it usually is. *My Baby* is also a surprise return to the show spiced up by Ian's guitar solo and extra vocals from Jimmy in the final choruses. *Hold Me Tight* is a powerful rendition - the newer material obviously inspiring the band.

The overall feeling in this show is that the band is tired. After hearing and writing about so many shows for this book (and I was at this one), it is very rare that I've had to say that - even for the German shows from the second tour (after which Steve left the band), but at certain points in this show they do sound tired. This was the end of a gruelling tour; it must have been difficult to return to venues they had played more than six years ago. *Painted Doll* sounds fresh and vital, possibly as it's a new song. *Bow River* is also a powerful delivery, really lifting the gig to another plane. *Let's Go Get Stoned* moves the show into a blues feel setting the mood for the intro to

(172

One Long Day, which is played at a similar speed to the first album version. The tiredness seems gone now and this is the Chisel we are more familiar with. *When Something Is Wrong With My Baby* doesn't sound quite right about *You Got Nothing I Want* (it's one that Ray Arnott just couldn't seem to master) although Ian and Jimmy really work hard. *Rising Sun* and *Only Make Believe* sound as fresh as ever.

Following *Goodbye* the band return, Jimmy asks, "What are you doin' you fuckin' arseholes? Thought you'd never make any fuckin' noise". *Sing To Me* is a reminder that they are looking to the future, a soulful, atmospheric performance with a stunning solo from Ian. One of the night's highlights. The following encores including *Khe Sanh* ensure that the audience goes home satisfied after a night which has had it's moments but falls short of the lofty expectations audiences have for Cold Chisel performances.

AUGUST 5	Lake Jindabyne
AUGUST 6	Lake Jindabyne
AUGUST 7	Lake Jindabyne

At the end of this tour the band's tour manager, Mark Pope quits.

● Cold Chisel . . . warm farewell.

By ANTHONY O'GRADY

ROCK band Cold Chisel created pandemonium — an a record — in Sydney when tickets went on sale

AUGUST 12

Recording at Richmond Recorders with producer Tony Cohen. Songs recorded: Saturday Night, Ghost Town, Feel This Love, Twentieth Century, Keep The Change and Temptation.

AUGUST 13	Recording continues: Janelle and Show Me A Light.
AUGUST 14	Recording: Build This Love

AUGUST 17 - BAND MEETING AT DON WALKER'S

In a move which surprised even Steve Prestwich himself, the band call him and announce their intention to disband, going out with a final tour and album and ask if he would like to play on the tour. Steve was not aware of much of what was happening regarding the recording of the final album, playing only on *Flame Trees*, which he co-wrote, *No Sense* and *The Game*, which used a backing track from '81/'82 sessions.

The decision had been sudden - Ray Arnott had even been given a work schedule of further live dates he was to do with the band.

AUGUST 22 - PRESS RELEASE:

Cold Chisel have today announced that on their 10th anniversary in October 1983, they will be disbanding following a final tour. The band's last studio album is being prepared. The tour will take in the major cities of Australia and New Zealand. Rod Willis Management. For and on behalf of Cold Chisel

(22 AUGUST 1983.)

No official reason was given for the split, and silence would be maintained until 1988 when Jimmy first began to talk and the others followed, almost in response. Prior to this the only 'reasons' given were along the lines of musical creativity being taken as far as it could go, but all were very vague in the few interviews which were done.

"We just felt we had covered everything we wanted to do, at least musically. At this point the things we want to do musically are more and more separating. We had this situation developing in the band whereby there were several writers, all writing in very different styles. It got to the point where we felt we were playing on other peoples songs, as session players rather than as members of a group. Suddenly we realised that Cold Chisel had become an outlet for a very small part of what we all wanted to do,

but it was taking up most of our time. "When you first get up on stage and play Wild Thing or whatever at the Mawson Hotel to 300 people when the place really only holds ten, it's inspiring, inspiring for everybody. It blows the roof off. When you're playing it four years later for the thousandth time, you may play it better but it means nothing. Anything repeated continually becomes just a sound, a gesture. When I wrote 'Choirgirl' it meant something to me; now it means nothing. The longer we stayed together the more these songs became burdens, because people wanted to hear them all the time. What they can't understand is that they won't get off on a song if the band isn't getting off on a song."

(Don talking to Rolling Stone Magazine)

AUGUST/SEPTEMBER

Rumours abound that Jimmy is planning a post-Chisel collaboration with his brother John. Juke even named musicians who had been involved in a project, which it stated, had already been shelved due to "politics". The story went on to say that all concerned parties had denied the rumours and were busy with their own careers and that if anything did happen it would be at least six months away.

The band commence recording what would become the Twentieth Century album.

"The album was a nightmare. It was one of the two or three worst nightmares of my life. It took a long time. During the time that we were recording it we were also doing our final tour. At that time relations within the band, between several parties within the band were barely above speaking terms. The business and the money side of it were incredibly bitter between several people. And in the midst of all this we're trying to do a massive national tour and record an album. Loaded on top of that we were trying to do half the album with Ray Arnott.

"Loaded on top of that three of the songs that we had used we had recorded one night in a studio in Melbourne where they had been recorded through a piece of sound reduction equipment of which the only copy was in that studio in Melbourne, in the Southern Hemisphere. So in order to hear that stuff back, and we knew from the tapes that they were very good recordings, I think that was Painted Doll, Hold Me Tight and Sing To Me.

"We knew those recordings were great recordings. I had to have that piece of equipment which was a flat-bed truck piece of equipment, shipped up to Sydney and hot-wired into the desk of Rhinosaurus studios up there.

"On top of that, like a fool, instead of recording an album in a normal way I wanted to go to some kind of new heights in rock and roll, so instead of putting down the basic tracks in a studio, we hired the Capitol Theatre, parked a mobile studio out the front, and recorded the basic tracks for a number of other tracks, like the band playing live. And I hired Tony Cohen who engineered a number of Birthday Party albums to handle that recording, which didn't really work because Tony had never really dealt with anything above four tracks before. Do you want any more problems?"

(Don Walker, talking to Billy Pinnell, 1991.)

In addition to this, different writers in the band were using different producers and recording techniques, further eroding unity within the band.

SEPTEMBER 4

Hundreds of people queue for Cold Chisel tickets for their Last Stand concert at the Sydney Entertainment Centre.One show quickly became two and then three before sales were halted before a fourth show went on sale at 2 pm. The band also sold 20,000 tickets in Melbourne.

SEPTEMBER 12-17 Recording at the Capital Theatre.

THE LAST STAND TOUR

SEPTEMBER 20 - AUCKLAND, LOGAN CAMPBELL CENTRE

(support Martial Law)

Set list (incomplete): Wild Colonial Boy/Star Hotel/ Merry-Go-Round/Khe Sanh/My Turn To Cry/One Long Day/Wild Thing/Cheap Wine/Goodbye Astrid

"The audience sounded as if it was trying to emulate the crowds on Swingshift and screams of "we want Chisel" increased as the evening went on.With very little of the props used by today's bands- grand lighting scale, or films, or giant effects to detract from the music, Chisel powered straight into Wild Colonial Boy with a furious energy that never let up.Steamroller - that's the only word to describe them. The crowds came to hear Chisel play their numbers in that ferocious manner, and that's exactly what they got. For a bit over two hours they crashed through Star Hotel, Merry-Go-Round, My Turn To Cry...Ian Moss, the

delicate, introverted Ian Moss, stepped into the spotlight, and caressed his axe into One Long Day, sparking off enough dynamics so the second part of the show visibly lifted. The energy level and Barnes magnetic presence is the main asset of the show: it's like a gym workout. They never let up. Virtually no pauses between numbers. By the end of the show they were an uncontrollable runaway engine, the rhythm section punching viciously on the heels of the front-line, most of Barnes lyrics disappearing in the white blur as they pounded out Wild Thing, got called back to ship steel through three encores and finally bowed out with Goodbye Astrid.

(MICHAEL MORRIS, JUKE)

SEPTEMBER 21	Wellington, Logan Campbell Centre
SEPTEMBER 23	Christchurch

Set List (included): Wild Colonial Boy /Khe Sanh/ One Long Day /Only Make Believe / Star Hotel /Merry-Go-Round / Wild Thing / Don't Let Go / Goodbye Astrid

SEPTEMBER 24	Dunedin
SEPTEMBER 27	Newcastle Workers Club

Chisel employee, Scott Howlett is involved in car accident on the way home from this gig , killing his girlfriend.

SEPTEMBER 28	Newcastle Workers Club
SEPTEMBER 29	Newcastle Workers Club
OCTOBER 1	Canberra, Bruce Stadium
OCTOBER 4	Brisbane, Festival Hall
OCTOBER 5	Brisbane, Festival Hall
OCTOBER 6	Bombay, Surfers Paradise
OCTOBER 7	Bombay, Surfers Paradise
OCTOBER 9	Melbourne, Sports & Entertainment Centre
OCTOBER 10	Hold Me Tight/No Sense single released.
OCTOBER 10	Melbourne, Sports & Entertainment Centre

175)

OCTOBER 11 - MELBOURNE, SPORTS & ENTERTAINMENT CENTRE

Set List (for either 9th, 10th or 11th-probably complete)

Wild Colonial Boy/ Standing On The Outside/ Merry-Go-Round/Letter To Alan/Cheap Wine/My Turn To Cry/Janelle/Khe Sanh/Hold Me Tight/Ghost Town/Hound Dog/Flame Trees/My Baby/One Long Day/You Got Not Nothin I Want/Bow River/Only Make Believe/Star Hotel/Star Spangled Banner/Wild Thing/Knockin' On Heaven's Door/River Deep, Mountain High/Painted Doll/Don't Let Go/Goodbye Astrid

The band was in fine form for the Melbourne dates, as a tape of this show indicates. Jimmy's voice sounds as good as it ever has, absolutely savage. It's an unfortunate irony that in four weeks time his voice would crack up completely and the shows immediately before and after this were those recorded and filmed. These Melbourne dates were far superior to those which appear on the *Last Stand* CD, not just because of Jimmy's voice - the band had been charging through its final tour and had played itself into fine form, the break in November meant that momentum was lost.

The set opens with *Wild Colonial Boy*, as did most shows on this tour. A lack-lustre version of this song was released as part of the Three Big Hits ,single triple pack in 1994 which unfortunately fails to capture the spirit that is present in this performance. *Merry-Go-Round* sounds like 1980 again and *Letter To Alan* retains all its primitive force- another song not included in an official live release (forget the version on Three Big Hits for the same reasons at the previously mentioned *Wild Colonial Boy*). *My Turn To Cry* is a sparkling version but it is noticeable that there is little overlap between Swingshift and the two *Last Stand* live albums so we didn't get to hear this on those albums.

A trio of new songs follows (along with *Khe Sanh*), *Ghost Town* has Jimmy timing it on his wristwatch, "minute five maybe" he announces at the songs completion. *Hound Dog* is played minus its bridge section while *Flame Trees* includes lyrics about "a GM assembly out-of-worker" and only one chorus repeat at the end instead of the usual one and a half (the record has two) causes Jimmy to comment:

"That's a new ending that one".

For all the new material previewed at this stage, it is the power in the delivery of older songs such as *One Long Day, Star Hotel*, and *Bow River* which stands out in these performances. Hendrix's *Star Spangled Banner* intros *Wild Thing* on this night (it would be *Foxy Lady* on the final Melbourne night) and we are also given powerful versions of *River Deep, Mountain High, Knocking' On Heaven's Door* and *Don't Let Go* in the encores.

Overall this is classic Chisel, the band at its very best.

OCTOBER 12 - MELBOURNE, SPORTS & ENTERTAINMENT CENTRE

Set List-(almost complete)*Wild Colonial Boy/ Standing On The Outside/ Merry-Go-Round/Cheap Wine/Khe Sanh/Hold Me Tight/Four Walls/One Long Day/Got Nothin' I Want/Bow River/Only Make Believe/Star Hotel/medley: Foxy Lady-Wild Thing-Purple Haze/Taipan/River Deep Mountain High/Ghost Town/Knocking' On Heaven's Door/Cheap Wine/Goodbye Astrid*

This was the last ever Chisel show in Melbourne, and it was a good one. The opening *Wild Colonial Boy* is particularly intense, the initial yells from Jimmy (he always seems to do this before the opening line, perhaps to test the PA and foldback) ensure us that the voice is in fine shape tonight. The show is by now a professional operation, the standard overall is most impressive with the band well oiled and the improvisation left to numbers like *Wild Thing* and *Goodbye Astrid*. *Wild Thing* tonight includes bits from *Foxy Lady* and an almost complete *Purple Haze*. Other highlights from this performance include *One Long Day* and the encore *Taipan*.

During the upcoming Adelaide shows Jimmy's voice would start to go, completely failing during the first Sydney show, making these Melbourne dates the last ones the band would play at full strength.

OCTOBER 15 - PERTH, ENTERTAINMENT CENTRE

"They were superb as they played a large cross-section of songs from their five top selling albums, interspersed with several covers at a frightful pace. The band played all its classics, such as Breakfast At Sweethearts, Cheap Wine, Forever Now, and Choir Girl Ian Moss is regarded as one of Australia's finest guitarists. He and the powerful voice of Jim Barnes had the crowd on their feet and screaming for more."

(THE WEST AUSTRALIAN, OCT 17, 1983)

(176

New Zealand
Last Stand Tour

OCTOBER 20	Adelaide, Apollo Stadium
OCTOBER 21	Adelaide, Apollo Stadium
OCTOBER 22	Adelaide, Apollo Stadium
OCTOBER 23	Adelaide, Apollo Stadium
OCTOBER 25	Sydney, Entertainment Centre

(support Choir Boys) This show sold out in 37 minutes and in seven and a half hours the band sold 37,000 tickets in Sydney.

OCTOBER 26	Sydney, Entertainment Centre (postponed)

"Well, terribly sorry, last night's farewell concert by Cold Chisel was cancelled because the lead singer had a bad throat (how could they tell?) and it will now be held at the Entertainment Centre on Saturday. The concert scheduled for Saturday will be held on Sunday, which seems a complicated way to do things."

(SYDNEY MORNING HERALD, "STAY IN TOUCH" COLUMN, EDITED BY DAVID DALE. 26 OCT)

From the above announcement, Jimmy obviously believed that his throat problems could be overcome with just a couple of days' rest. Sounds like David was really upset! The band also made a public announcement to the same effect, adding that: "The band would like to apologise to all concerned but as these are their final concerts they wish them to be memorable."

OCTOBER 27	Sydney, Entertainment Centre with Divinyls (postponed on the day of the show)
OCTOBER 28	Sydney, Entertainment Centre (postponed)
OCTOBER 29	Sydney, Entertainment Centre postponed)

"As most frustrated Sydney punters will already know, another long awaited megatour got truncated last week. Cold Chisel have had to reschedule the remaining four entertainment centre dates till early December after Jim Barnes' throat succumbed to laryngitis (otherwise known as singing your heart out on twenty farewell gigs in a row)

RAM MAGAZINE

NOVEMBER 7-18	Recording at Rhinosaurus Studios.
NOVEMBER 14	Hold Me Tight/No Sense single peaks nationally at No. 14.
NOVEMBER 21- 25	Recording at Rhinosaurus Studios

NOVEMBER 27

The band continue recording (with Ray Arnott), at the Capital Theatre on this day. Among the songs recorded that day was Twentieth Century. Obviously Jimmy's voice had made some sort of a recovery as this song is not exactly easy on the vocal chords !

DECEMBER 6-15	Recording continues at the Capitol Theatre.
DECEMBER 9	Thirroul Leagues Club

DECEMBER 11

The Sydney Morning Herald reports:

"Cold Chisel will begin their final four nights of live work tomorrow night at the Entertainment Centre. Two of the four final shows are now to be filmed so we can look forward to a cinema release of Chisel in concert sometime next year." The final re-arranging of the tickets went as follows:

Tues 25 Oct tickets now valid only for Mon 12 Dec
Thurs 27 Oct tickets now valid only for Tues 13 Dec
Fri 28 Oct tickets now valid only for Wed 14 Dec
Sat 29 Oct tickets now valid only for Thurs 15 Dec

DECEMBER 12

Sydney, Entertainment Centre Juke's Mark Cromelin said that this show was so bad that some people walked out in disgust.

The Sydney Morning Herald's Katherine Tulich saw it differently (despite having a little trouble with the name of a couple of songs and a harmonica player):

"Cold Chisel's Last Stand concert at the Sydney Entertainment Centre made you realise the Australia will be losing an outstanding rock'n'roll band. The concerts, which run until Friday, will be the last time Cold Chisel play together. The operative word with the band is "tight". While the charismatic Jim Barnes steals the show, the other members certainly contribute no less, particularly the lead guitarist, Ian Moss. His guitar work is the backbone of all their songs, from the introduction of My Turn To Cry to Tomorrow, Merry Go Round and Hold Me Tight, the Chisel's new single which comes across far more energetically in a live performance. Moss' forte is the blues. He fronts on vocals as well in One Long Day (featuring the excellent harmonica of David Blake and My Baby. His voice is not as strong as Barnes's and the best Moss songs featured Barnes on harmony, such as Bow River and a new song, China. Actually, they compliment each other well. Barnes' gesture at

177)

guitar playing, as in No Sense, greatly needed Moss' support.

"The Chisel's cover version of The Wild Thing, again featuring Moss' guitar, seemed a much better performance than the original by The TroggsBarnes gave credence to the "wild thing". He is the archetypal rock performer. His voice seems gravel and undisciplined. It can be emotive on blues like Choir Girl and Khe Sanh, or blast through the frenetic Star Hotel and Don't Let Go (no longer a sedate disco song with Barnes). He carouses around the stage, swiggering from a vodka bottle (even if the contents are water) and risking his safety by precariously balancing on speakers and monitors, throwing himself into the audience and running through the crowd to complete a song from the back of the hall on top of the sound mixing desk. Cold Chisel, always exciting to watch on stage, seemed to give everything, and the capacity crowd didn't want the group to leave the stage even after two and a half hours. It's a shame to see this band break up."

| DECEMBER 13 | Sydney, Entertainment Centre |
| DECEMBER 14 | Sydney, Entertainment Centre |

DECEMBER 15 - SYDNEY, ENTERTAINMENT CENTRE

"Cold Chisel's concerts tonight and tomorrow night (?) are sold out."

(SYDNEY MORNING HERALD, DEC 15)

Set list (complete): Wild Colonial Boy/ Merry-Go-Round/ Letter To Alan/ Cheap Wine/ My Turn To Cry/ Tomorrow/ Janelle/ / Khe Sanh / Twentieth Century / No Sense/ Hold Me Tight / Choir Girl/ / Standing On The Outside / My Baby/ Tomorrow/ Rising Sun/ One Long Day/ / You Got Nothing I Want/ Bow River/Only Make Believe/ Star Hotel/ / Wild Thing

Encore 1: Saturday Night/ Build This Love/ River Deep Mountain High/ Four Walls/ / Twist And Shout

Encore 2: Georgia/ Taipan/ Conversations / Forever Now / When Something's Wrong with my Baby / Goodbye (Astrid Goodbye)/ Don't Let Go

The Frank Sinatra song continued to play over the P.A. system until the first strains of *Wild Colonial Boy* cut through the pitch black darkness of the Sydney Entertainment Centre and yellow backlights revealed Cold Chisel, with David Blight, for the last time. It starts sluggishly, but builds to a dramatic climax as Ian and David trade notes in the outro. Purple backlights on the otherwise bare stage

(this will be the pattern all night, only the color changing) and we have *Merry-Go-Round*, always an energetic song, there seems to be a cloud handing over the band at times, as though they are trying to ensure tonight is a party and not a wake. This was evident on *Letter To Alan*, the lyrics as poignant as ever, "we believed, and I still do" has a question mark over it and Jimmy makes eye contact with Don as he sings this line.

Things begin to warm up in *My Turn To Cry* and the party begins. *Janelle* is the first new song; an emotion charged rendition followed immediately by *Khe Sanh*. The party takes off.

"How you all feelin'. I hope you all got well and truly pissed before you came in, before you came through the body search that is. By the way this is not my new American look (referring to his open shirt). I got here tonight and all the buttons were gone."

(178

Twentieth Century is the version that will later be issued on the Barking Spiders Live album, along with an edited version of the above dialogue. This is the first song from tonight's performance to be issued on either of the live albums or video. *No Sense* is a little rough around the edges, but *Hold Me Tight* is stunning. Short and sharp.

Standing On The Outside sees the party in full swing. Tonight's performance will grace the Barking Spiders and last stand albums as well as opening the video of the same name. *My Baby* is a spirited performance and a highlight of the show so far. *Tomorrow* is also impressive, as a listen to the *Last Stand* album or video will testify, as this is the version that appears on these. *Rising Sun* is a favourite with the crowd. You can feel the anticipation as Don begins a blues intro to *One Long Day*, with David Blight and Ian joining in as it builds. This is one of the longest versions ever, Ian even doing some scat singing during the intro. When the verse starts it is slow, sparse and even more laid back than the first album rendition.

Bow River is the version used in the film and live album, a great performance only rivalled by the circus tent '82 performance of the song. *Star Hotel* is captivating and also used in the film and album. Like the film, it runs straight into *Wild Thing*, the version used in the CD and video, with a few small edits. Jim almost has his shirt ripped off during his run into the crowd and Ian improvises beautifully when Jim is making his way back to the stage, Jim taking the classic arm around Ian's neck position when he returns. Ian finishes the song with guitar held high; one handed trills (ala Jimmy Page) and slides the strings along the mic stand, ala Jimi Hendrix. The last *Wild Thing*.

After approximately four minutes (which seemed like an eternity for the audience), Cold Chisel returns and introduce Venetta Fields and Renee Geyer on backing vocals. *Saturday Night* is performed, this performance is used in the album and filmed, with Ian improvising the lyrics- "cigarettes to ease my mind"? *Build This Love* follows. A powerful rendition, more complete than the one included on the 'Three Big Hits' CD. "They were two new ones. Any requests?" Jim asks. *River Deep, Mountain High* is played superbly, using the backing vocalists to great effect. Renee Geyer sings lead on the second verse, changing places with Jim. This magical performance was issued as the B-side to the *Flame Trees* single and later as part of the 'Three Big Hits' CD pack. "Any requests" is again asked, and after asking for quiet, so he can hear someone in the front rows, *Four Walls* is played.

Twist and Shout is intro'd by Jim, after asking where the girls (Renee & Venetta) are. Billy Rogers on saxophone joins them, along with David Blight and "the girls". Press reports had this version as running for 20 minutes, a slight exaggeration. Solos from almost everyone on the stage and a quiet interlude did extend it to over eight minutes. Whilst played at almost every show in the first half of 1982, *Twist and Shout* was indeed a rarity in 1983.

The band again leaves the stage, returning about four minutes later with *Georgia*. The song Ian did with Don at the audition to join the band in 1973. *Georgia* never really left the set, always a possibility as an encore number as it is, appropriately, tonight. Rarely was it played with the feel and soul of this version, later issued on the Barking Spiders Live album. As it does on The Barking Spiders album, *Taipan* follows. Not as intense as the live renditions of the *Circus Animals* period, powerful nonetheless.

Another call for requests, "What do you fancy?" finds the band attempting *Conversations*. "That'll be a laugh, we can't remember that one." Don

179)

remembers the piano intro, and Phil the bass line, while Ian is improvising the intro. Jim gets the first line and a half right, then cuts to the second verse and chorus, before things slow, as Jim asks if anyone knows what the next verse is and Don cleverly segues and ends the song. Steve quickly starts *Forever Now*, rescuing everyone from a sticky situation. Tonight's rendition is not the version issued on Barking Spiders Live. Ian plays an almost manic solo on the end of tonight's version. *When Something Is Wrong With My Baby* is next, a song which would serve Jim well in the future. This version sees solos from Don, David Blight, Jimmy Sloggett and Ian.

Goodbye Astrid and *Don't Let Go*, as appearing on the soundtrack album, complete a marathon show, with Ian using a mic as a slide in the latter song.

The band again leaves the stage. A crowd that refuse to budge, continue to chant "Chisel" and whistle. The house lights are still down and hopes are high for a last Chisel encore. The chant increases, even when the house lights are turned on.

"Ladies and gentlemen, on behalf of the band, thank you for supporting Cold Chisel. Goodnight and goodbye." This is announced over the P.A. and Cold Chisel are no more. Tour manager Chris Bastic recalls that the rest of the band were keen to do another encore, but Jimmy, whose voice would have been feeling the strain of the three previous nights, on top of this one, was not keen.

The last show epitomised Cold Chisel's strongest points and thankfully glossed over their cracks. Chisel's magic has centred around the angle on the tension between rock'n'roll's overwhelming sense of community and solidarity (whether it's with thousands or with three of your best mates, it's there) and rock's omnipresent sense of alienation and loneliness.

Even if on record Chisel kept on re-inventing themselves, live they remained a stamping stud. Even if most of the visual focus went on to the curly haired Adonises, fighting for dominance by competing lines on Merry-Go-Round, My Turn To Cry, Tomorrow, or oozing compatibility on Bow River or even some of the newies like Janelle, Saturday Night, and No Sense where Barnes would attempt to supplement Moss' near virtuoso with some pedestrian rhythm chords. So damn sharp, an agility and crispness borne not only out of a decade of hard touring but of a confidence wedded to a weight of solidarity and conviction. All the musicianship channeled straight into the songs

(Moss' solos of course are so tastefully administered there is now an iota of superflousness in them) with no room for self indulgence. Even their Hold Me Tight single was worryingly dispensable and nonchalant (admittedly it transforms better live than on the recorded version) their very last set never lost it's deftness and anger. It's a clich'e, of course, but this was one of those really magical nights where there was an almost unflawed fusing of intension and affect.: everything contributed to the impact of the songs, which took on a 3D life and sported a depth and intensity that surpassed all their recorded incarnations. There's never been anything innovative about Chisel's styles: it was the attitude, the guts personifying the understating of each number which made the whole enterprise strike home with a vengeance. And when everyone in that crowd held up lighted matches and lighters to denote the ultimate thumbs-up that a Rock Audience Can Bestow On A Rock Performer, it made for a very emotional night indeed. The tender moments of the Chisel soul were there, of course Choirgirl, My Baby, and One Long Day featuring harmonica player David Blythe - but the band preferred to concentrate on the runaway locomotive action, combining newies like Build This Love and 20th Century with the more familiar fare of Khe Sanh, Star Hotel and Goodbye. If it was anyone's night, not that there was any competition - it was Barnes'. Very much in control of his primitive instincts (and of his band) he as usual had the drop on the fans. Embracing the dark, primitive elemental forces latent in an audience, he made frequent trips - not only across the stage swigging from his vodka bottle (the Sydney Morning Herald claimed it was actually full of water; forget it! This is Jimmy Barnes who many, many years ago sacked a roadie for watering his vodka!) jumped on speakers and monitors and ran through the crowd to serenade them from the back of the room - like a deity in search of something to sacrifice, and exploited these forces to very subtle effect; like a magician...they communicated the ritualistic implications of rock and roll in a way that very, very few bands can pull off convincingly. It was hard to work out which was the highlight of the night. Conversations when the crowd exploded at the beginning of the gentle piano riff ?

(180

Or Wild Thing when they stormed and blistered through one of the wildest versions ever and positively cut the Troggs' original to shreds. Was it during their three encores when Renee Geyer and Venetta Fields joined them for a rip roaring run through their influences, from Twist and Shout (which ran for the best of twenty minutes) Georgia and Don't Let Go? Or was it even after their third encore, when the band slunk exhausted off the stage, and the crowd pleading for them to return, refusing to budge. Whether Chisel should have split up remains a moot point. The important thing is they left with their heads high; both the band and the audience did each other proud until the very end.

(MARK CROMELIN, JUKE MAGAZINE.)

The final show is even reviewed by German music press:

"Nobody wanted to believe it. When Cold Chisel returned from their European tour in August, a rumour circulated that the band wanted to split up after eight (sic) years together. This seemed even more unbelievable when one considers they have been one of Australia's top acts along with Men At Work for years now.

As there was no personal quarrel between the band members, it was decided to add a farewell tour through Australia and record a final studio LP. In Sydney Chisel broke all records for the venue: the Entertainment Centre, capacity 12,000, was sold out in only twenty minutes and four additional shows were sold out in the next two hours. An impressive 60,000 tickets sold! At 9.15 pm it finally happens: the four (sic) rocking Chiselers appear on the sparsely but effectively lit stage. Thousands call, Chisel, Chisel. Singer Jimmy Barnes is grinning almost from ear to ear while Steve Prestwich is slamming the first beats on the drum skins. Guitarist Ian Moss grips the strings to great effect. In combination with Jimmy Barnes' voice, shaped by more than a few drinks, and Don Walkers' sporadic E-piano staccatos, the typical Aussie rock of Cold Chisel is arising. The set consists of material from all four studio LPs: Khe Sanh, Breakfast At Sweethearts, Cheap Wine, and You Got Nothin' I Want. Also included are two brand new songs : Hold Me Tight and the reggae orientated No Sense. Both are scheduled to be on the next LP. Visually the set is dominated by Jim Barnes who is running from one end of the stage to the other and the calm lead guitarist, Ian Moss. Each one has his own charisma and both are the absolute darlings of the public.

181)

Sydney
Jim and Renee Geyer backstage on the Last Stand Tour.

The first encore is their ever popular version of the old Troggs standard Wild Thing. Barnes acts like a wild man and climbs down into the audience. The crowd doesn't want to part with him again and he has to be pulled out by the roadies to get him back on stage again. After three encores the band take a bow for the last time. Jimmy and Ian are wet through. The crowd give standing ovations.

(Robert Schaetti in *Music Express* thanks to Peer Meyer for translation)

These last shows are filmed and material taken from the shows of December 13 & 15 surfaces later in The *Last Stand* movie and soundtrack CD/album. The basic tracks had been completed for the final studio album although a lot of overdubbing and production work was still required. From a public point of view, and for all intents and purposes, other than completing the final record, Cold Chisel were no more.

There are three things required for success in rock, viz; (1) good music (2) good presentation (3) good luck.

Chisel's music and just as importantly, their lyrics, came at a perfect time in Australia's rock history. Don's lyrics on Australia and the music driving them was totally unique, aggressive and signified a change of guard and a change of generation, and so they were on the button.

The new generation of Oz rockers had been used to bands like Sherbert, John Paul Young etc, a pop sensibility that was outdated and non Australian. Chisel were the antichrists at the time, totally Australian, and totally irreverent. I have no doubt this was by design and not by accident.

Despite what they may have thought or pretended to others, they were very thoughtful about their presentation, their image, and they worked on it a lot, always pushing the envelope, always ensuring nobody could accuse them of selling out.

They experienced perfectly good luck and timing. Had they been at any other time in Oz rock history I believe they would not have forged through the barrier, would not have garnered the support they received.

Cold Chisel's impact was unique and significant. They spearheaded an entirely new generation of rockers, for an entirely new generation of rockers, they lampooned the media until the media eventually submitted under their onslaught. The media had no choice really, but to join the throng, for one thing's for sure about Cold Chisel...it was the public who made them, not the media...the media were the also rans and there is no doubt that eventually any media outlet had to join the throng or be left behind. This really was our version of punk rock, not musically, but socially Cold Chisel represented a new generation of people, they were symbols, and that, along with their music was what made them legends.

Their impact on Oz rock and a generation of people can never be overplayed. The fact that they never made it overseas was not a sign of their failure so much, as their totally unique Australian take on stance, profile and music. They would never make it overseas unless they lived there and they would never do that because they saw it as some kind of compromise. It was the world's loss, but Chisel must take some blame for this.

Vince Lovegrove

[1984 - '88]

The Party's Over

DESPITE THE BAND BEING OFFICIALLY FINISHED WHEN THE LAST DRINK HAD BEEN PUT DOWN AFTER THE LAST STAND TOUR, OTHER THAN PLAYING LIVE, 1984 WAS STILL A BIG YEAR FOR THE BAND IN EVERY RESPECT. AS A MATTER OF FACT, WHEREAS THE PREVIOUS YEAR HAD SEEN ONLY ONE SINGLE RELEASED BY THE BAND (HOLD ME TIGHT/ NO SENSE), 1984 SAW THREE SINGLES, TWO ALBUMS AND A FEATURE FILM RELEASED.

1984

183)

Ray Arnott had only to wait a couple of months before he got a call from Jim, just as he had done twice before, asking him to join his solo band on the eve of a tour of Queensland. Ray stayed for two albums and later had one of his songs, *Flaming Heart* recorded by Stephen Stills on one of his solo albums, with Jimmy Page (who had selected the song from a pile of demos), playing guitar on it.

FEBRUARY

Press reports that Don Walker is working on two Chisel-related projects, the *Twentieth Century* album and a 90 minute movie that looks at the band's illustrious career. The movie is tipped to include "superb footage from two shows from its final run of farewell shows at the Sydney Entertainment Centre." Rod Willis was still not sure how the movie would be distributed, adding that the band had considered showing it through clubs and halls of about 2500 capacity, in lieu of a Chisel performance.

MARCH - RELEASE

Saturday Night/Painted Doll single.

"Another of those sparse, atmospheric songs that enable Cold Chisel to evoke a strong vision of life at eye-level. One thing it captures very successfully is the sense of isolation and alone-ness that a Saturday night can have if you aren't in with the crowd. They haven't lost their edge over all these years, which is really sayin' something."

(JUKE MAGAZINE)

APRIL

Twentieth Century, the band's final studio album is released. For more on the making of *Twentieth Century*, see August/September 1983. Ian Moss holidays in India while Steve Prestwich is reportedly writing songs at home and spending a lot of time at the beach, amidst rumours that he has been offered the drum seat with a number of top bands. Jimmy Barnes and Don Walker do some press for the album, including an interview (together) with 2-MMM's Dave Carlson.

"With the band splitting up I think the best any of us can do is to contribute towards the making of an album that sounds good to us now. It's never very easy to make an album conscious of where it fits into your own development. All I know is that East and Circus Animals sounded good when we made them. The first two didn't even achieve that. The last studio album is basically an attempt to emphasize our strengths and avoid our weaknesses.

"Our basic weakness, when it comes to making records, is that we're not the kind of band that thrives on being shoved into the studio for six weeks. We're not Pink Floyd; our music doesn't slowly gestate. On the other hand, we can all sit together and play, and it will sound much better than any of us individually. That's what we're trying to capture on record."

(Don Walker, Rolling Stone Magazine)

"I was very pleased with a lot of the writing on the Twentieth Century album, though the production was terrible."

(Don Walker talking to Glenn A. Baker in 1988)

"Then we have Saturday Night, an appealing track with many of Chisel's best qualities filtered through a clever mix. The melody relies heavily on Phil Small's excellent bass lines. The mood is mellow, reflective until a typical Chisel chorus crashes through the undergrowth. But the party's over too soon and we're back on the race track for Painted Doll. The same unrelenting pace, but some delightful licks from Ian Moss who demonstrates his already familiar dexterity on the fretboard."

"As a showcase of Cold Chisel's techniques and abilities Twentieth Century is a mixed bag. Certainly with 13 tracks, it represents true value for money in this day and age. Reading back, I seem more critical that appreciative of this effort. But the question lingers: Cold Chisel being among Oz's best exponents of driving rock and a top live band, why so much emphasis on thrashing the beat to death? For a band that had developed subtlety, so much haste gives the album an unpalatable raw edge.

"Cold Chisel's consistently high quality, both live and on vinyl, over the past few years has been concurrent with Australia's emergence from a musical backwater to industry front-runners. Maybe other critics will find Twentieth Century more memorable than I did. After all, it's beefy and loud and bound to satisfy Chisel's more metal inclined supporters."

(Stephen Waldon, Juke magazine)

Although I have not included all of Stephen's review (three of 12 paragraphs), it does give no mention at all to three of the album's better songs, *Build This Love, Flame Trees* and *The Game,* none of

which suffer from the "emphasis on thrashing the beat to death" which is Stephen's main criticism of the album. As a matter of fact, in his fifth paragraph Stephen writes, "Only the single, *Saturday Night, Sing To Me* and *Janelle* provide any real relief from what seems like a competition to produce the fastest paced tracks ever recorded."

I have not made it my role to make comment on the critics, but I can't help but feel that perhaps a few more listens were required on this occasion.

"It's cruel that a band should make its last album its best, and it seems remarkable that while the members of the band were planning their individual futures they were able to present such a cohesive sound. Don Walker dominates the songwriting, as usual, but his style has matured. He now combines what could be sentimental lyrics with an awesome power and pace. He is reflective, introspective and succinct. On keyboard, he provides a lush backing to his words-words which are interpreted superbly with by Jimmy Barnes and Ian Moss. Barnes is using his voice better and his songwriting has also improved, which augers well for the proposed solo album. As for Moss, his magnificent voice has never been utilized to the fullest. On this album he takes the lead only twice, the single Saturday Night being one occasion. But when you play guitar as brilliantly as he does, I guess you don't have to push your vocal ability.

"As for the two remaining members of the band, bassist Phil Small and drummer Steve Prestwich, their performances are solid. Small's bass work is extremely imaginative."

(Pat Bowring, Melbourne Sun)

MAY 12

Saturday Night single is No. 9 (No. 6 the previous week) on the national (Australian) chart. The Twentieth Century album is No. 2 on the national chart.

Jimmy Barnes officially launches his new solo band, opening the set with *Rising Sun* and including another half a dozen Chisel songs, although only drawing from those he wrote, at this stage.

JUNE

Release: *Twentieth Century / Only One* single. Stephen Prestwich (now with the Little River Band), is reportedly working on songs for a solo LP. It is also reported that he has recovered from a painful back injury sustained in a 1979 car accident, a factor (reportedly !) in forcing him to quit the band last year after a European tour.

1984
Rod Willis & Jim, Bowral.

185)

JULY 19   Release of Last Stand film

The film opens for a two week season ($5 admittance) at Sydney's Village Cinema, City and Parramatta, Melbourne's Village East End and Frankston and Adelaide's Academy Cinema. A 1000 watt stereo sound system is used at these venues with other states being added later. For details see video appendix.

AUGUST

Release of Flame Trees / River Deep, Mountain High single.

DECEMBER

Barking Spiders Live album is released. This album is intended as a final statement from the band. Interestingly the composition of this record has little in common with the film from the *Last Stand* shows, all the gloss of the latter being deliberately avoided on this release, right down to the cover being a copy of the standard bootleg album cover and the cover liner notes following a similar, virtually nonsensical vein. All versions except the vinyl version contain the additional track *Only Make Believe*.

In a joint review with The Who's *Who's Last* live album, Christie Eliezer observed,

"Neither Who's Last nor Barking Spiders Live particularly capture the two bands at the height of their power; then on the other hand, they were so above the norm that there are moments on the LPs that are absolutely spine-chilling. It's impossible to listen to either of these LPs without a sense of nostalgia: people, places, and faces come flooding back with each track. As Don Walker opined to me once, THAT is the sign of great rock and roll- so powerful that it creates an inextinguishable mark on someone's memory bank. Flashes of Chisel images, the precarious hold on reality, the failures of communication, the inevitability of violence and exploitation, the humiliation of self and others as a response to a humiliating intolerable society. Seemingly fighting for its life, the band crash through Merry Go Round, You've Got Nothing I Want, Forever Now, Standing On The Outside, and Taipan- a painful and sometimes hysterical frustrated soundtrack, a facing of facts, a searching for the past to define the present. At their crassest, Cold Chisel are disgusting and bleeding in a magnificent way; when Moss exudes his bittersweet guitar or when the vocal rendition of "Georgia" tugs your very heartstrings, then you're witnessing a very real love affair between a band of

five and an audience of several thousand. What is this thing called love?

"It's true these LPs were made by men beginning to sound tired. It's true that both bands were not always fulfilled, and at times they were confused. But as these live sets show, there were the moments when the cobwebs and exhaustion were swept away to sheer exhilaration and stimulation. There are the moments of their prime where when the magic flared, these two were all but untouchable."

(CHRISTIE ELIEZER, JUKE MAGAZINE)

"This album only highlights the loss. Brilliant production from Mark Opitz of 1983 performances at the Sydney Entertainment Centre. Jimmy Barnes in full flight on the rock and rolls tracks, Twentieth Century, Standing On The Outside and You Got Nothing I Want. Georgia is a sensitive contrast. Bootleg posing cover promises bonus of a full color poster - not worth getting excited about, unlike the album. (9 out of 10)

(NEIL MOYSE, SMASH HITS MAGAZINE)

"Far and away the best live band in Australia, the Chisels are in Scintillating form on this album. Jimmy Barnes delivers his scorching vocals, Ian Moss displays blinding guitar runs and class vocals, and the rhythm section is rock solid. When it comes to tough and intelligent rock, they don't come any better than these lads."

(TV SCENE)

1985 MARCH

The Mirror, reports that,

"Three members of the legendary rock band Cold Chisel recently had a reunion at the Mosman Hotel. The occasion was a triple celebration. Lead guitarist Ian Moss was celebrating his 30th birthday, bassist Phil Small was showing of his new group, Pound, and drummer Steve Prestwich was having a final night out before leaving for America where he will join LRB."

NOVEMBER

Release of Radio Songs compilation

"This isn't really too bad an introduction to a band that became something of a legend here over the years. For a group that earned something of a reputation as hell-raisers they could put down some delicate sounds in the studio."

(JAMES MANNING IN SMASH HITS MAGAZINE)

(186

"a single album doesn't seem long enough to include every great Chisel track. "

(Steve Bibb, The (Melbourne) Sun, 18/12/85)

1986 DECEMBER

Release of Seeing Is Believing video. See video Appendix.

1988

Release of Razor Songs album. Tracks: Home and Broken Hearted / Standing On The Outside / Conversations / Hold Me Tight / Ghost Town / My Turn To Cry / Houndog / Painted Doll / Rising Sun / Merry Go Round / Wild Thing

All the tracks on this compilation had been previously released, although the tracks from *You're Thirteen, You're Beautiful and You're Mine* had not been available on CD before, and had not been available in any form since that EP was deleted. It was a collection of the band's more aggressive songs, those often overlooked by radio programmers, particularly since the release of the Radio Songs compilation. The two releases virtually balance each other out in that they display two different sides of the band. All the songs on this CD were important parts of the band's live show at some point in their development, from *Home and Broken Hearted*, which appeared on the band's demo tape in 1977 to *Ghost Town* and *Hold Me Tight*, which were staples in the band's last shows. Jimmy does an interview with Scott Howlett in *Playboy* magazine where, for the first time some of the reasons for the band's split are aired. Jimmy has obviously breached an agreed silence maintained by the band, but his comments draw a response from Rod Willis. Ian Moss and Don Walker start work on solo careers (see discography for details).

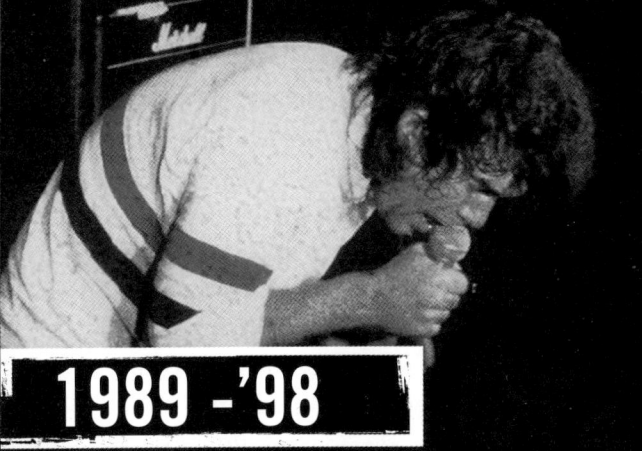

1989 -'98
Can't believe it's over with you

THE '90S SAW A CHANGE IN THE GENERAL PERCEPTION OF COLD CHISEL, WITH THE RELEASE OF PREVIOUSLY UNISSUED, OR RARE MATERIAL AND A GENERALLY POSITIVE ATTITUDE TOWARDS EACH OTHER BY THE BAND MEMBERS. APPARENT EVIDENCE OF THIS WAS THE FIRST PHOTOS OF THE BAND TOGETHER IN NEARLY TEN YEARS AND THE GENERALLY POSITIVE COMMENTS COMING FROM THEM ABOUT THE BAND. THE PRESS THEMSELVES SEEMED ALSO TO BE RE-EVALUATING THE BAND'S IMPORTANCE IN THE OVERALL SCHEME OF AUSTRALIAN MUSIC. NEEDLESS TO SAY THE SUCCESS OF THE RELEASES IN THE '90S ALSO HELPED.

1991 SEPTEMBER

Release of Misfits / Mona and the Preacher (live) / Four Walls (live) single. Misfits had been previously released as the B-side to My Baby, Mona and the Preacher was from the You're Thirteen... EP and Four Walls came from the Swingshift set.

SEPTEMBER RELEASE OF CHISEL ALBUM

This release is the first to showcase digitally remastered recordings of Cold Chisel material, something which was particularly effective on the songs from earlier albums, which were also remixed. The version of *Khe Sanh* which appears on this, which is listed as being from the US version of *East* is not the same as the US take. The remixing process, which has altered the length of the song, as well as the mix renders this as another version again. For more on this see the appendix of original songs. Billy Pinnell asked Don about the process used to select which songs made it onto the album, "The process was that we deliberately excluded ourselves, that is the members of the band. Rod Willis sat down, with various members of the record company and they went through and statistically figured out which had been the most popular songs or the ones

that people most wanted to hear. That way they figured that, and I agreed wholeheartedly that there would be no chance that there would be arguments about inclusions of which songs. Besides, at the time most of the members of the band were very busy with other projects, I was busy with the Catfish stuff and I was happy to leave the selection of songs to those people and then not to face any argument or hassle over which songs had been chosen."

1992 - OCTOBER 19

Release of *Last Stand* soundtrack CD as well as a re-release of the video (with digitally remixed and remastered sound) and a CD and video pack. The soundtrack album has a different track listing to the *Barking Spiders* album released previously, the latter bearing only scant relation to the film.

1994 - APRIL

Press reports that Cold Chisel may re-unite for a one-off tour this year. The reformation is to coincide with the release of a new CD *Never To Be Released*, a collection of tracks originally recorded for the East and *Circus Animals* albums. Also rumoured to be on the new album are tracks recorded in Adelaide when the band were relatively unknown.

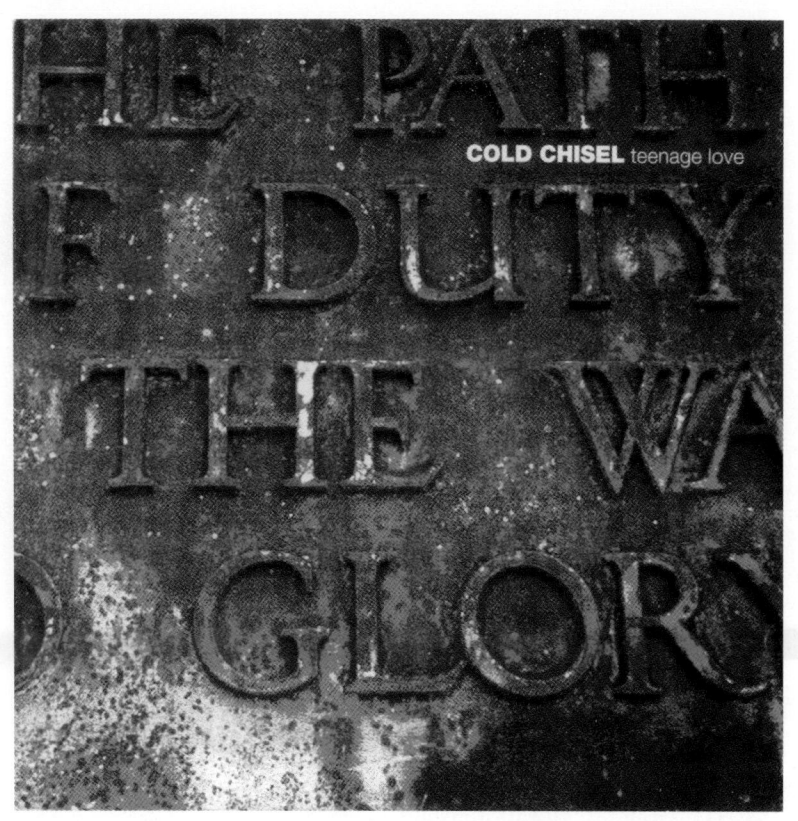

The tapes were reportedly discovered by the owner of a studio when cleaning out old boxes. Also reported was the expected release of a boxed set for the Christmas market.

AUGUST 29 - RELEASE OF PART 1 OF THREE BIG HITS

Disc 1 - Hands Out Of My Pocket/ Teenage Love Affair/It Aint Wrong/ H-Hour Hotel/ On The Road

These were the first tracks from the *Teenage Love Affair* album to be released, and perhaps more importantly, this contains two songs which were not released on the album. *H-Hour Hotel* comes from Peppers in June 1976 and demonstrates that even at this early stage the band had a knack for complex arrangements and impressive playing. *On The Road* crams more into a three minute song than you'll ever hear and is the first of the songs which featured a couple of early verses from Ian before Jim would take the last verse and complete it. It also features a complete change of pace in the coda. This version comes from the first album sessions.

Disc 2 - Nothing But You/When The Sun Goes Down/River Deep Mountain High* (live)/ Let's Go Get Stoned* (live)

Disc 3 - Yesterdays/Wild Colonial Boy* (live)/Only One* (live)/ Build This Love* (live)/ Letter To Alan* (live)

*All live tracks are taken from the Last Stand shows of the 13th and 15th December, 1983.

Unfortunately, from a performance point of view, some of these live tracks are not representative of the band at their best, due to the circumstances leading up to the final Sydney shows. Exceptions to this are *River Deep Mountain High, Only One* and *Let's Go Get Stoned* which make these CDs worth picking up. The fact that many of these songs (or versions of) are not available elsewhere makes these CD singles a must-have for the serious Cold Chisel fan. *On The Road* is one of the most important songs in the band's development, and this is the only official release of the song as the tape was not considered to be of high enough sound quality to see it included on the album.

OCTOBER 31 - RELEASE OF TEENAGE LOVE LP

The album was a collection of previously recorded tracks, which for one reason or another had not been released before. Within this was the stipulation that a song should not have been previously released in another form and that no overdubs were to be done. Exceptions were made for some tracks on the first of these stipulations, as *The Party's Over* had been released on a limited edition single with the *East* album, *Mona And The Preacher* had been issued in live format and *Daylight* had been issued by Jimmy Barnes as a solo artist. Of the stipulation that there be no overdubs, well that nearly didn't happen either as Don Walker explained, "I intercepted a couple of people with guitars, and Jim came in one night to do some vocals. That's a slippery slope that has only one end, which is the entire band setting up in the studio and that wasn't going to happen."

Many of the tapes had disintegrated so badly that they had to be baked in an oven then given a final pass through the tape heads to be transferred to digital. To coincide with this release, Don did an interview with JJJ where he discussed the album track by track. For more on the songs from *Teenage Love* see Appendix One. During this interview he mentioned that the assembling of this album had been:

"…the first time since about 1983 that all the band has been together in one room and enthusiastic about Cold Chisel stuff and actually working on something together… Even though we were just in the studio mixing, there's a lot of enthusiasm around the band for the way the stuff sounds and, a lot of

excitement that there should be a whole albums worth of stuff there. "

Speaking about the album to Toby Creswell in *Juice* Magazine, Don Walker observed,

"I know that most of the charm in this is that it's not all tight. If you made this tight it wouldn't sound half as good.

"If we were recording an album we could have tightened some of these songs up and in the process spoiled them. That's why this, in many ways sounds better and truer to the band than many of the tracks which did come out as serious studio records. It really is the band with no clothes on, doing what they did, and even in that relaxed state the band still plays tighter and better than most modern bands' overdubbed and over-produced recordings."

1995 AUGUST

Release of the double CD pack of the Chisel album and, for the first time in any form since its original limited vinyl release, *You're 13, You're Beautiful and You're Mine*. The cover incorrectly dates the recording as being at the Regent Theatre in 1977. It was recorded on October 14, 1978.

Recorded at Sydney's Regent Theatre, the EP is worth it's weight in gold just for the classics *One Long Day* and *Wild Thing*.

This CD set is a must have for all Cold Chisel fans.

(LYALL JOHNSON, SUNDAY HERALD SUN, 13 AUGUST)

1996 - SEPT 14

Following a story on the Internet a couple of months earlier from Rod Willis, *TV WEEK* reports that Cold Chisel (and Australian Crawl) are set to reform:

"Two of Australia's most loved bands are set to reform. Cold Chisel and Australian Crawl have been negotiating secret deals that would see them back on the road at the start of 1997. The Chisel tour has been pencilled in for March-April, and would be their first gigs since the Last Stand shows in 1983. "It's not locked in, but it's very close," a source close to the band says. "It'll be massive." Cold Chisel may also record a new album to coincide with the tour."

The source adds that the tour won't happen until next year, because singer Jimmy Barnes has a greatest hits

album, Barnes Hits, coming out next month. And guitarist Ian Moss is promoting his new album Petrolhead."

The Herald Sun of September 20 reported:

"Australian rocker Jimmy Barnes has returned to Australia amid rumours his former band Cold Chisel may get together for a summer tour......The band was seen this week at a city recording studio and has reportedly met for lunch."

A Cold Chisel spokesman yesterday said : "They're all getting on at the moment, so who knows?"

A week later Jimmy was asked about these rumours on live radio where he commented that it would be impossible for them to have been seen leaving a studio together as they all live in different states. He did add that if the band ever did get back it would be great and it would be no half hearted thing and they would definitely tour as they were a live band.

NOVEMBER

The CD version of the *Freedom* soundtrack is issued, receiving two and a half stars in a Rolling Stone review which described it as "very interesting." Both Ian and Jimmy continue tours around the country to promote their latest solo efforts, Jimmy's *Greatest Hits* package peaks at No. 1 on the charts.

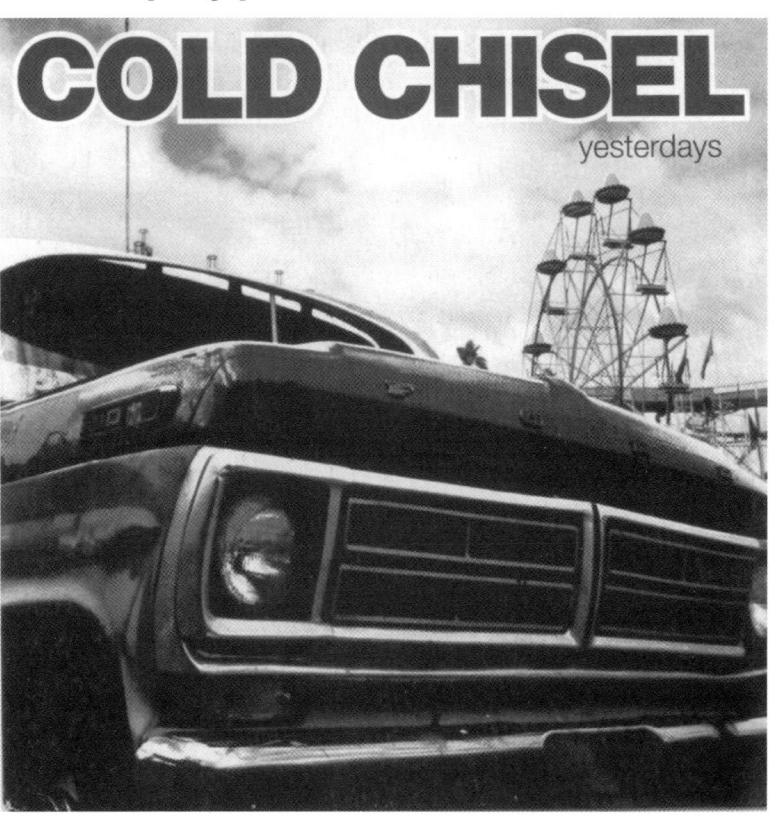

Rumours circulate of a Cold Chisel reunion at the Largs Pier Hotel on New Years Eve, very nostalgic but untrue.

1997 - JANUARY 1

The Melbourne *Age* reports:

"Rumors that Australian super-group Cold Chisel will re-form this year have been denied by the band's management, sparking confusion in the rock industry." A front page story in yesterday's Adelaide Advertiser reported that the band- arguably Australia's most popular in the late 1970s and early 1980s- would be considering a new album with a full reunion tour to follow. According to the article, lead singer Jimmy Barnes said the band had agreed to get together to write new songs early this year."

"We feel it's a good time to do it... if we do a great record we'll go out on tour", Barnes was quoted as saying. "The way we left it was, if we write a bunch of songs that are great, we're going to get together."

But Mr. Ray Smith from Rod Willis management, the band's managers, said the talk was "pure speculation."

He said he hadn't heard of any new plans for the band to get together and write new songs, let alone release an album and go on tour. He said any plans were "definitely not" confirmed and he had "no idea where that story would have come from."

"If they're Jim's words, they're Jim's words...I haven't spoken to him for a couple of weeks," he said of the singers comments.

MARCH

Jimmy tells the Melbourne *Herald Sun* that he has written songs with Don Walker and passed on his own work to other Chisel members, with a view to a reunion.

"We haven't sat and had dinner as a unit since we broke up, but we are looking at re-forming. If we end up with the right material and we feel good about it it's going to happen.

"One of the things Cold Chisel was great for was doing everything from blues to rock to ballads to jazz. That was the beauty of the band. You couldn't diversify enough. I want that chemistry. Cold Chisel wasn't all about Jimmy Barnes, I didn't have to carry the torch myself. In Cold Chisel we had the ability to let go - Mossy would sing and you had Don

Walker's songs of amazing depth and capability."

"I think what we have to do is exactly the same as we did when we were recording back then. That is, push the envelope and do something new and different and varied and intense. Push ourselves all the time. "We shouldn't be restricted to playing blues or live. We should be using everything. We should be using loops occasionally - you don't necessarily need a drummer on every track, just as you don't need guitar or bass on some things. We should do whatever the song demands."

MARCH

A couple of Don's new songs are demoed at Jim's home studio, including *Fallin' Angel*, a mid-paced bluesy tune which could be Cold Chisel in 1978. These demos have electric drums and bass, only Don, Ian and Jim being present on them.

MAY 1

Cold Chisel begins two weeks rehearsals below the Sydney Opera House. The band aim to do two weeks on and two weeks off for twelve weeks, trying as much new material as possible and ensuring that if things don't work out, it's not for want of trying. Right from the beginning these sessions take place on the proviso that if the results are not equal to or better than what the band was doing before, nothing more will happen as far as Cold Chisel are concerned. All band members, with the exception of Ian have large stockpiles of songs, with both Steve and Phil not having any regular outlet for their material and Don being quite prolific. In the first two weeks fourteen or fifteen songs are completed and the band are happy with them, the only concern being that they'd like to have more uptempo rock songs.

JUNE 2

The Melbourne *Herald Sun*, under the headline, Chisel Barnstorms Back reports that : 'Top rock band Cold Chisel has reformed after splitting up more than 13 years ago. Guitarist Ian Moss told the *Herald Sun* the original lineup - fronted by Jimmy Barnes - had been rehearsing and hoped to have an album out by the end of the year. A national tour will follow in February or March.

"We've done some rehearsing and so far it feels pretty good," Moss said.

"There was definitely a bit of nervousness about whether people could still play and whether we still had it. But I think the magic is still there." The five members of Cold Chisel - Barnes, Moss, keyboard player Don Walker, bass player Phil Small and drummer Steve Prestwich - spent two weeks holed up in a rehearsal room below the Sydney Opera House early last month…"

The article went on to say that Moss had in a lot of ways been looking forward to getting back to playing with the guys for a long time. "It took splitting up and getting away from them to realise how good they were. And the playing we've done so far has proved that's the case. We haven't touched one old song at all; it was straight into new songs. If it gets as far as live touring, we'll obviously be playing a lot of the old stuff. We couldn't go out there and tour and not play the old stuff." While many may have taken this story as an announcement of a more permanent future for Cold Chisel, the writer had in fact been talking to Ian about other things and the discussion had drifted onto the subject of Cold Chisel and was put into print. A number of radio stations, taking their cues from the newspaper, also reported the story on their news bulletins.

1997 - JULY 22

Newspapers report under the headline *Bids run hot for Cold Chisel* that Cold Chisel have become the most sought-after band in the country.

AUGUST 13

Cold Chisel sign to Mushroom Records in a deal described by Mushroom's Michael Gudinski as more of a partnership than a deal. The band have reportedly turned down a million dollar offer which was part of a bidding war between four record companies in return for creative control. "It says they are back together for the music." Gudinski added. "In the last few months negotiations veered right off that track. It was more important to structure a business relationship that gave the band total creative control."

The report also said that the band had written some 50 new songs, Gudinski adding, "From what I've heard personally, it sounds like they want to take that whole sound, and the Cold Chisel legend, even further."

AUGUST 20

"There was definitely a bit of nervousness about whether we could still play and whether we still had it. But I think the magic is still there. The scary thing is it doesn't feel like 13 years. It took splitting up from them to realise how good they were, and the playing we have done so far has proved that's the case."

(Don Walker)

SEPTEMBER/OCTOBER

Cold Chisel record in Megaphone Studios with engineer/producer Paul McKercher. Reports are good but the band are still reluctant to commit themselves to further sessions with this combination (producer and studio). Ian heads to Queensland for a short series of solo shows.

NOVEMBER 22

On the day that Michael Hutchence passes away Cold Chisel make their first live appearance since 1983. The occasion is manager Rod Willis' 50th birthday and the venue, Avalon RSL. Cold Chisel play six songs: *Merry-Go-Round, Roadhouse Blues, Bow River, Green River, Cry Me A River* (Ian vocals) and *Baby's On Fire*. The latter is one of the new originals the band are in the process of recording. The Creedence classic *Green River* goes right back to Ian's first band The Scene, in Alice Springs, 1969 and was also played by Ian's solo cover band, the Pye Dogs in 1991. *Cry Me A River* was also done by the Pye Dogs and as a solo guitar/vocal number has been a highlight of Ian's '96-'97 gigs.

The passing of Hutchence is a sad note in what was a most enjoyable evening. Band members attend Michael's funeral later in the week.

Now past the demo stage and into the serious recording, the band have laid down 21 new songs at Q Studios in Sydney with Nashville engineer Rick Will. The tracks are described as awesome, although Rod Willis is cautious, aware that there are many more songs to be recorded and the album they see at the moment may be quite different to the final product. They take a break from recording as Jim rehearses for a tour to support the re-release of the *Soul Deep* album and Ian heads to Italy for a quick holiday.

(192

Jimmy's *Soul Deep* Tour runs until the 5th of January, 1998. Highlights include guest appearances from his sons Jack and David Campbell. Jimmy is singing as well as he ever has, and Ian's guitar work at recent live shows has been excellent. Cold Chisel plan to continue recording the album in February, a release appears. likely in June/July, with a tour coinciding. Plans are also in place for a German tour, news reports of the band's reformation are reported in the press over there.

One of the songs intended for the new Cold Chisel is given to David Campbell and included on his *Taking The Wheel* CD release through Polydor. Don Walker plays piano on the track. David performs the song, *It Will Always Be You*, in New York, dedicating it to his father who is in the audience.

FEBRUARY 20/21/22

The band surprise everyone by playing a series of surprise shows in Broken Hill, Bourke and Dubbo. Press coverage is minimal, as intended. These shows really only serve as a chance to play some of the new material to an audience before returning to the studio for another intensive recording session.

APRIL

The band have demoed nearly 100 songs and have reduced those to about thirty finished (or in some cases , almost finished) tracks to be considered for a new album. Listed below are details on 28 of these.

Way Down - (Prestwich)

This catchy Prestwich ballad was played in the February sets in country NSW. Vocals are handled by Ian, with harmonies from Jim. A classy song which may not make it onto the album for no other reason than the strength of the other songs and the fact that it is virtually another ballad.

Bal-a-Versailles - (Walker)

A classic to be. At a similar pace to *Flame Trees*, with captivating lyrics and haunting melody. One of the most durable and effective choruses Don has written. I really can't say enough about this one, a few listens and you'll see why.

Fallin' Angel - (Walker)

One of the first songs prepared for Cold Chisel Mk.11, this one goes back to a demo Don, Ian and Jim did at Jim's house in Sydney in Feb/March 1997. Complete with drum machine.

This version, with the entire band is similar in feel to songs like *Numbers Fall* - that Australian Blues feel Don does so well. And Jim sings so well. A great guitar solo from Ian also on this one, which is a good chance to make the album. Some may know this one from the ABC television series where a version featuring Don on vocals was used as the theme.

Red Sands - (Moss)

When I recently spoke with Ian he was planning to rewrite the lyrics to this one(the current lyrics are along the line of *Tucker's Daughter*, as is the tempo) and re-record the vocal. Possibly one of the best numbers Ian has written since *Bow River*. A favourite of mine. The title may also change with the lyric.

One Life - (Small)

An Ian Moss vocal over a Stevie Ray Vaughan-ish guitar line. A very deep South mid-tempo blues feel, which features some fine playing from Ian, including some tasty Wah Wah pedal. This one was not tipped to make the album.

It Will Always Be You - (Walker)

Already issued on David Campbell's *Taking The Wheel* album (two versions) and unlikely to make the new Cold Chisel album for that reason and the fact that it is a slow ballad. This cut features a nice organ solo and a surprisingly effective (it's not the type of song he's known for) vocal from Jim. I must admit, this song didn't move me at first, but it really does grow on you.

Since You've Been Gone - (Prestwich)

This is Steve's vocal debut, and a better one I could not imagine. This is simply an amazingly catchy ballad. haunting, hypnotizing, beautiful, atmospheric, get the thesaurus-it's all here.

By My Side - (Barnes)

A fine song from Jim, whose songwriting is as good as it's ever been. This medium paced song has a catchy chorus and a fine vocal. At the time of writing, this one was not favoured to make the album.

Long Night Cold/Once Around the Sun (Small)/(Small/Barnes)

The first version of this one has Ian on vocals and is a fine song an almost soul influence in a cptivating rhythm which just seems to grab you. The band were never really happy with the vocal melody and it was recorded in late June with a new vocal (the rhythm track remains) from Jim and the title Once *Around The Sun*.

A certain for the album, and new musical territory for Cold Chisel. Maybe we'll see *Long Night Cold* as a B-side sometime.

Baby's On Fire - (Walker)

A real belter, sounds as though it was written to replace *Wild Thing* in the live set. Check out the twist in the slow tempo guitar solo. Destined to be a live favourite.

Silence - (Prestwich)

The first song rehearsed when the band assembled at the Opera House in may '97. A great soul groove which is quite different to anything else Steve has written. What makes this one so instantly appealing is the chorus which has that Cold Chisel sound where Ian and Jim sing together. A great chorus and some fine performances from everyone on this track, which unfortunately may not make the album.

The Last Wave Of Summer - (Walker)

In the style of *Taipan*, another of those Australian Blues feels Don Walker virtually invented (also see *Freedom* Soundtrack album). The intro is deceptive before the song literally lifts up and takes you somewhere else. Played at the 'secret' gigs earlier this year, this is a certain inclusion on the album.

This Big Old Car - (Walker)

In the style of *Hold Me Tight* and *Ghost Town*. This one will ensure that the intensity Cold chisel live shows are famous for, remains.

Mr. Crown Prosecutor - (Walker)

The fine wine of the album, along with Bal-a-Versailles. Written from the point of view of the accused addressing the crown prosecutor. A great shimmering tremolo guitar and another very intense vocal from Jim.

The Beast - (Moss/Walker)

A riff-based song of Ian's which Don also worked on, ulikely to appear on the album.

Water Into Wine - (Prestwich)

From very early in the piece this song was touted as a possible single. A catchy ballad with sees acoustic guitar appearing in a Cold Chisel song for the first time since *Khe Sanh*.

Yakuza Girls - (Walker)

Highly regarded song from the first recording sessions. Played at breakneck speed in the style of *Hold Me Tight*. Superb lyrics. Performed in Don's solo sets in '98.

He Can't Believe It's Over - (Walker)

Very catchy song, midpacaed rocker which could be a radio favourite. Played at Dubbo in Febru ary.

(194

I'll Never Stop Lovin' You - (Barnes)

One of Jim's better compositions in recent times, a possible hit single. Parts of this were re-recorded in June. Played at Dubbo in February.

No Reason - (Walker)

Don's first vocal for Cold Chisel although at the time of writing it appears that this will most likely appear on a Don Walker solo album. Already appearing in Don's solo sets.

Pretty Little Thing - (Walker)

A buesy song, played in all the February gigs.

The Things I Love In You - (Walker)

Probably the most Cold Chisel sounding of all the new songs, this one could have sat comfortably on the *East* album. Destined to be a classic. On the set list for the Dubbo show in February.

Small Town Motel Blues - (Moss/Walker/Barnes)

A likely B-side, a song which originally came from a writing session between Jim and Ian. Don added lyrics to finish it. Vocals from Ian.

So Hard - (Barnes)

Another quality song from Jim, whose writing is exceptional on these new songs. Played at the February shows, this song stands some chance of appearing on the album. It is said that record company execs virtually cried when they heard this song.

This Time Around - (Walker)

In the style of *When The War Is Over*, I must confess to initially being unimpressed with this song, but I have changed my mind after a number of listenings. It's a medium/slow number, with Ian singing the first verses and Jim taking over for a final rousing verse and chorus.

Better Time/Better Place - (Prestwich/Small/Walker)

Like Things I Love…, this one captures the classic Chisel sound by having an almost chanted chorus with all band members singing together. Originally an idea of Phil's, Steve provided the hook and Don added to the verses. Played at some shows in february and a certain inclusion on the album.

Angel In My Room - (Barnes)

A tender ballad which may possibly miss out for that reason alone.

Blind Can't Lead The Blind - (Barnes)

Possibly one of the finest songs Jim has ever written, and featuring some amazing singing which really shows just how he has improved as a vocalist in the last few years.

Caught My Eye - (Prestwich)

Another touching ballad, I particularly like the coda on this one.

JULY - 7

Yakuza Girls is released on the internet. The web site receives 228, 596 hits in the 12 hours following the songs release.

AUGUST - 24

Things I Love In You is released in a number of formats, including remixes and tracks such as Yakuza Girls and Small Town Motel Blues.

What can you say about reformations? What can you say about legends reforming? Is it a good thing? Is it a bad thing? The only thing I can say is that Don Walker, here, is the bench mark. If all the others wanted to get together and Don didn't want to get together, it wouldn't have happened. He would not have wanted to get together unless the songs were there. Then he would have wanted the music to be there. Clearly both fulfilled his bench mark. He is the key man, a fastidious man, a man who is hard to please and whose principles are up there with the best of them. If his principles have been satisfied then it must be OK with anyone else.

Vince Lovegrove, July, 1998.

195)

APPENDIX ONE

ORIGINAL SONGS '73-'83

Although the band made a decision to do original material back in the Adelaide days, they were still doing a large percentage of cover material (more than half) when they first moved to Sydney. The turning point came at a gig at the Bondi Lifesaver where RAM magazine editor Anthony O'Grady saw the band play their Zeppelin/ Free covers and sound-alike originals to an audience of about fifty people. He spoke to their then manager Sebastian Chase (who later managed Dragon) and told him that they seemed a "tight, powerful band who probably wouldn't get anywhere being a heavy metal jukebox." Don Walker finishes the story: "Sebastian came backstage and told us 'Anthony O'Grady doesn't think you'll make it'. It was a turning point actually, we decided to concentrate on nothing but originals."

Although generally happy to talk about his songs, Don Walker can be reluctant to get into too much detail, as he told Roadrunner magazine in 1980: "You get guys coming backstage and they say stuff like they lay a general over the top rave about Cold Chisel's position in their lives, which I always find pretty acutely embarrassing. And they can see that and get into some more down to earth topic."

Don is one of those rare songwriters who does the writing in his head, and can translate this to the band before even laying hands on an instrument, "I usually hear a section of a song pretty complete - as it would sound played by a band; I can sort of play it as I'll record it virtually straight off. But that may only last for eight bars, then the rest might be complete bullshit - I've got it orchestrated, the band's playing away but I don't know where the next bit goes.

"So you file away at the good bit and try to join it up with another bit later on. Some of them can hang about for a long time"

A Little Bit Of Daylight - (J. Barnes) Written about the flat Jimmy was living in at the time. He would arrive there in the wee hours of the morning from a show or recording session and try to sleep through the day, which was virtually impossible as it had no curtains. Better known as a Barnes solo song although it was demoed by Cold Chisel a couple of years before Barnes recorded it (see Oct '81). No references to it ever appearing in the Chisel live sets. Don felt so strongly about Cold Chisel's rendition of this song that he convinced the rest of the band that it should be included on the 'Teenage Love' album.

All In Trouble - (S. Prestwich) Demoed in September 1981, never released.

Best Kept Lies - (S. Prestwich) "I got the riff and it just grew from there. This was the first song I brought to the band, although certainly not the first idea I had had for a song." (Steve Prestwich)

"We were going to a beach resort south of Sydney (Nowra) to spend a couple of weeks writing, and he wrote this in his head on the bus trip there. It's hard for a drummer to do that, but he thought up the arrangement and taught it to the band. Steve's from Liverpool in England - his dad used to play drums at places like the Cavern - and in the songs Steve's been writing I can really hear that Liverpudlian sense of melody, the Swinging Blue Jeans, The Merseybeats and bands like that." (Don Walker)

This was the first song that Steve ever wrote, although there had been a few less successful songs, usually collaborations in the mid-1970s. First appeared in live shows during the Set Fire To The Town tour of late 1979 and rehearsed in Nowra in July of that year. Considered by many to be the highlight of the set

at that point. Played for most of 1980 and during the Summer Offensive and US Tours, before being dropped, never to return. Early live versions (late 1979) featured an extended guitar solo. The 1980 Manly Vale show is the only video reference. Never released in live form.

Blue Movies (Never Make Me Cry) - (Barnes) Played live during the Set Fire To The Town tour and no doubt demoed for the East album, this song was played in the live sets from 1978 also. Never released. Rod Willis stated that the song was considered for the Teenage Love album (he thought it was on it!) but was vetoed by Jimmy. Described as having a catchy descending guitar riff and hard-hitting drums. Don described it as: "one of several very good rockers Jim wrote at the time, in the explosion of writing among the other band members surrounding our writing holiday on the south coast. (See July 1979) It, and some others were considered for 'Teenage Love', but the recording quality was a bit beyond the line." A somewhat sexist song as the title suggests (the lyrics are very explicit!) and the subject of many onstage jokes from Jimmy. (See Sept 5 '79)

Bow River - (I.Moss) Ian told Ram's Annie Burton that Bow River was, in many ways, about his hometown Alice Springs, which he says is "too hard to sing."

"It (Alice Springs) keeps my feet on the ground, brings me back to earth - people in the Territory have a very realistic attitude, very level . 'Goin' for the heat babe In a place where no man's puttin' on the dog for me."

Bow River began as Anytime You Want, a much longer song with quite different lyrics which was virtually written in the studio with the help of the band.

Speaking about songwriting , Ian says that he locks himself in a room with an acoustic guitar and a tape recorder. "Hopefully ideas come into your head if you leave the tape running. Quite often a couple of days later when you play the tape back, you discover interesting things that you've done. Then you drag them out and start developing them, so that the song's finished before the rest of the boys are called in." First released on the Circus Animals album and as the B-side to the Forever Now single, a live version can be found on both the Barking Spiders and Last Stand albums, both from the final Last Stand show. Bow River is available on video from the Last Stand show, on the video of the same name and also in an alternative form which uses footage from both the Last Stand show and the Wentworth Park Circus Animals show from April '82, with the sound coming from the former show. An even rarer video has footage and live sound from Wentworth Park. This song is also included on the German video (only screened in Germany- see Appendix 3) in Hamburg, 3/12/82. See also Ian Moss solo.

Breakfast At Sweethearts - (D.Walker) Don wrote the chorus part for the song Breakfast At Sweethearts on the organ at Trafalgar Studios during demo sessions for the second album. First played in live sets in 1978, a live rendition of this track surfaced on Swingshift and the song remained at least an occasional encore piece right till the end. One of the finest performances comes from the July '83 La Trobe University show where it becomes a vehicle for some exceptional Ian Moss wizardry. On video this song can be found on Seeing Is Believing, (this version is credited as being from 1979, but it is in fact from August 1978- see the Video Appendix) and also on the German TV broadcast. See also Jimmy Barnes solo. "It was a sort of a bohemian establishment, that, it wasn't as big as this room here (radio studio), which your listeners can hear how small this room is, and it had gone back decades. It had gone back decades; it was the kind of place that, it had the reputation that when Nureyev was in Sydney he would always have his coffee at Sweethearts and stuff like that. There was a beautiful middle

aged woman who used to serve coffee there and never say anything and she was reputed to be the girlfriend of quite a dangerous guy around the Cross, so it was like look but don't touch. It was the sort of local. They closed it down a good ten years ago now and made it into a McDonalds, and the proprietors who are a Yugoslav family with whom I became friends then opened another establishment across the road and called that Sweethearts."(Walker talking to Billy Pinnell in 1991)

Brisbane Daylight Express - (?)
A never released number played on occasion by the band from 1974 through to early 1977. Mentioned in a live gig review from August of that 1976 where it was described as a "gut rock number....a fast moving song which stops for no-one." Ian always liked the main riff for this one and has suggested to Don that it would be a good song to rearrange. There appear to be no recordings of this song in existence.

Build This Love - (D.Walker)
Very under-rated song from the final studio album. First demoed in late 1982. Played live at the final show in Sydney of the Last Stand tour, although it may have got an airing on the second last night also. A live take from the final night was issued as part of the Three Big Hits singles pack and although the arrangement is slightly different, it is a strong performance deserved of a place on one of the live albums from the final shows. One of the strongest songs on the **Twentieth Century** LP and an insight into where Cold Chisel may have gone later in the 80's.

Bunny's Blues ('Blues From A Suitcase') - (Walker)
A song from the demo tape which got the band signed to WEA. Sung by Moss in the style of Georgia. This song was obviously in the live set also as when asked in 1996 about it Ian couldn't recall ever recording it, yet he was able to hum a few bars of it. "Bunny's Blues was written while I was at university for a song competition judged by Mike MacLellen. Cold Chisel weren't involved. I played and sang it myself and won. I believe, but can't be absolutely sure that this may have been in the latter half of 1974, after the rest of the band had returned to Adelaide from Armidale. The lyrics will always be a little embarrassing." Bunny's Blues was considered for the Teenage Love album, although the version considered was not the one from the demo tape and was not considered to be up to standard in sound quality. A very classy song. One of the best of the unreleased Cold Chisel songs. (See also July 1977)

Cheap Wine - (D.Walker)
"About someone who's on the skids, but still having a great time. I can relate to that - in the seven years Cold Chisel have been together, we've only had enough money to eat the last two and a half. If you get into that lifestyle and start to enjoy it, you tend to stay that way even when the money comes in. The song was written in the studio, I had a short time with nothing to do while the others were writing, so I put it together." (Don Walker, 1981)

Recorded in one or two takes with no demo, Don had the virtually complete song ready for the band to record during the East sessions. Live versions of the song appeared on both the Swingshift and Last Stand albums. The song first appeared in the live set around April of 1980 and was quickly relegated to encore status (if played) by 1982. It appeared occasionally during the Ray Arnott period of '83 and was brought back, in slightly re-arranged form for the Last Stand tour. Apart from the promotional video clip (available on Seeing Is Believing) a live clip of this song can be found from the 1980 Manly Vale show and also from the Last Stand video.

Choirgirl - (D.Walker)
WEA's A&R man, David Sinclair, recalls that Don studied what was required to have a hit song in Australia, in terms of arrangement and length etc. and then wrote Choirgirl. First rehearsed in Nowra in July 1979. Don recalls, "It was the very first thing we did with Mark (Opitz). Choirgirl had the best sound we'd been able to get- it was the sort of thing that had a lot of room to move

around in. The melody is R&B influenced. After our second Australian album, I realised we needed stronger melodies and I started to listen to people like Marvin Gaye for that. The lyric is about a pretty young girl - I'll leave it at that. Played almost always in the live set until the final show, although it was rare in 1983 with the exception being the Last Stand tour. It appears on the East album and in live form on the Swingshift and Last Stand albums. It is also on the Last Stand video. A cover version of Choir Girl appears on the soundtrack to Paradise Beach.

Cold Chisel - (Walker)
Ian explained this circa 1974 song, "The song itself was written when Don was still at uni - and he was experimenting - it had real weird sort of lyrics. We stuck a whole heap of phrases together and fitted them in lines, pot luck, and we called it Cold Chisel." I have not been able to trace any recordings of this song.

Conversations - (D.Walker)
Introduced as a new song in June 1978 and played as the opening number from 1980 to '82. Live versions of this song can be found on Swingshift and on the 12" single version of Choir Girl. On video it can be found on the early 1979 and German television broadcasts- only on the long version of the latter. It was not a regular in '83 sets but it did make occasional encore appearances and was played at the last show in Sydney on December 15. "The chorus of Conversations, that's straight from I'm A Man", Don told Anthony O'Grady in 1979.

Daskarzine - (D.Walker)
Inspired by the Led Zeppelin song Achilles Last Stand, which has the same frantic rhythm. Played live from mid 1976 (when it was written) to early '78. Did not return to the live set until 1980, where it was played on the last night of the Youth In Asia Tour, and then again at the Wentworth Park, Circus Animals shows. First demoed in June 1976, and again for the first album in September 1977, for which it was later recorded and released. Both of these early demo versions were significantly longer, including extra verses and solos. No video references. No live release.

Dresden - (D.Walker)
Dresden is supposed to be a nuclear song. It should have been called something like Hiroshima, something like Hiroshima Blues. Dresden when you get into the words is a pretty weird song. I suppose the thread running through it is a guy escaping some kind of nuclear bombing.

This song took quite a bit of arranging from the band and Richard Batchens. Don commented at the time (Feb '79) that the song was almost impossible to play onstage. This song appears on the August 1978 television broadcast, and also on the 3XY April '79 broadcast from Melbourne's Bombay Rock. No live release.

Drinking In Port Lincoln - (D.Walker)
Recorded at Peppers Studio in June 1976 (the band also played the Port Lincoln Hotel that same month), this song was in the live set when the band played in Melbourne in August - October of that year. Released on the Teenage Love Affair album in 1994. No video references.

F-111- (D.Walker)
Played in the live sets of 1978 and tipped to be the next single at the time, F-111 was also demoed for the first album.These early versions were quite different from the 80's one which was released on Teenage Love. The chorus was about the only constant. For some reason this track was overlooked for the subsequent Breakfast At Sweethearts album. It was eventually released on the Teenage Love album in a version from demo sessions for Circus Animals from which it was apparently omitted because the lyrical content didn't sit with the rest of the album. No video references.

197)

Faust- According to German legend a Faust is a magician or alchemist who sells his soul to the devil in exchange for power and knowledge. Originally a Ron Carpenter song for which Don wrote new lyrics. Played by the band in 1974-6 (see Shandon Hotel, June '75). A mid paced melodic rock song, an example of the more obscure material the band played, another example being Redwing's Underground Railway (see Cover Appendix) No other references.

Fire - **(Barnes)** Demoed by Cold Chisel in January 1983. Recorded by Jimmy Barnes for his first solo album. No other Cold Chisel references.

Fit To Bust Blues - A 12 bar rock song from '75-'76. Phil Small recalls this one as being a favourite of his. Demoed at Peppers in June 1976, with a lyric about "speaking to the nurse at the VD clinic." It was also demoed in March 1976 with Ian singing. Never released although played live regularly.

Five Thirty E.T.A.- Don described this as a truck driving story song with too many lyrics. Don rearranged the music and added new lyrics to make Unlimited Address on the first Catfish album of the same name. It was a '75-'77 era song.

This song was also played in the live sets of 1977, Steve Hands (from WEA)recalls the song well from shows he saw at this time. Five Thirty E.T.A. was also considered for the Teenage Love album, but as one of the criteria was that the song should not have been released previously, this one's appearance, in re-arranged form on the Catfish album may have excluded it. A very mature, classy sounding song which would have sat nicely on the first or second albums, although it does not contain the aggression present on later albums. Demoed at Peppers in June 1976 and again in September 1977 for the first album. Ian recalls that the band never felt that they were at home with its almost funky feel.

Flame Trees - **(S.Prestwich/D.Walker)** "This was a song I wrote on the bass (I used to write a lot on the bass), after having got the initial melodic idea. I never really had any lyrics to speak of, but luckily Don related to it enough to spend a sleepless night writing the lyrics, which enabled it to appear on the Twentieth Century album.

The song had already been recorded at a much earlier demo session, and we kept the drum track and built on that." (Steve Prestwich)

Steve's music and Don's lyric. Played live in early '83 and then dropped for the Ray Arnott tour, (as was all Steve's material) only to be brought back later in the same tour and remaining in the set for the Last Stand tour. Flame Trees was released on the Twentieth Centuryalbum and also as the band's last single in 1984.

Appears in the Last Stand video and the promotional video, the band's last, appears in the Seeing Is Believing video compilation. A compilation video, featuring excerpts from many different sources is also in circulation, distinguished by rare interview footage of a very young Jimmy saying that they're really just a heavy rock band. See also Jimmy Barnes solo.

Forever Now - **(S.Prestwich)** "This song was born out of an emotional feeling, which appeared in the form of the guitar intro melody line, and expanded from that point on. Ian played perfectly the melody I had in my head.Most, if not all the songs I write are born out of an initial melody. A melody comes to me and I build on it. If I'm lucky a few snippets of lyric will accompany that melody, allowing me an insight into what the song should be about, but usually it's hard work matching the sentiment of the melody with a lyric.Because I was not very proficient on any other instrument than the drums, a lot of my ideas for songs would have to be verbally conveyed the other band members-which they were very good at interpreting." (Steve Prestwich)

Played in the live sets of mid '81, '82 and '83 except for the period when Steve was not with the band. A live version was issued on the Barking Spiders Live LP although the song was strangely absent from the later Last Stand LP and film. The only live version to appear on video is from the December '82 German show (see Video Appendix or Dec '82) The promotional video can be found on Seeing Is Believing. This song was released in more countries than any other Cold Chisel single, and enjoyed more chart success than any other. Issued as a single in the US with the title Forever Now (All My Love).

Four Walls - **(D.Walker)** "I wrote Four Walls because I always wanted to write a state-of-the-art Ray Charles blues song. Four Walls is about as close as I'm gonna get."

This song appeared in vastly different form on the demo tape which got the band signed. (see July 1977 and below). It was most probably demoed for the first album, but not released until it had been completely revamped both musically and lyrically for the East album. It was however omitted from the U.S version of this album in favour of a remixed Khe Sanh. Played with some regularity in live sets from '80 through to the end in '83. Four Walls appears on the 1982 German video. Released on Swingshift in live form.

"I went to Parramatta Gaol and met some prisoners who'd written songs about gaol. When I told them I'd written a song about being inside, they told me there was no way I could write such a song. But although their songs might get closer to the truth, I maintain that Four Walls is a better crafted song. Unless I'm sentenced - and I wouldn't do that for a song - there'll always be a gap which really can't be bridged; you've just got to live with it." (Don talking to RAM's Greg Taylor)

Four Walls, Washbasin, Double Bed- In Don's own words, "This was the prototype of the song that appeared on "East", and was a description of my hotel room at the Plaza in Kings Cross and the life surrounding that hotel. I haven't heard it since then, but some of the lyrics are funny and not half bad." This version of the song appeared on the demo tape which the band (successfully) presented to WEA in 1977.

Fuck You Jack - Less than serious song demoed for the East album.

Ghost Town - **(D.Walker)** Don told Glenn A. Baker about this song in 1988, "I particularly like Ghost Town because I think it was the finest and most over the top rockin' roll song we ever did." Played live in early 1983 (an early arrangement) and again on the Last Stand tour. Ghost Town was first demoed by the band in October 1982, with Ian on vocals.

The take released on the Twentieth Century album is one of Ray Arnott's favourite songs, "We used a couple of Vanda & Young tricks on that one, putting a fast echo on the hi-hat to get it quick enough." An under-rated song, notably very short and fast . Like many of the songs from the Twentieth Century album, Ghost Town has not achieved the status it would have had the band been able to play it live in 1984. No video references. See also Catfish.

Goodbye (Astrid Goodbye)- **(D.Walker/J.Barnes)** "Well it's obvious he's (the main character in the song) married to a nuclear bomb" (Don Walker, Feb, 1979) Barnes also commented in the same interview that this was designed to be a live song. The single and album versions of this song are different takes, for details see September 1978.

The origins of this song go back to October 1975 when Don was working on a song called Open The Door Astrid, but this version was very different musically to the version released. Jim believes that Ian sang this early version. In 1978 Don gave the lyrics of the song to Jimmy who wrote the music for the song as we now know it.

(198

Played in the live set from '78 (late that year) to the final show in 1983. The lyrics came from Don, who told me that there was no Astrid, it was just a name that he had heard, probably in relation to one of Bill Wyman's wives. Jimmy wrote the music for this piece which has always been one of his favourite lyrics. This song appears on every available live video of the band! See video Appendix. See also Jimmy Barnes solo. Live versions are available on Swingshift and the Last Stand albums

Goodbye To All That - (Moss/Walker)
Don wrote the lyric and Ian the music to this '75-'77 era song which was sung by Jimmy, although Ian sang it in the '75/'76 period when Jim was not with the band. Ian recalls that the song was demoed for EMI sometime in early 1977. For a descrption of the song see Shandon Hotel, 1975.

Hands Out Of My Pocket - (J.Barnes)
According to Don Walker this song was only really played once and Jimmy can be heard calling the arrangement on the master tape as the band follow him. A promotional video was issued. Released on the Teenage Love Affair album.

H-Hour Hotel - (D.Walker)
Don recalls that this song was influenced by Chain's Black and Blue. No video references. The version on the Three Big Ones single comes from Peppers in June 1976 and has a verse and a guitar solo edited out.

Hold Me Now - (Walker)
Unreleased song which did not make the Teenage Love album due to the fact that the tape had deteriorated badly and the quality was not up to broadcast standard. Don describes it as a great song, with great playing and vocals, but nobody can remember the song or the recording of it, although he suspects that he wrote it as it comes from the early period when he was the only one writing. Hold Me Now has a great chorus and catchy verses. Recorded at the demo sessions for the first album and probably left off that album because it was too commercial and not really representative of the band's sound at the time. From the lack of knowledge about the song it is unlikely that it was played live often . One of the finest unreleased songs from the band.

Hold Me Tight - (D.Walker)
Influenced by fifties rock'n' roll songs although the song didn't really strike a chord with radio programmers. Played live throughout 1983. Available on The Barking Spiders Live and Razor Songs albums in addition to Twentieth Century. The mix on the single version is different to that on the Twentieth Century album, the latter having a little more reverb. A promotional video is available on Seeing Is Believing.

Houndog - (D.Walker)
Steve Prestwich recalls that Houndog was inspired by a line his brother Laurence used, "I've got the Houndog sittin" by the side of the road blues." Released on the Circus Animals album and later on the Razor Songs album. Played live just before and occasionally during the US Tour, with slightly altered lyrics (see Utica, August 10 1981 & Austin, Texas) until the end. The quiet bridge section was dropped from '83 versions, during the period when Gary Young was filling in on drums (see March '83). Ian explained this change in the songs arrangement as being due to the audience demand for faster, harder numbers. The only video reference is on the German '82 show.

Home And Broken Hearted - (D.Walker)
One of the first songs rehearsed with Jim after his return to the band in 1976. This song appeared on the demo tape which got the band signed in 1977. The early demo version doesn't differ a lot from the first album track. The live version of this song was re-arranged in late 1979 and it remained in the live set for much of 1980. It was played as an encore, by request in April '83 although Ian and Jimmy appeared to have forgotten some of the words! Released in live form on You're Thirteen You're Beautiful and You're Mine. (see July '77) No video

An alternative version of this was recorded, with altered lyrics for use as a single from the first album but radio"s playing of Khe Sanh put an end to that plan.

Idleness - (Walker)
Played live in late 1978 and demoed in late 1979, it was in and out of the live set during this period. See When The Sun Goes Down this appendix. Don stated that this was his attempt at writing a Dragon song which was in and out of live sets throughout '78-'79 due to the fact that the band was never completely happy with the arrangement, eventually recorded as When The Sun Goes Down in 1983 and released under that title on the Teenage Love Affair CD. No video references.

I'm Gonna Roll Ya - (D.Walker)
I'm Gonna Roll Ya is a pretty black and white sort of song, you'd have to be stupid to take it too seriously because obviously nobody could really think like that. It's obviously a tongue in cheeky ,dogmatic song about how marriage is fucked and it's just not true, but I just think it's a funny song. At least I hope it's funny. Jimmy regards it as his favourite on the album. This song was played as far back as 1975, when it was one of the first original songs to really strike a chord with audiences. (see Shandon Hotel, June '75) in an earlier form. Played from 1975 until (and including much of) 1980, into the Summer Offensive Tour of early 1981, at the Circus Animals shows at Wentworth Park in April 1982 and again in early 1983. Demoed for the first album, but not released until the second album. The only video reference comes from the August 1978 television broadcast.

Into The Night - (Swan)
One of the songs written by John Swan when he was sharing vocals with Jim in Armidale. A pop song with complicated timing changes.

Ita - (D.Walker)
David Sinclair, who worked with the band at this time, said that Ita Buttrose was something of a sexual fantasy figure to the band at the time and the song was a humorous way of expressing this. "We had all the songs together for the album, and I just thought to myself, 'Hey these songs are all serious! So I decided to inject some light humor. The problem is that people have decided to take it seriously. It was only intended for our record buyers to have a quiet giggle." (The Chronicle, Toowoomba, 28, June 1980)

"I don't think its well arranged - in fact when I'm listening to the album, about the middle of Ita I start to lose concentration."(Don Walker, 1980)

This song did not appear on the U.S. version of East ("It's a bit too much of a fluffy song." - Don) although it was on all other versions, being dropped in favour of a remixed Khe Sanh. Played live during the latter part of 1980 (August-October) and during the Summer Offensive tour. A promotional video was issued.

Ita was covered by an artist from Denmark, described as Denmark's answer to David Bowie in the early '80s.

It Aint Wrong - (D.Walker)
Demoed for the first album, but as producer Peter Walker was under pressure from the record company to deliver a rock'n' roll album, slower numbers like this had to miss out. A surprisingly religious lyrical content. No video references.

Janelle - (D.Walker)
Originally titled Danielle, after Don's daughter. Played live at some of the Sydney Last Stand shows where it was mistakenly called China by some reviewers. Live versions can be heard on the Last Stand CD and video. Recorded by Don Walker on the Tex Perkins, Don Walker , Charlie Owens CD, Sad But True in 1993, it also appeared on that trio's live CD Monday Mornin' Comin Down.

Juliet - (D.Walker/ J.Barnes)
Lyrics from Don, music from Jim. Played live for most of 1978 (it was opening song), part of '77 and 1979, 1980 and 1981, this song

tour and possibly during the Sydney Last Stand shows. No video references or live releases.

Just How Many Times - (D.Walker) An early version of this song was recorded in early 1977 for an ABC surf movie starring Beau Bridges, called A Shimmering Light. The band was required to play the song in the background of a party in an expensive Whale Beach house. However the overseas branch of the production required Don to surrender copyright on the song, which he had no hesitation refusing. The band's appearance in the movie was cut down to only a few seconds and the song not used at all.

Just How Many Times goes right back to the days when Les Kasmarek played bass with the band, although it was not always a regular in live sets as this type of song was not always felt suitable for pub rock audiences.

A jazz/rock style ballad which is very similar in feel to Stevie Wonder/Jeff Beck (Blow By Blow/ Wired period). Played live on the Summer Offensive Tour as an encore number, where it featured a great guitar solo from Ian. The only video appearance for this song is a compilation (bits from everywhere) clip at the end of the Seeing Is Believing video.

Khe Sanh - (D.Walker) Released on self titled album in April 1978. Released as a single in May '78. It is fascinating to hear Khe Sanh played on the Foreigner tour (see April '78), before the album (or single) had been issued and the song is played to an audience who have never heard it before. The original single version has a very prominent acoustic guitar, particularly in the introduction which is not obvious on the later, re-mixed version, as released on the Radio Songs and Chisel albums. Also released in live form on both Swingshift and the Last Stand album and video. A promotional video of the song was shot and is available on the Seeing Is Believing and the later Chisel Seeing Is Believing video. Khe Sanh also appears on video in the Feb '79 and December '82 German television broadcasts. Perhaps the most interesting (and noticeably different) version is the one which appeared on the U.S version of East. It starts with only acoustic guitar, leaving out the eight bar piano intro (there is no piano until the drums enter !) and starting just a few seconds before the opening vocal line. The sleeve notes on the Chisel album state This re-mixed version from the U.S. version of East, which is not entirely true ! Live versions of this song sometimes feature a guitar solo (Aug '78 TV), a keyboard solo (organ sound), as on the first album or a mouth organ (harp) solo, as on Swingshift.

Don has said that the song was not written about any particular individual, although he has admitted that Rick Morris, a Vietnam vet who played with Adelaide band Salvation Airforce in 1975. Rick filled in for Jim when he had laryngitis with Cold Chisel on at least one occasion. The demo version of the song, recorded in September 1977 featured a number of lyrical differences to the take later released:

I left my heart to the sappers round Khe Sanh,

And my soul was sold with my cigarettes to the black market man,

I've had the Vietnam cold turkey from the ocean to the Silver City,

And it's only other vets could understand.

How we sailed into Sydney Harbour, home and free (But) There were no V-day heroes back in nineteen seventy three;

How I bought a King's Cross whisper, I found an old friend but I couldn't kiss her,

She said "Boy I'm glad you didn't see no harm."

She was like so many others from then on

Their lives were all so empty

'Till they found their chosen one

And their legs were often open,

But their minds were always closed

And they had something cotton wool instead of brains

And the legal pads were yellow,

And my swivel chair was green

And the telex writers clattered

Where the gunships once had been:

And carparks make me jumpy

And I"ll never forget the dreams,

I've got red-hot peppers running through my veins.

So I roamed around the country from end to end,

Tried to find a place to settle down,

Where my mixed up life could mend,

Held a job on an oil rig,

Flying choppers when I could,

But the nightlife nearly drove me 'round the bend.

So I sailed a round the world from year to year,

But each new water's just as fine as a Port Jackson beer.

And I've been back to South-East Asia,

You know the answer sure ain't there,

But I'm drifting North,

To check things out again.

(200

The last plane out of Sydney's almost gone,

The last plane out of Sydney's almost gone,

And there ain't nothin' like the kisses,

From a slant-eyed Chinese princess

I"m gonna hit some Hong Kong mattress all night long

Well (honey) the last plane out of Sydney's almost gone,

You know the last plane out of Sydney's almost gone,

And it's really got me worried,

I'm goin' nowhere and I"m in a hurry,

You know the last plane out of Sydney's almost gone. (Repeat last verse one more time)

(Reprinted by permission Don Walker)

"No, (it's not about me) it's the result of talking to an old friend of mine, and being in an area like Kings Cross is conductive to writing a song like that." (Don Walker 1978)

"There seems to have been some problem with us releasing 'Khe Sanh' as a single. Some of the radio stations are objecting to lines like "and their legs were often open" and "or the growing need for speed and Novocain".(Don Walker)

"The only reason Khe Sanh was released as a single was because radio stations were already playing it from the album. When we released the album we didn't intend releasing a single because we're not a singles band." (Don Walker 1978)

"I originally wrote it as a punk song, but we found it worked better with a country-rock approach. Strangely enough, people who are into the Australian bush and folk tradition like the song, so there must be a connection there too. It's about the guys who went to Vietnam - we've known quite a few who served over there. The song didn't get played on Australian radio because they objected to the line, Their legs were often open. That was the reason they told us, which wasn't necessarily the real one." (Don Walker in the USA, 1981) "Every DJ in the country begged us to release Khe Sanh as a single. Then they banned it two weeks later. They had to ban something once a week to keep the Catholic Church happy. You see the main chain of radio stations in Australia is owned by the Catholic Church." (Jimmy talking to the Gazette Telegraph, Denver, July 1981)

"It was a time where we had been going nowhere for about 12 months, we were just playing one show a week, occasionally maybe, once every six months we'd get a trip down to Melbourne for a week and we were going nowhere." It occurred to me, although it should have been obvious - this is shortly after Rod took over management and he suggested "well it's been a long time since you had any fresh original songs."

"So I set about to do some writing because at that time I was the only person writing, and wrote that song fairly quickly around what used to be Sweethearts Caf'e in the Cross, it's not the current Sweethearts Caf'e, but it was an old establishment. I just sat in there on a rainy afternoon and wrote it and taught it to the band in the rehearsals we were doing at the time and we started playing it."(Don Walker talking to Billy Pinnell in 1991)

"This country-rock ballad about the soldiers who went to Vietnam is highly overrated. Australian radio stations wisely refused to play it because of its controversial lyrics." (Sue Simon, The Missourian, Columbia. Missouri, June 1981)

See also Jimmy Barnes solo and Catfish.

Kings Cross Kid - (Walker) Hard rock song played in the live sets of 1978, never released. The intro features a Kevin Borich-like slide guitar while the body of the song sounds like Smokin' In The Boys Room meets Mona And The Preacher. Don described this song as an attempt to write "a Rose Tattoo style song." The lyrics feature verses from the later Plaza, although Jimmy is singing and in a vastly different style. Very much a guitar track, unlike Plaza and there are no similarities in the melodies of the two songs. Demoed for the second album.

Don describes this song as a boogie, put together because that type of song was needed. On listening to it he described one section as terrible! No other references.

Lean and Hungry - (Walker) Circa 1975 song.

Letmenotforgetme - (Walker) See The Party's Over.

Letter To Alan - (D.Walker) Originally titled, Billy and Alan. First played in Darwin in 1981 and remaining in the set from then on. A live version was issued on the Three Big Hits singles set. The only video reference is the 1982 German show.

Merry-Go-Round - (D.Walker) First rehearsed in the first week of October, 1978 and its second performance was recorded for the You're Thirteen E.P. A song which remained in the set, sometimes as opening number until the bands last shows. This song appears in video form on the Manly Vale '80 and Hamburg, Germany '82 videos (see Appendix 3). The song appears on the Breakfast.. LP and in live form on the Barking Spiders and You're Thirteen records.

Metho Blues - (D.Walker) An early Walker song which he admitted has strong Stevie Wonder influences "in the melody and everything". This song was demoed for the first album, it is this demo which appears on Teenage Love and

was written "a couple of years earlier" according to Don. Another classy song in the "pseudo sophisticated" style. This song probably missed a place on the first album, as the band was conscious of putting forth a rock 'n' roll image and too many non-rock songs would detract from this. Phil Small recalled that Metho Blues was not a regular in the live set, being played only occasionally as a substitute for Georgia.

Misfits - (D.Walker) Originally issued as the B-side to My Baby; this was eventually issued as a single to accompany the Chisel album. The track was originally written to accompany a documentary on homeless children, which was never aired. Performed during the latter part of the Youth In Asia Tour and also on the Summer Offensive Tour when the band were experimenting with the set for a tour which really didn't have an album to promote, being six months after East and a few months before Swingshift was released.

No Video references or live release.

Mona And The Preacher - (D.Walker) Peter Moss recalls this song being one of the songs played when the band decided to go original soon after their return from Armidale in late 1974. Demoed for the first album (this demo can be found on the Teenage Love LP) and eventually issued in I've form on the You're Thirteen E.P. No video references.

Monica - (S.Prestwich) "Written in transit on the way to Wagga Wagga. I had all the melody and the arrangement and the lyrics came spontaneously." (Steve Prestwich)

Don does not play on this track as he claims to be unable to play with a latin feel. Never played live although often played at soundchecks. Released on the Teenage Love album, no other references.

My Baby - (P.Small) Phil wrote the basic idea for My Baby during a break in the recording of East and took the idea to Ian and Steve who helped him develop it further, Ian supplying the chorus lyric ("My Baby"). Phil recalls that the song was recorded on the second or third take. The sax sound came about accidentally due to a problem with the mic used to record it. Apparently this song was quite a hit in Denver, Colorado during the band's U.S tour. The record was marketed to U.S. radio stations by wrapping it in a baby's nappy, a plan which Rod Willis at first thought was a joke. Played live through the Youth in Asia and Summer Offensive tours and on occasion until the Last Stand tour when it came back into the set permanently. No video references although the song was performed on Countdown.

My Turn To Cry - (J.Barnes) Jimmy Barnes: "This is the first song we did that I'd written on my own. I didn't really take the idea behind the lyrics all that seriously except as a subject to write about - the story's something I can relate to. We put a lot of work into this track. We tried a couple of different arrangements until we hit on this one."

The subject of the song is Jim's sweetheart at the time, a lovely blonde called Brihony. When Jim left Adelaide with Cold Chisel to conquer the east coast, she said she would wait for him. Jim told her not to be ridiculous and to have a good time. Soon after she was engaged. Played live from 1979 (Set Fire To The Town) up to and including the Last Stand shows. First rehearsed in Nowra in July 1979 and demoed with Richard Batchens later that month. My Turn To Cry was also recorded with Mark Opitz at the same time as Choirgirl in October 1979, a version, which was rejected as a single as it, was considered too commercial. The most famous performance would no doubt be the March 1981 Countdown Awards performance where the latter part of the song (after the quieter bridge section) was altered (e.g. "I never saw you at the Largs Pier Hotel. And now you're tryin' to use my face to sell 'TV Week'") as the band expressed their opinions of the awards.

201)

Mark Opitz recalls that he was not happy with the guitars in the intro "Who like bits, adding that the accents weren't punchy enough", when he was mixing the record. As the band were all overseas he had no choice but to use what he had and for this reason 'buried' My Turn To Cry on the end of the album.

Necrophiliacis Blues- (Walker/Kacmarek/Prestwich/Barnes/M oss) A rare band composition with Jim taking words and melody, refining from Steve and Ian, riffs from Don and the concept from Les and Steve. A circa 1975 song with dubious lyrical content, no references.

Need Love Tonight - Demoed for the second album, never released.

Never Before - (I.Moss) Don Walker: Mark Opitz recalls that this was the last track completed for the East album, as the idea was still being developed right up to the last minute. Mark was very happy with the finished product, and had good reason to be. It was also Mark who connected the opening drum lines of this to the closing ones on Standing On The Outside to create the effect of the two songs sounding as though they are meant to be back to back. Only available on the East album and only played live in 1980 on the Youth in Asia tour. See also Ian Moss solo.

Never Say Goodbye - Uptempo rock song played live around 1978 but never released. Possibly an early version of Blue Movies (Never Make Me Cry) which was played in late 1979.(see Oct '78)

New Car - Demoed for the final studio album with producer Peter Walker.

No Good For You - (I.Moss) Originally considered and demoed for the East album, with both Jim and Ian trying the different sections on vocals before it was finally completed for the Circus Animals album. Played in live sets of early '82 . No video references or live release.

Northbound - (D.Walker) Played as second song in the live sets of 1978 and obviously considered a highlight of the sets as it was also included in the shortened sets the band did when they were supporting other artists, (see Foreigner tour, April 1978). Demos show that the song originally had a longer piano intro and a guitar solo both during the intro and in the middle. Also demoed in March 1976 with Ian on vocals. Peter Walker used tape speed manipulation to create a subtle chorus effect on the intro of this song. Northbound Train was written in November of 1975 and made its live debut at the Largs Pier on the 23rd of that month, with Ian on vocals.

No Sense - (J.Barnes) Written about a fan from Woolongong who used to write letters to Jimmy (through the band's office) in which she would suggest everything from "You don't love me, I'm going to commit suicide" to pages of 'I love you.' Although demoed in October '82 and again in January '83, No Sense didn't enter the live set until late in the Last Stand Tour. A live version was issued on the Barking Spiders Live album. A promotional video can be found on the Seeing is Believing video.

Notion For You- (P.Small) Demoed for the Circus Animals album.

Nothing But You - (S.Prestwich) "Written on the bass guitar having come up with the riff. This saw me and Ian doing backing vocals together in the studio. And a great spontaneous guitar solo from Ian." (Steve Prestwich)

Originally demoed with a working title of That One or Yeah That One, this song was even demoed with Jim doing the vocal and may have been included on the final studio album but for Steve not being with the band.

Numbers Fall - (D.Walker) Played from early '82 to after the Circus Animals shows (where its presentation featured dancers), from which point it was brought back on occasion. Also the B-side to the You Got Nothing I Want single. Numbers Fall is typical of the type of rhythmic ideas Don experimented with in 1981 on both the Freedom soundtrack and the Circus Animals album.

One Long Day - (D.Walker) Written during 1974. First demoed, in quite different form in March 1976 where it included a piano solo and different lyrics, such as "Bus is packed, fare is cheap" and "Boss is found hung in office with tear stained face.' This song remained in the live set (with few exceptions) until the very end. it first appeared on the self titled first album, then as a live take on the You're 13" EP and then again on the Swingshift album. It is a difficult one to find in video form, appearing on the early '79 TV broadcast and again on the Nov '82 German TV broadcast. (See Appendix 3)

Only One - (J.Barnes) A song about Jim's wife, Jane. Not included in live sets until the final shows of the Last Stand tour. See also Jimmy Barnes solo.

Only A Fool - (Walker) Gem of a ballad which dates right back to 1975 (written November and in the set December), written by Don and sung by Ian, who was handling all vocals at this point. Considered for the Teenage Love album but not included due to the source being a poor tape. One of their best never-issued tracks.

On The Road - (D.Walker) Recorded at Slaters in November 1975 and again in demos for the first album, this great little song was not released until 1994 as part of the Three Big Hits singles pack. A classy song with a complex arrangement, the first album demo version features vocals from both Ian and Jim although I have heard versions with only Ian singing, from November 1975 when Jimmy was not with the band (see also Shandon Hotel, June 1975). One of the better of the unreleased tracks to appear in the 1994 (on the Three Big Hits singles pack), On The Road again is one of the earliest Cold Chisel tracks for which a recording is still in existence. Not included on the Teenage Love Affair album because the quality of the recording was considered to be inferior. One of the most important songs in the band's development. Played in most live sets from '75-'77.

Painted Doll - (Walker) A traditional Chisel blues rock song, played through latter 1983, though not on all dates of the Last Stand tour (to make way for the return of some of the older material). A stinging live number, one the more frequently performed songs from the Twentieth Century album and a very under-rated Chisel number. Don Walker also performed this song as a solo artist.(see Appendix 4)

Payday in A Pub - (J.Barnes) Demoed for East in March 1980.

Plaza - (D.Walker) The lyrics from Plaza originally were part of a song called Kingis Cross Kid played during 1978. Live renditions linked Plaza with One Long Day, as can be heard to great affect on the 1979, 3XY radio broadcast.

Promise Me You'll Call - Better known as a Barnes solo song.

Rising Sun - (J.Barnes) "I came up with the hook line first - 'The rising sun just stole my girl away'. The lady I was living with was going back to Japan because her parents were there. Then came the music, it has a rockabilly feel which I like a lot. I'm a bit of a Jerry Lewis fanatic. We just went into the studio and cut it in one take. We later only re-did the piano and vocal." See also Jimmy Barnes solo.

(202

Rosaline - (D.Walker) An early version of this song appears on the July '77 demo tape, complete with guitar intro and piano and guitar solos. An even earlier version was recorded in March 1976, this one being a much faster arrangement in an attempt to make the song more acceptable in the live situation. One of the more under-rated Cold Chisel songs. One of the reasons why the first album is not the rock'n'roll album many thought it should have been is because great songs like this simply had to be included.

Saturday Night - (D.Walker) issued as a single in March 1984, Saturday Night was played live during the final shows from the Last Stand Tour in Sydney, as documented in the video and CD, the former of which shows a snippet of the song in rehearsal. One of Don Walker's more complex songs, featuring sections for both Ian and Jim, a key change and guest musicians, it is also deceptively simple and easy to listen to. Ray Arnott was particularly pleased with the drum arrangement he did for this song.

Shipping Steel - (D.Walker) First appeared in live sets in 1978, Shipping Steel was played live until the middle of 1981. Used as the opening number for much of 1979. Released as a single in June 1979. There is a video fragment from the Civic Hotel in 1978 (see Last Stand video) and a version from the Manly Vale in 1980.

Showtime - (D.Walker) in 1988 Don Walker told Glenn A. Baker, "I remember a lot of resistance from all quarters to Showtime, and that was the only occasion when I jacked up and said to everyone "hey, you owe me this one." I had to be a bit of prima donna. it was a very down song providing an accurate description of the frustration of playing the clubs without a record contract for four to five years. No-one wanted to know about down songs at the time." In February 1979 he described the musical ideas tried with this song, "The original idea was to do a disco track with a slide guitar and harmony. Because of what the words are I wanted to make the music disco but unfortunately, or fortunately we are not a very good band to play disco music. The band just can't play it." Showtime was also considered a likely single. Early versions of this song (as it was played live in 1977) feature a slower verse section, an extra verse and a much longer arrangement. Richard Batchens and the band worked particularly hard on this one during the Breakfast sessions. (See Breakfast At Sweethearts) Showtime was played live in most 1979 sets, a superb version is included on the 3XY radio broadcast from April '79.

Sing in The Band - Demoed for the second album, never released.

Sing To Me - (D.Walker) Written in Germany during the second tour of that country and first played in live sets during that tour and later during the Ray Arnott tour. Dropped for the Last Stand Tour No live or video references for this bluesy ballad which would have become an audience favourite had the band stayed together as it received great responses on the 'Ray Arnott' tour as an unknown song. Covered by Renee Geyer on the 'Sing To Me' album and also by Kate Ceberano and Wendy Matthews on the album You've Always Got The Blues.

Sorbonne Fender Chrome - (Walker) Demoed for the first album, a song which dates back to 1975 (Les Kasmarek played it) and featured vocals from both Ian and Jimmy on the chorus. A melodic rock song which was considered for the Teenage Love album. Peter Walker recalls that he wanted to include this song on the first album but Don was not satisfied with the lyrics and the record company felt the title was a little too bizarre.

Standing On The Outside - (D.Walker) "This is about the unemployment situation in Australia - right now about 20% of the work force under 20 in this country doesn't

have a job. The young person who's Standing On The Outside these days is just an average person. We had a number of demo sessions for the song, trying several arrangements. We finally kept the piano, bass, and drums from the original demo and re-did a rhythm guitar track." (Don Walker in phone interview to the US prior to the band's tour there) "Everybody says you can't go out and pull a job on a bank because you have to obey society's laws, because you owe certain things to society. Well there are a lot of young kids around now that society has given nothing. What do they owe ? They're not even part of it - so the rules don't apply" (Don Walker talking around the time of the Parramatta Gaol gig, June 1980)

From the rehearsal sessions at Nowra in July 1979 and making its live debut at Nowra roller-skating rink. Used as the opening number throughout the Youth in Asia and Summer Offensive tours and remaining in live sets until the final show. Written during the bandis writing holiday at Nowra in July 1979 while the band were recreationally listening to "Who's Next" and Ronny Wood's "Gimme Some Neck", which you can hear in the rhythm guitar arrangements for Standing On The Outside and My Turn To Cry. Demoed with Richard Batchens in July 1979 when it included the line, "I know, that's why I want to testify."

Mark Opitz was particularly happy with the snare drum sound achieved with a digital reverb unit during the recording of this track. A live version of this song can be found on the Barking Spiders Live album and on the Last Stand CD. On video it can be found on the Last Stand video and on the German TV broadcast from 1982.

Star Hotel - (D.Walker) "The Star Hotel in Newcastle, the second biggest industrial city in New South Wales, was a rather incredible gathering point for different sorts of people, but particularly the young and unemployed. The place had three bars - the back bar was frequented by off-duty military people, petty crooks and pimps, the middle bar featured drag shows and was favored by homosexuals and the front bar held about 600 people and featured local Newcastle bands. Only beer was sold in the front bar, and it was served from huge tin bathtubs behind the bar. There was a lot of energy in the place. Then the brewery that owned the hotelis license, Tooths & Co., was told by the government to make major alterations or the license would not be renewed. Tooths figured those alterations would be too expensive and opted to close the bars instead. When the police arrived on the last night, Sept. 19, 1979, to close the place down, a riot started. Most of the young people in Newcastle saw the closure as oppressive and still another infringement on their liberty. incidents like that are generally hushed up in the Australian press, but we find out about them while we're touring."

(Don Walker talking to the Entertainer, Milwaukee) This song was demoed with quite different lyrics in or around October of 1979. (see Oct '79) The song first appeared on the East album and live versions appear on both Swingshift and the Last Stand albums. Star Hotel was a regular (and usually a highlight) in all set lists from 1980 to 1983. The video file for this song is extensive. The June '80 Manly Vale gig (available on Seeing is Believing) is the first . Another 1980 video, from a different date has inserts from the Newcastle riot during the middle section. Jimmy is wearing a red head band in the Manly Vale video and a white one in the other. The song also appears on the Last Stand video from Sydney in December 1983. A rarer video of Star Hotel was broadcast on German television from a show in Hamburg in December 1982. (see Appendix 3).

Suicide Sal - (J.Barnes) Jim was in a gay bar in Adelaide, getting extremely serious with a lady friend in a quiet corner, when the barmaid, a very large woman known as Suicide Sal threw a bucket of water over the pair. No live or video references.

Taipan - (D.Walker) First performed in Darwin in 1982 and remaining in the set from then on. On video this song can be found both as a live clip (footage from Wentworth Park '82) with live sound and as a live clip with studio sound (same footage). The latter was included on the Seeing is Believing video. A disappointing (far below their best performance) live rendition from the Last Stand Sydney shows appeared on the Barking Spiders Live album. For an inspired live performance look for the video with live sound from the Wentworth Park Circus Animals shows.

Teenage Love Affair - (D.Walker) "Teenage Love Affair' would appear in live sets right up to 1979. Ian recalls singing a slower version of the song during the period (late '75 to early '76-see Shandon Hotel, 1975) when Jimmy was not with the band. Demoed for the first album in September '77 but not released until the album of the same name in 1994. By the time it was recorded the band had been playing it in the live set for two and a half years. It was designed to be "faster /harder/louder than anything else going" by any other band at the time, to be used as a set closer.

"Teenage Love wasn't a piece of music - It was a military assault. it has all these key changes in it so you milk the band of all the power you can get out of it to a certain point, whether that be eight bars or sixteen bars, and then you just find somewhere else to go that just notches it up another gear again. By the time we got to record albums we were totally sick of it, but I haven't heard it since 1976 and I think it sounds great, maybe the best thing on the album" (Don talking to Toby Creswell in 1994) I have heard a roaring live version of this song from 1978/9 which was even more manic than the recorded version and included Jimmy telling those married people in the audience that they had made the biggest mistake of their lives and that the audience had been fucking pathetic for so many people together in one place! A short (approx. 20 seconds) bridge section was edited from the version released on the Teenage Love Affair album. Teenage Love Affair was also played during the period when Jimmy had left the band and Ian was doing the lead vocals. (see Shandon Hotel, June 1975)

Temptation - (J.Barnes) A song about the constant temptations of women encountered on the road. First demoed by the band in October 1982. First appeared in the live sets of March/April of '83 and never again, although it was included on the Twentieth Century album. See also Jimmy Barnes solo.

The Ballad of Nick and Tiny - (Walker) A never recorded original which made it's debut at the Shandon Hotel on the 10th October, 1975. The band had learnt the song the week before. Vocals for this were done by Ian as it was during the period when Jim was with Fraternity. See also Shandon Hotel, 17th October, 1975.

The Backdoor Man - (Walker) Never-released song played in live sets on the Melbourne tour of late '76. Described as a bluesy rocker, with harmonies. Don recalled this song as a 6/8 time blues song sung by Ian with somewhat sexually explicit lyrics about screwing someone else's wife, lyrics which he confessed were very throwaway and written by himself.

The Door - (D.Walker) Played in the live sets of 1978-79 only to disappear from the live repertoire thereafter. The only video reference for The Door is from the August 1978 television broadcast.

The Dummy - (Moss/Walker) This song appeared on the Australian Guitar Album, released in January of 1980, although it was recorded more than a year earlier. it was also played live - about four times according to Ian, around the time it was recorded (see Dec 25 1979). Sung by Ian, this number has a strong Jeff Beck influence, and at the time of itis release was the finest example if Ian's guitar playing

talents available. The Dummy was also issued as the B-side to the Mr. Rain single from ianis first solo album.

The Game - (P.Small/D.Walker) Released only on Twentieth Century, no live or video references for this greatly under-rated song. "He (Phil) had a song on the final album that was a musical idea of his that was quite an old one that I took and wrote some words for so he got another go (at getting a song on an album) towards the end. And its a shame that Phil has never written more, he is a great writer." (Don Walker talking with Billy Pinnell in 1991)

Phil Small recalls that the music had been around for many years (it was originally titled "Misadventure") and that he wrote much of the melody while Don contributed the words and some parts of the melody needed to complete the song. Phil also thinks that the rhythm track used on the Twentieth Century album is the one recorded at the Circus Animals sessions. No other references.

The Man From Yesterday - (J. Swan) An original song of John Swan's which the band continued to include in sets for some time after John's time with the band - it was played at the Uriah Heap support gig in November 1974. John recalls that it was a pop song with a number of complex timing changes.

The Party's Over - (D.Walker) Don Walker states that this was the first song he ever wrote, originally titled Letmenotforgetme, after deciding that the band could go all the way and it was time to write some original material. "initially it was called Let Me Not Forget Me and I changed the lyrics sometime later. I've never been able to figure what it was about, except that all the words fell into it and made their own kind of sense. I still have no idea what it means, but the words are in the right place and they feel right when they go past" (Don Walker talking to Toby Creswell in 1994)

Demoed at Slaters in November 1975. The first release of this song (it was demoed for the first album, and again for the second) was on the bonus single with the East album, the next was a live version on the Swingshift album and then the first mentioned version came out on the Teenage Love album. A German Best Of Cold Chisel album contains a different version again, (possibly the first album demo ?) this time produced by Peter Walker (the other versions were produced by Mark Opitz, see March 1980.) Played live on occasion (not always) from 1980 through to December 1982 and almost certainly in early sets as far back as 1975. it was one of what Don refers to as his "pseudo sophisticated" songs, which he also added were virtually useless in the Australian pub rock scene at the time. The only video reference comes from the German 1982 video.

"We've got a long list of slow material which we rotate in the set from night to night 'cause you can only do one or two slow ones otherwise we'd become a laid back band. You always end up with more ballads than you can use. In some ways it's more fun to write a ballad than a rock and roll number. But they're just not as much fun to play." (Don Walker talking to RAM's Greg Taylor in 1981)

The Smacko Queen - (Walker) Played in the live sets of early/mid 1978, see March 1978, Bondi Lifesaver. Don does not recall much about the song, although he does recall the title.

Tomorrow - (D.Walker) From the Nowra rehearsals in July 1979 and making it's live debut at Nowra roller-skating rink. Remained in the live set until the last shows. Although played live almost always (it was rarely played in early/mid '83) from late '79 onwards, the only live release has been on the Last Stand album and video.

(204

Twentieth Century - (D.Walker) influenced by The Who, Twentieth Century was meant to be a gentle prod at the many political bands which seemed to be doing good business at the time. Played live in the final shows of the Last Stand Tour. Released on the album of the same name and also as a single. A video (live footage with studio sound) was issued to promote this song and is included on the Seeing is Believing video release.

Week Away From Paradise - (Barnes) Demoed by the band in October 1982. No other references. Later recorded by Jimmy for his first solo album.

When The Sun Goes Down - (a.k.a. idleness)- (D.Walker) This song was in the live sets in 1978 and was probably demoed for the Breakfast. album See idleness for additional information, also October '78 and October '79.

When The War is Over - (S.Prestwich) "I got the first verse of melody and lyric quite spontaneously, and that coupled with the verse guitar melody brought it all together. However, I had to write the middle eight in the studio just prior to it being recorded." (Steve Prestwich, 1997)

"I just write them in the back of my head, really. I could be doing anything at all, and then suddenly I'll get a melody, usually that'll come first. I'll like the melody and stick with it, and eventually end up with some words. After sort of pulling my hair out I'll get some words and then we'll arrange it. I've been pretty lucky with Forever Now. On this album, Circus Animals, I've written Forever Now and When The War is Over, which I think is the next single. I sort of dabble on a bit of bass and a little bit of guitar, but like I said I mostly get everything in my head and I'll sort of put it to the bass and then I'll really just parrot fashion show the other guys or sing to them or tell them exactly what I'd like them to do." (Steve talking to New Zealand television, August 1982)

What They Wanted - (Prestwich) Very impressive rock song from the East period which was never released.

Why Don't You Call Me - Almost a disco song, probably written with the commercial market in mind. Never released although it was probably demoed for the second album. Played in the live set of late 1978 alongside other 'new' numbers which would surface on the second album. (see Oct '78) No other references.

Wild Colonial Boy - (D.Walker) Don was having trouble with the lyrics on this one. He knew he wanted to write a song with the title, but always felt the song lacked the lyrical depth he would have liked. One of the songs designed by Don to take the band away from a more structured pop sound towards an improvised, free arrangement style. Used as the opening number for most of the Last Stand shows, it was in the set from Darwin '82 until the final show. Released in live form as part of the Three Big Hits CD single pack, this was a disappointing version, not indicative of the power the song inspired in earlier performances. A video can be found on the German '82 TV broadcast.

Won't Be Back For Long - (Barnes) Mid-paced rock song of Jim's with a Shipping Steel- like intro. Demoed but never released.

Work My Fingers - (?) Funk/disco song with vocals from Ian. Never released.

Yesterdays - (D.Walker) A superb song, released as the last of the Three Big Hits trilogy of singles, deserving to be a hit but perhaps missing the boat as third single from the album. No live references for this song and I am not aware of a promotional video being made for it. Available also on the Teenage Love album. In my estimation this is the finest Cold Chisel song released since the group disbanded.

You and Me - (Barnes) Demoed but never released.

You Got Nothing I Want - (J.Barnes) Don described the motivation for this song as coming from their experiences in America:

"When we went down to master the second single in their mastering studios, we listened to it and there was something dreadfully wrong. It was horrible, there was noise all over it and cracks and pops. Something had happened. We took this back to Marty Schwartz and, I think there was Jim and Ian and I standing across from his desk and he looked at us cooly and said 'Have you considered that it may not be the fault of the mastering engineer at all. Have you considered that it may just be that you guys can't play?' I have to tell you we had never considered that. After we came back Jim wrote You Got Nothing I Want more or less as a personal tribute to Marty Schwartz." You Got Nothing Want remained in the live set from the Darwin '82 show until the final show. A promotional video was made and is available on Seeing is Believing. Live versions can be found on the Last Stand video and CD as well as on the German TV broadcast. See also Jimmy Barnes solo.

APPENDIX TWO

COVER SONGS

Cold Chisel always played some cover material- it was very rare for them to play a show of 100% original material. Phil Small recalls that when he first joined the band (July 1975) they only played two or three original songs Below are many of the cover songs played by Cold Chisel. Thanks to Billy Pinnell for his assistance on the background of some of these songs.

All Along The Watchtower - Bob Dylan classic, played in a heavy rock style which featured Moss' soloing. Mentioned in a review from Melbourne in October 1976. This song was a highlight of the Fraternity sets when Jim was in the band, and was played by Cold Chisel during their Armidale days and into 1975 - see Shandon Hotel, 1975.

Alright Now - Free standard Free were one of Jimmy's favourite bands and this standard was played in the '75 period and earlier.

Black Dog - The band played many Zeppelin numbers, although by the late seventies most had been relegated to encore positions.

Cause We've Ended As Lovers - Stevie Wonder song, although the version played by Cold Chisel was the instrumental version as appearing on Jeff Beck's Blow By Blow album. Beck was one of Ian's favourite guitarists and Stevie Wonder was a favourite of the whole band. Played in the live set of 1977.

Come On (a.k.k. Let The Good Times Roll) (Earl King) Written by New Orleans guitarist Earl King, it was almost certainly the Jimi Hendrix version which was covered by the band during 1977. (see April '77, Chequers)

Crossroads - Robert Johnson blues standard, popularized by Cream.

Don't Let Go - (J.Stone) Jerry Lee Lewis song first played in 1980 and brought back occasionally (including German shows and Ray Arnott shows) right up to and including Last Stand shows. Officially released on the live Swingshift and Last Stand albums and included in the Last Stand video. Has the distinction of being the last song the band played live together on the Last Stand tour. Video references include the Last Stand video and Germany 1982.

205)

Foxy Lady - Jimi Hendrix song which could appear at any gig, usually in the middle of Wild Thing, as it did on the last night in Melbourne of the Last Stand tour.

Georgia On My Mind - (Carmichael/Gorrell) The first song rehearsed by Don and Ian at Les Kaczmarek's house in 1973. Released only as B-side (to Goodbye) in studio form in September 1978 and as a live track in 1984 on The Barking Spiders Live album, from the December '83 Last Stand shows, December 15 to be exact.

First played at the band's first rehearsals and last played in the band's final shows in December 1983. Played as part of the main set until 1979 when it was moved to an encore position, where it remained. When the band were doing five sets at Chequers in April '77, Georgia was played as part of a more laid back, final (late) set. The contrast between this number and the band's more full on material always surprised audiences and added a level of sophistication which broadened the band's appeal. Don states that he first heard the song on a Jerry Reid (country and Western guitarist) album. The only video reference is in the August 1978 television broadcast, and this song is a lot harder to find than the rest of the broadcast as it was often left out for some reason.

Green River - (Fogarty) One of the songs played in the first live show from Cold Chisel 1997 at Rod Willis' birthday party. Also played by Ian in solo sets in the early '90s and very probably by early Cold Chisel.

Heartbreak Hotel - (Axton-Durden-Presley) Elvis cover played in August 1980.

Honky Tonk Woman - (Jagger/Richards) Rolling Stones standard played as an encore, often with support band INXS on the January 1982 New Zealand Tour.

I'm A Man - Spencer Davis Group standard dating back to 1975, also done during the period when Ian was handling all the vocals.

It's Only Make Believe - (July -December '83) The first hit for country legend Conway Twitty in 1958. Played on the Ray Arnott tour and most of the Last Stand tour. issued on all formats of the Barking Spiders Live album, except for the vinyl version. No other references.

Keep Playin' That Rock'n'Roll - (Winter) Written and recorded by Edgar Winter. Played by Cold Chisel circa '74 to '76.

Knocking On Heaven's Door - Dylan classic played late '79 and 1980. Returned again for the Last Stand tour. it appears on the Swingshift album and also on the bonus single with early pressings of East (both are different live versions)- Mark Opitz speaks highly of the single version (which apparently came from a Bondi Lifesaver show in late 1979), due to it possessing a freshness lacking on the Swingshift version. On video it can only be found on the Manly Vale 1980 show. (See Video Appendix)

Lazy - Deep Purple standard, played in 1973 to '76. Phil Small recalls this one as being a highlight of the band's early sets and one of the songs he had to learn when he first joined the band. This was one of the first songs the band learnt as Ian knew how to play it all as he was a big fan of Deep Purple guitarist Ritchie Blackmore. See also Shandon Hotel, June 1975.

Let's Go Get Stoned - (Ashford/Simpson) Ray Charles performed and recorded this song. Cold Chisel played it as a duet between Moss and Barnes on the Ray Arnott tour of 1983 and during the Last Stand tour, possibly only in Sydney. it is available on the Three Big Hits CD single package as a live cut from the Last Stand shows. No other references.

Long As I Can See The Light - Creedence Clearwater Revival song played in the latter part of the Youth in Asia Tour and on the Summer Offensive Tour, released on the Swingshift live album. The version released on the Swingshift album lacks the piano intro as tape reels were being changed during this part of the song as the mobile recording took place at the Capital Theatre. As everyone was keen to include the song on the live album, Mark Opitz edited out the small section of the intro which was recorded, creating an impressive sounding start where everyone comes in together. No video references.

Mozambique - (Dylan) Bob Dylan song, from the Desire album. Performed by Cold Chisel in 1975/6. No other references.

Pearly Queen - (Winwood/ Capaldi) A classic by the band Traffic (from their self-titled album) which Cold Chisel played regularly in mid-70s sets.

Purple Haze - (Hendrix) Hendrix song which could appear (usually as part of Wild Thing) in the set at any time. A popular soundcheck piece. (see Aug '79, Oct '83, 1/1/82) No other references.

Rat Bat Blue - Deep Purple song (from the Who Do We Think We Are? album) played at the Gawler Raceway gig in 1973 as well as in sets from 1974.

Red House - Jimi Hendrix classic often played at soundchecks and with some regularity on the Summer Offensive Tour. No other references.

Rip it Up - (Blackwell/ Marascalco) (March-August '83) Elvis/ Little Richard standard played at great speed in most '83 shows although not appearing on the Last Stand tour. Never released, no video references.

River Deep, Mountain High - (Greenwich/Spector/Barry) Played occasionally in live sets from April '83-December '83. issued as a B-side to the single Flame Trees in 1984 and again as part of the Three Big Hits CD singles package or on the CD single of Nothing But You in 1994, all from the same source of 13th or 15th December, 1983. No other references.

Roadhouse Blues - Doors classic covered by the band in '76-'77, '74 in Armidale, and occasionally in later shows. (see April '77, Chequers) No other references.

Rock'n'Roll - The most often played of the band's Led Zeppelin covers.

Rock'n'Roll Hoochie Coo - (Rick Derringer) Performed by Johnny Winter on an album called Johnny Winter And. Later recorded by Edgar Winter and then Rick Derringer himself. Performed by Cold Chisel in the '74/5 period. Sung by Jim.

Rocky Mountain Way - (Walsh) Covered by the band in '75-'77. Don recalls feeling that the band had gotten past doing songs like this but Jim, determined to fire up a sluggish audience at one gig, introduced the song anyway, causing Don to walk off and watch from the wings.

Shake, Rattle and Roll - Reviews from the Wentworth Park Circus Animals show suggest that this was played at that time.

Shakin' All Over - (Heath) Originally by Johnny Kidd and the Pirates, later covered by the Guess Who and Normie Rowe. Outstanding Cold Chisel live performances of this song featured an extended 'rave up' in the middle. Probably one of the band's most effective covers to never be released. Played in the latter part of 1979 and on much of the Youth in Asia tour in 1980 (see Townsville '80 or Pooled Resources '79). No other references.

Show Me - (Tex) Joe Tex song played on occasion during late 1979. Later covered by Jimmy as a solo artist. No other references.

(206

**Smoke On The Water -
(Blackmore/Gillian/Glover/Lord/Paice)**
Deep Purple standard played in '75 and during the Armidale
period. Peter Moss remembers that this song became
something of a problem for the band as it became associated
with them and audiences always called for the band to play it.
Ritchie Blackmore was one of Ian's favourite guitar players and
a number of Deep Purple songs were played by the band at
different times. No other references.

Solitaire - (Durant) One only public performance on
19/8/80 at the Andrew Durant Memorial Concert at the the
Palais Theatre in Melbourne by Don and Ian in the style of
Georgia. Released on both the album (now on CD) and video
of the same name. No other references.

Star Spangled Banner - (12/10/83) Jimi Hendrix
style interpretation, the sort of thing often heard at
soundchecks, which only occasionally crept into the show.

Superstition - Stevie Wonder song played by the band
during the Armidale period.

The Stealer - Free song covered by the band circa 1974.

The Wind Cries Mary- Jimi Hendrix song played by
the band during the Armidale period.

This Guy's in Love - (Bacharach / David) A
snippet of this song was occasionally played in the intro to
Georgia in early '83. (See April i83)

**Tonight I'll Be Staying Here With You -
(Dylan)** Played by the band in '77 (see Chequers, April),
probably more like the Jeff Beck Group version than the
Dylan version.

Twist and Shout - (Medley/Russell) A twenty
minute version of this Beatles favourite (originally done by the
isley Brothers) was played at the last show in Sydney of the
Last Stand tour (a small snippet can be heard on The Barking
Spiders Live album, immediately after Forever Now) as well as
appearing as an encore occasionally in other shows such as the
An Evening With The Circus Animals at Wentworth Park.
Played as an encore number on the Summer Offensive Tour.
Also played (as an encore) with support band INXS on the
January 1982 New Zealand tour and again at the final show in
Sydney. A standout cover version never officially released by
the band. No other references.

Ubangi Stomp - (Warren Smith) Recorded on
Jerry Lee Lewisi first album, Ubangi Stomp is the only song to
be sung by a Cold Chisel drummer. Played as an encore
during the six shows in March 1983 when Gary Young played
drums with the band.

Underground Railway - Song by an obscure group,
Redwing, played by the band during the Armidale period

**When Something is Wrong With My Baby
- (Isaac Hayes/David Porter)** When Cold Chisel
supported Rod Stewart in February 1979, Rod suggested to
Jimmy that he should listen to Sam and Dave and that is most
likely where this song came from. Probably first played in
Darwin in October 1981, and occasionally right through to
the final show. (See La Trobe Uni, 12/7/83, Sawtell RSL,
16/3/83 and Germany 9/11/82 as well as Barnes solo.) No
video references.

**Whole Lotta Love -
(Page/Plant/Jones/Bonham/Dixon)** Billy
Pinnell recalls the band playing this song when he saw them at
the Station Hotel in Melbourne in 1977, Peter Moss recalls
that it was played often, but not every night during the early
days. No other references.

Wild Thing - First played by the band as a request at a
gig in Armidale in 1974 although not becoming a regular in
the set until 1977 when it was played as an encore at a

Mawson Hotel show, this spontaneous version being so well
received that it became a regular in the set. Wild Thing almost
accidentally became one of the band's signature songs and was
always in the sets until 1980, it disappeared for the Summer
Offensive Tour, was played occasionally on the US tour, and
again on the first German tour. it again was omitted from sets
until the Last Stand Tour, from which it also appears on the
video and album of the same name. The first release was on
the You're Thirteen EP in 1978. No other references.

Wishing Well - Free classic covered by the band in the
early days. Jim was always keen to sing anything by Paul
Rogers.

You Keep On Knockin'- Choruses from this Little
Richard standard were added to early '83 versions of I'm
Gonna Roll Ya.

Your Cheatin' Heart - (Hank Williams) "We
were all sort of dabbling in Country a little bit. Jim always
listens to lots of things - like when he's driving in the car he'll
pick a favourite song and then throw it in the set just for a bit
of fun." (Ray Arnott, 1988)

Rarely played (12/7/83) soul/C&W standard, the only
reference being La Trobe University at Ray Arnott's public
debut. This was almost certainly not the only time it was
played but it did not become a regular on the set list. No other
references.

APPENDIX THREE

I TOOK MY BABY TO A MOVIE SHOW

COLD CHISEL ON VIDEO

Apart from the Last Stand video promotional video clips were
made of the following songs: Cheap Wine*, Forever Now*,
Khe Sanh*, One Long Day, No Sense*, Hold Me Tight*,
Saturday Night*, You Got Nothing I Want*, Flame Trees*.
Both Khe Sanh and One Long Day were recorded on the
same day in 1978, the latter being one of the most difficult to
find Cold Chisel clips. Compilation clips (bits and pieces)
were made for Just How Many Times*, Hands Out Of My
Pocket, and Misfits*.Live clips have been issued for: Star Hotel
from the Manly Vale* (2 different 1980 versions, see Appendix
One for details- there is also the Last Stand version) Taipan
from Wentworth Park "A Night With The Circus Animals" in
1982 (2 versions of this, the main differences being that one
has live sound and the other studio sound*)Bow River-
available from both Circus Animals (April '82) and Last Stand,
as well as a compilation of the two*. Only One - Live footage
from the Last Stand. *(This song does not appear in the Last
Stand video.)

Twentieth Century*- Live footage from the Last Stand

OTHERS:

1978 - August 27, ABC Studios, Sydney. Songs
broadcast are Khe Sanh / One Long Day / Goodbye /
Conversations / Dresden / The Door / I'm Gonna Roll Ya /
Shipping Steel / Breakfast At Sweethearts* / Georgia

Parts of this video were released on the Seeing is Believing
video (the one song "Breakfast At Sweethearts"). The footage
shows the band in a pub environment, doing the type of gig
that was standard for them before they really made it big. The
version of Georgia from this show is a lot harder to find, and
often of inferior quality. Broadcast recently on Australian cable
TV, minus Georgia.

1980 - APRIL 12 - Manly Vale Filmed as a live
promo for the East album. The footage shows the band during
a very exciting point in its development, having enjoyed
success with its second album and about to release a new
album that they knew was by far the best thing they had done.
The live versions of the new songs such as Star Hotel have

something special, which could not be captured on the album. This show is a wonderful document of the point when the band became the best band in the country, but had not yet enjoyed the mass success that would follow almost immediately after the release of East. A still from the Goodbye clip from this show was used for the cover of Swingshift.Cheap Wine/ Rising Sun/ Best Kept Lies/ Shipping Steel/ Choir Girl/ Star Hotel/ Merry-Go-Round*/ Knocking On Heavens Door/ Goodbye Astrid* *Songs marked with asterisk are available on the Seeing is Believing video.

1982 - DECEMBER 3 - Markthalle, Hamburg, Germany (referred to as the 'German TV Broadcast) Set List-Merry-Go-Round/Khe Sanh/Wild Colonial Boy/Taipan/Bow River/One Long Day/You Got Nothin' I Want/My Turn To Cry/Forever Now/Letter To Alan/Hound Dog/Four Walls/Standing On The Outside/Don't Let Go/Star Hotel/Goodbye Astrid/The Partyis Over/Rising Sun/Conversations

This show was filmed and broadcast on German television as part of the Rockpalast show, a show that each week featured a band playing live. Cold Chisel's performance was initially broadcast as a 45 minute special in April 1983, but a longer version was re-broadcast in 1993. The set list above is from the latter broadcast.

OFFICIAL RELEASES:

SEEING IS BELIEVING - Features the following songs: Khe Sanh/ Breakfast At Sweethearts/ Merry-Go-Round/ Cheap Wine/ Star Hotel/ No Sense/ Forever Now/ Taipan/ Hold Me Tight/ Saturday Night/ You Got Nothing I Want/ Bow River/ Only One/ Twentieth Century/ Goodbye (Astrid Goodbye)/ Flame Trees/ Just How Many Times The versions appearing on the Seeing is Believing video are marked in the earlier part of this appendix with an asterisk *. CHISEL- A re-issue of Seeing is Believing with the additional Misfits clip. LAST STAND- Contains footage from the Last Stand concerts from the 13th and 15th of December 1983 in Sydney as well as archival footage (fragments only) from many other earlier sources, in addition to many interviews and backstage sequences. Songs from the Last Stand concerts are: Standing On The Outside/ Cheap Wine/ Rising Sun/ Janelle/ Khe Sanh/ Twentieth Century/ You Got Nothing I Want/ Tomorrow/ Star Hotel/ Choir Girl/ Bow River/ Flame Trees/ Saturday Night/ Wild Thing/ Goodbye (Astrid Goodbye)/ Don't Let Go

APPENDIX FOUR

OTHER RECORDINGS OR GUEST APPEARANCES '76-'84

* For some appearances in the post Cold Chisel period, see the solo discography section.

Freedom Soundtrack - Featuring all the members of Chisel except Jimmy playing Don Walker songs. Issued on CD in 1996. (See March /April '81)

Australian Guitar Album - 1979 Razzle Records Productions -L37052 SMK-54717) The track The Dummy is a Cold Chisel song, sung by Ian. The entire band, with the exception of Jim appear on this Peter Walker produced track written by Walker and Moss. The sleeve notes for the album describe The Dummy as a Cold Chisel track and it was played briefly in the band's live set. This track was also released on the B-side of the Mr. Rain single, taken from Ian's first solo album..

Short Note - **Matt Finish** Don plays keyboards on the track Younger Days from this album.

Andrew Durant Memorial Concert - Don, Ian and Jimmy appear on the video and album. (See August 19, 1980)

Rude Dudes - **Ray Arnott** - (EMI APLP 039) Jimmy and John Swan appear together on two tracks on this album - Some Feelings and K.O.Love.

Icehouse - **Flowers** - Ian appears on the track Skin.

The Great Escape - **Richard Clapton** Ian plays on (and sings backing vocal) on a number of tracks on this album, although he is not given (at his request) a credit on the sleeve. At that stage the band had a policy of not appearing ('guesting') on non Cold Chisel projects.

Afterglow - **Daryl Braithwaite** - single, Ian plays on this record from 1978.

Ain't Love The Strangest Thing - **Joe Camilleri** Ian plays guitar on this 1992 single.

You're Gonna Get Caught - **Jenny Morris** Ian plays guitar on this 1986 single.

APPENDIX FIVE

COLD CHISEL SONGS PERFORMED BY JIMMY, DON & IAN AS SOLO ARTISTS

The name in brackets indicates which former Cold Chisel member actually performed that song in his live set.

A LITTLE BIT OF DAYLIGHT - (Barnes)

BOW RIVER - Performed live by Ian Moss during the late '80s - early '90s and re-recorded for the World's Away album in 1991. A live version is also on the Live At The Hordern video.

BREAKFAST AT SWEETHEARTS - (Barnes)

DON'T LET GO - (Barnes)

FLAME TREES - (Barnes)

FOUR WALLS - (Barnes)

GHOST TOWN - (Walker) Performed live by Catfish.

HOLD ME TIGHT - (Barnes)

GOODBYE (ASTRID GOODBYE) - (Barnes)

JANELLE/ DANIELLE - Recorded as Danielle by Don Walker on the Tex Perkins, Don Walker , Charlie Owens CD in 1993. This title also appeared on the live album, Monday Morning Comes Down by the same artists in 1995.

KHE SANH - Performed live by Catfish (circa 1988) and Jimmy Barnes.

MERRY GO ROUND - (Barnes) 1987

MY TURN TO CRY - (Barnes)

NEVER BEFORE - Performed live by Ian Moss during the late '80s - early '90s and released as a live 'B' side to She's A Star and also on the Live At The Hordern video.

NO GOOD FOR YOU - Performed by Ian Moss on his first solo tour- before the release of the Matchbook album.

PAINTED DOLL - A live version of this track appeared as a 'B' side to a Catfish CD single (Johnny's Gone) in 1991.

RISING SUN - (Barnes)

RIVER DEEP MOUNTAIN HIGH - (Barnes)

STANDING ON THE OUTSIDE - (Barnes) 1987

TEMPTATION - (Barnes)

TOMORROW - (Barnes) 1987

YOU GOT NOTHING I WANT - (Barnes)

(208

APPENDIX SIX

DISCOGRAPHY

** 7"** CAT

KHE SANH/JUST HOW MANY TIMES
ATLANTIC-1OOO73

GOODBYE (ASTRIDGOODBYE)/ GEORGIA ON MY
MIND   ELECTRA -1OOO78

BREAKFAST AT SWEATHEARTS/ PLAZA
ELECTRA-1OOO85

SHIPPING STEEL/ SHOWTIME   W.E.A.-1OOO9O

CHOIR GIRL/ CONVERSATIONS (live) W.E.A.-OO113

CHEAP WINE/RISING SUN   W.E.A.-OO133

KNOCKING ON HEAVENS DOOR/PARTY'S OVER
W.E.A.-1OO134

MY BABY/MISFITS   W.E.A.-1OO148

YOU GOT NOTHING I WANT/NUMBERS FALL
W.E.A.-1OO191

FOREVER NOW/BOW RIVER   W.E.A.-1OO2O2

WHEN THE WAR IS OVER/WILD COLONIAL
W.E.A.-1OO216

HOLD ME TIGHT/NO SENSE   W.E.A.-7-259773

SATURDAY NIGHT/PAINTED DOLL W.E.A.- 7-259621

TWENTIETH CENTURY/ONLY ONE W.E.A.-7-259492

FLAME TREES/RIVER DEEP MOUNTAIN HIGH
(LIVE)   W.E.A.-7-25941O

KHE SANH/MY BABY (REISSUE) FLAMINGO
FLA-1OO1

KHE SANH/CHEAP WINE (REISSUE)
SUNDOWN-O526

FLAME TREES/CHOIR GIRL (REISSUE)
SUNDOWN-O535

** U.S.A **

MY BABY/MYBABY   ELECTRA-E-47141

KHE SANH/MY TURN TO CRY   ELECTRA-E-47194

FOREVER NOW (ALL MY LOVE)   ELECTRA-E-47458

** GERMANY **

CHEAP WINE/ MY BABY   VINYL-6.12924

CHEAP WINE/ MY BABY (PROMO)   VINYL-6.12924

CHEAP WINE/KNOCKING ON HEAVENS DOOR
LINE- 6.13759

FOREVER NOW/BOW RIVER   POLYDOR 2OO2 154

** HOLLAND **

CHEAP WINE/MY TURN TO CRY   W.E.A.-7O.OOO7

** UK **

CHEAP WINE/MY TURN TO CRY   W.E.A.-K7OO7

YOU GOT NOTHING I WANT/LETTER TO ALEN
POLYDOR-POSP-469

FOREVER NOW/NO GOOD FOR YOU
POLYDOR-POSP-514

** FRANCE **

FOREVER NOW (1 SIDED PROMO)
POLYDOR-2814338

** SPAIN **

FOREVER NOW   2002154

**NEW ZEALAND **

BOW RIVER

WHEN THE WAR IS OVER

** 12" MAXI SINGLES **

** AUSTRALIA**

YOUR THIRTEEN YOUR BEAUTIFUL AND YOUR
MINE   ELECTRA-EP12OO1

CHOIR GIRL/ KHE SANH (LIVE)   W.E.A.-SP 718

DON'T LET GO/ FOUR WALLS   W.E.A.-XS 721

GEORGIA/ ONLY MAKE BELIEVE W.E.A.-MX 21OO58

KHE SANH/ BREAKFAST AT SWEETHEARTS/
GOODBYE   W.E.A.-MX 21O829

WILD THING/ WILDTHING (RAZOR SONGS
PROMO)   W.E.A.-MX 214O22

RADIO SONGS (INTERVIEW DISC) W.E.A.-MX 211214

** GERMANY **

YOUR THIRTEEN YOUR BEAUTIFUL AND YOUR
MINE   LINE-MLSLP 4O1O AN

** USA **

FOREVER NOW (ALL MY LOVE)/ SAME
ELECTRA AS-11571

COLD CHISEL-LIVE (FOUR TRACK PROMO)
ELECTRA AS-11513

CD SINGLES

** AUSTRALIA**

MISFITS/MISFITS (RADIO VERSION)-PROMO
EAST WEST PRO-CD-CCI

MISFITS/MONA AND THE PREACHER/ FOUR WALLS
EAST WEST-9O3175547-2

KHE SANH/ JUST HOW MANY TIMES
EAST WEST-45O99 52842

THREE BIG HITS (3 CD singles)

Disc 1- Hands Out Of My Pocket/ Teenage Love Affair/
EAST WEST   It Aint Wrong/ H-Hour Hotel/ On The Road
45O99 73742

Disc 2- Nothing But You/ When The Sun Goes Down/
River Deep Mountain High (live)/ Let's Go Get Stoned (live)
4509975152

Disc 3- Yesterdays/ Wild Colonial Boy (live)/ Only One (live)/
Build This Love (live)/ Letter To Alan (live)   4509975162

** ALBUMS **

AUSTRALIA

COLD CHISEL	ATLANTIC-6OOO38
BREAKFAST AT SWEETHEARTS	ELECTRA-6OOO42
BREAKFAST AT SWEATHEARTS	W.E.A.-6OOO42
EAST (1st 10,000 CAME WITH BONUS 7')	W.E.A.-6OOO64
SWINGSHIFT	W.E.A.-8OOOO3
CIRCUS ANIMALS	W.E.A-6OO113
TWENTIETH CENTURY (1st I,000 CAME WITH POSTER)	W.E.A.-25O39O.1
BARKING SPIDERS (WITH OBI STRIP AND POSTER)	W.E.A.-251525.1
RADIO SONGS	W.E.A.-252362.1
RAZOR SONGS (WITH RAZOR COVER)	W.E.A.-6OO148.1
RAZOR SONGS	W.E.A.-6OO148.1

** CANADA **

BREAKFAST AT SWEETHEARTS	ELECTRA-Q6E 9OOO1
CIRCUS ANIMALS	ELECTRA-XE1-6O119

** FRANCE **

CIRCUS ANIMALS	POLYDOR-2311 147

** GREECE **

EAST	W.E.A-9OOO3

HOLLAND

SWINGSHIFT	W.E.A.-900.26

** GERMANY **

COLD CHISEL	ATLANTIC-ATL5O517
COLD CHISEL (WHITE VINYL) *	LINE-LILP-4.OO155
COLD CHISEL (BLACK VINYL)*-LINE	
BREAKFAST AT SWEETHEARTS (BLACK VINYL)	MAINLINE-MLLP 5I99
BREAKFAST AT SWEETHEARTS (WHITE VINYL)*	LINE-LILP-4.OO152
SWINGSHIFT (BLACK VINYL) *	LINE
SWINGSHIFT (WHITE VINYL) *	LINE
EAST	W.E.A-9O.OO
EAST (WHITE VINYL)*	LINE-LILP-4.OO148
EAST	VINYL-6.24446
CIRCUS ANIMALS	POLYDOR-2311 147
NORTHBOUND (THE BEST OF COLD CHISEL) *	LINE-6.254224

GERMAN ONLY RELEASE FEATURING-CHEAP WINE/ CHOIR GIRL/ SHIPPING STEEL

BREAKFAST AT SWEETHEARTS/ HOME AND BROKEN HEARTED/ MY BABY/ STAR HOTEL

NORTHBOUND/ STANDING ON THE OUTSIDE/ DRESDEN/ THE PARTY'S OVER(alternate take).

*The albums released on the Line label can virtually be considered to be bootlegs as the band were never paid any royalties for these, and never will be as the company has since ceased operation, making it virtually impossible to determine the band's sales in Germany although reports from Germany suggest that sales were good, with most record stores reporting sales of Chisel records on the Line label. I am also told that Chisel records on Line are not hard to find at record fairs, which suggests that a lot of them were in circulation. It appears as though any 'new' releases in German, in the immediate future, will be imported from Australia, although not necessarily in the same form as the local versions.

NEW ZEALAND

EAST	

** JAPAN **

EAST	W.E.A.- P-1O919J
CIRCUS ANIMALS (White label promo)	28MM 0189
CIRCUS ANIMALS	28MM 0189

** U.S.A. **

EAST	ELECTRA-6E-336
CIRCUS ANIMALS	ELECTRA-E1-6O119

SOUTH AFRICA

BREAKFAST AT SWEETHEARTS	ELEKTRA EKC6074
EAST	WEA-WIC5015
CIRCUS ANIMALS	POLYDOR-2311147

** CDS **

AUSTRALIA

COLD CHISEL	W.E.A.-6OOO38-2
BREAKFAST AT SWEETHEARTS	W.E.A.-6OOO42-2
EAST	W.E.A.-6OOO64-2
SWINGSHIFT	W.E.A.-8OOOO3-2
CIRCUS ANIMALS	W.E.A.-6OO113-2
TWENTIETH CENTURY	W.E.A.-25O39O-2
BARKING SPIDERS	W.E.A.-251525-2
RADIO SONGS	W.E.A.-252362-2
RAZOR SONGS	W.E.A.-6OO148-2
CHISEL (The first 1,000 came with a gold backed disc)	W.E.A.-9O3175O21-2
LAST STAND	W.E.A -45O99O71O-2
TEENAGE LOVE	W.E.A.-45O998O55-2
EAST/CIRCUS ANIMALS	W.E.A.-229254868-2
CHISEL/YOU'RE THIRTEEN,YOU'RE BEAUTIFUL	EAST/WEST-O63O11446-2

GERMANY

COLD CHISEL	LINE-MLCD 9.OO155
BREAKFAST AT SWEETHEARTS	LINE-MLCD-9.OO152
EAST	LINE-MLCD 9.OO148
EAST	W.E.A. 2292-5493O-2
SWINGSHIFT	LINE-LICD 9.OO416
CIRCUS ANIMALS	W.E.A-2292549312
TWENTIETH CENTURY	W.E.A.-2292-5O39O-2
RAZOR SONGS	W.E.A-2292568272
CHISEL	W.E.A.-9O31-75O21-2
LAST STAND	EAST/WEST-45O9-9O71O-2

DON WALKER SOLO

ALBUMS

1981

FREEDOM-Released 1981   WEA-600119-LP

Re-released 1996 in remastered form, Origin Records
ORO26 - CD

1988

CATFISH - UNLIMITED ADDRESS Released 17/10/88
WEA 255916-4

Re-released 1996,   Salt Records-Salt02 CD

Produced and mixed by Peter Walker and Don Walker. Engineered by Peter Walker. The track When You Dance was part of Ian's early solo sets and did appear on the Ian Moss Live At The Hordern video. The title track is a rewrite of the early, never released Cold Chisel song Five-Thirty ETA.

CATFISH - RUBY   EAST/WEST Records-903174797-2

CD   903174796-2

CASS Re-released 1996   Salt Records - Salt03 CD

1993

TEX PERKINS DON WALKER CHARLIE OWEN- SAD BUT TRUE   POLYGRAM-521 183-2

(This album contains 6 songs written by Walker and one co-written by Walker. Of interest to Cold Chisel fans is the re-recording of Janelle as Danielle, the name of Walker's daughter and the title it originally had before Jimmy altered it. The Walker track Sitting In A Bar was recorded by Jimmy Barnes in 1993 and issued as a 'B' side to the Sweat It Out single with the title Sitting At A Br.)

WE'RE ALL GONNA DIE   released 7/8/95
SALT RECORDS-SALT 01

1995

TEX, DON AND CHARLIE - MONDAY MORNING COMING DOWN (LIVE)   POLYDOR 5270892

(Features 6 Walker compositions, one co-written.. Danielle is also included on this live set, as is Sitting In A Bar.)

* Don Walker has also appeared on the albums "Lullaby and Goodnight" (LULLCD001, Flip Records) performing the track Danielle and on "Fuse Box AC/DC Tribute" (BMG

76896402522) where he performs There's Gonna Be Some Rockin' with Peter Walker on guitar. Tex, Don and Charlie also had a song (Danielle) appear on the 1992 JJJ Live At The Wireless album.

SINGLES

WHEN YOU DANCE / SEE YOU AGAIN (non-album track 'B' side) Released 18/4/88   WEA-7.10015

WHEN YOU DANCE / WHEN YOU DANCE + SEE YOU AGAIN Released 26/4/88   WEA-010011

EARLY HOURS / ELECTION MAN   Released 19/9/88
WEA 7257931

EARLY HOURS / ELECTION MAN 12" Released 19/9/88   WEA 0.257931

HI-WIRE GIRL / MY BACKYARD Released 13/3/89
WEA 7257664

1991

JOHNNY'S GONE/PAINTED DOLL (Live)
EAST/WEST   903174797-2

Cassingle   9031747974

Also available as a CD single, same number as the 7" single.

CROOKED SMILE / HI-WIRE GIRL (live) Cassingle Released 4/11/91   EW Records - 9031758954

CROOKED SMILE / HI-WIRE GIRL / ONE NIGHT IN SOVIET RUSSIA   EW 903175895-2

IAN MOSS SOLO

ALBUMS

1989

MATCHBOOK   MUSHROOM-TVC93307-RMC53307

(This album has 9 songs which were written or co-written by Don Walker, including one, I've Got You which was written by Moss/Walker/Prestwich. Steve Prestwich also plays drums on a couple of songs while Don plays keyboards on Such A Beautiful Thing.)

1991

WORLDS AWAY MUSHROOM-TVD93350 RMD53350

(This album was produced by Peter Walker (who produced Cold Chisel's debut) with Ian and features a re-recording of Bow River as well as six Walker compositions (some with Moss) and a Steve Prestwich song , Only Love).

1996

PETROLHEAD   TWAD107

This album features 5 Don Walker songs and not a single Moss song.

*Ian has also appeared on Jimmy Barnes' Stone Cold single and also as "Kid Groove" on Don Walker's second solo album Ruby, playing guitar on the songs Too Long and Jericho Road. On Don's third solo album, (his first under his own name) We're All Gonna Die, Ian played guitar on the title track.

PETROLHEAD (RE-ISSUE WITH BONUS LIVE 10
TRACK CD)   TWAD404

Five of the 10 live tracks on the bonus CD were previously
available on the All Alone On A Rock (see below) single,
production details are the same)

SINGLES

All of Ian's singles contain non-album 'B' sides making them
well worth chasing up.

1988

TUCKER'S DAUGHTER MUSHROOM-K690 MX-70835

1989

TELEPHONE BOOTH   MUSHROOM K881 MX-71918

OUT OF THE FIRE   MUSHROOM-C937

(The 'B' side of this is an old jazzy standard Angel Eyes
(popularized by Frank Sinatra) done in Georgia style and
produced by Ian with Peter Walker.)

MR.RAIN   MUSHROOM-C1065

(This is a gem due to the 'B' side, The Dummy, a
Moss/Walker song recorded in 1978 with Cold Chisel and
produced by Peter Walker.)

1991

SLIP AWAY   MUSHROOM-011004

SHE'S A STAR   MUSHROOM-010498

(This single features three live tracks on the 'B' side including
an extended Never Before, in addition to Tucker's Daughter
and Mr.Rain.)

NEVER GIVE UP   MUSHROOM-D11023

Ian has also released two videos, one a compilation of his
promotional clips and the other part of a live show at the
Hordern Pavilion from 1990. The only Cold Chisel reference
on either of these are live versions of Never Before- a most
impressive extended version on the Hordern Pavilion video,
along with Bow River. Both were issued on Virgin video.

1996

POOR BOY   TWASO18

ALL ALONE ON A ROCK (This CD single comes with 5
live tracks on the B-side, alrecorded in Jan and Sept. 1996.
Engineered and mixed by Ian's manager, Mick Mazzone and
mastered by Don Bartley, who mastered all of Cold Chisel's,
Ian's and Don's '90s releases.)

STEVE PRESTWICH

Although Steve has not released a solo album (although he did
begin work on one on at least one occasion), he did appear, or
have his songs appear on a number of records by other artists.
Steve's song When The War Is Over appeared on both John
Farnham's Age Of Reason and live Full House albums and
became almost as well known as the Cold Chisel version.

Steve also played on two Little River Band albums (1984's
Playing To Win and No Reins) also accompanying the band
on two US tours. A song of Steve's also appeared on the
Crocodile Dundee film soundtrack.

JIMMY BARNES SOLO

BARNES DISCOGRAPHY

7"SINGLES

NO SECOND PRIZE	K-9468-AUSTRALIA
NO SECOND PRIZE	928 672-7- GERMANY
PROMISE ME YOULL CALL	K-9538-AUSTRALIA
DAYLIGHT	K-9582-AUSTRALIA
I'D DIE TO BE WITH YOU	K-9819-AUSTRALIA
I'D DIE TO BE WITH YOU	7-28693-A-USA
I'D DIE TO BE WITH YOU	928 693-7-GERMANY
WORKING CLASS MAN	K-9883-AUSTRALIA
WORKING CLASS MAN	28748-7-USA
WORKING CLASS MAN/SAME	728749-A USA-PROMO
WORKING CLASS MAN	928749-7-UK
WORKING CLASS MAN	928 749-7-GERMANY
WORKING CLASS MAN	P-2077-JAPAN
RIDE THE NIGHT AWAY	K-9931-AUSTRALIA
RIDE THE NIGHT AWAY	K-9931-NEW ZEALAND
GOODTIMES	K-202AUSTRALIA
GOODTIMES/SAME	7-89237- USA-PROMO
GOODTIMES	7-89237-USA
GOODTIMES/SAME	SAM 75O-UK-PROMO
GOODTIMES	A7751-UK
TOO MUCH AIN'T ENOUGH	K-424-AUSTRALIA
TOO MUCH AIN'T ENOUGH	27920-7-USA
TOO MUCH AIN'T ENOUGH/SAME	USA-PROMO
TOO MUCH AIN'T ENOUGH	927 920-7-UK
TOO MUCH AIN'T ENOUGH	927 920-7-GERMANY
TOO MUCH AIN'T ENOUGH	2 79207CANADA
DRIVING WHEELS	K-488AUSTRALIA
I'M STILL ON YOUR SIDE	K-527AUSTRALIA
I'M STILL ON YOUR SIDE/SAME	7-27727-DJ- USA-PROMO
I'M STILL ON YOUR SIDE	27727-7-USA
I'M STILL ON YOUR SIDE	92 77277-A-CANADA
WAITING FOR THE HEARTACHE	K-532-AUSTRALIA
WHEN A MAN LOVES A WOMAN	K-683-AUSTRALIA
LAST FRONTIER	K-784 AUSTRALIA
LAY DOWN YOUR GUNS	K-1OO133-AUSTRALIA
LAY DOWN YOUR GUNS	K-1OO133-AUSTRALIA-BLACK PROMO COVER
LETS MAKE IT LAST ALL NIGHT	K-1O2O7AUSTRALIA
LETS MAKE IT LAST ALL NIGHT	7567-87836-7-GERMANY
LETS MAKE IT LAST ALL NIGHT	7567-87722-7-UK

(212

LITTLE DARLING	K1O289-AUSTRALIA
LITTLE DARLING-TOUR PAK	K-1O289-AUSTRALIA
WHEN YOUR LOVE IS GONE	K-1O321-AUSTRALIA
LOVE IS ENOUGH	K-1O436-AUSTRALIA
I GOTCHA	K-11045-AUSTRALIA
WHEN SOMETHING IS WRONG WITH MY BABY	K11O48-AUSTRALIA
AIN'T NO MOUNTAIN HIGH ENOUGH-K-11O9O AUSTRALIA	
THE BEST	K-11189- AUSTRALIA
SWEAT IT OUT-BLACK VINYL	K-11351-AUSTRALIA
SWEAT IT OUT-RED VINYL	K-11351-AUSTRALIA
STAND UP/STONE COLD 7'JUKE BOX SINGLE	SUN O547-AUSTRALIA

CD SINGLES

WAITIN' FOR THE HEARTACHE	AUSTRALIA-D-532
WHEN A MAN LOVES A WOMAN	AUSTRALIA-D-683
TOO MUCH AIN'T ENOUGH LOVE	JAPAN-3"PROMO CD-1OSW-61
TOO MUCH AIN'T ENOUGH LOVE	USA-I TRACK PROMO-GHS 24146
TOO MUCH AIN'T ENOUGH LOVE	USA 1 TRACK PROMO{LPVER}PROCD3054
TOO MUCH AIN'T ENOUGH LOVE	USA-2 TRACK PROMO-PROCD 3033
LAY DOWN YOUR GUNS	AUSTRALIA-D-1O133
LAY DOWN YOUR GUNS	USA- PROMO-PRCD 3673
WHEN YOUR LOVE IS GONE	AUSTRALIA-D-1O321
LET'S MAKE IT LAST ALLNIGHT	USA- PROMO-PRCD 351O-2
I'M STILL ON YOUR SIDE	USA-PROMO-PRO-CD3244
LOVE IS ENOUGH	AUSTRALIA-D-1O436
GOOD TIMES	UK-7567-86O78-2
I GOTCHA	AUSTRALIA-D-11O45
WHEN SOMETHING IS WRONG WITH MY BABY	AUSTRALIA-D-11O48
AIN'T NO MOUNTAIN HIGH ENOUGH	AUSTRALIA-D-11O9O
SIMPLY THE BEST	AUSTRALIA-D-11189
HEAT-4 TRACK PROMO	UK-BARNES-1
SWEAT IT OUT-#369	AUSTRALIA-1 TRAK GOLD PROMO-WET-1
SWEAT IT OUT	AUSTRALIA-TOUR EDITION-D11351
SWEAT IT OUT	AUSTRALIA-D-11351
STAND UP	AUSTRALIA-1 TRACK PROMO
STAND UP	AUSTRALIA-D-12O94

STAND UP	UK-D-12094
STONE COLD	AUSTRALIA-D-12111
STONE COLD	AUSTRALIA-D-115O4-[BONUS- TRACKS]
STONE COLD	UK-D-115O4
STONE COLD	GERMANY-74321 18494 2
MMM PROMO	AUSTRALIA-PRD93/27
GONNA SEE MY BABY TONIGHT	AUSTRALIA- PROMO COVER
GONNA SEE MY BABY TONIGHT	AUSTRALIA-TOBY 1OO
RIGHT BY YOUR SIDE 2 TRACK	AUSTRALIA-D-16O72
RIGHT BY YOUR SIDE 3 TRACK	AUSTRALIA-D-11529
THE WEIGHT DIGI PAK	AUSTRALIA-D-116O6
THE WEIGHT CARDBOARD COVER	AUSTRALIA-D-116O6
YOU CAN'T MAKE LOVE WITHOUT A SOUL	AUSTRALIA-D1167O
YOU CAN'T MAKE LOVE WITHOUT A SOUL	GERMANY-74321 21499 2
IT WILL BE ALRIGHT	AUSTRALIA-D1179O
STILL GOT ALONG WAY TO GO	AUSTRALIA- PROMO
STILL GOT ALONG WAY TO GO-2 CD SET	AUSTRALIA-D11714
PSYCLONE SAMPLER	UK-PSYCPROO1
CHANGE OF HEART LIMITED EDITION	AUSTRALIA-D1198O
CHANGE OF HEART	AUSTRALIA-D1198O
CHANGE OF HEART LIMITED EDITION	UK-DX1198O
CHANGE OF HEART	UK-D1198O
CHANGE OF HEART	GERMANY-74321 27619 2
COME UNDONE	AUSTRALIA-1 TRACK PROMO -PRD 95/70
COME UNDONE	AUSTRALIA-D12158
COME UNDONE	HOLLAND-74321 348712
EVERYBEAT	AUSTRALIA-D1224
LOVER LOVER	AUSTRALIA-1 TRACK PROMO- PRD96/78
LOVER LOVER-JEWEL CASE	AUSTRALIA-D12164
LOVER LOVER-CARDBOARD COVER	AUSTRALIA-D12164

CASSINGLES

WHEN A MAN LOVES A WOMAN

I'D DIE TO BE WITH YOU

TOO MUCH AIN'T ENOUGH LOVE

TOO MUCH AIN'T ENOUGH LOVE   USA

213)

LAY DOWN YOUR GUNS

LITTLE DARLING

LETS MAKE IT LAST ALLNIGHT

WHEN YOUR LOVE IS GONE

LOVE IS ENOUGH

I GOTCHA

WHEN SOMETHING IS WRONG WITH MY BABY

AIN'T NO MOUNTAIN HIGH ENOUGH

THE BEST

I GOTCHA

SWEAT IT OUT

STAND UP

STAND UP   UK

STONE COLD

STONE COLD

YOU CAN'T MAKE LOVE WITH OUT A SOUL

RIGHT BY YOUR SIDE- 2 TRACK

RIGHT BY YOUR SIDE- 3 TRACK

THE WEIGHT

 STILL GOT A LONG WAY TO GO

PSYCLONE SAMPLER   UK

CHANGE OF HEART- LIMITED EDITION
AUSTRALIA

CHANGE OF HEART   AUSTRALIA

CHANGE OF HEART- 6 TRACK PROMO   UK

CHANGE OF HEART- 1 TRACK PROMO   UK

CHANGE OF HEART   UK

COME UNDONE- PROMO -1 TRACK   UK

COME UNDONE   AUSTRALIA

EVERYBEAT   AUSTRALIA

LOVER LOVER   AUSTRALIA

12" SINGLES

NO SECOND PRIZE   X-14109-AUSTRALIA

NO SECOND PRIZE   PRO-A24148-USA

I'D DIE TO BE WITH TONIGHT   X-4248-AUSTRALIA

I'D DIE TO BE WITH TONIGHT   PRO A 2488-USA

TOO MUCH AIN'T ENOUGHX-14519   AUSTRALIA

WORKING CLASS MAN   PRO A 2452-USA

DRIVING WHEELS   X-13308-AUSTRALIA

I WANNA GET STARTED WITH YOU
                   AUSTRALIA -3 TRACK PROMO

I'M STILL ON YOUR SIDE-X13313   AUSTRALIA

WAITING FOR THE HEARTACHE
                          X14600-AUSTRALIA

WHEN A MAN LOVES A WOMAN
                          X13360-AUSTRALIA

LAST FRONTIER   X13360-AUSTRALIA

GOOD TIMES   PR 2050-USA-PROMO

GOODTIMES   A 7751 (T)-UK

LAY DOWN YOUR GUNS   SAM-696 -UK

LET'S MAKE IT LAST ALL NIGHT   A7722T-UK

I GOTCHA   X13458-AUSTRALIA

STAND UP   T12094-UK

ALBUMS

BODYSWERVE-INTERVIEW DISC   RML-53138-
AUSTRALIA

BODYSWERVE WITH BONUS 7"   53138-AUSTRALIA

FOR THE WORKING CLASS MAN
                       51003/4-AUSTRALIA

JIMMY BARNES-   GH 524089-USA

JIMMY BARNES   P 13254-JAPAN-PROMO

JIMMY BARNES   P 13254-JAPAN

JIMMY BARNES   924 089-1-GERMANY

FREIGHT TRAIN HEART
                   INTERVIEW DISC -AUSTRALIA

FREIGHT TRAIN HEART   TVL-98001/2-AUSTRALIA

FREIGHT TRAIN HEART   G. S. PROMO-USA

FREIGHT TRAIN HEART   GHS 24146- USA

FREIGHT TRAIN HEART   924 146-1-GERMANY

FREIGHT TRAIN HEART   P-8656 - JAPAN

BARNESTORMING   TVL98001/2-AUSTRALIA

TWOFIRES   TVL93318-AUSTRALIA

TWOFIRES   7567-82141-1- GERMANY

SOUL DEEP   TVD93344-AUSTRALIA

SOUL DEEPINTERVIEW DISC
                   DMX 795656-AUSTRALIA

HEAT-WHITE LABEL   TVL93372A-UK-PROMO

HEAT-TVL93372   UK

CD'S

BODYSWERVE   CD 53138-AUSTRALIA

FOR THE WORKING CLASS MAN
                       CD5316/7-AUSTRALIA

FOR THE WORKING CLASS MAN
                       TVD91015-AUSTRALIA

FREIGHT TRAIN HEART   CD53238-AUSTRALIA

FREIGHT TRAIN HEART   9 24146-2-U.S.A.

FREIGHT TRAIN HEART   GED 21416-GERMANY

FREIGHT TRAIN HEART   25XD 1079-JAPAN

BARNESTORMING   TVD 98001/2-AUSTRALIA

(214

BARNESTORMING	74321 2O832 2-	GERMANY
TWO FIRES	TVD93318-	AUSTRALIA
TWO FIRES	TVD91016-	AUSTRALIA
TWO FIRES	7 82141-2-	USA
TWO FIRES	ATLANTIC 7567-82141-2-	GERMANY
TWO FIRES	MUSHROOM 74321-2O831 2-	GERMANY
TWO FIRES	(AMCY-188)-	JAPAN
SOUL DEEP-STANDARD	TVD93344-	AUSTRALIA
SOUL DEEP-LIMITED EDITION		
	TVD93344-	AUSTRALIA
SOUL DEEP-STANDARD & LIVE TRACKS		
	TVD93344-	AUSTRALIA
HEAT-INTERVIEW DISC	(PRO 93/15)-	AUSTRALIA
HEAT-16 TRACK RED COVER		
	(TVD 93372)-	AUSTRALIA
HEAT-1O TRACK CLEAR COVER		
	(TVD 93372)-	AUSTRALIA
HEAT-16TRACK-RED COVER		
	(TVD91O5O)-	AUSTRALIA
HEAT-& 1O TRACK BONUS DISC		
	(74321-1907-2)	GERMANY
HEAT	(74321 17765 2)-	GERMANY
HEAT	(BVCP 719)-	JAPAN
HEAT&FLESH AND WOOD	(D45O45)-	GERMANY
FLESH AND WOOD	TVD9339O	AUSTRALIA
EURO SUMMER 94-PROMO-EURO THANK I		UK
PSYCLONE-ADVANCE COPY	TVD93433	AUSTRALIA
PSYCLONE	TVD93433-	AUSTRALIA
PSYCLONE & BONUS DISC	TVD93433-	AUSTRALIA
PSYCLONE IN HAMBURG	(BOOTLEG)-	GERMANY
A WEEK A WAY/FREIGHT TRAIN HEART		
	GED 24559	GERMANY
BARNES HITS-WITH LIVE EURO CD BONUS		
	TVD93465	AUSTRALIA

The second CD (rarities and B-sides), contains a new mix of No Second Prize which has Don Walker playing organ on it.

JIMMY BARNES HITS INTERVIEW DISC-PRD 96/1O1 AUSTRALIA

CASSETTES

BODYSWERVE	
JIMMY BARNES	GERMANY
FOR THE WORKING CLASS MAN	
FREIGHT TRAIN HEART	
FREIGHT TRAIN HEART	INDONESIA
BARNESTORMING	
BARNESTORMING	THAILAND
TWO FIRES	

TWO FIRES	THAILAND
SOUL DEEP	
SOUL DEEP-LIMITED EDITION	
HEAT	
FLESH &WOOD	
HEAT /FLESH&WOOD	UK

OTHERS

SPIRIT OF CHRISTMAS	AUSTRALIA-1993
SPIRIT OF CHRISTMAS	AUSTRALIA-1995
EARTH MUSIC	
SMOKEY DAWSON	

VIDEOS

TAKE I

TAKE 1-{DIFFERENT COVER}

TAKE 2

AUSTRALIAN MADE

SOUL DEEP

FLESH&WOOD

BARNES HITS-

MISSING

UK12" WORKING CLASS MAN

UK12"TOO MUCH AIN'T ENOUGH LOVE

UK CASSINGLE GOODTIMES

CANADA LP FREIGHT TRAIN HEART

NEW ZEALAND NO SECOND PRIZE

NEW ZEALAND PROMISE ME YOU'LL CALL

GERMAN CD SOUL DEEP

215)